LANGUAGE
in Thought and Action

SECOND EDITION

S. I. Hayakawa *Samuel Ichiye* , 1906 –

IN CONSULTATION WITH

Leo Hamalian and Geoffrey Wagner
The City College of New York

Harcourt, Brace & World, Inc.

NEW YORK ■ CHICAGO ■ SAN FRANCISCO ■ ATLANTA

Library of Congress Catalog Card Number: 64-10333

Printed in the United States of America

ACKNOWLEDGMENTS

The author wishes to thank the following publishers and copyright holders for their permission to reprint the material listed below:

Anderson & Ritchie: Excerpt from *Words and Their Meanings* by Aldous Huxley.

Appleton-Century-Crofts, Inc.: Excerpts from *The Illiteracy of the Literate* by H. R. Huse, copyright, 1933, by D. Appleton-Century Company, Inc.; from *Political Ideals* by Bertrand Russell, copyright, 1917, by the Century Company.

The Bell Syndicate, Inc.: Excerpt from Dorothy Dix's column for December 15, 1948. Reprinted by special permission of The Bell Syndicate, Inc., and the Chicago *Sun-Times*.

Brandt & Brandt: Excerpt from "Rain after a Vaudeville Show" by Stephen Vincent Benét. Copyright, 1918, 1920, 1923, 1925, 1929, 1930, 1931, by Stephen Vincent Benét.

Jonathan Cape Limited: "Naming of Parts" from *A Map of Verona and Other Poems* by Henry Reed. Reprinted by permission of the publishers.

Constable and Company Limited: Excerpt from Barbara Tuchman's *August 1914* (published in America under the title *The Guns of August*).

Doubleday & Company, Inc.: Excerpts from *Literary Taste: How to Form It* by Arnold Bennett; from *Country Squire in the White House* by John T. Flynn; from "The Ballad of East and West" by Rudyard Kipling.

ETC.: A Review of General Semantics: Excerpts from the writings of S. I. Hayakawa.

Faber and Faber Ltd., Publishers: "Poem, or Beauty Hurts Mr. Vinal" from *Selected Poems* by E. E. Cummings.

Fawcett Publications, Inc.: Excerpts from *True Confessions*, August 1948. Courtesy of *True Confessions*. Copyright 1948 Fawcett Publications, Inc.

Harcourt, Brace & World, Inc.: Excerpts from T. S. Eliot; from *The Meaning of Meaning*, 3rd Edition, by C. K. Ogden and I. A. Richards; from *The Child's Conception of the World* by Jean Piaget; from *Theory of Literature* by René Wellek and Austin Warren, copyright, 1949, by Harcourt, Brace & World, Inc.; "Naming of Parts" from *A Map of Verona and Other Poems* by Henry Reed, copyright, 1947, by Henry Reed; from *Modern Man in Search of a Soul* by Carl Jung; "Poem, or Beauty Hurts Mr. Vinal," copyright, 1926, by Horace Liveright; renewed, 1954, by E. E. Cummings, reprinted from *Poems 1923–1954* by E. E. Cummings by permission of Harcourt, Brace & World, Inc.

iv ■

Harper & Row, Publishers, Incorporated: Excerpts from *People in Quandaries* by Wendell Johnson; from *The Mind in the Making* by James Harvey Robinson; from *Union Now with Britain* by Clarence Streit; from *Quo Vadimus?* by E. B. White; "Commuter" from *The Lady Is Cold* by E. B. White, copyright 1929 by Harper & Row, Publishers, Incorporated, reprinted with their permission.

Holt, Rinehart and Winston, Inc.: Excerpts from *Language* by Leonard Bloomfield; "Terence, This Is Stupid Stuff" from "A Shropshire Lad"—Authorised Edition—from *Complete Poems* by A. E. Housman, copyright © 1959 by Holt, Rinehart and Winston, Inc., reprinted by permission of Holt, Rinehart and Winston, Inc.; "Happiness" from *Chicago Poems* by Carl Sandburg, copyright 1916 by Holt, Rinehart and Winston, Inc., copyright renewed 1944 by Carl Sandburg, reprinted by permission of Holt, Rinehart and Winston, Inc.; editorial "Forty-nine Per Cent Sympathy" from *Forty Years on Main Street* by William Allen White, copyright 1937 by William Allen White, reprinted by permission of Holt, Rinehart and Winston, Inc.

A. J. Liebling: Excerpts from *The Wayward Pressman*.

Liveright Publishing Corporation: Excerpts from: *Lunacy Becomes Us* by Adolf Hitler and his Associates, edited by Clara Leiser. By permission of Liveright, Publishers, N.Y. Copyright © 1939, by Liveright Publishing Corp.

The Macmillan Company: "The Snare," reprinted with permission of the publisher from *Collected Poems* by James Stephens, copyright 1915 by The Macmillan Company, renewed 1943 by James Stephens; excerpt reprinted with permission of The Macmillan Company from *The Guns of August* by Barbara W. Tuchman, copyright 1962 by Barbara W. Tuchman.

Masses & Mainstream: Excerpt from "The Cult of the Proper Word" by Margaret Schlauch, *New Masses*, April 15, 1947.

David McKay Company, Inc.: Excerpt from *Pragmatism* by William James, copyright, 1907.

Hughes Mearns: "The Man Who Wasn't There." Reprinted by permission of the author.

The Nation: Excerpt from *The Nation*, June 26, 1948 (book review by Rolfe Humphries, Jr.).

New Directions: "Salutation" from *Selected Poems* by Ezra Pound.

New Statesman & Nation: Excerpt from *New Statesman & Nation*, June 5, 1948.

Pittsburgh *Courier:* Excerpt from an article by Rose Wilder Lane, May 13, 1944.

Political Science Quarterly: Excerpt from "An American Dilemma" by Frank Tannenbaum, *Political Science Quarterly*, September 1944.

Laurence Pollinger Limited: Excerpt from "Morality and the Novel" (in *Phoenix*) by D. H. Lawrence, published in England by William Heinemann Ltd., used by permission of Laurence Pollinger Limited and the Estate of the Late Mrs. Frieda Lawrence; "Happiness" from *Chicago Poems* by Carl Sandburg, published in England by Jonathan Cape Limited.

Random House: "Buick" by Karl Shapiro. Copyright 1941 by Karl Shapiro. Reprinted from *Poems 1940–1953*, by Karl Shapiro, by permission of Random House, Inc.

The Reporter: Excerpt from "The Case of the Orange Orange" by Marya Mannes, *The Reporter*, March 8, 1956.

Routledge & Kegan Paul Ltd.: Excerpt from *Modern Man in Search of a Soul* by Carl G. Jung.

W. B. Saunders Company, Publishers: Excerpt from *Principles of Dynamic Psychiatry* by Jules Masserman.

Charles Scribner's Sons: "Invictus" by W. E. Henley; excerpts from "Haircut" in *Round Up* by Ring Lardner; from *A Farewell to Arms* by Ernest Hemingway.

Simon and Schuster, Inc.: Excerpt from *Mathematics and the Imagination* by permission of Simon and Schuster, Publishers. Copyright, 1940, by Edward Kasner and James Newman.

The Society of Authors: "Terence, This Is Stupid Stuff" by A. E. Housman, by permission of The Society of Authors as the literary representative of the Estate of the late A. E. Housman and Messrs. Jonathan Cape Ltd., publishers of A. E. Housman's *Collected Poems;* extract from "The Listeners" by Walter de la Mare, by permission of The Literary Trustees of Walter de la Mare and The Society of Authors as their representative.

St. Martin's Press Incorporated: "The Snare" from *Collected Poems* by James Stephens, published by Macmillan & Company Ltd. Reprinted by permission of St. Martin's Press Incorporated and Mrs. James Stephens.

Time: Excerpts from *Time,* October 7, 1929, January 24, 1949. Courtesy of *Time,* Copyright Time Inc., 1929 and 1949.

The Viking Press, Inc.: Excerpt from "Morality and the Novel" (in *Phoenix*) by D. H. Lawrence.

A. P. Watt & Son: Excerpt from "The Ballad of East and West" by Rudyard Kipling from *Barrack Room Ballads*. Used by permission of Mrs. George Bambridge, the Macmillan Company of Canada Ltd., and Messrs. Methuen & Co. Ltd.

E. B. White: "Commuter" from *The Lady Is Cold* by E. B. White.

Preface

To learn to think more clearly, to speak and write more effectively, and to listen and read with greater understanding—these have been the goals of the study of language from the days of the medieval trivium to present-day high school and college English. This book tries to approach these traditional goals by the methods of modern semantics, that is, through an understanding in biological and functional terms of the role of language in human life, and through an understanding of the different uses of language: language to persuade and control behavior, language to transmit information, language to create and express social cohesion, and the language of poetry and the imagination. Words that convey no information may nevertheless move carloads of shaving soap or cake-mix, as we all know from television commercials. Words can start people marching in the streets—and can stir others to stoning the marchers. Words that make no sense as prose can make a great deal of sense as poetry. Words that seem simple and clear to some may be puzzling and obscure to others. With words we sugarcoat our nastiest motives and our worst behavior, but with words we also formulate our highest ideals and aspirations. To understand how language works, what pitfalls it conceals, what its possibilities are, is to understand what is central to the complicated business of living the life of a human being. To be concerned with the relation between language and reality, between words and what they stand for in the speaker's or the hearer's thoughts and emotions, is to approach the study of language as both an intellectual and a moral discipline.

Perhaps an illustration will clarify the writer's position. What is the teacher's duty when a child says in class, "Taters ain't doin' good this year"? Traditionally, teachers of English and speech have seen their first duty as that of correcting the child's grammar, pronunciation, and diction in order to bring these up to literate standards. The teacher with a semantic orientation will give priority to a different task. He will ask the student such questions as "What potatoes do you mean? Those on your father's farm, or those throughout the county? How do you know? From personal observation? From reports from credible sources?" In short, the teacher of semantics will concern himself, and teach his students to concern themselves, first of all with the truth, the adequacy, and the degree of trustworthiness of statements. Often, when students who are bored with studying grammar and diagraming sentences become interested in the content and purposes of communication, their hostility to linguistic instruction vanishes, and problems of grammatical and syntactical propriety are solved in passing.

Today the public is aware, perhaps to an unprecedented degree, of the role of communication in human affairs. This awareness arises in large part out of the urgency of the tensions existing everywhere between nation and nation, class and class, individual and individual, in a world that is undergoing rapid change and reorganization. It arises too out of the enormous powers for good and evil—powers apparent to even the least reflective members of society—that lie in the media of mass communication: the press, motion pictures, radio, and television.

The vacuum tube especially has produced in the twentieth century a revolution in communication, a revolution probably more far-reaching in its effects than the invention of printing, which ushered in the Renaissance. The rising expectations of the people of Asia, Africa, and Latin America are due to advances in transportation and communication: the airplane, the jeep, the helicopter, bringing newspapers, magazines, motion pictures, and especially the radio. In thousands of remote villages, my African students tell me, people who formerly had no cultural contacts beyond the next village gather today around portable battery-operated radios to hear the news from London, New York, Tokyo, and Moscow—and start wanting to become citizens of a larger world than they have ever known before.

Television, too, is helping to change the world. In the United States, for example, commercial television invites everyone to participate fully in the benefits of an industrial and democratic culture by buying toothpastes and detergents and automobiles, by taking an interest in national and international affairs, by sharing the emotions and dreams and aspirations and values that are depicted in the entertainment. What television communicates to whites, it also communicates, perhaps absentmindedly, to Negroes, who constitute one-tenth of the nation. There is nothing to be surprised at, therefore, in the increased urgency of Negro demands, not only for better job opportunities, but for full rights as consumers to eat, drink, wear, and enjoy what all other Americans are daily urged to eat, drink, wear, and enjoy. A revolution in the patterns and techniques of communication always has more consequences than are dreamed of at the time the innovations are introduced. The increased density of the communication network in the nation and in the world resulting from technological advances means an increased tempo of social change—and therefore an increased need for semantic sophistication on the part of everyone.

The original version of this book, *Language in Action,* published in 1941, was in many respects a response to the dangers of propaganda, especially as exemplified in Adolf Hitler's success in persuading millions to share his maniacal and destructive views. It was the writer's conviction then, as it remains now, that everyone needs to have a habitually critical attitude towards language—his own as well as that of others—both for the sake of his personal well-being and for his adequate functioning as a citizen. Hitler is gone, but if the majority of our fellow-citizens are more susceptible to the slogans of fear and race hatred than to those of peaceful accommodation and mutual respect among human beings, our political liberties remain at the mercy of any eloquent and unscrupulous demagogue.

Semantics is the study of human interaction through communication. Communication leads sometimes to cooperation and sometimes to conflict. The basic ethical assumption of semantics, analogous to the medical assumption that health is preferable to illness, is that cooperation is preferable to conflict. This assumption, implicit in *Language in Action,* was made explicit as a central and unifying theme in *Language in Thought and Action,* an expansion of the earlier work, published in 1949. It remains the central theme of the present revised edition.

The principal changes in the present edition are of two kinds. First, much new material has been added under the heading of "Applications" at the end of each chapter. A book on semantics is not something simply to be read and put aside. Its principles, to be meaningful, must be tried out in one's own thinking and speaking and writing and behavior; they must be tested against one's own observations and experience. The "Applications" therefore have a double purpose: they offer a means whereby the reader may, in addition to reading *about* semantics, absorb the semanticist's point of view by undertaking actual semantic investigations and exercises. They are also a way of urging the reader not to take the writer's word for anything that is in this book. (It is further hoped that the reader will find the "Applications" amusing. The world is fortunately full of people who say and write wonderfully preposterous things for the semanticist's notebook.)

Second, the present edition has been much revised in order to take into account recent writings and developments in the field of semantics. The treatment of the "two-valued orientation" has been expanded and elaborated in the light of current thought on the subject, especially in social psychology. The account given of "intensional orientation" has been rewritten in the interests of greater clarity. Advertising has long been a prominent feature of the American semantic environment, but with the growth of television it has become even more prominent, so that it enters our lives more profoundly now than ever before. A new chapter on "Poetry and Advertising" has been added in order to stimulate discussion, both in literary and psychological terms, of exactly what it is that advertising does for and to us.

My deepest debt in this book is to the General Semantics ("non-Aristotelian system") of Alfred Korzybski. I have also drawn heavily upon the works of other contributors to semantic thought: especially C. K. Ogden and I. A. Richards, Thorstein Veblen, Edward Sapir, Leonard Bloomfield, Karl R. Popper, Thurman Arnold, Jerome Frank, Jean Piaget, Charles Morris, Wendell Johnson, Irving J. Lee, Ernst Cassirer, Anatol Rapoport, Stuart Chase. I am also deeply indebted to the writings of numerous psychologists and psychiatrists with one or another of the dynamic points of view inspired by Sigmund Freud: Karl Menninger, Trigant Burrow, Carl Rogers, Kurt Lewin, N. R. F. Maier, Jurgen Ruesch, Gregory Bateson, Rudolph Dreikurs, Milton Rokeach. I have also found extremely helpful the writings of cultural anthropologists, especially those of Benjamin Lee Whorf, Ruth Benedict, Clyde Kluckhohn, Leslie A. White, Margaret Mead, Weston La Barre.

Insight into human symbolic behavior and into human interaction through symbolic mechanisms comes from all sorts of disciplines: not only from linguistics, philosophy, psychology, and cultural anthropology, but from attitude research and public opinion study, from new techniques in psychotherapy, from physiology and neurology, from mathematical biology and cybernetics. How are all these separate insights to be brought together and synthesized? This is a task which I cannot claim to have performed here, but I have examined the problem long enough to believe that it cannot be done without some set of broad and informing principles such as is to be found in the General Semantics of Korzybski.

Since anything approaching a full citation of sources would have made these pages unduly formidable in appearance, I have appended, in lieu of detailed documentation, a list of books (pp. 331–36) which I have found especially useful. However, none of the authors whose works I have profited by is to be held accountable for the errors or shortcomings of this book or for the liberties I have taken in the restatement, application, and modification of existing theories.

Professors Leo Hamalian and Geoffrey Wagner of the Department of English of the City College of New York, my friends and collaborators in the preparation of this edition, have gone over every page of the manuscript and have provided most of the new "Applications." Their suggestions and contributions, based on many years of teaching semantics in the classroom as well as on their extraordinarily broad reading and interests, have enriched this volume throughout. Acknowledgment is also due to the late Professor Basil H. Pillard of Antioch College, who was consultant on the 1949 edition of *Language in Thought and Action;* many of his suggestions and additions remain in this edition not only as contributions to content, but to structure. I am also indebted to many students; to innumerable colleagues in the teaching profession; to business executives, training directors, and advertising men; to friends in medicine, law, labor relations, and government (especially in the diplomatic service) whose criticisms and discussions have helped to clarify and enlarge my views.

S. I. H.

San Francisco State College

Contents

Directives and Disillusionment
APPLICATIONS

BOOK ONE The Functions of Language

BOOK ONE

The Functions of Language

A great deal of attention has been paid . . . to the technical languages in which men of science do their specialized thinking. . . . But the colloquial usages of everyday speech, the literary and philosophical dialects in which men do their thinking about the problems of morals, politics, religion and psychology—these have been strangely neglected. We talk about "mere matters of words" in a tone which implies that we regard words as things beneath the notice of a serious-minded person.

This is a most unfortunate attitude. For the fact is that words play an enormous part in our lives and are therefore deserving of the closest study. The old idea that words possess magical powers is false; but its falsity is the distortion of a very important truth. Words do have a magical effect—but not in the way that the magicians supposed, and not on the objects they were trying to influence. Words are magical in the way they affect the minds of those who use them. "A mere matter of words," we say contemptuously, forgetting that words have power to mould men's thinking, to canalize their feeling, to direct their willing and acting. Conduct and character are largely determined by the nature of the words we currently use to discuss ourselves and the world around us.

—ALDOUS HUXLEY, *Words and Their Meanings*

Foreword

Red-Eye and the Woman Problem:
A Semantic Parable

> *Whenever agreement or assent is arrived at in human*
> *affairs, . . .* THIS AGREEMENT IS REACHED BY LIN-
> GUISTIC PROCESSES, OR ELSE IT IS NOT REACHED.
> —BENJAMIN LEE WHORF

Once, long ago, tens of thousands of years before history began, people were worried, as they have often been since, about the chaotic condition of their lives. For in those days men took by force the women they desired. There was no way of stopping them.

If you wanted a woman but found that she was already the partner of another man, all you needed to do was to kill him and drag her home. Naturally, someone else might slug you a little later to get her away from you, but that was the chance you took if you wanted a woman at all.

Consequently there wasn't much of what you could call family life. The men were too busy suspiciously watching each other. And time that might have been spent fishing or hunting or otherwise raising the general standard of living was wasted in constant and anxious measures to defend one's woman.

Many people saw that this was no way for human beings to live. As they said among themselves: "Truly we are strange creatures. In some ways we are highly civilized. We no longer eat raw flesh, as did our savage ancestors. Our technical men have perfected stone arrowheads and powerful bows so that we can slay the fastest deer that runs. Our medicine men can foretell the running of the fish in the streams, and our sorcerers drive away illnesses. At the Institute for Advanced Studies at Notecnirp, a group of bright young men are said to be working out a dance that will make the rain fall. Little by little, we are mastering the secrets of nature, so that we are able to live like civilized men and not like beasts.

■ 5

"Yet," they continued, "we have not mastered ourselves. There are those among us who continue to snatch women away from each other by force, so that every man of necessity lives in fear of his fellows. People agree, of course, that all this killing ought to be stopped. But no one is stopping it. The most fundamental of human problems, that of securing a mate and bringing up one's children under some kind of decent, orderly system, remains unsolved. Unless we can find some way of placing the man-woman relationship on a decent and human basis, our pretensions to civilization are hollow."

For many generations the thoughtful men of the tribe pondered this problem. How could men and women, living peacefully together with their children, be protected from the lusts of the few, who went around killing other men in order to possess their women?

Slowly, and only after centuries of groping discussion, they evolved an answer. They proposed that men and women who have decided to live together permanently be bound by a "contract," by which they meant the uttering, before the priests of the tribe, of solemn promises, binding on their future behavior. This contract was to be known as "marriage." The man in the marriage was to be known as a "husband," the woman as a "wife."

They further proposed that this contract be observed and honored by all the people of the tribe. In other words, if a given woman, Slendershanks, was known to be the "wife" of a given man, Beetlebrow, everyone in the tribe was to agree not to molest their domestic arrangements. Furthermore, they proposed that if anyone failed to respect this contract and killed another man to possess his "wife," he was to be punished by the collective force of tribal authority.

In order to put these proposals into effect, a great conference was called, and delegates arrived from all branches of the tribe. Some came with glad hearts, filled with the hope that humanity was about to enter a new era. Some came with faint hearts, not expecting much to come out of the conference, but feeling that it was at least worth a try. Some came simply because they had been elected delegates and were getting their expenses paid; they were willing to go along with whoever proved to be in the majority.

All the time the conference was going on, however, a big, backward savage called Red-Eye the Atavism, who was so loud-mouthed that he always had a following in spite of his unprepossessing personality, kept shouting scornful remarks from the sidelines. He called the delegates "visionaries," "eggheads," "impractical theorists," "starry-eyed dreamers," "crackpots," and "pantywaists." He gleefully pointed out that many of the delegates had themselves been, at an earlier date, women-snatchers. (This, unfortunately, was true.)

He shouted to Hairy Hands, who was one of the delegates, "You don't think Brawny Legs is going to leave your woman alone just because he makes an agreement, do you?" And he shouted to Brawny Legs, "You don't think Hairy Hands is going to leave your woman alone just because he makes an agreement, do you?" And he poured derision on all the delegates, referring to their discussion as "striped-pants kind of talk, like who ever heard of 'husband,' and 'wife,' and 'marriage' and all that double-dome Choctaw!"

Then Red-Eye the Atavism turned to his following, the crowd of timid and tiny-minded people who always found their self-assurance in the loudness of his voice, and he yelled, "Look at those fool delegates, will you? They think they can change human nature!"

Thereupon the crowd rolled over with laughter and repeated after him, "Haw, haw! They think they can change human nature!"

That broke up the conference. It was another two thousand years, therefore, before marriage was finally instituted in that tribe—two thousand years during which innumerable men were killed defending their women, two thousand years during which men who had no designs on their neighbors' women killed each other as a precaution against being killed themselves, two thousand years during which the arts of peace languished, two thousand years during which people despaired as they dreamed of a distant future time when a man might live with the woman of his choice without arming himself to the teeth and watching over her day and night.

* * *

Perhaps you find this little fiction depressing. Whether or not you find it so depends on what you abstract from it as the most important point. Red-Eye the Atavism, it is true, scored a victory on that occasion. But it is also true that marriage (however imperfect an institution *that* may be) was finally established.

However, as for instituting the social agreements to prevent international violence in today's world, we don't have two thousand years to find the solution. Indeed, we don't have two hundred years. Nor even twenty. Perhaps not even two.

And *that's* our problem.

1 Language and Survival

One cannot but wonder at this constantly recurring phrase "getting something for nothing," as if it were the peculiar and perverse ambition of disturbers of society. Except for our animal outfit, practically all we have is handed to us gratis. Can the most complacent reactionary flatter himself that he invented the art of writing or the printing press, or discovered his religious, economic, and moral convictions, or any of the devices which supply him with meat and raiment or any of the sources of such pleasures as he may derive from literature or the fine arts? In short, civilization is little else than getting something for nothing. —JAMES HARVEY ROBINSON*

Whenever agreement or assent is arrived at in human affairs . . . this agreement is reached by linguistic processes, or else it is not reached.
—BENJAMIN LEE WHORF

What Animals Shall We Imitate?

People who think of themselves as tough-minded and realistic, among them influential political leaders and businessmen as well as go-getters and hustlers of smaller caliber, tend to take it for granted that human nature is selfish and that life is a struggle in which only the fittest may survive. According to this philosophy, the basic law by which man must live, in spite of his surface veneer of civilization, is the law of the jungle. The "fittest" are those who can bring to the struggle superior force, superior cunning, and superior ruthlessness.

The wide currency of this philosophy of the "survival of the fittest" enables people who act ruthlessly and selfishly, whether in personal rivalries, business competition, or international relations, to allay their consciences by telling themselves that they are only obeying a law of nature. But a disinterested observer is entitled to ask whether the ruthlessness of the tiger, the cunning of the ape, and obedience to the law of the jungle are, in their *human* applications, actually evidences of *human* fitness to survive. If human beings are to pick up pointers on behavior from the lower animals, are there not animals other than beasts of prey from which we might learn lessons in survival?

We might, for example, point to the rabbit or the deer and define fitness to survive as superior rapidity in running away from our enemies. We might point to the earthworm or the mole and define it as the ability to keep out of sight and out of the way. We might point to the oyster or the housefly and define it as the ability to propagate our kind faster than our enemies can eat us up. If we are looking to animals for models of behavior, there is also the pig, an animal which many human beings have tried to emulate since time immemorial. (It will be remembered that in the *Odyssey* Circe gave ingenious and practical encouragement to those inclined this way.) In Aldous Huxley's *Brave New World,* we see a world designed by those who would model human beings after the social ants. The world, under the management of a super-brain-trust, might be made as well-integrated, smooth, and efficient as an ant colony and, as Huxley shows, just about as meaningless. If we simply look to animals in order to define what we mean by "fitness to survive," there is no limit to the subhuman systems of behavior that can be devised: we may emulate lobsters, dogs, sparrows, parakeets, giraffes, skunks, or the parasitical worms, because they have all obviously survived in one way or another. We are still entitled to ask, however, if *human* survival does not revolve around a different kind of fitness from that of the lower animals.

Because of the wide prevalence of the dog-eat-dog, survival-of-the-fittest philosophy in our world (although the H-bomb has awakened *some* people to the need for a change in philosophy), it is worth while to look into the present scientific standing of the phrase "survival of the fittest." Biologists distinguish between two kinds of struggle for survival. First, there is the *interspecific* struggle, warfare between different species of animals, as between wolves and deer, or men and bacteria. Second, there is the *intraspecific* struggle, warfare among members of a single species, as when rats fight other rats, or men fight other men. A great deal of evidence in modern biology indicates that those species which have developed elaborate means of intraspecific competition often unfit themselves for interspecific competition, so that such species are either already extinct or are threatened with extinction at any time. The peacock's tail, although useful in sexual competition against other peacocks, is only a hindrance in coping with the environment or competing against other species. The peacock could therefore be wiped out overnight by a sudden change in ecological balance. There is evidence, too, that strength and fierceness in fighting and killing other animals, whether in interspecific or intraspecific competition, have never been enough of themselves to guarantee the survival of a species. Many a mammoth reptile, equipped with magnificent offensive and defensive armaments, ceased millions of years ago to walk the earth.[1]

If we are going to talk about human survival, one of the first things to do, even if we grant that men must fight to live, is to distinguish between those qualities that are useful to men in fighting the environment and other species (for example, floods, storms, wild animals, insects, or bacteria) and those qualities (such as aggressiveness) that are useful in fighting other men.

The principle that if we don't hang together we shall all hang separately was discovered by nature long before it was put into words by man. Cooperation within a species (and sometimes with other species) is essential to the survival of most living creatures. Man, moreover, is the *talking* animal—and any theory of human survival that leaves this fact out of account is no more scientific than would be a theory of beaver survival that failed to consider the interesting uses a beaver makes of its teeth and flat tail. Let us see what talking—human communication—means.

Cooperation

When someone shouts at you, "Look out!" and you jump just in time to avoid being hit by an automobile, you owe your escape from injury to the fundamental cooperative act by which most of the higher animals survive, namely, communication by means of noises. You did not see the car coming; nevertheless, someone did, and he made certain *noises to communicate* his alarm to you. In other words, although your nervous system did not record the danger, you were un-

[1] "For example, the brain of the massive [about two tons] stegosaur weighed only about 70 grams, or 2½ ounces. . . . By contrast, even the brain of the sheep—which is not a particularly brilliant animal—weighs 130 grams, greater both in absolute size and even more so relatively to body size. . . . So far as strength is concerned, nothing could stop one of the great dinosaurs when it was on its way; but while it is all very well to be able to go where you are going, the reasons for going and what is seen and understood on the way are even more important." Weston La Barre, *The Human Animal* (1954), pp. 24–25.

harmed because another nervous system did. You had, for the time being, the advantage of someone else's nervous system in addition to your own.

Indeed, most of the time when we are listening to the noises people make or looking at the black marks on paper that stand for such noises, we are drawing upon the experiences of others in order to make up for what we ourselves have missed. Obviously the more an individual can make use of the nervous systems of others to supplement his own, the easier it is for him to survive. And, of course, the more individuals there are in a group cooperating by making helpful noises at each other, the better it is for all—within the limits, naturally, of the group's talents for social organization. Birds and animals congregate with their own kind and make noises when they find food or become alarmed. In fact, gregariousness as an aid to survival and self-defense is forced upon animals as well as upon men by the necessity of uniting nervous systems even more than by the necessity of uniting physical strength. Societies, both animal and human, might almost be regarded as huge cooperative nervous systems.

While animals use only a few limited cries, however, human beings use extremely complicated systems of sputtering, hissing, gurgling, clucking, cooing noises called *language,* with which they express and report what goes on in their nervous systems. Language is, in addition to being more complicated, immeasurably more flexible than the animal cries from which it was developed—so flexible indeed that it can be used not only to report the tremendous variety of things that go on in the human nervous system but also *to report those reports.* That is, when an animal yelps, he may cause a second animal to yelp in imitation or alarm; the second yelp, however, is not *about* the first yelp. But when a man says, "I see a river," a second man can say, "He says he sees a river"—which is a statement about a statement. About this statement-about-a-statement further statements can be made—and about these, still more. *Language, in short, can be about language.* This is a fundamental way in which human noisemaking systems differ from the cries of animals.

The Pooling of Knowledge

In addition to having developed language, man has also developed means of making, on clay tablets, bits of wood or stone, skins of animals, and paper, more or less permanent marks and scratches which *stand for* language. These marks enable him to communicate with people who are beyond the reach of his voice, both in space and in time. There is a long course of evolution from the marked trees that indicated Indian trails to the metropolitan daily newspaper, but they have this in common: They pass on what one individual has known to other individuals, for their convenience or, in the broadest sense, instruction. Many of the lopstick trails in the Canadian woods, marked by Indians long since dead, can be followed to this day. Archimedes is dead, but we still have his reports on what he observed in his experiments in physics. Keats is dead, but he can still tell us how he felt on first reading Chapman's Homer. From our newspapers and radios we learn with great rapidity facts about the world we live in. From books and magazines we learn how hundreds of people whom we shall never be able to see have felt and thought. All this information is helpful to us at one time or another in throwing light on our own problems.

A human being, then, is never dependent on his own experience alone for his information. Even in a primitive culture he can make use of the experience of his neighbors, friends, and relatives, which they communicate to him by means of language. Therefore, instead of remaining helpless because of the limitations of his own experience and knowledge, instead of having to discover what others have already discovered, instead of exploring the false trails they explored and repeating their errors, he can *go on from where they left off*. Language, that is to say, makes progress possible.

Indeed, most of what we call the human characteristics of our species are expressed and developed through our ability to cooperate by means of our systems of making meaningful noises and meaningful scratches on paper. Even people who belong to backward cultures in which writing has not been invented are able to exchange information and to hand down from generation to generation considerable stores of traditional knowledge. There seems, however, to be a limit both to the amount and to the trustworthiness of knowledge that can be transmitted orally.[2] But when writing is invented, a tremendous step forward is taken. The accuracy of reports can be checked and rechecked by successive generations of observers. The

[2] This is so despite the fact that preliterate people often exhibit remarkable feats of memory, such as the ability to remember every landmark and detail of a journey that may extend for hundreds of miles, or the ability to recall verbatim folk tales and sagas that may take days to recite. Literate people, who rely on notebooks and reference books, have relatively very poor memories.

amount of knowledge accumulated ceases to be limited by people's ability to remember what has been told them. The result is that in any literate culture of a few centuries' standing, human beings accumulate vast stores of knowledge—far more than any individual in that culture can read in his lifetime, let alone remember. These stores of knowledge, which are being added to constantly, are made widely available to all who want them through such mechanical processes as printing and through such distributive agencies as the book trade, the newspaper and magazine trade, and library systems. The result is that all of us who can read any of the major European or Asiatic languages are potentially in touch with the intellectual resources of centuries of human endeavor in all parts of the civilized world.

A physician, for example, who does not know how to treat a patient suffering from a rare disease can look up the disease in the *Index Medicus,* which will send him in turn to medical journals published in all parts of the world. In these he may find records of similar cases as reported and described by a physician in Rotterdam, Holland, in 1913, by another physician in Bangkok, Siam, in 1935, and by still other physicians in Kansas City in 1954. With such records before him, he can better handle his own case. Again, if a person is worried about ethics, he is not limited to the advice of the pastor of the Elm Street Baptist Church; he may go to Confucius, Aristotle, Jesus, Spinoza, and many others whose reflections on ethical problems are on record. If he is worried about love, he can get insights not only from his mother or best friend but from Sappho, Ovid, Propertius, Shakespeare, Havelock Ellis, or any of a thousand others who knew something about it and wrote down what they knew.

Language, that is to say, is the indispensable mechanism of human life—of life such as ours that is molded, guided, enriched, and made possible by the accumulation of the *past* experience of members of our own species. Dogs and cats and chimpanzees do not, so far as we can tell, increase their wisdom, their information, or their control over their environment from one generation to the next. But human beings do. The cultural accomplishments of the ages, the invention of cooking, of weapons, of writing, of printing, of methods of building, of games and amusements, of means of transportation, and the discoveries of all the arts and sciences come to us as *free gifts from the dead.* These gifts, which none of us has done anything to earn, offer us not only the opportunity for a richer life than our forebears enjoyed but also the opportunity to add to the sum total of human achievement by our own contributions, however small they may be.

To be able to read and write, therefore, is to learn to profit by and take part in the greatest of human achievements—that which makes all other achievements possible—namely, the pooling of our experiences in great cooperative stores of knowledge, available (except where special privilege, censorship, or suppression stand in the way) to all. From the warning cry of primitive man to the latest newsflash or scientific monograph, language is social. Cultural and intellectual cooperation is the great principle of *human* life.

This is by no means an easy principle to accept or to understand —except as a kind of pious truism that we should like, because we are well-meaning people, to believe. We live in a highly competitive society, each of us trying to outdo the other in wealth, in popularity or social prestige, in dress, in scholastic grades or golf scores. As we read our daily papers, there is always news of conflict rather than of cooperation—conflict between labor and management, between rival corporations or movie stars, between rival political parties and nations. Over us all hangs the perpetual fear of another war even more unthinkably horrible than the last. One is often tempted to say that conflict, rather than cooperation, is the great governing principle of human life.

But what such a philosophy overlooks is that, despite all the competition at the surface, there is a huge substratum of cooperation *taken for granted* that keeps the world going. The coordination of the efforts of engineers, actors, musicians, cameramen, utilities companies, typists, program directors, advertising agencies, writers, and hundreds of others is required to put on a single television program. Hundreds of thousands of persons cooperate in the production of motor cars, including suppliers and shippers of raw materials from different parts of the earth. Any organized business activity whatsoever is an elaborate act of cooperation, in which every individual worker contributes his share. A lockout or a strike is a *withdrawal of cooperation:* things are regarded as "back to normal" when cooperation is restored. We may indeed as individuals compete for jobs, but our function in the job, once we get it, is to contribute at the right time and place to that innumerable series of cooperative acts that eventually result in automobiles being manufactured, in cakes appearing in pastry shops, in department stores being able to serve their customers, in the trains and airlines running as scheduled. And what is important for our purposes here is that all this coordination of effort necessary for the functioning of society is *of necessity achieved by language or else it is not achieved at all.*

The Niagara of Words

And how does all this affect Mr. T. C. Mits? [3] From the moment he switches on an early-morning news broadcast until he falls asleep at night over a novel or a magazine, he is, like all other people living in modern civilized conditions, swimming in words. Newspaper editors, politicians, salesmen, disc jockeys, columnists, luncheon-club speakers, and clergymen; colleagues at work, friends, relatives, wife and children; market reports, direct-mail advertising, books, and billboards—all are assailing him with words all day long. And Mr. Mits himself is constantly contributing to that verbal Niagara every time he puts on an advertising campaign, delivers a speech, writes a letter, or even chats with his friends.

When things go wrong in Mr. Mits' life—when he is worried, perplexed, or nervous, when family, business, or national affairs are not going as he thinks they should, when he finds himself making blunder after blunder in personal or financial matters—he blames a number of things as responsible for his difficulties. Sometimes he blames the weather, sometimes his health or the state of his nerves, sometimes his glands; if the problem is a larger one, he may blame his environment, the economic system he lives under, a foreign nation, or the cultural pattern of his society. When he is pondering the difficulties of other people, he may attribute their troubles too to causes such as these, and he may add still another, namely, "human nature." (He doesn't blame his own "human nature" unless he is in a very bad way indeed.) It rarely, if ever, occurs to him to investigate, among other things, the nature and constituents of that daily verbal Niagara as a possible source of trouble.

Indeed, there are few occasions on which Mr. Mits thinks about language as such. He pauses from time to time over a grammatical point. Sometimes he feels an uneasiness about his own verbal accomplishments, and so begins to consider improving his vocabulary. Occasionally, he runs into advertisements on "how to increase your

[3] Lillian and Hugh Lieber, of Long Island University, are responsible for christening this gentleman, The Celebrated Man In The Street. Mits' wife's name is, of course, Wits. See *The Education of T. C. Mits* (1944) and *Mits, Wits, and Logic* (1960).

word power," and wonders if he shouldn't take steps to become a more effective persuader—and he may buy a book or take a course, which may make him feel better for a while. Confronted by the Niagara of words—the magazines he hasn't time to keep up with and the books he knows he should read—he wonders if it wouldn't help to take a course in speed-reading.

Once in a while he is struck by the fact that some people (although he never includes himself among these) twist the meanings of words, especially during the course of arguments, so that words are often very tricky. Occasionally, too, he notices, usually with irritation, that words sometimes mean different things to different people. This condition, he feels, could be corrected if people would only consult their dictionaries oftener and learn the "true meanings" of words. He knows, however, that they will not—at least, not any oftener than he does, which is not very often—so that he puts this failure down as another instance of the weakness of human nature.

This, unfortunately, is about the limit of Mr. Mits' linguistic speculations. And here Mr. Mits is representative not only of the general public, but also of many scientific workers, publicists, and writers. Like most people, he takes words as much for granted as the air he breathes, and gives them about as much thought. (After all, he has been talking ever since he can remember.) Mr. Mits' body automatically adjusts itself, within certain limits, to changes in climate or atmosphere, to shifts from cold to warm, from dry to moist, from fresh to foul; no conscious effort on his part is required to make these adjustments. Nevertheless, he is ready to acknowledge the effect that climate and air have upon his physical well-being, and he takes measures to protect himself from unhealthy air, either by getting away from it, or by installing air-conditioning systems to purify it. But Mr. Mits, like the rest of us, also adjusts himself automatically to changes in the verbal climate, from one type of discourse to another, from one set of terms to another, from the listening habits of one kind of social occasion to those of another kind of social occasion, without conscious effort. He has yet, however, to acknowledge the effect of his verbal climate on his mental health and well-being.

Nevertheless, Mr. Mits is profoundly involved in the words he absorbs daily and in the words he uses daily. Words in the newspaper make him pound his fist on the breakfast table. Words his superiors speak to him puff him out with pride, or send him scurrying to work harder. Words about himself, which he has overheard being spoken behind his back, worry him sick. Words which he spoke before a clergyman some years ago have tied him to one woman for life. Words written down on pieces of paper keep him at his job, or bring bills in his mail every month which keep him paying and paying. Words written down by other people, on the other hand, keep them paying him month after month. With words woven into almost every detail of his life, it seems amazing that Mr. Mits' thinking on the subject of language should be so limited.

Mr. Mits has also noticed that when large masses of people, for example under totalitarian regimes, are permitted by their governments to hear and read only carefully selected words, their conduct becomes so strange that he can only regard it as mad. Yet he has observed that some individuals who have the same educational attainments and the same access to varied sources of information as he has, are nevertheless just as mad. He listens to the views of some of his neighbors and he cannot help wondering, "How can they think such things? Don't they see the same things happening that I see? They must be crazy!" "Does such madness," he asks, "illustrate again the 'inevitable frailty of human nature'?" Mr. Mits, who, as an American, likes to regard all things as possible, does not like the conclusion that "nothing can be done about it," but often he can hardly see how he can escape it. Occasionally, timidly, Mr. Mits approaches one more possibility: "Maybe I'm crazy myself. Maybe we're all nuts!" Such a conclusion leads to so complete an impasse, however, that he quickly drops the notion.

One reason for Mr. Mits' failure to get any further in his thinking about language is that he believes, as most people do, that words are not really important; what is important is the "ideas" they stand for. But what is an "idea" if it is not the *verbalization* of a cerebral itch? This, however, is something that has rarely, if ever, occurred to Mr. Mits. The fact that the implications of one set of terms may lead inevitably into blind alleys while the implications of another set of terms may not; the fact that the historical or sentimental associations that some words have make calm discussion impossible so long as those words are employed; the fact that language has a multitude of different kinds of use, and that great confusion arises from mistaking one kind of use for another; the fact that a person speaking a language of a structure entirely different from that of English, such as Japanese, Chinese, or Turkish, may not even think the same thoughts as an English-speaking person—these are unfamiliar notions to Mr. Mits, who has always assumed that the important thing is always to get one's "ideas" straight first, after which the words would take care of themselves.

Whether he realizes it or not, however, Mr. Mits is affected every hour of his life not only by the words he hears and uses, *but also by his unconscious assumptions about language.* If, for example, he likes the name Albert and would like to christen his child by that name but superstitiously avoids doing so because he once knew an Albert who committed suicide, he is operating, whether he realizes it or not, under certain assumptions about the relationship of language to reality.[4] Such unconscious assumptions determine the effect that words have on him—which in turn determines the way he acts, whether wisely or foolishly. Words—the way he uses them and the way he takes them when spoken by others—largely shape his beliefs, his prejudices, his ideals, his aspirations. They constitute the moral and intellectual atmosphere in which he lives—in short, his *semantic environment.*

This book is devoted, then, to the study of the relationships between language, thought, and behavior. We shall examine language and people's linguistic habits as they reveal themselves in thinking (at least nine-tenths of which is talking to oneself), speaking, listening, reading, and writing. *It will be the basic assumption of this book that widespread intraspecific cooperation through the use of language is the fundamental mechanism of human survival. A parallel assumption will be that when the use of language results, as it so often does, in the creation or aggravation of disagreements and conflicts, there is something linguistically wrong with the speaker, the listener, or both.* Human "fitness to survive" means the ability to talk and write and listen and read in ways that increase the chances for you *and fellow-members of your species* to survive *together.*

APPLICATIONS

Since one of the purposes of this book is to help the reader understand more clearly how language works and how this understanding can be applied to the practical situations of life, the reader will find at the end of each chapter a section entitled "Applications." Some of these Applications are designed to enable the reader to test how

---

[4] What were the assumptions about language operative in the parents of the two children who were named John Glenn the day after that astronaut circled the globe? What of the people who name their children by fictitious titles of nobility, such as Duke, Baron, and Lord?

clearly he has understood what the author is saying in the chapter; others suggest operations or activities by which the reader can experimentally test out some of the ideas set forth.

In those Applications where the reader is invited to analyze examples of language in action, it should be emphasized that there is seldom one—and only one—"right answer." The point is, rather, to become conscious of what is going on: what silent assumptions of the speaker or writer and of the listener or reader appear to be involved in a given example.

If the reader discusses his analyses or experiments with others who are reading this book, he should try to avoid hairsplitting and verbal free-for-alls. It is well to be able to give a clear account of one's reasons for reaching a certain result, but one can learn a great deal by listening carefully to what others did and what *their* reasons are for *their* conclusions.

The ideas in this book will be helpful in proportion as the reader puts them to the test of actual experience and decides for himself how valid and useful they are for his own thinking and living. The Applications throughout the book are simply starters in this direction, but it *is* important that what is read here be put to the test of experience.

I. We all tend to assume that what we have read without too much difficulty, we have understood. This assumption is not, of course, always justified. The reader may find it interesting to check his own interpretative processes (and perhaps also the clarity of the writer's exposition) by going over the following list and indicating which statements *agree with,* which statements *disagree with,* and which statements *have no relation to* what has been said in this chapter.

1. Human beings should study the entire animal kingdom in order to to find out which animals are most worth imitating.
2. Heathens believe in the law of the jungle; Christians do not.
3. The Battle of the Bulge is an example of *intraspecific* struggle.
4. Cockroach powder and DDT are weapons of *interspecific* struggle.
5. Intraspecific struggle must be replaced by cooperation if man is to survive as a species.
6. So far as we can observe, animals do not increase their store of knowledge from one generation to the next.
7. If you fall in love, you should read a good book.

8. Through language man is able to profit by the experience of the dead as well as the living members of his species.

9. There ought to be laws prohibiting strikes and lockouts.

10. Cultural and intellectual cooperation is the great principle of human life.

11. However, there is little prospect that human nature can be so altered as to make cooperation possible on a wide scale.

12. Because we are overdeluged with words, everybody should keep his mouth shut.

13. Man has little or no way of controlling his semantic environment.

14. Because language is so important, people have got to learn to think more logically if they want to solve their problems.

15. Because language is so important, learning the correct definitions of words is basic to human survival.

16. Language, thought, and behavior are intimately related to each other.

17. When a discussion leads to increasing disagreement, there is something wrong with the language habits of one or more of the persons involved.

II. The following anecdotes or situations might be discussed in the light of what you have read in this chapter.

1. Two young girls were introduced to each other at a party. The host gave their names as Carol and Patricia. Carol immediately replied, "Oh, she doesn't look like a Patricia at all; she looks just like a Mary."

2. Nellie Dewey, in *The Psychology of Your Name* (1924), claims that by virtue of being composed of straight lines and angles, the letter *A* indicates energy and organization.

3. In *Naming-Day in Eden* (1959), Noah Jonathan Jacobs lists criteria for naming that Adam had at his disposal, e.g., place of origin (Great Dane); size (horsefly); means of sustenance (anteater); characteristic sound emitted (bullfrog); shape (ringworm); method of locomotion (grasshopper); color (redbreast); odor (muskrat).

   (Give further examples for each of the foregoing categories. Can you think of other criteria for selecting names? For insects, birds, animals? For racehorses? For people?) There is a wealth of information on names and naming in H. L. Mencken's *The American Language, Supplement II* (1948), Chapter 10, "Proper Names in America."

4. Protective names were once given warriors going into battle. Starlets and show-business people choose such names as Rock, Gale Storm (there is a stripper called Tempest Storm), Tuesday Weld, Nat "King" Cole. Hurricanes are given women's names. There is a Jewish tradition of changing a sick person's name to confuse the Angel of Death.

And what of the primitive habit of characterizing by naming? Shakespeare's Malvolio, Hotspur, Blunt, and the like. Fielding's Allworthy, Dickens' Pumblechook and Scrooge. Trollope's Mrs. Bold. (Chapter 16 of René Wellek and Austin Warren's *Theory of Literature* [1956] contains some interesting comments on this subject. A curious discussion of the relation between names and the character of people bearing them is to be found in A. A. Roback, *Destiny and Motivation in Language* [1954].)

5. Often there were fights merely because people did not speak the same language. Words that were not understood were taken as insults and were answered with blows. When a Frenchwoman spoke to a Russian, the latter would almost invariably reply, *"Nie ponimayu"* ("I do not understand"). Once I saw a little Frenchwoman throw herself against a Russian with fists doubled, furiously shouting, *"Ni-pou-ni-maille* yourself, you brute." Fortunately I knew Polish and enough of the other Slavic languages to be able sometimes to prevent trouble. But the fact remains that the natural intonation of some Russians and Ukrainians has a harsh and unpleasant ring to French ears. —MICHELINE MAUREL, *An Ordinary Camp*

III. You might ask yourself the question, "What constitutes *my* daily Niagara of words?" To whom do you listen from day to day? At home? At work? At church? At your club? Which of these are influential in forming your opinions? What newspapers and magazines do you read? What plays and movies do you see? What radio and television programs do you hear? Which of these do you absorb attentively, and to which of these do you expose yourself thoughtlessly, just to kill time?

What important communications come to you from the past? The Bible? Classic literature? History? Science? Opera? To what advertisements do you pay special attention? Newspaper and magazine ads? Billboards? Radio and television commercials? Direct mail? How do you *select* what to listen to, what to read carefully, out of all the hundreds of thousands of words directed at you daily by all the many channels of communication? What do the channels of communication you prefer reveal about the kind of person you are?

IV. You may wish to use these suggestions and references as the basis for discussion, debate, and written exercises:

1. The question of the origin of language has long fascinated people, and continues to do so. Nothing can be proved about the beginnings of language, because speech leaves no physical traces for archeologists to dig up and interpret. If you imagine that primitive or preliterate people speak a simple, subhuman gibberish of squawks and grunts, you are very much mistaken, because the languages of all primitive peoples studied so far show extreme complexities of grammar, declension, conjugation, and syntax. There are no primitive languages, if by "primitive" we mean something between the cries of animals and human language. Hence the question of how language developed from its presumably simple beginnings to its present complexity remains unanswered and perhaps unanswerable.

   Some readings in this connection: Margaret Schlauch, *The Gift of Tongues* (1942), which is interesting on the relationships between languages and on the origins of language; Noah Jonathan Jacobs, *Naming-Day in Eden* (1959); Joseph Vendryes, *Language: A Linguistic Introduction to History*, trans. by Paul Radin (1951); C. F. Hockett, *A Course in Modern Linguistics* (1958), especially pp. 580–85; Weston La Barre, *The Human Animal* (1954), especially Chapters 10, 11, 12.

2. The relations between language and thought are discussed in Stuart Chase, *Power of Words* (1954), especially Chapter 10; the important sourcebooks in this area are Alfred Korzybski, *Science and Sanity: An Introduction to Non-Aristotelian Systems and General Semantics*, 4th ed. (1958), and John B. Carroll, ed., *Language, Thought, and Reality: Selected Writings of Benjamin Lee Whorf* (1956).

3. Is man by nature competitive or brotherly? What is the basic law of life, conflict or cooperation? The point of view of this book has been much influenced by such works as Petr Kropotkin's *Mutual Aid: A Factor of Evolution,* with foreword by Ashley Montagu (1955), and W. C. Allee's *Cooperation Among Animals, with Human Implications* (1938).

2 Symbols

This basic need, which certainly is obvious only in man, is the need of symbolization. The symbol-making function is one of man's primary activities, like eating, looking, or moving about. It is the fundamental process of the mind, and goes on all the time.

—SUSANNE K. LANGER

Man's achievements rest upon the use of symbols.

—ALFRED KORZYBSKI

The Symbolic Process

Animals struggle with each other for food or for leadership, but they do not, like human beings, struggle with each other for things that *stand for* food or leadership: such things as our paper symbols of wealth (money, bonds, titles), badges of rank to wear on our clothes, or low-number license plates, supposed by some people to stand for social precedence. For animals, the relationship in which one thing *stands for* something else does not appear to exist except in very rudimentary form.[1]

[1] One investigator, J. B. Wolfe, trained chimpanzees to put poker chips into an especially constructed vending machine ("chimpomat") which supplied grapes, bananas, and other food. The chimpanzees proved to be able to distinguish chips of different "values" (1 grape, 2 grapes, zero, and so on) and also proved to be willing to work for them if the rewards were fairly immediate. They tended, however, to stop work as they accumulated more chips. Their "money system" was definitely limited to rudimentary and immediate transactions. See Robert M. Yerkes' *Chimpanzees: A Laboratory Colony* (1943).

Other examples of animals successfully learning to react meaningfully to things-that-stand-for-other-things can readily be offered, but as a general rule these animal reactions are extremely simple and limited when contrasted with human possibilities in this direction. For example, it appears likely that a chimpanzee might be taught to drive a simplified car, but there would be one thing wrong with its driving: its reactions are such that if a red light showed when it was halfway across a street, it would stop in the middle of the crossing, while, if a green light showed when another car was stalled in its path, it would go ahead regardless of consequences. In other words, so far as such a chimpanzee would be concerned, the red light could hardly be said to *stand for* stop; it *is* stop.

The process by means of which human beings can arbitrarily make certain things *stand for* other things may be called the *symbolic process*. Whenever two or more human beings can communicate with each other, they can, by agreement, make anything stand for anything. For example, here are two symbols:

$$X \qquad\qquad Y$$

We can agree to let X stand for buttons and Y stand for bows; then we can freely change our agreement and let X stand for the Chicago White Sox and Y for the Cincinnati Reds; or let X stand for Chaucer and Y for Shakespeare, X for North Korea, and Y for South Korea. *We are, as human beings, uniquely free to manufacture and manipulate and assign values to our symbols as we please.* Indeed, we can go further by making symbols that stand for symbols. If necessary we can, for instance, let the symbol M stand for all the X's in the above example (buttons, White Sox, Chaucer, North Korea) and let N stand for all the Y's (bows, Cincinnati Reds, Shakespeare, South Korea). Then we can make another symbol, T, stand for M and N, which would be an instance of a symbol of symbols of symbols. This freedom to create symbols of *any* assigned value and to create *symbols that stand for symbols* is essential to what we call the symbolic process.

Everywhere we turn, we see the symbolic process at work. Feathers worn on the head or stripes on the sleeve can be made to stand for military rank; cowrie shells or rings of brass or pieces of paper can stand for wealth; crossed sticks can stand for a set of religious beliefs; buttons, elks' teeth, ribbons, special styles of ornamental haircutting or tattooing, can stand for social affiliations. The symbolic process permeates human life at the most primitive and the most civilized levels alike. Warriors, medicine men, policemen, doormen, nurses, cardinals, and kings wear costumes that symbolize their occupations. American Indians collected scalps, college students collect membership keys in honorary societies, to symbolize victories in their respective fields. There are few things that men do or want to do, possess or want to possess, that have not, in addition to their mechanical or biological value, a symbolic value.

All fashionable clothes, as Thorstein Veblen has pointed out in his *Theory of the Leisure Class* (1899), are highly symbolic: materials, cut, and ornament are dictated only to a slight degree by considerations of warmth, comfort, or practicability. The more we dress up in fine clothes, the more we restrict our freedom of action. But by means of delicate embroideries, easily soiled fabrics, starched shirts, high heels, long and pointed fingernails, and other such sacrifices of comfort, the wealthy classes manage to symbolize, among other things, the fact that they don't have to work for a living. On the other hand, the not-so-wealthy, by imitating these symbols of wealth, symbolize their conviction that, even if they do work for a living, they are just as good as anybody else.

With the changes in American life since Veblen's time, many changes have taken place in our ways of symbolizing social status. Except for evening and party wear, fashionable clothes nowadays are often designed for outdoor life and therefore stress comfort, informality, and, above all, freedom from the conventions of business life —hence the gaily colored sports shirts for men and capri pants for women.

In Veblen's time a deeply tanned skin was indicative of a life spent in farming and other outdoor labor, and women in those days went to a great deal of trouble shielding themselves from the sun with parasols, wide hats, and long sleeves. Today, however, a pale skin is indicative of confinement in offices and factories, while a deeply tanned skin suggests a life of leisure—of trips to Florida, Sun Valley, and Hawaii. Hence, a sun-blackened skin, once considered ugly because it symbolized work, is now considered beautiful because it symbolizes leisure. "The idea is," as Stanton Delaplane said in the San Francisco *Chronicle,* "to turn a color which, if you were born with it, would make it extremely difficult to get into major hotels." And pallid people in New York, Chicago, and Toronto who cannot afford midwinter trips to the West Indies find comfort in browning themselves with drugstore tanning solutions.

Food, too, is highly symbolic. Religious dietary regulations, such as those of the Catholics, Jews, and Mohammedans, are observed in order to symbolize adherence to one's religion. Specific foods are used to symbolize specific festivals and observances in almost every country—for example, cherry pie on George Washington's birthday; haggis on Burns' Nicht. And eating together has been a highly symbolic act throughout all of man's known history: "companion" means one with whom you share your bread.

The white Southerner's apparently illogical attitude toward Negroes can also be accounted for on symbolic grounds. People from outside the South often find it difficult to understand how many white Southerners accept close physical contact with Negro servants and yet become extremely upset at the idea of sitting beside Negroes in restaurants or buses. The attitude of the Southerner rests on the fact that the ministrations of a Negro servant—even personal care, such as nursing—have the symbolic implication of social inequality; while admission of Negroes to buses, restaurants, and nonsegregated schools has the symbolic implication of social equality.

We select our furniture to serve as visible symbols of our taste, wealth, and social position. We often choose our residences on the basis of a feeling that it "looks well" to have a "good address." We trade in perfectly good cars for later models, not always to get better transportation, but to give evidence to the community that we can afford it.[2]

Such complicated and apparently unnecessary behavior leads philosophers, both amateur and professional, to ask over and over again, "Why can't human beings live simply and naturally?" Often the complexity of human life makes us look enviously at the relative simplicity of such lives as dogs and cats lead. But the symbolic process, which makes possible the absurdities of human conduct, also makes possible language and therefore all the human achievements dependent upon language. The fact that more things can go wrong with motorcars than with wheelbarrows is no reason for going back to wheelbarrows. Similarly, the fact that the symbolic process makes complicated follies possible is no reason for wanting to return to a cat-and-dog existence. A better solution is to understand the symbolic process so that instead of being its victims we become, to some degree at least, its masters.

Language as Symbolism

Of all forms of symbolism, language is the most highly developed, most subtle, and most complicated. It has been pointed out that human beings, by agreement, can make anything stand for anything. Now, human beings have agreed, in the course of centuries of mutual dependency, to let the various noises that they can pro-

[2] The writer once had an eight-year-old car in good running condition. A friend of his, a repairman who knew the condition of the car, kept urging him to trade it for a new model. "But why?" the writer asked. "The old car's in fine shape still." The repairman answered scornfully, "Yeah, but what the hell. All you've got is transportation."

Recently, the term "transportation car" has begun to appear in advertisements; for example, " '48 Dodge—Runs perfectly good; transportation car. Leaving, must sell. $100." (Classified section of the *Pali Press,* Kailua, Hawaii.) Apparently it means a car that has no symbolic or prestige value and is good only for getting you there and bringing you back—a miserable kind of vehicle indeed!

duce with their lungs, throats, tongues, teeth, and lips systematically stand for specified happenings in their nervous systems. We call that system of agreements *language*. For example, we who speak English have been so trained that, when our nervous systems register the presence of a certain kind of animal, we may make the following noise: "There's a cat." Anyone hearing us expects to find that, by looking in the same direction, he will experience a similar event in his nervous system—one that will lead him to make an almost identical noise. Again, we have been so trained that when we are conscious of wanting food, we make the noise "I'm hungry."

There is, as has been said, *no necessary connection between the symbol and that which is symbolized*. Just as men can wear yachting costumes without ever having been near a yacht, so they can make the noise "I'm hungry" without being hungry. Furthermore, just as social rank can be symbolized by feathers in the hair, by tattooing on the breast, by gold ornaments on the watch chain, or by a thousand different devices according to the culture we live in, so the fact of being hungry can be symbolized by a thousand different noises according to the culture we live in: *"J'ai faim,"* or *"Es hungert mich,"* or *"Ho appetito,"* or *"Hara ga hetta,"* and so on.

However obvious these facts may appear at first glance, they are actually not so obvious as they seem except when we take special pains to think about the subject. Symbols and things symbolized are independent of each other; nevertheless, we all have a way of feeling as if, and sometimes acting as if, there were necessary connections. For example, there is the vague sense we all have that foreign languages are inherently absurd: foreigners have such funny names for things, and why can't they call things by their right names? This feeling exhibits itself most strongly in those tourists who seem to believe that they can make the natives of any country understand English if they shout loud enough. Like the little boy who was reported to have said, "Pigs are called pigs because they are such dirty animals," they feel that the symbol is inherently connected in some way with the thing symbolized. Then there are the people who feel that since snakes are "nasty, slimy creatures" (incidentally, snakes are *not* slimy), the word "snake" is a *nasty, slimy word*.

The Pitfalls of Drama

Naïveté regarding the symbolic process extends to symbols other than words, of course. In the case of drama (stage, movies, television), there appear to be people in almost every audience who never quite fully realize that a play is a set of fictional, symbolic representations. An actor is one who symbolizes other people, real or imagined. In a movie some years ago, Fredric March enacted with great skill the role of a drunkard. Florence Eldridge (Mrs. March) reports that for a long time thereafter she got letters of advice and sympathy from women who said that they too were married to alcoholics. Also some years ago it was reported that when Edward G. Robinson, who used to play gangster roles with extraordinary vividness, visited Chicago, local hoodlums would telephone him at his hotel to pay their professional respects.

One is reminded of the actor, playing the role of a villain in a traveling theatrical troupe, who, at a particularly tense moment in the play, was shot by an excited cowpuncher in the audience. But this kind of confusion does not seem to be confined to unsophisticated theatergoers. In recent times, Paul Muni, after playing the part of Clarence Darrow in *Inherit the Wind,* was invited to address the American Bar Association; Ralph Bellamy, after playing the role of Franklin D. Roosevelt in *Sunrise at Campobello,* was invited by several colleges to speak on Roosevelt. Also, there are those astonishing patriots who rushed to the recruiting offices to help defend the nation when, on October 30, 1938, the United States was "invaded" by an "army from Mars" in a radio dramatization.[3]

The Word Is Not the Thing

The above, however, are only the more striking examples of confused attitudes toward words and symbols. There would be little point in mentioning them if we were *uniformly and permanently aware* of the independence of symbols from things symbolized, as all human beings, in the writer's opinion, *can be* and *should be.* But we are not. Most of us have, in some area or other of our thinking, improper habits of evaluation. For this, society itself is often to blame: most societies systematically encourage, concerning certain topics, the habitual confusion of symbols with things symbolized. For example, if a Japanese schoolhouse caught on fire, it used to be obligatory in the days of emperor-worship to try to rescue the emperor's *picture* (there was one in every schoolhouse), even at the risk of one's life. (If you got burned to death, you were

[3] See Hadley Cantril's *The Invasion from Mars* (1940); also John Houseman's "The Men from Mars," *Harper's* (December 1948).

posthumously ennobled.) In our society, we are encouraged to go into debt in order that we may display, as symbols of prosperity, shiny new automobiles. Strangely enough, the possession of shiny automobiles even under these conditions makes their "owners" *feel* prosperous. In all civilized societies (and probably in many primitive ones as well), the symbols of piety, of civic virtue, or of patriotism are often prized above actual piety, civic virtue, or patriotism. In one way or another, we are all like the brilliant student who cheats on his exams in order to make Phi Beta Kappa: it is so much more important to have the symbol than the things it stands for.

The habitual confusion of symbols with things symbolized, whether on the part of individuals or societies, is serious enough at all levels of culture to provide a perennial human problem.[4] But with the rise of modern communications systems, the problem of confusing verbal symbols with realities assumes peculiar urgency. We are constantly being talked at, by teachers, preachers, salesmen, public-relations counsels, governmental agencies, and moving-picture sound tracks. The cries of the hawkers of soft drinks, detergents, and laxatives pursue us into our homes, thanks to radio and television—and in some houses the sets are never turned off from morning to night. The mailman brings direct-mail advertising. Billboards confront us on the highway, and we even take portable radios with us to the seashore.

We live in an environment shaped and largely created by hitherto unparalleled semantic influences: mass-circulation newspapers and magazines which are given to reflecting, in a shocking number of cases, the weird prejudices and obsessions of their publishers and owners; radio programs, both local and network, almost completely dominated by commercial motives; public-relations counsels who are simply highly paid craftsmen in the art of manipulating and reshaping our semantic environment in ways favorable to their clients. It is an exciting environment, but fraught with danger: it is only a slight exaggeration to say that Hitler conquered Austria by radio. Today, the full resources of advertising agencies, public-relations counsels, radio, television, and slanted news stories are brought to bear in order to influence our decisions in election campaigns, especially in years of presidential elections.

Citizens of a modern society need, therefore, more than that ordi-

---

[4] The charge against the Pharisees, it will be remembered, was that they were obsessively concerned with the symbols of piety at the expense of an adequate concern with its spirit.

nary "common sense" which was defined by Stuart Chase as that which tells you that the world is flat. They need to be systematically aware of the powers and limitations of symbols, especially words, if they are to guard against being driven into complete bewilderment by the complexity of their semantic environment. The first of the principles governing symbols is this: The symbol is NOT the thing symbolized; the word is NOT the thing; the map is NOT the territory it stands for.

Maps and Territories

There is a sense in which we all live in two worlds. First, we live in the world of happenings which we know at first hand. This is an extremely small world, consisting only of that continuum of the things that we have actually seen, felt, or heard—the flow of events constantly passing before our senses. So far as this world of personal experience is concerned, Africa, South America, Asia, Washington, New York, or Los Angeles do not exist if we have never been to these places. Jomo Kenyetta is only a name if we have never seen him. When we ask ourselves how much we know at first hand, we discover that we know very little indeed.

Most of our knowledge, acquired from parents, friends, schools, newspapers, books, conversation, speeches, and television, is received *verbally*. All our knowledge of history, for example, comes to us only in words. The only proof we have that the Battle of Waterloo ever took place is that we have had reports to that effect. These reports are not given us by people who saw it happen, but are based on other reports: reports of reports of reports, which go back ultimately to the first-hand reports given by people who did see it happening. It is through reports, then, and through reports of reports, that we receive most knowledge: about government, about what is happening in Korea, about what picture is showing at the downtown theater—in fact, about anything that we do not know through direct experience.

Let us call this world that comes to us through words the *verbal world,* as opposed to the world we know or are capable of knowing through our own experience, which we shall call the *extensional world.* (The reason for the choice of the word "extensional" will become clear later.) The human being, like any other creature, begins to make his acquaintance with the extensional world from infancy. Unlike other creatures, however, he begins to receive, as soon as he can learn to understand, reports, reports of reports, reports of reports of reports. In addition he receives inferences made from reports, inferences made from other inferences, and so on. By the time a child is a few years old, has gone to school and to Sunday school, and has made a few friends, he has accumulated a considerable amount of second- and third-hand information about morals, geography, history, nature, people, games—all of which information together constitutes his verbal world.

Now, to use the famous metaphor introduced by Alfred Korzybski in his *Science and Sanity* (1933), this verbal world ought to stand in relation to the extensional world as a *map* does to the *territory* it is supposed to represent. If a child grows to adulthood with a verbal world in his head which corresponds fairly closely to the extensional world that he finds around him in his widening experience, he is in relatively small danger of being shocked or hurt by what he finds, because his verbal world has told him what, more or less, to expect. He is prepared for life. If, however, he grows up with a false map in his head—that is, with a head crammed with error and superstition— he will constantly be running into trouble, wasting his efforts, and acting like a fool. He will not be adjusted to the world as it is; he may, if the lack of adjustment is serious, end up in a mental hospital.

Some of the follies we commit because of false maps in our heads are so commonplace that we do not even think of them as remarkable. There are those who protect themselves from accidents by carrying a rabbit's foot. Some refuse to sleep on the thirteenth floor of hotels—a situation so common that most big hotels, even in the capitals of our scientific culture, skip "13" in numbering their floors. Some plan their lives on the basis of astrological predictions. Some play fifty-to-one shots on the basis of dream books. Some hope to make their teeth whiter by changing their brand of tooth paste. All such people are living in verbal worlds that bear little, if any, resemblance to the extensional world.

Now, no matter how beautiful a map may be, it is useless to a traveler unless it accurately shows the relationship of places to each other, the structure of the territory. If we draw, for example, a big dent in the outline of a lake for, let us say, artistic reasons, the map is worthless. But if we are just drawing maps for fun without paying any attention to the structure of the region, there is nothing in the world to prevent us from putting in all the extra curlicues and twists we want in the lakes, rivers, and roads. No harm will be done *unless someone tries to plan a trip by such a map.*

Similarly, by means of imaginary or false reports, or by false inferences from good reports, or by mere rhetorical exercises, we can manufacture at will, with language, "maps" which have no reference to the extensional world. Here again no harm will be done unless someone makes the mistake of regarding such "maps" as representing real territories.

We all inherit a great deal of useless knowledge, and a great deal of misinformation and error (maps that were formerly thought to be accurate), so that there is always a portion of what we have been told that must be discarded. But the cultural heritage of our civilization that is transmitted to us—our socially pooled knowledge, both scientific and humane—has been valued principally because we have believed that it gives us accurate maps of experience. The analogy of verbal worlds to maps is an important one and will be referred to frequently throughout this book. It should be noticed at this point, however, that there are two ways of getting false maps of the world into our heads: first, by having them given to us; second, by creating them ourselves when we misread the true maps given to us.

APPLICATIONS

The reader who wants to put to work the ideas that are presented in this book would do well to start keeping a scrapbook or a filing folder or a set of 5×7 filing cards. Start a collection of quotations, newspaper clippings, editorials, anecdotes, and so forth, that illustrate in one way or another the confusion of symbols with things symbolized. The ensuing chapters of this book will suggest other kinds of confusion to look for. Look for those instances in which people seem to think that there are *necessary* connections between symbols and things symbolized—between words and what words stand for.

After a few such examples are collected and studied, the reader will be able to recognize readily similar patterns of thought in his contemporaries and friends and, perhaps, even in himself.

I. The following examples of language in action, taken from a variety of sources, indicate what one should be on the lookout for. The reader should try to state explicitly what silent, unconscious assumptions about the relation of words (maps) to things (territories) seem to be guiding the writer or speaker in each case.

1. The gates of the 1933 Century of Progress Exposition at Chicago were opened, through the use of the photoelectric cell, by the light of the star Arcturus. It is reported that a woman, on being told this, remarked, "Isn't it wonderful how those scientists know the names of all those stars."

> SAMPLE ANALYSIS: Apparently this woman, on the basis of an unconscious assumption that there are necessary connections between names and things, believes that scientists discover a star's name by observing it very carefully. Come to think of it, how *do* stars get their names? Obviously, every star that has a name was *given* its name by somebody at some time. Apparently in ancient times people named stars after gods and goddesses, and star-clusters on the basis of accidental resemblances to known objects, like the Dipper and the Scales. Query: Do scientists have any more systematic ways of naming stars today? Surely they must. Check and find out. *Webster's New International Dictionary* or the *Encyclopædia Britannica* will help.

2. (A child is being questioned.) "Could the sun have been called 'moon' and the moon 'sun'?—*No.*—Why not?—*Because the sun shines brighter than the moon.* . . . But if everyone had called the sun 'moon' and the moon 'sun,' would we have known it was wrong? —*Yes, because the sun is always bigger, it always stays like it is and so does the moon.*—Yes, but the sun isn't changed, only its name. Could it have been called . . . etc.?—*No . . . Because the moon rises in the evening, and the sun in the day."*
   —JEAN PIAGET, *The Child's Conception of the World*

3. The City Council of Cambridge, Massachusetts, unanimously passed a resolution (December 1939) making it illegal "to possess, harbor, sequester, introduce or transport, within the city limits, any book, map, magazine, newspaper, pamphlet, handbill or circular containing the words Lenin or Leningrad.

4. State Senator John McNaboe of New York bitterly opposed a bill for the control of syphilis in May, 1937, because "the innocence of children might be corrupted by a widespread use of the term. . . . This particular word creates a shudder in every decent woman and decent man."   —STUART CHASE, *The Tyranny of Words*

5. A picture in the magazine *Life* shows the backs of a sailor's hands, with the letters "H-O-L-D F-A-S-T" tattooed on the fingers. The caption explains, "This tattoo was supposed to keep sailors from falling off yardarm."

6. The Ukrainian delegate charged Greece had "anti-democratic" motives in wanting to demilitarize the Bulgarian border. Philip Dra-

goumis, Greek undersecretary of foreign affairs, tartly replied, "Democracy is a Greek word and Greece knows better than anyone else how to interpret it." —Unidentified newspaper clipping

7. If you spell it backwards, it spells Nature's!
—Patent medicine advertisement

8. It was very big to think about everything and everywhere. Only God could do that. He tried to think what a big thought that must be but he could only think of God. God was God's name just as his name was Stephen. *Dieu* was the French for God and that was God's name too; and when anyone prayed to God and said *Dieu* then God knew at once that it was a French person that was praying. But though there were different names for God in all the different languages in the world and God understood what all the people who prayed said in their different languages still God remained always the same God and God's real name was God.
—JAMES JOYCE, *A Portrait of the Artist as a Young Man*

9. Sigmund Freud once pointed out in a lecture on hysteria that men as well as women were often subject to its symptoms. A distinguished Viennese professor upon hearing this walked angrily out of the hall.

"Never have I heard such nonsense," he fussed. "Men subject to hysteria! Why the word 'hysteria' is derived from the Greek word for *womb*!" —ANATOL RAPOPORT, *Science and the Goals of Man*

10. "Looky here, Jim; does a cat talk like we do?"

"No, a cat don't."

"Well, does a cow?"

"No, a cow don't, nuther."

"Does a cat talk like a cow, or a cow talk like a cat?"

"No, dey don't."

"It's natural and right for 'em to talk different from each other, ain't it?"

"Course."

"And ain't it natural and right for a cat and a cow to talk different from *us*?"

"Why, mos' sholy it is."

"Well, then, why ain't it natural and right for a *Frenchman* to talk different from *us*? You answer me that."

"Is a cat a man, Huck?"

"No."

"Well, den, dey ain't no sense in a cat talkin' like a man. Is a cow a man?—er is a cow a cat?"

"No, she ain't neither of them."

"Well, den, she ain' got no business to talk like either one er the yuther of 'em. Is a Frenchman a man?"

"Yes."

"*Well,* den! Dad blame it, why doan' he *talk* like a man? You answer me *dat!*   —SAMUEL L. CLEMENS, *Huckleberry Finn*

11. The British had adopted khaki after the Boer War, and the Germans were about to make the change from Prussian blue to field-gray. But in 1912 French soldiers still wore the same blue coats, red kepi, and red trousers they had worn in 1830 when rifle fire carried only two hundred paces and when armies, fighting at these close quarters, had no need for concealment. Visiting the Balkan front in 1912, Messimy saw the advantages gained by the dull-colored Bulgarians and came home determined to make the French soldier less visible. His project to clothe him in gray-blue or gray-green raised a howl of protest. . . . To banish "all that is colorful, all that gives the soldier his vivid aspect," wrote the *Echo de Paris,* "is to go contrary both to French taste and military function." Messimy pointed out that the two might no longer be synonymous, but his opponents proved immovable. At a parliamentary hearing a former War Minister, M. Etienne, spoke for France.

"Eliminate the red trousers!" he cried. "Never! *Le pantalon rouge c'est la France!*"

"That blind and imbecile attachment to the most visible of colors," wrote Messimy afterward, "was to have cruel consequences."
    —BARBARA W. TUCHMAN, *The Guns of August*

II. Select a word which has a strong emotional charge (negative or positive), such as "spider," "gun," "math," "blonde," or "Mexican," and describe the feelings which are associated with the term. Where did they come from? To what extent are these feelings based on reactions to the "map" and to what extent on an actual acquaintance with the "territory"?

III. Take an orange or an apple that bears no special distinguishing marks. Write a description of it in a couple of hundred words. Put your orange or apple in with a dozen or so similar oranges or apples, give the description to a friend and see if he can readily pick the one described from the others. Then let him write a description of another one and try to pick out the one he has described.

IV. What makes a map a "good" map or a "bad" one, anyway? If an outline map of the United States had the following cities arranged in this fashion (the left standing for the west):

| St. Louis | Washington | San Francisco |

people would say it was an incorrect map. What would be the result of trying to follow such a map? What needs to be done to make it a correct map? Is it simply a matter of putting the names in the "right places"? How do we know what the "right places" are? The map is certainly *not* the territory, but aren't there some similarities between a correct map and the territory it stands for? Try to put into words some of these similarities and see how well they apply to words and the things that words stand for.

For further discussion see Alfred Korzybski, *Science and Sanity* (1933), p. 750, or Wendell Johnson, *People in Quandries* (1946), pp. 131–33.

V. It is not easy to distinguish between knowledge gained at first hand and knowledge gained from reading. A thoughtful commentator on current journalism writes:

> A newspaper gives the reader the impression of being closer to life than a book, and he is likely to confuse what he has read in it with actual experiences he has not had.
>
> "You should have seen Charlie White," a middle-aged bore may say to me in a bar. "*He* had a left hook."
>
> I too know that White had a left hook, because I read about it so often, but it is no more or less likely that the fellow talking saw him than that I saw Ty Cobb, about whose base-running I talk with the same knowing ease. I don't think I ever did see Cobb, personally, but I do know I saw Hans Wagner and Christy Mathewson in a game between the Pirates and Giants when I was small, and I can't remember what either of them looked like on that particular day or what he did. What I *know* about them, like what I know about Cobb, is simply the cumulative product of newspaper stories and newspaper photographs, and in that way I know as much about Cobb as I do about either.
>
> In the same way, the first President I actually saw was Warren Gamaliel Harding, but he is a paler memory to me than the first Roosevelt, or Taft or Wilson. And it is incredible to me even now that I never saw Franklin D. Roosevelt, who was nearly as much of a personal experience as my own father.
>
> —A. J. LIEBLING, *The Wayward Pressman*

How much of what Mr. Liebling "knows" is "map-knowledge" and how much is "territory-knowledge"? Recall some similar experiences from your own reading and background.

VI. Checking the relationship between "maps" and "territories" is a limitless endeavor, because we see around us constantly the daily substitution of fictitious maps for reality. For example, what would happen if you really tried to keep house as is shown on television commercials—vacuum-cleaning in a tight sheath dress, the wash hanging itself white and sparkling from a line outdoors, mud and raspberry-jam stains vanishing at a touch, and not a task to be done that cannot be accomplished in two smiling, effortless minutes? Think, too, of the discrepancies between the ideals of college athletics (the inculcation of sportsmanship, the building of character, etc.) and what actually goes on in many colleges overeager for victory.

Discrepancies between maps and territories have been the subject matter of comedy, satire, and general outbursts of moral indignation throughout most of human history. The following are a small sampling of many books in this area:

Vilhjalmur Stefansson, *The Standardization of Error* (1927). How people seem to prefer nonsense to fact—a witty and disturbing work.

Bergen Evans, *The Natural History of Nonsense* (1946). An amusing catalogue of errors, superstitions, and mistaken folk beliefs.

Martha Wolfenstein and Nathan Leites, *Movies: A Psychological Study* (1950). A classic study of the ways in which movies create false maps of reality in our heads.

Robert Lindner, *The Fifty-Minute Hour* (1955). Case studies of individuals with extremely distorted maps of reality. Many psychiatric and psychological books in addition to those of Dr. Lindner provide examples of pathologically fictitious map-making.

Albert D. Biderman, *March to Calumny: The Story of American POW's in the Korean War* (1963). We have been led to think that the behavior of American soldiers who were captured in the Korean War constituted a shameful episode. We were told that American prisoners collaborated wholesale with their captors, were too cowardly to resist or escape, too undisciplined to organize effectively for survival. This book challenges these commonly accepted assertions about the American fighting force in Korea.

3 Reports, Inferences, Judgments

To put it briefly, in human speech, different sounds have different meanings. To study this co-ordination of certain sounds with certain meanings is to study language. This co-ordination makes it possible for man to interact with great precision. When we tell someone, for instance, the address of a house he has never seen, we are doing something which no animal can do. —LEONARD BLOOMFIELD

Vague and insignificant forms of speech, and abuse of language, have so long passed for mysteries of science; and hard or misapplied words with little or no meaning have, by prescription, such a right to be mistaken for deep learning and height of specu-lation, that it will not be easy to persuade either those who speak or those who hear them, that they are but the covers of ignorance and hindrance of true knowledge. —JOHN LOCKE

For the purposes of the interchange of information, the basic sym-bolic act is the *report* of what we have seen, heard, or felt: "There is a ditch on each side of the road." "You can get those at Smith's hard-ware store for $2.75." "There aren't any fish on that side of the lake, but there are on this side." Then there are reports of reports: "The longest waterfall in the world is Victoria Falls in Rhodesia." "The Battle of Hastings took place in 1066." "The papers say that there was a smash-up on Highway 41 near Evansville." Reports adhere to the following rules: first, they are *capable of verification;* second, they *exclude,* as far as possible, *inferences* and *judgments.* (These terms will be defined later.)

Verifiability

Reports are verifiable. We may not always be able to verify them ourselves, since we cannot track down the evidence for every piece of history we know, nor can we all go to Evansville to see the remains of the smash-up before they are cleared away. But if we are roughly agreed on the names of things, on what constitutes a "foot," "yard," "bushel," and so on, and on how to measure time, there is relatively little danger of our misunderstanding each other. Even in a world such as we have today, in which everybody seems to be quarreling with everybody else, *we still to a surprising degree trust each other's reports*. We ask directions of total strangers when we are traveling. We follow directions on road signs without being suspicious of the people who put them up. We read books of information about science, mathematics, automotive engineering, travel, geography, the history of costume, and other such factual matters, and we usually assume that the author is doing his best to tell us as truly as he can what he knows. And we are safe in so assuming most of the time. With the interest given today to the discussion of biased newspapers, propagandists, and the general untrustworthiness of many of the communciations we receive, we are likely to forget that we still have an enormous amount of reliable information available and that deliberate misinformation, except in warfare, is still more the exception than the rule. The desire for self-preservation that compelled men to evolve means for the exchange of information also compels them to regard the giving of false information as profoundly reprehensible.

At its highest development, the language of reports is the language of science. By "highest development" we mean greatest general usefulness. Presbyterian and Catholic, workingman and capitalist, East German and West German, *agree* on the meanings of such symbols as $2 \times 2 = 4$, $100°$ C., HNO_3, 3:35 A.M., *1940* A.D., *1000 kilowatts, Quercus agrifolia*, and so on. But how, it may be asked, can there be agreement about even this much among people who disagree about political philosophies, ethical ideas, religious beliefs, and the survival of my business *versus* the survival of yours? The answer is that circumstances *compel men to agree,* whether they wish to or not. If, for example, there were a dozen different religious sects in the United States, each insisting on its own way of naming the time of the day and the days of the year, the mere necessity of having a dozen different calendars, a dozen different kinds of watches, and a dozen sets of schedules for business hours, trains, and television programs, to say nothing of the effort that would be required for translating terms from one nomenclature to another, would make life as we know it impossible.[1]

The language of reports, then, including the more accurate reports of science, is "map" language, and because it gives us reasonably accurate representations of the "territory," it enables us to get work done. Such language may often be dull or uninteresting reading: one does not usually read logarithmic tables or telephone directories for entertainment. But we could not get along without it. There are numberless occasions in the talking and writing we do in everyday life that *require that we state things in such a way that everybody will be able to understand and agree with our formulation.*

Inferences

The reader will find that practice in writing reports is a quick means of increasing his linguistic awareness. It is an exercise which will constantly provide him with his own examples of the principles of language and interpretation under discussion. The reports should be about first-hand experience—scenes the reader has witnessed himself, meetings and social events he has taken part in, people he knows well. They should be of such a nature that they can be verified and agreed upon. For the purpose of this exercise, inferences will be excluded.

Not that inferences are not important—we rely in everyday life and in science as much on *inferences* as on reports—in some areas of thought, for example, geology, paleontology, and nuclear physics,

[1] According to information supplied by the Association of American Railroads, "Before 1883 there were nearly 100 different time zones in the United States. It wasn't until November 18 of that year that . . . a system of standard time was adopted here and in Canada. Before then there was nothing but local or 'solar' time. . . . The Pennsylvania Railroad in the East used Philadelphia time, which was five minutes slower than New York time and five minutes faster than Baltimore time. The Baltimore & Ohio used Baltimore time for trains running out of Baltimore, Columbus time for Ohio, Vincennes (Indiana) time for those going out of Cincinnati. . . . When it was noon in Chicago, it was 12:31 in Pittsburgh; 12:24 in Cleveland; 12:17 in Toledo; 12:13 in Cincinnati; 12:09 in Louisville; 12:07 in Indianapolis; 11:50 in St. Louis; 11:48 in Dubuque; 11:39 in St. Paul, and 11:27 in Omaha. There were 27 local time zones in Michigan alone. . . . A person traveling from Eastport, Maine, to San Francisco, if he wanted always to have the right railroad time and get off at the right place, had to twist the hands of his watch 20 times en route." Chicago *Daily News* (September 29, 1948).

reports are the foundations, but inferences (and inferences upon inferences) are the main body of the science. An inference, as we shall use the term, is *a statement about the unknown made on the basis of the known*. We may *infer* from the material and cut of a woman's clothes her wealth or social position; we may *infer* from the character of the ruins the origin of the fire that destroyed the building; we may *infer* from a man's calloused hands the nature of his occupation; we may infer from a senator's vote on an armaments bill his attitude toward Russia; we may *infer* from the structure of the land the path of a prehistoric glacier; we may *infer* from a halo on an unexposed photographic plate that it has been in the vicinity of radioactive materials; we may *infer* from the sound of an engine the condition of its connecting rods. Inferences may be carelessly or carefully made. They may be made on the basis of a broad background of previous experience with the subject matter, or no experience at all. For example, the inferences a good mechanic can make about the internal condition of a motor by listening to it are often startlingly accurate, while the inferences made by an amateur (if he tries to make any) may be entirely wrong. But the common characteristic of inferences is that they are statements about matters which are not directly known, statements made on the basis of what has been observed.

The avoidance of inferences in our suggested practice in report-writing requires that we make no guesses as to what is going on in other people's minds. When we say, "He was angry," we are not reporting; we are making an inference from such observable facts as the following: "He pounded his first on the table; he swore; he threw the telephone directory at his stenographer." In this particular example, the inference appears to be fairly safe; nevertheless, it is important to remember, especially for the purposes of training oneself, that it is an inference. Such expressions as "He thought a lot of himself," "He was scared of girls," "He has an inferiority complex," made on the basis of casual social observation, and "What Russia really wants to do is to establish a world communist dictatorship," made on the basis of casual newspaper reading, are highly inferential. We should keep in mind their inferential character and, in our suggested exercises, should substitute for them such statements as "He rarely spoke to subordinates in the plant," "I saw him at a party, and he never danced except when one of the girls asked him to," "He wouldn't apply for the scholarship although I believe he could have won it easily," and "The Russian delegation to the United Nations has asked for *A*, *B*, and *C*. Last year they voted against *M* and *N*, and voted for *X* and *Y*. On the basis of facts such as these, the newspaper I read makes the inference that what Russia really wants is to establish a world communist dictatorship. I agree."

In spite of the exercise of every caution in avoiding inferences and reporting only what is seen and experienced, we all remain prone to error, since the making of inferences is a quick, almost automatic process. We may watch a car weaving as it goes down the road and say, "Look at that *drunken driver*," although what we *see* is only *the irregular motion of the car*. The writer once saw a man leave a one-dollar tip at a lunch counter and hurry out. Just as the writer was wondering why anyone should leave so generous a tip in so modest an establishment, the waitress came, picked up the dollar, put it in the cash register as she punched up ninety cents, and put a dime in her pocket. In other words, the writer's description to himself of the event, "a one-dollar tip," turned out to be not a report but an inference.

All this is not to say that we should never make inferences. The inability to make inferences is itself a sign of mental disorder. For example, the speech therapist Laura L. Lee writes, "The aphasic [brain-damaged] adult with whom I worked had great difficulty in making inferences about a picture I showed her. She could tell me what was happening at the moment in the picture, but could not tell me what might have happened just before the picture or just afterward." [2] Hence the question is not whether or not we make inferences; the question is whether or not we are aware of the inferences we make.

Judgments

In our suggested writing exercise, judgments are also to be excluded. By judgments, we shall mean *all expressions of the writer's approval or disapproval of the occurrences, persons, or objects he is describing*. For example, a report cannot say, "It was a wonderful car," but must say something like this: "It has been driven 50,000 miles and has never required any repairs." Again statements such as "Jack lied to us" must be suppressed in favor of the more verifiable statement, "Jack told us he didn't have the keys to his car with him. However, when he pulled a handkerchief out of his pocket a

[2] "Brain Damage and the Process of Abstracting: A Problem in Language Learning," *ETC.: A Review of General Semantics*, XVI (1959), 154–62.

few minutes later, a bunch of car keys fell out." Also a report may not say, "The senator was stubborn, defiant, and uncooperative," or "The senator courageously stood by his principles"; it must say instead, "The senator's vote was the only one against the bill."

Many people regard statements such as the following as statements of "fact": "Jack *lied* to us," "Jerry is a *thief*," "Tommy is *clever*." As ordinarily employed, however, the word "lied" involves first an inference (that Jack knew otherwise and deliberately misstated the facts) and second a judgment (that the speaker disapproves of what he has inferred that Jack did). In the other two instances, we may substitute such expressions as, "Jerry was convicted of theft and served two years at Waupun," and "Tommy plays the violin, leads his class in school, and is captain of the debating team." After all, to say of a man that he is a "thief" is to say in effect, "He has stolen *and will steal again*"—which is more of a prediction than a report. Even to say, "He has stolen," is to make an inference (and simultaneously to pass a judgment) on an act about which there may be difference of opinion among those who have examined the evidence upon which the conviction was obtained. But to say that he was "convicted of theft" is to make a statement capable of being agreed upon through verification in court and prison records.

Scientific verifiability rests upon the external observation of facts, not upon the heaping up of judgments. If one person says, "Peter is a deadbeat," and another says, "I think so too," the statement has not been verified. In court cases, considerable trouble is sometimes caused by witnesses who cannot distinguish their judgments from the facts upon which those judgments are based. Cross-examinations under these circumstances go something like this:

WITNESS: That dirty double-crosser Jacobs ratted on me.

DEFENSE ATTORNEY: Your honor, I object.

JUDGE: Objection sustained. (Witness's remark is stricken from the record.) Now, try to tell the court exactly what happened.

WITNESS: He double-crossed me, the dirty, lying rat!

DEFENSE ATTORNEY: Your honor, I object!

JUDGE: Objection sustained. (Witness's remark is again stricken from the record.) Will the witness try to stick to the facts.

WITNESS: But I'm telling you the facts, your honor. He did double-cross me.

This can continue indefinitely unless the cross-examiner exercises some ingenuity in order to get at the facts behind the judgment. To the witness it is a "fact" that he was "double-crossed." Often patient questioning is required before the factual bases of the judgment are revealed.

Many words, of course, simultaneously convey a report and a judgment on the fact reported, as will be discussed more fully in a later chapter. For the purposes of a report as here defined, these should be avoided. Instead of "sneaked in," one might say "entered quietly"; instead of "politicians," "congressmen" or "aldermen" or "candidates for office"; instead of "bureaucrat," "public official"; instead of "tramp," "homeless unemployed"; instead of "dictatorial set-up," "centralized authority"; instead of "crackpots," "holders of nonconformist views." A newspaper reporter, for example, is not permitted to write, "A crowd of suckers came to listen to Senator Smith last evening in that rickety firetrap and ex-dive that disfigures the south edge of town." Instead he says, "Between seventy-five and a hundred people heard an address last evening by Senator Smith at the Evergreen Gardens near the South Side city limits."

Snarl-Words and Purr-Words

Throughout this book, it is important to remember that we are not considering language as an isolated phenomenon. Our concern, instead, is with language in action—language in the full context of the nonlinguistic events which are its setting. The making of noises with the vocal organs is a muscular activity and, like other muscular activities, often involuntary. Our responses to powerful stimuli, such as to things that make us very angry, are a complex of muscular and physiological events: the contracting of fighting muscles, the increase of blood pressure, a change in body chemistry, clutching of our hair, *and* the making of noises, such as growls and snarls. We are a little too dignified, perhaps, to growl like dogs, but we do the next best thing and substitute series of words, such as "You dirty double-crosser!" "The filthy scum!" Similarly, if we are pleasurably agitated, we may, instead of purring or wagging the tail, say things like "She's the sweetest girl in all the world!"

Speeches such as these are, as direct expressions of approval or disapproval, judgments in their simplest form. They may be said to be human equivalents of snarling and purring. "She's the sweetest girl in all the world" is not a statement about the girl; it is a purr. This seems to be a fairly obvious fact; nevertheless, it is surprising how often, when such a statement is made, both the speaker and the hearer feel that something has been said about the girl. This error is especially common in the interpretation of utterances of orators and editorialists in some of their more excited denunciations of "Reds," "greedy monopolists," "Wall Street," "radicals," "foreign ideologies," and in their more fulsome dithyrambs about "our way of life." Constantly, because of the impressive sound of the words, the elaborate structure of the sentences, and the appearance of intellectual progression, we get the feeling that something is being said about something. On closer examination, however, we discover that these utterances merely say, "What I hate ('Reds,' 'Wall Street,' or whatever) I hate very, very much," and "What I like ('our way of life') I like very, very much." We may call such utterances "snarl-words" and "purr-words." They are not reports describing conditions in the extensional world in any way.

To call these judgments "snarl-words" and "purr-words" does not mean that we should simply shrug them off. It means that we should be careful to *allocate the meaning correctly*—placing such a statement as "She's the sweetest girl in the world" as a revelation of the speaker's state of mind, and not as a revelation of facts about the girl. If the "snarl-words" about "Reds" or "greedy monopolists" are accompanied by verifiable reports (which would also mean that we have previously agreed as to who, specifically, is meant by the terms "Reds" or "greedy monopolists"), we might find reason to be just as disturbed as the speaker. If the "purr-words" about the sweetest girl in the world are accompanied by verifiable reports about her appearance, manners, character, and so on, we might find reason to admire her too. But "snarl-words" and "purr-words" as such, unaccompanied by reports, offer nothing further to discuss, except possibly the question, "Why do you feel as you do?"

It is usually fruitless to debate such questions as "Is President Kennedy a great statesman or merely a skillful politician?" "Is the music of Wagner the greatest music of all time, or is it merely hysterical screeching?" "Which is the finer sport, tennis or baseball?" "Could Joe Louis in his prime have licked Bob Fitzsimmons in his prime?" To take sides on such issues of conflicting judgments is to reduce oneself to the same level of stubborn imbecility as one's opponents. But to ask questions of the form, "Why do you like (or dislike) Kennedy (or Wagner, or tennis, or Joe Louis)?" is to learn something about one's friends and neighbors. After listening to their opinions and their reasons for them, we may leave the discussion slightly wiser, slightly better informed, and perhaps slightly less one-sided than we were before the discussion began.

How Judgments Stop Thought

A judgment ("He is a fine boy," "It was a beautiful service," "Baseball is a healthful sport," "She is an awful bore") is a conclusion, summing up a large number of previously observed facts. The reader is probably familiar with the fact that students almost always have difficulty in writing themes of the required length because their ideas give out after a paragraph or two. The reason for this is that those early paragraphs contain so many judgments that there is little left to be said. When the conclusions are carefully excluded, however, and observed facts are given instead, there is never any trouble about the length of papers; in fact, they tend to become too long, since inexperienced writers, when told to give facts, often give far more than are necessary, because they lack discrimination between the important and the trivial.

Still another consequence of judgments early in the course of a written exercise—and this applies also to hasty judgments in everyday thought—is the temporary blindness they induce. When, for example, a description starts with the words, "He was a real Madison Avenue executive," or "She was a typical sorority girl," if we continue writing at all, we must make all our later statements consistent with those judgments. The result is that all the individual characteristics of this particular "executive" or this particular "sorority girl" are lost sight of; and the rest of the account is likely to deal not with observed facts but with the writer's private notion (based on previously read stories, movies, pictures, and so forth) of what "Madison Avenue executives" or "typical sorority girls" are like. The premature judgment, that is, often prevents us from seeing what is directly in front of us, so that clichés take the place of fresh description. Therefore, even if the writer feels sure at the beginning of a written account that the man he is describing is a "real leatherneck" or that the scene he is describing is a "beautiful residential suburb," he will conscientiously keep such notions out of his head, lest his vision be obstructed. He is specifically warned against describing *anybody* as a "beatnik"—a term (originally applied to literary and artistic Bohemians) which was blown up by sensational journalism and movies into an almost completely fictional and misleading stereotype. If a writer applies the term to any actual living human being, he will have to spend so much energy thereafter explaining what he does *not* mean by it that he will save himself trouble by not bringing it up at all.

Slanting

In the course of writing reports of personal experiences, it will be found that in spite of all endeavors to keep judgments out, some will creep in. An account of a man, for example, may go like this: "He had apparently not shaved for several days, and his face and hands were covered with grime. His shoes were torn, and his coat, which was several sizes too small for him, was spotted with dried clay." Now, in spite of the fact that no judgment has been stated, a very obvious one is implied. Let us contrast this with another description of the same man. "Although his face was bearded and neglected, his eyes were clear, and he looked straight ahead as he walked rapidly down the road. He seemed very tall; perhaps the fact that his coat was too small for him emphasized that impression. He was carrying a book under his left arm, and a small terrier ran at his heels." In this example, the impression about the same man is considerably changed, simply by the inclusion of new details and the subordination of unfavorable ones. Even if explicit judgments are kept out of one's writing, implied judgments will get in.

How, then, can we ever give an impartial report? The answer is, of course, that we cannot attain complete impartiality while we use the language of everyday life. Even with the very impersonal language of science, the task is sometimes difficult. Nevertheless, we can, by being aware of the favorable or unfavorable feelings that certain words and facts can arouse, attain enough impartiality for practical purposes. Such awareness enables us to balance the implied favorable and unfavorable judgments against each other. To learn to do this, it is a good idea to write two accounts of the same subject, both strict reports, to be read side by side: the first to contain facts and details likely to prejudice the reader in favor of the subject, the second to contain those likely to prejudice the reader against it. For example:

FOR	AGAINST
He had white teeth.	His teeth were uneven.
His eyes were blue, his hair blond and abundant.	He rarely looked people straight in the eye.
He had on a clean white shirt.	His shirt was frayed at the cuffs.
His speech was courteous.	He had a high-pitched voice.
His employer spoke highly of him.	His landlord said he was slow in paying his rent.
He liked dogs.	He disliked children.

This process of selecting details favorable or unfavorable to the subject being described may be termed *slanting*. Slanting gives no explicit judgments, but it differs from reporting in that it deliberately makes certain judgments inescapable. Let us assume for a moment the truth of the statement "When Clyde was in New York last November he was seen having dinner with a show girl. . . ." The inferences that can be drawn from this statement are changed considerably when the following words are added: ". . . and her husband and their two children." Yet, if Clyde is a married man, his enemies could conceivably do him a great deal of harm by talking about his "dinner-date with a New York show girl." One-sided or biased slanting of this kind, not uncommon in private gossip and backbiting, and all too common in the "interpretative reporting" of newspapers and news magazines, can be described as a technique of lying without actually telling any lies.

Discovering One's Bias

Here, however, a caution is necessary. When, for example, a newspaper tells a story in a way that we dislike, leaving out facts we think important and playing up important facts in ways that we think unfair, we are tempted to say, "Look how unfairly they've slanted the story!" In making such a statement we are, of course, making an inference about the newspaper's editors. We are assuming that what seems important or unimportant to us seems equally important or unimportant to them, and on the basis of that assumption we infer that the editors "deliberately" gave the story a misleading emphasis. Is this necessarily the case? Can the reader, as an outsider, say whether a story assumes a given form because the editors "deliberately slanted it that way" or because that was the way the events appeared to them?

The point is that, by the process of selection and abstraction imposed on us by our own interests and background, experience comes to all of us (including newspaper editors) already "slanted." If you happen to be pro-labor, pro-Catholic, and a stock-car racing fan, your ideas of what is important or unimportant will of necessity be different from those of a man who happens to be indifferent to all three of your favorite interests. If, then, some newspapers often seem to side with the big businessman on public issues, the reason is less a matter of "deliberate" slanting than the fact that publishers are often, in enterprises as large as modern urban newspapers, big businessmen themselves, accustomed both in work and in social life to associating with other big businessmen. Nevertheless, the best newspapers, whether owned by "big businessmen" or not, do try to tell us as accurately as possible what is going on in the world, because they are run by newspapermen who conceive it to be part of their professional responsibility to present fairly the conflicting points of view in controversial issues. Such newspapermen are *reporters* indeed.

The writer who is neither an advocate nor an opponent avoids slanting, except when he is seeking special literary effects. The avoidance of slanting is not only a matter of being fair and impartial; it is even more importantly a matter of making good maps of the territory of experience. The profoundly biased individual cannot make good maps because he can see an enemy *only* as an enemy and a friend *only* as a friend. The individual with genuine skill in writing—one who has imagination and insight—can look at the same subject from many points of view. The following examples may illustrate the fullness and solidity of descriptions thus written:

Adam turned to look at him. It was, in a way, as though this were the first time he had laid eyes on him. He saw the strong, black shoulders under the red-check calico, the long arms lying loose, forward over the knees, the strong hands, seamed and calloused, holding the reins. He looked at the face. The thrust of the jawbone was strong, but the lips were heavy and low, with a piece of chewed straw hanging out one side of the mouth. The eyelids were pendulous, slightly swollen-looking, and the eyes bloodshot. Those eyes, Adam knew, could sharpen to a quick, penetrating, assessing glance. But now, looking at that slack, somnolent face, he could scarcely believe that. —ROBERT PENN WARREN, *Wilderness*

Soon after the little princess, there walked in a massively built, stout young man in spectacles, with a cropped head, light breeches in the mode of the day, with a high lace ruffle and a ginger-coloured coat. This stout young man [Pierre] was the illegitimate son of a celebrated dandy of the days of Catherine, Count Bezuhov, who was now dying in Moscow. He had not yet entered any branch of the service; he had only just returned from abroad, where he had been educated, and this was his first appearance in society. Anna Pavlovna greeted him with a nod reserved for persons of the very lowest hierarchy in her drawing-room. . . .

Pierre was clumsy, stout and uncommonly tall, with huge, red hands; he did not, as they say, know how to come into a drawing-room and still less how to get out of one, that is, how to say something particularly agreeable on going away. Moreover, he was dreamy.

He stood up, and picking up a three-cornered hat with the plume of a general in it instead of his own, he kept hold of it, pulling the feathers until the general asked him to restore it. But all his dreaminess and his inability to enter a drawing-room or talk properly in it were atoned for by his expression of good-nature, simplicity and modesty.　　　　　　　　　　—COUNT LEO TOLSTOY, *War and Peace*
(Translated by Constance Garnett)

APPLICATIONS

I. Here are a number of statements which the reader may attempt to classify as judgments, inferences, or reports. Since the distinctions are not always clear-cut, a one-word answer will not ordinarily be adequate. Note that we are concerned here with the nature of the statements, not the truth or falsity of them; for example, the statement, "Water freezes at 10° centigrade," is, although inaccurate, a report.

1. She goes to church only in order to show off her clothes.

> SAMPLE ANALYSIS: In usual circumstances under which such a statement would be made, this would be an *inference,* since people ordinarily do not admit that they go to church for that reason. A *judgment* is also strongly implied, since it is assumed that one ought to have better reasons.

2. There is something essentially unclean about eating meat and fish.

3. Cary Grant has lots of personality.

4. Rough-grained Split Leather Brief Case; artificial leather gussets. 3 position lock with key. 16 × 11 in. Color: black or brown. Shpg. wt. 2 lbs. Price, $4.86.　　　　　—Sears, Roebuck and Company Catalog

5. 　　　　　Commuter—one who spends his life
　　　　　In riding to and from his wife;
　　　　　A man who shaves and takes a train
　　　　　And then rides back to shave again.
　　　　　　　　　　—E. B. WHITE

6. To commit murder is wrong under all circumstances.

7. The Russian people do not want war.

8. He is a typical bureaucrat.

9. An intelligent man makes his own opportunities.

10. The senator's support of the bill was a move to catch the veteran vote.

11. 　　　　　That time of year thou may'st in me behold
　　　　　When yellow leaves, or few, or none do hang

Upon those boughs that shake against the cold,
Bare ruined choirs where late the sweet birds sang.
—WILLIAM SHAKESPEARE

12. And Adam lived an hundred and thirty years, and begat a son in his likeness, after his image; and called his name Seth: And the days of Adam after he had begotten Seth were eight hundred years: and he begat sons and daughters: And all the days that Adam lived were nine hundred and thirty years: and he died.   —Genesis 5:3–5

13. Crisp as Jack Frost, crunchy and crackle-happy . . . redder than a fire sale of long-handle flannels. Your big delicious beauties arrive so fresh we don't guarantee they won't talk back to folks . . . in a flavor-full language all their own. Shipping weight about 9 pounds."
      —Advertising material accompanying
      a Fruit-of-the-Month Club delivery

14. William Jameson is a skinny, crippled, tuberculosis-ridden little man, weighing only 95 pounds and standing only 5 feet tall. And every ounce and inch of him is criminal—incorrigible, remorseless and vicious.   —New York *World-Telegram & Sun*

15. Research scientists proved that regular after-meal brushing with new Ipana reduced bacteria in the mouth—including decay and bad-breath bacteria—*by an average of 84%.*
      —Advertisement for Ipana toothpaste

16. *C'est Magnifique! Une maison Ranch très originale avec 8 rooms, 2½ baths . . . 2-Cadillac garage . . . $21,990 . . . No cash for veterans.*   —Advertisement for a Long Island development

17. Our shameful Justice of the Peace system allows many legal igno-ramuses—more intent on picking our pockets than on guarding our rights—to mishandle the law in rural areas.   —*Reader's Digest*

18. But the delegates [at the U.S. Chamber of Commerce convention] remained wary. "He [President Kennedy] gave a nice speech," said one of them afterward, "but actions speak louder than words. Nothing he said here this morning erased his actions taken against the steel industry." The business community had cause for concern. Kennedy is not ideologically against business; he probably thinks he is all for it. But the fact is that as a millionaire's son with no ex-perience in any calling but politics, the President has led an eco-nomically sheltered life—and he does not seem to understand business or businessmen too well.   —*Time*

II. In addition to trying such exercises in report-writing and the exclusion of judgments and inferences as are suggested in this chap-ter, the reader might try writing (a) reports heavily slanted *against* persons or organizations he *likes,* and (b) reports heavily slanted *in favor of* persons or organizations he *dislikes.* For example, imagine that your luncheon club or fraternity or lodge is a subversive organization and report the facts about its activities and members upon which unfavorable inferences could be made; or imagine that one of your most disagreeable neighbors has been offered a job two thousand miles away and write a factual letter of recommendation to help him get the job.

It is also amusing and instructive to write parodies of biased writing, i.e., to write with so strong a bias that you ridicule the bias. A strongly biased account consists, of course, of slanted reports and unqualified judgments. The following is a quotation from *Mad* magazine's attempt to see the Boy Scouts through *Pravda's* eyes:

> After three years of servitude in the Cub Scouts, the boys, now hooligan adolescents, are forced to join the older, more corrupt Boy Scouts. Here, they are snatched away from their families and taken to primitive forests where they must live in unheated tents.
>
> The most deceitful ritual is the shameful "Court of Honor," where the young warmongers are decorated with so-called "Merit Badges." It is here that they receive awards for their work in such insidious fields as "Swimming" (Underwater Demolition and Sabotage), "Chemistry" (Germ and Poison Gas Warfare), "Pathfinding" (Counter-espionage), and "Pioneering" (Exploitation of Undeveloped Nations).

III. "A youth and a man were killed and three teenagers seriously injured early today in two auto accidents." Write:

1. A *report* of these accidents, inventing names and places.
2. A *slanted report* for a newspaper campaigning for stricter laws against juvenile delinquency. (Be sure to use factual statements only, letting your reader make his own inferences and judgments.)
3. A *slanted report* for a newspaper highly critical of the local city administration. (Again, use factual statements only.)

IV. Discuss the use of inference in the following passage from Sir Arthur Conan Doyle. Are the inferences made by Sherlock Holmes the kind that are described in this chapter? Comment on the validity and verifiability of Holmes's inferences.

> With a resigned air and a somewhat weary smile, Holmes begged the beautiful intruder to take a seat, and to inform us what it was that was troubling her.

"At least it cannot be your health," said he, as his keen eyes darted over her; "so ardent a bicyclist must be full of energy."

She glanced down in surprise at her own feet, and I observed the slight roughening of the side of the sole caused by the friction of the edge of the pedal.

"Yes, I bicycle a good deal, Mr. Holmes. . . ."

My friend took the lady's ungloved hand, and examined it with as close an attention and as little sentiment as a scientist would show to a specimen.

"You will excuse me, I am sure. It is my business," said he, as he dropped it. "I nearly fell into the error of supposing you were type-writing. Of course, it is obvious that it is music. You observe the spatulate finger-ends, Watson, which is common to both professions? There is a spirituality about the face, however"—she gently turned it towards the light—"which the typewriter does not generate. This lady is a musician."

"Yes, Mr. Holmes, I teach music."

"In the country, I presume, from your complexion."

"Yes, sir, near Farnham, on the borders of Surrey."

V. "Harry Thompson visited Russia in 1958"; "Rex Davis is a millionaire"; "Betty Armstrong does not believe in God"; "Dr. Baxter is in disagreement with the policies of the American Medical Association." Accepting these statements as true, write several hundred words of unfounded inferences, and inferences upon inferences about these people. Of course, you don't know who they are, but don't let that stop you. Just go ahead and make inferences.

This exercise is also amusing and instructive for discussion groups, the members taking turns in adding inferences.

VI. Select a topic about which you have little information but many prejudices, such as "Whither Modern Youth?" "The Menace of Federal Encroachments on American Freedom," "The National Association of Manufacturers: A Threat to Democracy," "Big Unions: A Threat to Free Enterprise," "What's Wrong with Modern Women," "Let's Cut the Fads and Frills from Education," or "The South: Yesterday and Today," and write a one-thousand-word essay consisting solely of sweeping generalizations, broad judgments, and unfounded inferences. Use plenty of "loaded" words. Knock off five points (out of a possible 100) for each verifiable fact used. If you can consistently score 95 or better on all these and other such topics, and your grammar and spelling are plausible, leave your present job. Or quit school. Fame and fortune are within your grasp.

4 Contexts

How Dictionaries Are Made

It is widely believed that every word has a correct meaning, that we learn these meanings principally from teachers and grammarians (except that most of the time we don't bother to, so that we ordinarily speak "sloppy English"), and that dictionaries and grammars are the supreme authority in matters of meaning and usage. Few people ask by what authority the writers of dictionaries and grammars say what they say. The writer once got into a dispute with an Englishwoman over the pronunciation of a word and offered to look it up in the dictionary. The Englishwoman said firmly, "What for? I am English. I was born and brought up in England. The way I speak *is* English." Such self-assurance about one's own language is not uncommon among the English. In the United States, however, anyone who is willing to quarrel with the dictionary is regarded as either eccentric or mad.

* From *The Illiteracy of the Literate* by H. R. Huse, copyright, 1933, by D. Appleton-Century Company, Inc. Reprinted by permission of Appleton-Century-Crofts, Inc.

Let us see how dictionaries are made and how the editors arrive at definitions. What follows applies, incidentally, only to those dictionary offices where first-hand, original research goes on—not those in which editors simply copy existing dictionaries. The task of writing a dictionary begins with reading vast amounts of the literature of the period or subject that the dictionary is to cover. As the editors read, they copy on cards every interesting or rare word, every unusual or peculiar occurrence of a common word, a large number of common words in their ordinary uses, and also the sentences in which each of these words appears, thus:

> pail
> The dairy *pails* bring home increase of milk
> Keats, *Endymion*
> I, 44–45

That is to say, the context of each word is collected, along with the word itself. For a really big job of dictionary writing, such as the *Oxford English Dictionary* (usually bound in about twenty-five volumes), millions of such cards are collected, and the task of editing occupies decades. As the cards are collected, they are alphabetized and sorted. When the sorting is completed, there will be for each word anywhere from two or three to several hundred illustrative quotations, each on its card.

To define a word, then, the dictionary editor places before him the stack of cards illustrating that word; each of the cards represents an actual use of the word by a writer of some literary or historical importance. He reads the cards carefully, discards some, rereads the rest, and divides up the stack according to what he thinks are the several senses of the word. Finally, he writes his definitions, following the hard-and-fast rule that each definition *must* be based on what the quotations in front of him reveal about the meaning of the word. The editor cannot be influenced by what *he* thinks a given word *ought* to mean. He must work according to the cards or not at all.

The writing of a dictionary, therefore, is not a task of setting up authoritative statements about the "true meanings" of words, but a task of *recording,* to the best of one's ability, what various words *have meant* to authors in the distant or immediate past. *The writer of a dictionary is a historian, not a lawgiver.* If, for example, we had been writing a dictionary in 1890, or even as late as 1919, we could have said that the word "broadcast" means "to scatter" (seed and so on) but we could not have decreed that from 1921 on, the commonest meaning of the word should become "to disseminate audible messages, etc., by radio transmission." To regard the dictionary as an "authority," therefore, is to credit the dictionary writer with gifts of prophecy which neither he nor anyone else possesses. In choosing our words when we speak or write, we can be *guided* by the historical record afforded us by the dictionary, but we cannot be *bound* by it, because new situations, new experiences, new inventions, new feelings, are always compelling us to give new uses to old words. Looking under a "hood," we should ordinarily have found, five hundred years ago, a monk; today, we find a motorcar engine.[1]

Verbal and Physical Contexts

The way in which the dictionary writer arrives at his definitions merely systematizes the way in which we all learn the meanings of words, beginning at infancy, and continuing for the rest of our lives. Let us say that we have never heard the word "oboe" before, and we overhear a conversation in which the following sentences occur:

> He used to be the best *oboe* player in town. . . . Whenever they came to that *oboe* part in the third movement, he used to get very excited. . . . I saw him one day at the music shop, buying a new reed for his *oboe*. . . . He never liked to play the clarinet after he started playing the *oboe*. . . . He said it wasn't much fun, because it was too easy.

Although the word may be unfamiliar, its meaning becomes clear to us as we listen. After hearing the first sentence, we know that an "oboe" is "played," so that it must be either a game or a musical instrument. With the second sentence the possibility of its being a game is eliminated. With each succeeding sentence the possibilities as to what an "oboe" may be are narrowed down until we get a fairly clear idea of what is meant. This is how we learn by *verbal context.*

[1] *Webster's Third New International Dictionary* lists the word "hood" also as a shortened form of "hoodlum."

The time that elapsed between *Webster's Second Edition* (1934) and the *Third* (1961) indicates the enormous amount of reading and labor entailed in the preparation of a really thorough dictionary of a language as rapidly changing and as rich in vocabulary as English.

But even independently of this, we learn by physical and social context. Let us say that we are playing golf and that we have hit the ball in a certain way with certain unfortunate results, so that our companion says to us, "That's a bad *slice.*" He repeats this remark every time our ball fails to go straight. If we are reasonably bright, we learn in a very short time to say, when it happens again, "That's a bad slice." On one occasion, however, our friend says to us, "That's not a *slice* this time; that's a *hook.*" In this case we consider what has happened, and we wonder what is different about the last stroke from those previous. As soon as we make the distinction, we have added still another word to our vocabulary. The result is that after nine holes of golf, we can use both these words accurately—and perhaps several others as well, such as "divot," "number-five iron," "approach shot," *without ever having been told what they mean.* Indeed, we may play golf for years without ever being able to give a dictionary definition of "to slice": "To strike (the ball) so that the face of the club draws inward across the face of the ball, causing it to curve toward the right in flight (with a right-handed player)" (*Webster's New International Dictionary, Second Edition*). But even without being able to give such a definition, we should still be able to use the word accurately whenever the occasion demanded.

We learn the meanings of practically all our words (which are, it will be remembered, merely complicated noises), not from dictionaries, not from definitions, but from hearing these noises as they accompany actual situations in life and then learning to associate certain noises with certain situations. Even as dogs learn to recognize "words," as for example by hearing "biscuit" at the same time as an actual biscuit is held before their noses, so do we all learn to interpret language by being aware of the happenings that accompany the noises people make at us—by being aware, in short, of contexts.

The definitions given by little children in school show clearly how they associate words with situations; they almost always define in terms of physical and social contexts: "Punishment is when you have been bad and they put you in a closet and don't let you have any supper." "Newspapers are what the paper boy brings and you wrap up the garbage with it." These are good definitions. They cannot be used in dictionaries mainly because they are too specific; it would be impossible to list the myriads of situations in which every word has been used. For this reason, dictionaries give definitions on a high level of abstraction; that is, with particular references left out for the sake of conciseness. (The term "high level of abstraction" is more fully explained in Chapter 10.) This is another reason why it is a great mistake to regard a dictionary definition as telling us all about a word.

Extensional and Intensional Meaning

Dictionaries deal with the world of intensional meanings, but there is another world which a dictionary by its very nature ignores: the world of extensional meanings. *The extensional meaning of an utterance is that which it points to in the extensional (physical) world,* referred to in Chapter 2. That is to say, the extensional meaning cannot be expressed in words, because it is that which words stand for. An easy way to remember this is *to put your hand over your mouth and point* whenever you are asked to give an extensional meaning.

Of course, we cannot always point to the extensional meanings of the words we use. Therefore, so long as we are *discussing* meanings, we shall refer to that which is being talked about as the *denotation* of an utterance. For example, the denotation of the word "Winnipeg" is the prairie city of that name in southern Manitoba; the denotation of the word "dog" is a class of animals which includes dog_1 (Fido), dog_2 (Rex), dog_3 (Rover) . . . dog_n.

The *intensional meaning* of a word or expression, on the other hand, is that which is *suggested* (connoted) inside one's head. Roughly speaking, whenever we express the meaning of words by uttering more words, we are giving intensional meaning, or connotations. To remember this, put your hand over your eyes and let the words spin around in your head.

Utterances may have, of course, both extensional and intensional meaning. If they have no intensional meaning at all—that is, if they start no notions whatever spinning about in our heads—they are meaningless noises, like foreign languages that we do not understand. On the other hand, it is possible for utterances to have no extensional meaning at all, in spite of the fact that they may start many notions spinning about in our heads. The statement, "Angels watch over my bed at night," is one that has intensional but no extensional meaning. This does not mean that there are no angels watching over my bed at night. When we say that the statement has no extensional meaning, we are merely saying that we cannot see, touch, photograph, or in any scientific manner detect the presence of angels. The result is that, if an argument begins on the subject whether or not angels watch over my bed, *there is no way of ending the argument to the satisfaction of all disputants,* the Christians and the non-Christians, the pious and the agnostic, the mystical and the scientific. Therefore, whether we believe in angels or not, knowing in advance that any argument on the subject will be both endless and futile, we can avoid getting into fights about it.

When, on the other hand, statements have extensional content, as when we say, "This room is fifteen feet long," arguments can come to a close. No matter how many guesses there are about the length of the room, all discussion ceases when someone produces a tape measure. This, then, is the important difference between extensional and intensional meanings: namely, when utterances have extensional meanings, discussion can be ended and agreement reached; when utterances have intensional meanings only and no extensional meanings, arguments may, and often do, go on indefinitely. Such arguments can result only in conflict. Among individuals, they may result in the breaking up of friendships; in society, they often split organizations into bitterly opposed groups; among nations, they may aggravate existing tensions so seriously as to become real obstacles to the peaceful settling of disputes.

Arguments of this kind may be termed "non-sense arguments," because they are based on utterances about which no sense data can be collected. Needless to say, there are occasions when the hyphen may be omitted—that depends on one's feelings toward the particular argument under consideration. The reader is requested to provide his own examples of "non-sense arguments." Even the foregoing example of the angels may give offense to some people, despite the fact that no attempt is made to deny or affirm the existence of angels. Imagine, then, the uproar that might result from giving a number of examples from theology, politics, law, economics, literary criticism, and other fields in which it is not customary to distinguish clearly sense from non-sense.

The "One Word, One Meaning" Fallacy

Everyone, of course, who has ever given any thought to the meanings of words has noticed that they are always shifting and changing in meaning. Usually, people regard this as a misfortune, because it "leads to sloppy thinking" and "mental confusion." To remedy this condition, they are likely to suggest that we should all agree on "one meaning" for each word and use it only with that meaning. Thereupon it will occur to them that we simply cannot make people agree in this way, even if we could set up an ironclad dictatorship under a committee of lexicographers who would place censors in every newspaper office and microphones in every home. The situation, therefore, appears hopeless.

Such an impasse is avoided when we start with a new premise altogether—one of the premises upon which modern linguistic thought is based: namely, that *no word ever has exactly the same meaning twice.* The extent to which this premise fits the facts can be demonstrated in a number of ways. First, if we accept the proposition that the contexts of an utterance determine its meaning, it becomes apparent that since no two contexts are ever *exactly* the same, no two meanings can ever be exactly the same. How can we "fix the meaning" even for so common an expression as "to believe in" when it can be used in such sentences as the following:

I believe in you (I have confidence in you).

I believe in democracy (I accept the principles implied by the term democracy).

I believe in Santa Claus (It is my opinion that Santa Claus exists).

Second, we can take, for example, a word of "simple" meaning, like "kettle." But when John says "kettle," its intensional meanings to him are the common characteristics of all the kettles John remembers. When Peter says "kettle," however, its intensional meanings to him are the common characteristics of all the kettles he remembers. *No matter how small or how negligible the differences may be between John's "kettle" and Peter's "kettle," there is some difference.*

Finally, let us examine utterances in terms of extensional meanings. If John, Peter, Harold, and George each say "my typewriter," we would have to point to four different typewriters to get the extensional meaning in each case: John's new Olivetti, Peter's old Remington, Harold's Smith-Corona portable, and the undenotable intended "typewriter" that George plans some day to buy: "My typewriter, when I buy it, will be an electric." Also, if John says "my typewriter" today, and again "my typewriter" tomorrow, the extensional meaning is different in the two cases, because the typewriter is not exactly the same from one day to the next (nor from one minute to the next): slow processes of wear, change, and decay are going on constantly. Although we can say, then, that the differences in the meanings of a word on one occasion, on another occasion a minute later, and on still another occasion another minute later, are negligible, we cannot say that the meanings are *exactly* the same.

To insist dogmatically that we know what a word means *in advance of its utterance* is nonsense. All we can know in advance is *approximately* what it will mean. After the utterance, we interpret what has been said in the light of both verbal and physical contexts, and act according to our interpretation. An examination of the verbal context of an utterance, as well as the examination of the utterance itself, directs us to the intensional meanings; an examination of the physical context directs us to the extensional meanings. When John says to James, "Bring me that book, will you?" James looks in the direction of John's pointed finger (physical context) and sees a desk with several books on it (physical context); he thinks back over their previous conversation (verbal context) and knows which of those books is being referred to.

Interpretation *must* be based, therefore, on the totality of contexts. If it were otherwise, we should not be able to account for the fact that even if we fail to use the right (customary) words in some situations, people can very frequently understand us. For example:

A: Gosh, look at that second baseman go!
B (looking): You mean the shortstop?
A: Yes, that's what I mean.

A: There must be something wrong with the oil line; the engine has started to balk.
B: Don't you mean "gas line"?
A: Yes—didn't I say "gas line"?

Contexts often indicate our meaning so clearly that we do not even have to say what we mean in order to be understood.

Ignoring Contexts

It is clear, then, that the ignoring of contexts in any act of interpretation is at best a stupid practice. At its worst, it can be a vicious practice. A common example is the sensational newspaper story in which a few words by a public personage are torn out of their context and made the basis of a completely misleading account. There is the incident of a Veterans Day speaker, a university teacher, who declared before a high-school assembly that the Gettysburg Address was "a powerful piece of propaganda." The context clearly revealed that "propaganda" was being used, not according to its popular meaning, but rather, as the speaker himself stated, to mean "explaining the moral purposes of a war." The context also revealed that the speaker was a very great admirer of Lincoln. However, the local newspaper, ignoring the context, presented the account in such a way as to suggest that the speaker had called Lincoln a liar. On this basis, the newspaper began a campaign against the instructor. The speaker remonstrated with the editor of the newspaper, who replied, in effect, "I don't care what else you said. You said the Gettysburg Address was propaganda, didn't you?" This appeared to the editor complete proof that Lincoln had been maligned and that the speaker deserved to be discharged from his position at the university. Similar practices may be found in advertisements. A reviewer may be quoted on the jacket of a book as having said, "A brilliant work," while reading of the context may reveal that what he really said was, "It just falls short of being a brilliant work." There are some people who will always be able to find a defense for such a practice in saying, "But he did use the words, 'a brilliant work,' didn't he?"

People in the course of argument very frequently complain about words meaning different things to different people. Instead of complaining, they should accept such differences as a matter of course. It would be startling indeed if the word "justice," for example, were to have the same meaning to each of the nine justices of the United States Supreme Court; we should get nothing but unanimous decisions. It would be even more startling if "justice" meant the same to President Kennedy as to Nikita Khrushchev. If we can get deeply into our consciousness the principle that no word ever has the same meaning twice, we will develop the habit of automatically examining contexts, and this will enable us to understand better what others are saying. As it is, however, we are all too likely, when a word sounds familiar, to assume that we understand it even when we don't. In this way we read into people's remarks meanings that were never intended. Then we waste energy in angrily accusing people of "intellectual dishonesty" or "abuse of words," when their only sin is that they use words in ways unlike our own, as they can hardly help doing, especially if their background has been widely different from ours. There are cases of intellectual dishonesty and the abuse of words, of course, but they do not always occur in the places where people think they do.

In the study of history or of cultures other than our own, contexts take on special importance. To say, "There was no running water or electricity in the house," does not condemn an English house in 1570, but says a great deal against a house in Chicago in 1963. Again, if we wish to understand the Constitution of the United States, it is not enough, as our historians now tell us, merely to look up all the words in the dictionary and to read the interpretations written by Supreme Court justices. We must see the Constitution in its historical context: the conditions of life, the state of the arts and industries and transportation, the current ideas of the time—all of which helped to determine what words went into the Constitution and what those words meant to those who wrote them. After all, the words "United States of America" stood for quite a different-sized nation and a different culture in 1790 from what they stand for today. When it comes to very big subjects, the range of contexts to be examined—verbal, social, and historical—may become very large indeed.

In personal relations, furthermore, those who ignore psychological contexts often make the mistake of interpreting as insults remarks that are only intended in jest.

The Interaction of Words

All this is not to say, however, that the reader might just as well throw away his dictionary, simply because contexts are so important. Any word in a sentence—any sentence in a paragraph, any paragraph in a larger unit—whose meaning is revealed by its context, is itself part of the context of the rest of the text. To look up a word in a dictionary, therefore, frequently explains not only the word itself, but the rest of the sentence, paragraph, conversation, or essay in which it is found. All words within a given context interact upon one another.

Realizing, then, that a dictionary is a historical work, we should understand the dictionary thus: "The word *mother* has most frequently been used in the past among English-speaking people to indicate a female parent." From this we can safely infer, "If that is how it has been used, that is what it *probably* means in the sentence I am trying to understand." This is what we normally do, of course; after we look up a word in the dictionary, we reexamine the context to see if the definition fits. If the context reads, "Mother began to form in the bottle," one may have to look at the dictionary more carefully.

A dictionary definition, therefore, is an invaluable guide to interpretation. Words do not have a single "correct meaning"; they apply to *groups* of similar situations, which might be called *areas of meaning*. It is for defining these areas of meaning that a dictionary is useful. In each use of any word, we examine the particular context and the extensional events denoted (if possible) to discover the *point* intended within the area of meaning.

APPLICATIONS

I. If you were compiling a dictionary and had before you only the following quotations, what definition would you write for the word "shrdlu"? Don't just try to find a one-word synonym but write out a ten- to twenty-word definition.

1. He was exceptionally skillful with a shrdlu.
2. He says he needs a shrdlu to shape the beams.
3. I saw Mr. Jenkins yesterday buying a new handle for his shrdlu.
4. The steel head of Jenkins' shrdlu was badly chipped.
5. Don't bother with a saw or an ax; a shrdlu will do the job faster and better.

From the following quotations make up a definition in less than twenty words of "wanky."

1. He seems to be perpetually wanky.
2. Some people feel most wanky in the early morning but I get that way just before supper.
3. If you want to get over that wanky feeling, take Johnson's Homogenized Yeast Tablets.
4. Everybody feels more or less wanky on a hot, humid day.
5. . . . the wanky, wanky bluebell
   That droops upon its stem . . .
6. I am not cross, just wanky.

II. Two new terms—*extensional* and *intensional*—were introduced in this chapter and will be used frequently in the rest of this book. Some readers assume from the sound and the spelling that *extensional* comes from "extension" in the sense of "prolonging, stretching out" and that *intensional* comes from "intention" meaning "purpose or design." Those who are inclined to make such incorrect assumptions would do well to read again pages 58–60, asking, "What do these terms mean in this particular context?"

III. There are a number of words which, depending on their contexts, denote sometimes "the act of" and sometimes "the results of." For example, compare the word "building" in the following sentences:

a. The building of the stadium took three years.
b. The building which was completed in 1897 still stands.

In sentence *a* "building" refers to the "act of building," "the building process"; in sentence *b* it refers to a "finished building." Using the following words, compose parallel sentences in which the context makes clear a similar shift in meaning.

entertainment	creation
invention	destruction
painting	education

IV. In what contexts are the following questions likely to arise, and, in those contexts, which are non-sense questions and which not? Can you tell why?

1. Is democracy a failure?

   SAMPLE ANALYSIS: Unless there is reasonable agreement as to the extensional meaning of "democracy" and "failure," a discussion of this question is not likely to be fruitful. It might be broken up into smaller questions such as these: "Assuming that democracy is a success if 60 or more percent of those able to vote in presidential elections do vote, what was the percentage of voters in the elections of 1956, 1960, 1964 . . . ?" "Assuming that democracy may be said to be reasonably successful if intelligent but underprivileged children are given the opportunity to finish their schooling, what percentage of fourth grade children with I.Q.'s of over 125 finish high school?" If, however, we talk chiefly in terms of intensional meanings of the terms "democracy" and "failure," disagreement and ill-feeling are likely to result. In many contexts where such a question is brought up for discussion, it would seem to be a nonsense question.

2. Did Abraham Lincoln write the Gettysburg Address?

3. Why was I born?

4. Was Eisenhower a greater general than Napoleon?

5. Does Shirley MacLaine make more money than Kim Novak?

6. Should women work after marriage?

7. Why did this have to happen to *me*?

8. Are Negroes more intelligent than whites?

9. Where do flies go in the wintertime?

10. Am I the first girl you ever kissed?

11. Will the position of the stars on March 29 be such as to augur a successful business trip if I start out on that date? My birthday is November 6.

12. Is the universe expanding?

13. DEAR DOROTHY DIX: How can a wife tell when her husband loves her? I have been married ten years and my husband and I quarrel constantly. He beats me and swears at me, and then tells how much he loves me and cries over it all. Now I would like to leave him and go back to my folks, but he won't let me go. Says he can't bear to be separated from me. Please tell me what to do. Do you think he really loves me?   —UNHAPPY WIFE.   —Chicago *Sun-Times*

14. What's wrong with young people nowadays?

15. Are you honest?

V. Keep a record of some arguments you overhear in the next twenty-four hours with these questions in mind:

45380

1. What is the question at issue?

2. Is it a non-sense question or could it be answered by observation of the disputed facts?

3. To what extent do the participants reach agreement? If the argument ends in disagreement, can you think of any procedures that might have helped to bring about agreement?

VI. If you think you are clear about the "one word, one meaning" fallacy discussed in this chapter, try your hand at this problem:

> Some years ago, being with a camping party in the mountains, I returned from a solitary ramble to find everyone engaged in a ferocious metaphysical dispute. The corpus of the dispute was a squirrel —a live squirrel supposed to be clinging to one side of a tree-trunk; while over against the tree's opposite side a human being was imagined to stand. This human witness tries to get sight of the squirrel by moving rapidly around the tree, but no matter how fast he goes, the squirrel moves as fast in the opposite direction and always keeps the tree between himself and the man, so that never a glimpse of him is caught. The resultant metaphysical problem now is this: *Does the man go around the squirrel, or not?* He goes round the tree, sure enough, and the squirrel is on the tree; but does he go round the squirrel? In the unlimited leisure of the wilderness discussion had been worn threadbare. Everyone had taken sides, and was obstinate; and the numbers on both sides were even. Each side, when I appeared, therefore appealed to me to make it a majority. Mindful of the scholastic adage that whenever you meet a contradiction you must make a distinction, I immediately sought and found one, as follows. . . .   —WILLIAM JAMES

Make a distinction that would help end the argument and show clearly the source of the dispute. Note also the different meanings of the word "opposite" in this passage.

VII. In any good standard dictionary, words are defined in terms of areas of meaning and, for most words, there are many *different* areas of meaning. See if you can provide contexts (in this case, sentences) that will make clear the different areas of meaning of the following words:

frame	open	order
strike	pink	board
cut	point	interference

EXAMPLE: *pool.*

The brook formed a *pool* at the bend.

He lay in a *pool* of blood.

Let's go to the *pool* for a swim!

The wheat *pool* succeeded in sustaining the price of wheat.

He had the winning team in our baseball *pool.*

The balls clicked sharply on the *pool* table.

At the present time, it is not possible to *pool* the research findings of scientists all over the world.

VIII. Sit in a chair and say the words, "my chair," pointing to the object. Now, after moving to another chair, say again "my chair" and point to the object. Is the extensional meaning of the words still the same? Is the intensional meaning of the words still the same?

Take a sheet of paper and write your name half a dozen times. There are now before you six examples of the extensional meaning of the words "my signature." Compare them carefully. Are the extensional meanings in any two cases the same? Would they be the same if they were printed?

Take a piece of chewing gum from its wrapper and examine it carefully. Chew it for a time, then examine it again. Has the intensional meaning of "this chewing gum" been altered? How has the extensional meaning been affected?

IX. Here are some simple statements, the contexts of which are given upside down beneath each. Before reading the context, write down your immediate response to the statement. For example:

STATEMENT: He doesn't even know how to add one and one.
RESPONSE: How stupid can you get?

1. He hasn't washed himself for a month.

Water, for troops fighting in the desert in World War II, had to be conserved for drinking and for vehicles.

2. He looks at me blankly when I speak to him.

I therefore suppose that he is still unconscious from the blow.

3. Of course, son, I'll buy you a new sports car for Christmas.

In addition, I'll buy your sister two mink coats, your mother a villa in France, and your grandfather the Brooklyn Bridge.

5 The Language of Social Cohesion

> *Two little dogs sat by the fire*
> *Over a fender of coal dust;*
> *Said one little dog to the other little dog,*
> *"If you don't talk, why, I must."*
>
> —MOTHER GOOSE

> *Are words in Phatic Communion ["a type of speech*
> *in which ties of union are created by a mere ex-*
> *change of words"] used primarily to convey mean-*
> *ing, the meaning which is symbolically theirs? Cer-*
> *tainly not! They fulfil a social function and that is*
> *their principal aim, but they are neither the result*
> *of intellectual reflection, nor do they necessarily*
> *arouse reflection in the listener.*
>
> —BRONISLAW MALINOWSKI

Noises as Expression

What above all complicates the problems of interpretation is the fact that informative uses of language are intimately fused with older and deeper functions of language, so that only a small proportion of utterances in everyday life can be described as purely informative. We have every reason to believe that the ability to use language for strictly informative purposes was developed relatively late in the course of linguistic evolution. Long before we developed language as we now know it, we probably made, like the lower animals, all sorts of cries, expressive of such internal conditions as hunger, fear, loneliness, sexual desire, and triumph. We can recognize a variety of such noises and the conditions of which they are symptoms in our domestic animals. Gradually such noises seem to have become more and more differentiated; consciousness expanded. Grunts and gibberings became language. Therefore, although we have developed language in which accurate reports may be given, we almost universally tend to *express* our internal conditions *first,* then to follow up with a report if necessary: "Ow! (expression) My tooth hurts (report)." Many utterances are, as we have seen with regard to "snarl-words" and "purr-words," vocal equivalents of expressive gestures, such as crying in pain, baring the teeth in anger, nuzzling to express friendliness, dancing with delight, and so on. When words are used as vocal equivalents of expressive gestures, we shall say that language is being used in *presymbolic* ways. These presymbolic uses of language coexist with our symbolic systems, and the talking we do in everyday life is a thorough blending of symbolic and presymbolic.

Indeed, the presymbolic factors in everyday language are always most apparent in expressions of strong feeling of any kind. If we carelessly step off a curb when a car is coming, it doesn't much matter whether someone yells, "Look out!" or "Kiwotsuke!" or "Hey!" or "Prends garde!" or simply utters a scream, so long as whatever noise is made is uttered loudly enough to alarm us. It is the fear expressed in the *loudness* and *tone* of the cry that conveys the necessary sensations, and not the words. Similarly, commands given sharply and angrily usually produce quicker results than the same commands uttered tonelessly. The quality of the voice itself, that is to say, has a power of expressing feelings that is almost independent of the symbols used. We can say, "I hope you'll come to see us again," in a way that clearly indicates that we hope the visitor never comes back. Or again, if a young lady with whom we are strolling says, "The moon is bright tonight," we are able to tell by the tone whether she is making a meteorological observation or indicating that she wants to be kissed.

Very small infants understand the love, the warmth, or the irritation in a mother's voice long before they are able to understand her words. Most children retain this sensitivity to presymbolic elements in language. It even survives in some adults; they are the people credited with "intuition" or "unusual tact." Their talent lies in their ability to interpret tones of voice, facial expressions, and other symptoms of the internal condition of the speaker: they listen not only to *what* is said, but to *how* it is said. On the other hand, people who have spent much of their lives in the study of *written* symbols (scientists, intellectuals, bookkeepers) tend to be relatively deaf to everything but the surface sense of the words. If a lady wants a person of this kind to kiss her, she usually has to tell him to in so many words.

Noise for Noise's Sake

Sometimes we talk simply for the sake of hearing ourselves talk; that is, for the same reason that we play golf or dance. The activity gives us a pleasant sense of being alive. Children prattling, adults singing in the bathtub, are alike enjoying the sound of their voices. Sometimes large groups make noises together, as in group singing, group recitation, or group chanting, for similar presymbolic reasons. In all this, the significance of the words used is almost completely irrelevant. We may, for example, chant the most lugubrious words about a desire to be carried back to a childhood home in old Virginny, when in actuality we have never been there and haven't the slightest intention of going.

What we call social conversation is again largely presymbolic in character. When we are at a tea or dinner party, for example, we all have to talk—about anything: the weather, the performance of the Chicago White Sox, James Michener's latest book, or Natalie Wood's recent picture. Rarely, except among very good friends, are the remarks made during these conversations important enough to be worth making for their informative value. Nevertheless, it is regarded as rude to remain silent. Indeed, in such matters as greetings and farewells—"Good morning"—"Lovely day"—"And how's your family these days?"—"It was a pleasure meeting you"—"Do look us up the next time you're in town"—it is regarded as a social error not to say these things even if we do not mean them. There are numberless daily situations in which we talk simply because it would be impolite not to. Every social group has its own form of this kind of talking— "the art of conversation," "small talk," or the mutual kidding that Americans love so much.[1] From these social practices it is possible

[1] Among American men, this mutual kidding has something of the quality of an initiation rite. During World War II a Jewish scientist, recently fled from Germany, served as a professor of physics on the faculty of a Midwestern college. Also on the faculty was a professor of chemistry, a bluff, outgoing, cheerful man who was always kidding others in the faculty dining room. The chemist would joke with the physicist in what many of us felt to be a crude way: "Hey, Max, what did you Jews do that they kicked you out of Germany?" Professor Max, still sensitive and bitter after his persecution by the Nazis, would simply look miserable and not reply.

One day, however, Professor Max caught the idea. He said to the chemist, "Professor Schlemmer, isn't yours a *German* name?" "Why, yes," said Professor Schlemmer, "my grandparents came here from Germany in the 1880's." "Aha," said Professor Max, "they kicked your family out *two generations* before they kicked out mine!" Professor Schlemmer roared with laughter and put his arm around Professor Max's shoulder.

to state, as a general principle, that *the prevention of silence is itself an important function of speech,* and that it is completely impossible for us in society to talk only when we "have something to say."

This presymbolic talk for talk's sake is, like the cries of animals, a form of activity. We talk together about nothing at all and thereby establish friendships. The purpose of the talk is not the communication of information, as the symbols used would seem to imply ("I see the Dodgers are out in the lead again"), but the establishment of communion. Human beings have many ways of establishing communion among themselves: breaking bread together, playing games together, working together. But talking together is the most easily arranged of all these forms of collective activity. The *togetherness* of the talking, then, is the most important element in social conversation; the subject matter is only secondary.

There is a principle at work, therefore, in the selection of subject matter. Since the purpose of this kind of talk is the establishment of communion, *we are careful to select subjects about which agreement is immediately possible.* Consider, for example, what happens when two strangers feel the necessity or the desire to talk to each other:

> "Nice day, isn't it?"
> "It certainly is." (Agreement on one point has been established. It is safe to proceed.)
> "Altogether, it's been a fine summer."
> "Indeed it has. We had a nice spring, too." (Agreement on two points having been established, the second party invites agreement on a third point.)
> "Yes, it was a lovely spring." (Third agreement reached.)

The togetherness, therefore, is not merely in the talking itself, but in the opinions expressed. Having agreed on the weather, we go on to further agreements—that it is nice farming country around here, that it certainly is scandalous how prices are going up, that New York is certainly an interesting place to visit but it would be awful to have to live there, and so on. *With each new agreement, no matter how commonplace or how obvious, the fear and suspicion of the stranger wears away, and the possibility of friendship enlarges.* When further conversation reveals that we have friends or political views or artistic tastes or hobbies in common, a friend is made, and genuine communication and cooperation can begin.

Here is how these conversational exchanges are likely to go among young people:

BOY: Like to dance?
GIRL: Yes, I would.
BOY: My name's Charlie.
GIRL: I'm Joan. Nice party, isn't it?
BOY: Yes, it sure is. One of the best since I been in school.
GIRL: Oh, do you go to school here?
BOY: Yeah. You?
GIRL: No . . . well, I came with a friend who does, though. How many years have you been going here?
BOY: Two.
GIRL: What's your major?
BOY: I don't know yet.
GIRL: That's a pretty popular major around here, isn't it.
BOY: Guess so. How about a drink?
GIRL: Okay.
BOY: I'll be right back then.

The Value of Unoriginal Remarks

An incident in the writer's own experience illustrates how necessary it sometimes is to give people the opportunity to agree. Early in 1942, a few weeks after the beginning of the war and at a time when rumors of Japanese spies were still widely current, he had to wait two or three hours in a railroad station in Oshkosh, Wisconsin, a city in which he was a stranger. He became aware as time went on that the other people waiting in the station were staring at him suspiciously and feeling uneasy about his presence. One couple with a small child were staring with special uneasiness and whispering to each other. The writer therefore took occasion to remark to the husband that it was too bad that the train should be late on so cold a night. The man agreed. The writer went on to remark that it must be especially difficult to travel with a small child in winter when train schedules were so uncertain. Again the husband agreed. The writer then asked the child's age and remarked that the child looked very big and strong for his age. Again agreement—this time with a slight smile. The tension was relaxing.

After two or three more exchanges, the man asked, "I hope you don't mind my bringing it up, but you're Japanese, aren't you? Do you think the Japs have any chance of winning this war?"

"Well," the writer replied, "your guess is as good as mine. I don't know any more than I read in the papers. (This was true.) But the way I figure it, I don't see how the Japanese, with their lack of coal and steel and oil and their limited industrial capacity, can ever beat a powerfully industrialized nation like the United States."

The writer's remark was admittedly neither original nor well informed. Hundreds of radio commentators and editorial writers were saying exactly the same thing during those weeks. But just because they were, the remark *sounded familiar* and was *on the right side,* so that it was easy to agree with. The man agreed at once, with what seemed like genuine relief. How much the wall of suspicion had broken down was indicated in his next question, "Say, I hope your folks aren't over there while the war is going on."

"Yes, they are. My father and mother and two young sisters are over there."

"Do you ever hear from them?"

"How can I?"

"Do you mean you won't be able to see them or hear from them till after the war is over?" Both he and his wife looked troubled and sympathetic.

There was more to the conversation, but the result was that within ten minutes after it had begun they had invited the writer to visit them in their city and have dinner with them in their home. And the other people in the station, seeing the writer in conversation with people who *didn't* look suspicious, ceased to pay any attention to him and went back to reading their papers and staring at the ceiling.[2]

Maintenance of Communication Lines

Such presymbolic uses of language not only establish new lines of communication, but keep old lines open. Old friends like to talk even when they have nothing especially to say to each other. In the same way that long-distance telephone operators, ship radio officers, and army signal corps outposts chatter with each other even when there are no official messages to communicate, so do people who live in the same household or work in the same office continue to talk to each other even when there is nothing much to say. The purpose in both cases seems to be partly to relieve tedium, but partly, and more importantly, to keep the lines of communication open.

[2] Perhaps it should be added that the writer was by no means *consciously* applying the principles of this chapter during the incident. This account is the result of later reflection. He was simply groping, as anyone else might do, for a way to relieve his own loneliness and discomfort in the situation.

Hence the situation between many a married couple:

WIFE: Wilbur, why don't you talk to me?

HUSBAND (interrupted in his reading of Schopenhauer or *The Racing Form*): What's that?

WIFE: Why don't you talk to me?

HUSBAND: But there isn't anything to say.

WIFE: You don't love me.

HUSBAND (thoroughly interrupted, and somewhat annoyed): Oh, don't be silly. You know I do. (Suddenly consumed by a passion for logic.) Do I run around with other women? Don't I turn my paycheck over to you? Don't I work my head off for you and the kids?

WIFE (way out on a logical limb, but still not satisfied): But still I wish you'd say something.

HUSBAND: Why?

WIFE: Well, because.

Of course, in a way the husband is right. His actions are an extensional demonstration of his love. They speak louder than words. But, in a different way, the wife is right. How does one know that the lines of communication are still open unless one keeps them at work? When a sound engineer says into a microphone, "One . . . two . . . three . . . four . . . testing . . ." he isn't saying anything much. But it is nevertheless important at times that he say it.

Presymbolic Language in Ritual

Sermons, political caucuses, conventions, pep rallies, and other ceremonial gatherings illustrate the fact that all groups—religious, political, patriotic, scientific, and occupational—like to gather together at intervals for the purpose of sharing certain accustomed activities, wearing special costumes (vestments in religious organizations, regalia in lodges, uniforms in patriotic societies, and so on), eating together (banquets), displaying the flags, ribbons, or emblems of their group, and marching in processions. Among these ritual activities is always included a number of speeches, either traditionally worded or specially composed for the occasion, whose principal function is *not* to give the audience information it did not have before, *not* to create new ways of feeling, but something else altogether.

What this something else is, we shall analyze more fully in Chapter 7, the chapter on "The Language of Social Control." However, we can now analyze one aspect of language as it appears in ritual speeches. Let us look at what happens at a pep rally such as precedes college football games. The members of "our team" are "introduced" to a crowd that already knows them. Called upon to make speeches, the players mutter a few incoherent and often ungrammatical remarks, which are received with wild applause. The leaders of the rally make fantastic promises about the mayhem to be performed on the opposing team the next day. The crowd utters "cheers," which normally consist of animalistic noises arranged in extremely primitive rhythms. *No one comes out any wiser or better informed than he was before he went in.*

To some extent religious ceremonies are equally puzzling at first glance. The priest or clergyman in charge utters set speeches, *often in a language incomprehensible to the congregation* (Hebrew in orthodox Jewish synagogues, Latin in the Roman Catholic churches, Sanskrit in Chinese and Japanese temples), with the result that, as often as not, no information whatsoever is communicated to those present.

If we approach these linguistic events from a detached point of view, and if we also examine our own reactions when we enter into the spirit of such occasions, we cannot help observing that, whatever the words used in ritual utterance may signify, we often do not think very much about their signification during the course of the ritual. Most of us, for example, have often repeated the Lord's Prayer or sung "The Star-Spangled Banner" without thinking about the words at all. As children we are taught to repeat such sets of words before we can understand them, and many of us continue to say them for the rest of our lives without bothering about their signification. Only the superficial, however, will dismiss these facts as "simply showing what fools human beings are." We cannot regard such utterances as "meaningless," because they have a genuine effect upon us. We may come out of church, for example, with no clear memory of what the sermon was about, but with a sense nevertheless that the service has somehow "done us good."

What is the "good" that is done us in ritual utterances? It is the *reaffirmation of social cohesion:* the Christian feels closer to his fellow-Christians, the Elk feels more united with his brother Elks, the American feels more American and the Frenchman more French, as the result of these rituals. Societies are held together by such bonds of common reactions to sets of linguistic stimuli.

Ritualistic utterances, therefore, whether made up of words that have symbolic significance at other times, of words in foreign or obsolete tongues, or of meaningless syllables, may be regarded as consisting in large part of presymbolic uses of language: that is, *accustomed sets of noises* which convey no information, but to which feelings (often group feelings) are attached. Such utterances rarely make sense to anyone not a member of the group. The abracadabra of a lodge meeting is absurd to anyone not a member of the lodge. When language becomes ritual, that is to say, its effect becomes to a considerable extent independent of whatever significations the words once possessed.

Advice to the Literal-Minded

Presymbolic functions of language have this characteristic in common: their effectiveness does not depend on the use of words. They can even be performed without recognizable speech at all. Group feeling may be established, for example, among animals by collective barking or howling, and among human beings by college cheers, community singing, and other collective noise-making activities. Indications of friendliness such as we give when we say "Good morning" or "Nice day, isn't it?" can be given by smiles, gestures, or, as among animals, by nuzzling or sniffing. Frowning, laughing, smiling, jumping up and down, can satisfy a large number of needs for expression, without the use of verbal symbols. But the use of verbal symbols is more customary among human beings, so that instead of expressing our feelings by knocking a man down, we often verbally blast him to perdition; instead of forming social groups by huddling together like puppies, we write constitutions and bylaws and invent rituals for the vocal expression of our cohesion.

To understand the presymbolic elements that enter into our everyday language is extremely important. We cannot restrict our speech to the giving and asking of factual information; we cannot confine ourselves strictly to statements that are literally true, or we should often be unable to say even "Pleased to meet you" when the occasion demanded. The intellectually persnickety often tell us that we ought to say what we mean and mean what we say, and talk only when we have something to talk about. These are, of course, impossible prescriptions.

Ignorance of the existence of these presymbolic uses of language is not so common among uneducated people (who often perceive such things intuitively) as it is among the educated. The educated often listen to the chatter at teas and receptions, and conclude from the triviality of the conversation that all the guests (except themselves) are fools. They may discover that people often come away from church services without any clear memory of the sermon and conclude that churchgoers are either fools or hypocrites. Listening to political oratory, they may wonder "how anybody can believe such rot," and then conclude that people in general are so unintelligent that democracy is unworkable. Almost all such gloomy conclusions about the stupidity or hypocrisy of our friends and neighbors are unjustifiable on such evidence, because they usually come from applying the standards of symbolic language to linguistic events that are either partly or wholly presymbolic in character.

One further illustration may make this clearer. Let us suppose that we are on the roadside struggling with a flat tire. A not-very-bright-looking but friendly youth comes up and asks, "Got a flat tire?" If we insist upon interpreting his words literally, we will regard this as an extremely silly question and our answer may be, "Can't you see I have, you dumb ox?" If we pay no attention to what the words say, however, and understand his meaning, we will return his gesture of friendly interest by showing equal friendliness, and in a short while he may be helping us to change the tire.[3] In a similar way, many situations in life demand that we pay no attention to what the words say, since the meaning may often be a great deal more intelligent and intelligible than the surface *sense* of the words themselves. A great deal of our pessimism about the world, about humanity, and about democracy probably derives from the fact that unconsciously we apply the standards of symbolic language to presymbolic utterances.

APPLICATIONS

I. Try the following game with a group of friends. At an afternoon gathering or an evening party, set aside a period during which

[3] Dr. Karl Menninger, in *Love Against Hate* (1942), comments on this passage and offers the following translation of "Got a flat tire?" in terms of its psychological meaning: "Hello—I see you are in trouble. I'm a stranger to you but I might be your friend now that I have a chance to be if I had any assurance that my friendship would be welcomed. Are you approachable? Are you a decent fellow? Would you appreciate it if I helped you? I would like to do so but I don't want to be rebuffed. This is what my voice sounds like. What does your voice sound like?" Why does not the youth simply say directly, "I would be glad to help you"? Dr. Menninger explains: "But people are too timid and mutually distrustful to be so direct. *They want to hear one another's voices. People need assurance that others are just like themselves.*" (Italics added.)

the rules are that no one is permitted to say anything except the word "Urglu" (to be uttered with any variations of pitch or tone necessary to convey different meanings) and that anyone using ordinary language during that period is to be fined. Notice what *can* and *cannot* be communicated by the use of such a single nonsense-word, accompanied by whatever gestures or facial expressions seem necessary. (Incidental query: Why is it that party-games, although often interesting when played, sound so silly when described?)

II. At the next meeting of a club or committee where group discussion is expected, notice the occasions when presymbolic language is used. At what points of the meeting does it seem to help the group along? Are there times when it seems to stall the meeting?

Or observe the ways in which an effective chairman at a banquet, an orator at a Farm Bureau or Grange picnic, or a popular master of ceremonies at a night club operates. Don't be too "objective" about this sort of exercise—don't sit there deadpan and detached, like an ethnologist from a different civilization taking notes on native customs. Enter into the spirit of the occasion, observing your own reactions as well as the reactions of others to the meaningfully meaningless utterances that are made. The detached approach may be taken on the following day, when you are writing down your observations, with the speeches, the audience reactions, and your own reactions as objects of study.

III. Keep track some day of the number of times a meeting of friends is begun with remarks about the weather. Why does the weather make such an easy opening? Is it true that women are more likely than men to greet each other with complimentary remarks about each other's appearance—"What a lovely new hat!" "Where *did* you get that stunning dress?" Query: *Do men have special patterns of their own in greeting other men?*

It is the writer's impression that small children usually have not developed these presymbolic means of getting rapport with others. Observe with special care how a child and an adult who are strangers to each other get conversation started, if they do at all.

What does "How do you do?" really mean? Wouldn't the man you pass every morning be surprised if you answered his "How are you?" with "I'm running a temperature of 103"? Or would he just fail to notice your reply? Is the Frenchman who says *"Enchanté"* on introduction really as enchanted as he says? The complimentary close of a Spanish letter to a lady says that the sender kisses her feet—*Que besa sus pies*. The suffix "*-kun*" with which Japanese men address each other ("Hayakawa-*kun,* Yamada-*kun*") originally meant "prince." Such formulas are worth examining.

IV. Note the differences in forms of presymbolic usage in different classes of society, in different ethnic groups, in different countries. If the reader is well acquainted with more than one social class, or more than one nationality group, he might compare and contrast the different usages among the groups with which he is familiar. In the United States, there appear to the writer to be marked differences in the style and amount of presymbolic discourse between the general American middle-class culture and the cultures of immigrant groups who retain some of their Old World habits (Scandinavian farmers of the Midwest, Pennsylvania Dutch, Jews of the New York garment district, Italians, Poles, Germans of the Chicago northwest side, and so forth). There are also occupational and class differences: social usages among theatrical people, truck-drivers, women's clubs, artists and writers in urban Bohemias, and naval officers provide some sharp contrasts. An especially graceful ceremoniousness is often to be found in gatherings of American lower middle-class Negroes.

In an essay of 1000 to 1500 words, describe the differences in presymbolic usage among two or more different social groups.

V. In the United States, many books are published on how to "improve" on silence. Books of social guidance for young girls, for example, advise them to ask their dates fatuous questions in order to get them talking. For adults, there are "conversation" and "word power" courses:

> LESSON NO. 2—Getting Acquainted. Are you at a loss for words when you meet strangers? How to be at ease with anyone, anywhere, is the theme of this lesson: entertaining conversation in mixed company. . . .   —Advertisement for Conversation Studies

There are also inspirational books, such as those by Norman Vincent Peale and Rabbi Joshua Liebman, which show how to get ahead in life by talking. The most famous of these books is, of course, *How to Win Friends and Influence People,* in which the late Dale Carnegie advises, "Get the other person saying 'yes, yes' immediately."

Professor Geoffrey Wagner of the City College of New York,

who was brought up in England, observes that the English are not nearly as interested in the prevention of silence as Americans. "One of my uncles," he writes, "went up to London daily for twenty years with the same group of men who occupied the same carriage and never spoke to each other. Visit a West End club. Try London elevators (lifts). The British usually don't want to speak."

The reader is urged to think back over his own experiences with the customs, the conversation, and the etiquette of his own social group, to examine carefully those things which he ordinarily takes for granted, and to write a 1000-word essay describing those social rituals *for the benefit of a newcomer who has just arrived from a distant country in, say, Latin America or Asia.*

VI. Try to live a whole day without any presymbolic uses of language, restricting yourself solely to (a) specific statements of fact which contribute to the hearer's information; (b) specific requests for needed information or services. This exercise is recommended only to those whose devotion to science and the experimental method is greater than their desire to keep their friends.

6 The Double Task of Language

> *Tens of thousands of years have elapsed since we
> shed our tails, but we are still communicating with a
> medium developed to meet the needs of aboreal
> man. . . . We may smile at the linguistic illusions
> of primitive man, but may we forget that the verbal
> machinery on which we so readily rely, and with
> which our metaphysicians still profess to probe the
> Nature of Existence, was set up by him, and may
> be responsible for other illusions hardly less gross
> and not more easily eradicable?*
>
> —C. K. OGDEN AND I. A. RICHARDS

Connotations

Report language, as we have seen, is *instrumental* in character—
that is, instrumental in getting work done; but, as we have seen,
language is also used for the direct *expression* of the feelings of the
speaker. Considering language from the point of view of the *hearer,*
we can say that report language *informs* us but that these expressive
uses of language (for example, judgments and what we have called
presymbolic functions) *affect* us—that is, affect our feelings. When
language is affective, it has the character of a kind of force.[1] A
spoken insult, for example, provokes a return insult, just as a blow
provokes a return blow; a loud and peremptory command compels,
just as a push compels; talking and shouting are as much a display

[1] Such terms as "emotional" and "emotive," which imply misleading distinctions between the "emotional appeals" and "intellectual appeals" of language, should be carefully avoided. In any case, "emotional" applies too specifically to strong feelings. The word "affective," however, in such an expression as the "affective uses of language," describes not only the way in which
language can arouse strong feelings, but also the way in which it arouses
extremely subtle, sometimes unconscious, responses. "Affective" has the further advantage of introducing no inconvenient distinctions between "physical"
and "mental" responses.

of energy as the pounding of the chest. And the first of the affective elements in speech, as we have seen, is the tone of voice, its loudness or softness, its pleasantness or unpleasantness, its variations in volume and intonation during the course of the utterance.

Another affective element in language is rhythm. *Rhythm* is the name we give to the effect produced by the repetition of auditory (or kinesthetic) stimuli at fairly regular intervals. From the boom-boom of a childish drum to the subtle nuances of cultivated poetry and music, there is a continuous development and refinement of man's responsiveness to rhythm. To produce rhythm is to arouse attention and interest; so affective is rhythm, indeed, that it catches our attention even when we do not want our attention distracted. *Rhyme* and *alliteration* are, of course, ways of emphasizing rhythm in language, through repetition of similar sounds at regular intervals. Political-slogan writers and advertisers therefore have a special fondness for rhyme and alliteration: "Tippecanoe and Tyler Too," "Rum, Romanism, and Rebellion," "Keep Cool with Coolidge," "Order from Horder," "Better Buy Buick," "Take Tea 'n' See," "I Like Ike." These are totally absurd slogans so far as informative value is concerned, but by their sound they set up small rhythmic echoes in one's head that make them annoyingly difficult to forget.

In addition to tone of voice and rhythm, another extremely important affective element in language is the aura of feelings, pleasant or unpleasant, that surrounds practically all words. It will be recalled that in Chapter 4 a distinction was made between denotations (or extensional meaning) pointing to things, and connotations (or intensional meaning) consisting of "ideas," "notions," "concepts," and feelings suggested in the mind. These connotations can be divided into two kinds, the *informative* and the *affective*.

Informative Connotations

The informative connotations of a word are its socially agreed upon, "impersonal" meanings, *insofar as meanings can be given at all by additional words*. For example, if we talk about a "pig," we cannot give the extensional meaning of the word unless there happens to be an actual pig for us to point to. But we can give its informative connotations: "pig" for English-speaking people means "domesticated mammalian quadruped of the kind generally raised by farmers to be made into pork, bacon, ham, lard. . . ."

Informative connotations may include both the *definition* of a term ("pig" as a "domesticated mammalian . . .") and its *denotation* (pig₁, pig₂, pig₃ . . .). But some terms have a definition, yet lack denotation: for example, a "mermaid" exists by definition only ("a creature half woman and half fish"). The term has no denotation because an extensional mermaid is not to be found. Terms in mathematics which have "logical existence" but no extensional reference can also be said to have informative connotations, but no denotation.

Denotations would seem to offer few problems of interpretation, since we are dealing here with words apart from the personal feelings that they may arouse. But such is not the case, because the same word may denote different things to people in different occupations or in different parts of the English-speaking world. The names of birds, animals, and plants are an interesting example of confusion about denotations. The English "robin" is an entirely different species from the American bird of that name. Many different and unrelated kinds of fish are denoted by the word "bream" (pronounced "brim" in the South). Belgian hares, we are told, are "really rabbits," while the American jackrabbit is "really a hare." The term "crocus," as popularly used, refers in different parts of the country to different flowers. The writer has also heard from a bird-watcher that "The English sparrow is not a sparrow at all, but a weaver finch. House finches are often called linnets. The linnet is a European bird that we don't have in America."

Such differences in popular and regional terminology are among the reasons for establishing scientific names for plants and animals—names which are accepted and used by the entire international scientific community.

Affective Connotations

The affective connotations of a word, on the other hand, are the aura of personal feelings it arouses, as, for example, "pig": "Ugh! Dirty, evil-smelling creatures, wallowing in filthy sties," and so on. While there is no necessary agreement about these feelings—some people like pigs and others don't—it is the existence of these feelings that enables us to use words, under certain circumstances, *for their affective connotations alone,* without regard to their informative connotations. That is to say, when we are strongly moved, we express our feelings by uttering words with the affective connotations appropriate to our feelings, without paying any attention to the informative connotations they may have. We angrily call people "rats," "wolves," "old bears," "skunks," or lovingly call them "honey," "sugar," "duck," and "sweetie pie." Indeed, all verbal expressions of feeling make use to some extent of the affective connotations of words.

All words have, according to the uses to which they are put, some affective character. There are many words that exist more for their affective value than for their informative value; for example, we can refer to "that man" as "that gentleman," "that individual," "that person," "that gent," "that guy," "that hombre," "that bird," or "that bozo"—and while the person referred to may be the same in all these cases, each of these terms reveals a difference in our feelings toward him. Dealers in knickknacks frequently write "Gyfte Shoppe" over the door, hoping that such a spelling carries, even if their merchandise does not, the flavor of antiquity. Affective connotations suggestive of England and Scotland are often sought in the choice of brand names for men's suits and overcoats: "Glenmoor," "Regent Park," "Bond Street." Sellers of perfume choose names for their products that suggest France—"Mon Désir," "Indiscret," "Evening in Paris"—and expensive brands always come in "flacons," never in bottles. Consider, too, the differences among the following expressions:

> I have the honor to inform Your Excellency . . .
> This is to advise you . . .
> I should like to tell you, sir . . .
> I'm telling you, Mister . . .
> Cheez, boss, git a load of dis . . .

The parallel columns below also illustrate how affective connotations can be changed while extensional meanings remain the same.

Finest quality filet mignon.	First-class piece of dead cow.
Cubs trounce Giants 5–3.	Score: Cubs 5, Giants 3.
French armies in rapid retreat!	The strategic withdrawal of the French forces to previously prepared positions in the rear was accomplished briskly and efficiently.
Urban Redevelopment Bill steam-rollered through Senate.	Senate passes Urban Redevelopment Bill over strong opposition.
She has her husband under her thumb.	She takes a deep interest in her husband's affairs.

| The governor appeared to be gravely concerned and said that a statement would be issued in a few days after careful examination of the facts. | The governor was on the spot. |

The story is told that, during the Boer War, the Boers were described in the British press as "sneaking and skulking behind rocks and bushes." The British forces, when they finally learned from the Boers how to employ tactics suitable to veldt warfare, were described as "cleverly taking advantage of cover."

A Note on Verbal Taboo

In every language there seem to be certain "unmentionables"—words of such strong affective connotations that they cannot be used in polite discourse. In English, the first of these to come to mind are, of course, words dealing with excretion and sex. We ask movie ushers and filling-station attendants where the "lounge" or "rest room" is, although we usually have no intention of lounging or resting. "Powder room" is another euphemism for the same facility, also known as "toilet," which itself is an earlier euphemism. Indeed, it is impossible in polite society to state, without having to resort to baby-talk or a medical vocabulary, what a "rest room" is for. (It is where you "wash your hands.")

Money is another subject about which communication is in some ways inhibited. It is all right to mention *sums* of money, such as "ten thousand dollars" or "two dollars and fifty cents." But it is considered in bad taste to inquire directly into other people's financial affairs, unless such an inquiry is really necessary in the course of business. When creditors send bills, they practically never mention money, although that is what they are writing about. There are many circumlocutions: "We beg to call your attention to what might be an oversight on your part." "We would appreciate your early attention to this matter." "May we look forward to an early remittance?"

The fear of death carries over, quite understandably in view of the widespread confusion of symbols with things symbolized, into fear of the *words* having to do with death. Many people, therefore, instead of saying "died," substitute such expressions as "passed away," "gone to his reward," "departed," and "gone west." In Japanese, the word for death, *"shi,"* happens to have the same pronunciation as the word for the number four. This coincidence results in many linguistically awkward situations, since people avoid *"shi"* in the discussion of numbers and prices, and use *"yon,"* a word of different origin, instead.

Words having to do with anatomy and sex—and words even vaguely suggesting anatomical or sexual matters—have, especially in American culture, remarkable affective connotations. Ladies of the last century could not bring themselves to say "breast" or "leg"— not even of chicken—so that the terms "white meat" and "dark meat" were substituted. It was thought inelegant to speak of "going to bed," and "to retire" was used instead. In rural America there are many euphemisms for the word "bull"; among them are "he cow," "cow critter," "male cow," "gentleman cow." But Americans are not alone in their delicacy about such matters. When D. H. Lawrence's first novel, *The White Peacock* (1911), was published, the author was widely and vigorously criticized for having used (in innocuous context) the word "stallion." "Our hearts are warm, our bellies are full," was changed to "Our hearts are warm, and we are full" in a 1962 presentation of the Rodgers and Hammerstein musical *Carousel* before the British Royal Family.

These verbal taboos, though sometimes amusing, also produce serious problems—since they prevent frank discussion of sexual matters. Social workers, with whom the writer has discussed this question, report that young people of junior high school and high school age who contract venereal disease, become pregnant out of wedlock, and get into other serious trouble of this kind, are almost always profoundly ignorant of the most elementary facts about sex and procreation. Their ignorance is apparently due to the fact that neither they nor their parents have a vocabulary in which to discuss such matters: the nontechnical vocabulary of sex is to them too coarse and shocking to be used, while the technical, medical vocabulary is unknown to them. The social workers find, therefore, that the first step in helping these young people is usually linguistic: they have to be taught a vocabulary in which they can talk about their problems before they can be helped further.

The stronger verbal taboos have, however, a genuine social value. When we are extremely angry and we feel the need of expressing our anger in violence, the uttering of these forbidden words provides us with a relatively harmless verbal substitute for going berserk and smashing furniture; that is, they act as a kind of safety valve in our moments of crisis.

It is difficult to explain why some words should have such powerful affective connotations while others with the same informative connotations do not. Some of our verbal reticences, especially the religious ones, have the authority of the Bible: "Thou shalt not take the name of the Lord thy God in vain; for the Lord will not hold him guiltless that taketh his name in vain" (Exodus 21:7). "Gee," "gee whiz," "gosh almighty," "gee whillikens," and "gosh darn" are ways of avoiding saying "Jesus," "God Almighty," and "God damn"; and carrying the biblical injunction one step further, we also avoid taking the name of the Devil in vain by means of such expressions as "the deuce," "the dickens," and "Old Nick." It appears that among all the people of the world, among the civilized as well as the primitive, there is a feeling that the names of the gods are too holy, and the names of evil spirits too terrifying, to be spoken lightly.

The primitive confusion of word with thing, of symbol with thing symbolized, manifests itself in some parts of the world in a belief that the name of a person is *part of* that person. To know someone's name, therefore, is to have power over him. Because of this belief, it is customary among some peoples for children to be given at birth a "real name" known only to the parents and never used, as well as a nickname or public name to be called by in society. In this way the child is protected from being put in someone's power. The story of Rumpelstiltskin is a European illustration of this belief in the power of names.

Thomas Mann, in *Joseph and His Brethren,* gives the following dramatic account of the power of names, according to ancient Jewish belief:

> [Joseph, speaking of a lion.] "But if he had come, with lashing tail, and roared after his prey, like the voice of the chanting seraphim, yet thy child would have been little affrighted or not at all before his rage. . . . For knoweth not my father that the beasts fear and avoid man, for that God gave him the spirit of understanding and taught him the orders into which single things fall; doth he not know how Shemmael shrieked when the man of earth knew how to name the creation as though he were its master and framer . . . ? And the beasts too they are ashamed and put the tail between their legs because we know them and have power over their names and can thus render powerless the roaring might of the single one, by naming him. If now he had come, with long slinking tread, with his hateful nose, mewing and spitting, terror would not have robbed

me of my senses, nor made me pale before his riddle. 'Is thy name Blood-Thirst?' I would have asked of him, making merry at his expense. 'Or Springing Murder?' But there I would have sat upright and cried out: 'Lion! Lo, Lion art thou, by nature and species, and thy riddle lieth bare before me, so that I speak it out and with a laugh it is plain.' And he would have blinked before the name and gone meekly away before the word, powerless to answer unto me. For he is quite unlearned and knows nought of writing tools."

Words with Built-in Judgments

The fact that some words arouse both informative and affective connotations simultaneously gives a special complexity to discussions involving religious, racial, national, and political groups. To many people, the word "communist" means simultaneously "one who believes in communism" (informative connotations) *and* "one whose ideals and purposes are altogether repellent" (affective connotations). Words applying to occupations of which one disapproves ("pickpocket," "racketeer," "prostitute"), like those applying to believers in philosophies of which one may disapprove ("atheist," "heretic," "materialist," "Holy Roller"), likewise often communicate *simultaneously* a fact and a judgment on the fact.

In some parts of the southwestern United States, there is strong prejudice against Mexicans, both immigrant and American-born. The strength of this prejudice is indirectly revealed by the fact that newspapers and polite people have stopped using the word "Mexican" altogether, using the expression "Spanish-speaking person" instead. "Mexican" has been used with contemptuous connotations for so long that it has become, in the opinion of many people in the region, unsuitable for polite conversation. In some circles, the word is reserved for lower-class Mexicans, while the "politer" term is used for the upper class.

On subjects about which strong feelings exist, we are compelled to talk in roundabout terms if we wish to avoid arousing traditional prejudices which hinder clear thinking. Hence we have not only such terms as "Spanish-speaking persons" but also, in other contexts, "problem drinkers" instead of "drunkards," and "Hansen's disease" instead of "leprosy."

These verbal stratagems are necessitated by the strong affective connotations as well as by the often misleading implications of their blunter alternatives; they are not merely a matter of giving things fancy names in order to fool people, as the simple-minded often believe. Because the old names are "loaded," they dictate traditional patterns of behavior towards those to whom they are applied. When everybody "knew" what to do about "little hoodlums," they threw them in jail and "treated 'em rough." Once in jail, little hoodlums showed a marked tendency to grow up into big hoodlums. When thoughtful people began to observe such facts, they started rethinking the problem, using different terminologies. What is the best way of describing these troubled and troublesome youths? Shall they be described as "defectives" or "psychopathic personalities"? Or as "maladjusted" or "neurotic"? Shall we say they are "deprived," "frustrated," or "socially displaced"? Shall we say they are "troubled by problems of identity"? Are they in need of "confinement," "punishment," "treatment," "education," or "rehabilitation"? It is through trying out many, many possible terms such as these that new ways of dealing with the problem are discovered and devised.

The meaning of words, as we have observed, changes from speaker to speaker and from context to context. The words "Japs" and "niggers," for instance, although often used both as a designation and an insult, are sometimes used with no intent to offend. In some classes of society and in some geographical areas, there are people who know no other words for Japanese, and in other areas there are people who know no other words for Negroes. Ignorance of regional and class differences of dialect often results in feelings needlessly hurt. Those who believe that the meaning of a word is *in the word* often fail to understand this simple point of differences in usage. For example, an elderly Japanese woman of the writer's acquaintance used to squirm at the mention of the word "Jap," even when used in an innocuous or complimentary context. "Whenever I hear that word," she used to say, "I feel dirty all over."

The word "nigger" has a similar effect on most Negroes. A distinguished Negro sociologist tells of an incident in his adolescence when he was hitchhiking far from home in regions where Negroes are hardly ever seen. He was befriended by an extremely kindly white couple who fed him and gave him a place to sleep in their home. However, they kept calling him "little nigger"—a fact which upset him profoundly even while he was grateful for their kindness. He finally got up courage to ask the man not to call him by that "insulting term."

"Who's insultin' you, son?" said the man.

"You are, sir—that name you're always calling me."

"What name?"

"Uh . . . you know."

"I ain't callin' you no names, son."

"I mean your calling me 'nigger.' "

"Well, what's insultin' about that? You are a nigger, ain't you?"

As the sociologist says now in telling the story, "I couldn't think of an answer then, and I'm not sure I can now."

In case the sociologist reads this book, we are happy to provide him with an answer, although it may be twenty-five years late. He might have said to his benefactor, "Sir, in the part of the country I come from, white people who treat colored people with respect call them 'Negroes,' while those who wish to show their contempt for colored people call them 'niggers.' I hope the latter is not your intention." And the man might have replied, had he been kindly in thought as he was in deed, "Well, you don't say! Sorry I hurt your feelings, son, but I didn't know." And that would have been that.

Negroes, having for a long time been victims of unfair persecution because of race, are often even more sensitive about racial appellations than the Japanese woman previously mentioned. It need hardly be said that Negroes suffer from the confusion of informative and affective connotations just as often as white people—or Japanese. Such Negroes, and those white sympathizers with the Negro cause who are equally naïve in linguistic matters, tend to feel that the entire colored "race" is vilified whenever and wherever the word "nigger" occurs. They bristle even when it occurs in such expressions as "niggertoe" (the name of an herb; also a dialect term for Brazil nut), "niggerhead" (a type of chewing tobacco), "niggerfish" (a kind of fish found in West Indian and Floridan waters)—and even the word "niggardly" (of Scandinavian origin, unrelated, of course, to "Negro") has to be avoided before some audiences.

Such easily offended people sometimes send delegations to visit dictionary offices to demand that the word "nigger" be excluded from future editions, being unaware that dictionaries, as has already been said (Chapter 4), perform a historical, rather than legislative, function. (They will probably come to bother the publishers of this book, too.) To try to reduce racial discrimination by getting dictionaries to stop including the word "nigger" is like trying to cut down the birth rate by shutting down the office of the county register of births. When racial discrimination against Negroes is done away with, the word will either disappear or else lose its present connotations. By losing its present connotations, we mean (1) that people who need to insult their fellow men will have found more interesting grounds on which to base their insults, and (2) that people who are called "niggers" will no longer fly off the handle any more than a person from New England does at being called a "Yankee."

One other curious fact needs to be recorded about words applied to such hotly debated issues as race, religion, political heresy, and economic dissent. Every reader is acquainted with certain people who, according to their own flattering descriptions of themselves, "believe in being frank" and like to "call a spade a spade." By "calling a spade a spade" (the expression itself is a relic of the "right name" superstition discussed in Chapter 2), they usually mean calling anything or anyone by the term which has the strongest and most disagreeable affective connotations. Why people should pin medals on themselves for "candor" for performing this nasty feat has often puzzled the writer. Sometimes it is necessary to violate verbal taboos as an aid to clearer thinking, but more often "calling a spade a spade" is to provide our minds with a greased runway down which we may slide back into old *and discredited* patterns of evaluation and behavior.

Everyday Uses of Language

The language of everyday life, then, differs from "reports" such as those discussed in Chapter 3. As in reports, we have to be accurate in choosing words that have the informative connotations we want; otherwise the reader or hearer will not know what we are talking about. But in addition, we have to give those words the affective connotations we want in order that he will be interested or moved by what we are saying, and feel towards things the way we do. This double task confronts us in almost all ordinary conversation, oratory, persuasive writing, and literature. Much of this task, however, is performed intuitively; without being aware of it, we choose the tone of voice, the rhythms, and the affective connotations appropriate to our utterance. Over the informative connotations of our utterances we exercise somewhat more conscious control. Improvement in our ability to understand language, as well as in our ability to use it, depends, therefore, not only upon sharpening our sense for the informative connotations of words, but *also upon the sharpening of our insight into the affective elements in language through social experience, through contact with many kinds of people in many kinds of situations, and through literary study.*

The following, finally, are some of the things that can happen in any speech event:

1. The informative connotations may be inadequate or misleading, but the affective connotations may be sufficiently well directed so that we are able to interpret correctly. For example, when someone says, "Imagine who I saw today! Old What's-his-name—oh, you know who I mean—Whoosis, that old buzzard that lives on, oh—what's the name of that street!" there are means, certainly not clearly informative, by which we manage to understand who is being referred to.

2. The informative connotations may be correct enough and the extensional meanings clear, but the affective connotations may be inappropriate, misleading, or ludicrous. This happens frequently when people try to write elegantly: "Jim ate so many bags of *Arachis hypogaea,* commonly known as peanuts, at the ball game today that he was unable to do justice to his evening repast."

3. Both informative and affective connotations may "sound all right," but there may be no "territory" corresponding to the "map." For example: "He lived for many years in the beautiful hill country just south of Chicago." There is no hill country just south of Chicago.

4. Both informative and affective connotations may be *consciously* used to create "maps" of "territories" that do not exist. There are many reasons, only two of which need be mentioned now, why we should wish on occasion to do this. First, we may wish to give pleasure:

> Yet mark'd I where the bolt of Cupid fell:
> It fell upon a little western flower,
> Before milk-white, now purple with love's wound,
> And maidens call it, Love-in-idleness.
> Fetch me that flower; the herb I show'd thee once:
> The juice of it on sleeping eyelids laid
> Will make or man or woman madly dote
> Upon the next live creature that it sees.
> —*A Midsummer Night's Dream*

A second reason is to enable us to plan for the future. For example, we can say, "Let us suppose there is a bridge at the foot of this street; then the heavy traffic on High Street would be partly diverted over the new bridge; shopping would be less concentrated on High Street. . . ." Having visualized the condition that would result, we can recommend or oppose the bridge according to whether or not we like the probable results. The relationship of present words to future events is a subject we must leave for the next chapter.

APPLICATIONS

I. Read carefully the following five excerpts and write an essay (1000 words should be enough) on the problems involved in these cases and in similar ones that you know from your own experience:

1. The Arizona Lath and Plaster Institute has cried out for speakers of the language to cease and desist in the use of "plastered" as a synonym for "inebriated" or "drunk as a skunk." "Linking our trade with overindulgence," says the Institute by resolution, "detracts from the dignity of a respectable industry."

    —San Francisco *Chronicle*

2. WASHINGTON, Feb. 8 (AP)—Representative Matthews, Dem., of Florida, thinks the Navy ought to give its petty officers a new name. The dictionary defines petty as small, trifling, inferior, he said in remarks prepared for House delivery today, "but I am sure these names have no part in the magnificent work that the petty officers in our Navy perform." His advice: change the name to "enlisted officer."

    —Boston *Daily Globe*

3. FBI Chief J. Edgar Hoover suggested that policemen wouldn't have so many robbers to chase if only the robbers—and honest citizens, too—would stop using the word "cop." "As a career law-enforcement officer," Hoover wrote in an editorial in the FBI's monthly bulletin, "I abhor the word 'cop'. . . . The expression is degrading. . . . Especially deplorable is the use of this term—a standard derisive invective of the underword—in a careless and disdainful manner by . . . law-abiding individuals. . . . Poor adult example can only lead to youthful disrespect for police authority. . . ."

    —*Newsweek*

4. CHICAGO, August 31—The chefs of America are gloomy about the future of the culinary art in the country. The trouble, as they have reviewed in three days of sessions here, is that few young men want to become cooks—and that is the first step to becoming chefs. The sessions were those of the American Culinary Association. . . .

    One of the things the delegates found particularly annoying and damaging to the future of the profession was the insistence of the Department of Labor in classifying chefs as "domestics." Even the word "cook" is loathsome, declared Seymour Weiss, president of the Hotel Roosevelt in New Orleans, adding that it was "unfortunate a man must become a cook before he can become a chef."

He said that because of the concept that the word "cook" conjures in the minds of youth it is becoming more and more difficult to interest American youth in the study of cooking. Indicating how strongly he felt on this point, Mr. Weiss pledged his personal check of $1,000 to the federation if it could come up with a suitable substitute for the word, one that would connote the dignity the work merits. —New York *Times*

5. From time to time . . . delegations of teen-age hot rodders have visited the I-J office to complain that their good name and reputation was being impugned by associating the term hot rodder with juvenile delinquents. . . . If a fellow driving a junk heap gets involved in an accident . . . the policeman's report is liable to describe the junk heap as a hot rod. And our reporters are just as liable to describe the junk heap as a hot rod in their news accounts. This rubs the organized and enlightened hot rodders the wrong way. . . .

Some months ago . . . a Sausalito resident['s] . . . car was disabled at a dangerous turn. . . . One of the young fellows of the hot rod club happened by, stopped, helped the Sausalitan move his car to a safe place, and helped him make emergency repairs. Then the young fellow drove off, refusing the offer of a gift of money and declining to give his name. He did leave a card, however, advising the stranded motorist he had been helped by a member of the hot rod club. . . .

Earlier this week, a lady . . . telephoned to tell us the same kind of story. . . . Her husband, convalescing from surgery, was struggling to change a tire. Along came two young fellows who stopped to take over the tire-changing job. When they finished they refused to accept any payment and they handed the stranded couple a card explaining, "You have been helped by a member of the Nomads Auto Club, which is an organization of youth dedicated to safer and more courteous driving conditions."

We feel sure that if hot rod organizations . . . were to adopt this procedure and practice it intensively, they soon would "rewrite the public's definition" of the term "hot rodder," and win public respect and confidence in the process.

—San Rafael (California) *Independent Journal*

II. Bertrand Russell, on a British Broadcasting Company radio program called the Brains Trust, gave the following "conjugation" of an "irregular verb":

I am firm.

You are obstinate.

He is a pig-headed fool.

The *New Statesman and Nation,* quoting the above as a model, offered prizes to readers who sent in the best "irregular verbs" of this kind. Here are some of the published entries.

I am sparkling. You are unusually talkative. He is drunk.

I am righteously indignant. You are annoyed. He is making a fuss about nothing.

I am fastidious. You are fussy. He is an old woman.

I am a creative writer. You have a journalistic flair. He is a prosperous hack.

I am beautiful. You have quite good features. She isn't bad-looking, if you like that type.

I day dream. You are an escapist. He ought to see a psychiatrist.

I have about me something of the subtle, haunting, mysterious fragrance of the Orient. You rather overdo it, dear. She stinks.

"Conjugate," in a similar way, the following statements:

1. I am slender.
2. I am a trifle overweight.
3. I don't dance very well.
4. Naturally I use a little make-up.
5. I collect rare, old objects of art.
6. I don't like to play bridge with people who are too serious about it.
7. I don't claim to know all the answers.
8. I believe in old-fashioned, laissez-faire liberalism.
9. I need plenty of sleep.
10. I'm just an old-fashioned girl.
11. I don't care much about theories; I'm the practical type.
12. I believe in being frank.
13. I rarely find time to read books.

III. It is important to be able to sort out of any utterance *the information given* from *the speaker's feeling toward that information.* In order to sharpen one's perception in this respect, it is instructive sometimes to rewrite articles one reads, *using the same information given in the original and reversing the judgments.* For example, the following is a review by Rolfe Humphries of a book, *The Frieda Lawrence Collection of D. H. Lawrence Manuscripts: A Descriptive Bibliography,* by E. W. Tedlock, Jr. (1948), as published in *Nation:*

This is a remarkable bibliography. Not only does it examine, with the cool painstaking labor of scholarship, the 193 manuscripts in Mrs. Lawrence's collection—and nine others thrown in for good measure—but also, it is informed with warmth, a growing sympathy, admiration, understanding of its subject, never forgetting that that subject was a man, never seeking to claim him as a literary property, as so often tends to be the case when scholars figure they have learned more facts about somebody than anybody else. There is enough material in Professor Tedlock's book to fascinate those with an appetite for such items as that the paper measures eight and a half by ten and five-eighths inches, or that the pages are incorrectly numbered; there is also material for those who want to study how an artist improved, corrected, extended, his initial attempts; beyond all that, the book is interesting to any who care about Lawrence, so that, as Frieda Lawrence says in a brief foreword, the love and truth in him may rouse the love and truth in others. Professor Tedlock's study is a valuable help, and readable.

Now let us suppose for the purpose of our exercise the existence of a different reviewer, one who dislikes the works of Lawrence, dislikes those who admire Lawrence, and has a low opinion of painstaking literary scholarship. Such a reviewer, using the same facts, might write his review in somewhat the following way:

This bibliography examines, with the appalling industriousness of the professional pedant, the 193 manuscripts in Mrs. Lawrence's collection—and nine others thrown in for good measure. Professor Tedlock goes completely overboard for his subject. Like other worshipers at the Lawrence shrine, he is almost as much preoccupied with Lawrence the man as with his works—so much so, indeed, that it is surprising he does not take Lawrence over as a literary property, as so often tends to be the case when scholars figure they have learned more facts about somebody than anybody else. There is enough material in Professor Tedlock's book to fascinate those with an appetite for such items as that the paper measures eight and a half by ten and five-eighths inches, or that the pages are incorrectly numbered; there is also material for those who, not content with the study of finished works, want to pry into the processes by which an artist improved, corrected, and extended his initial attempts; beyond all that, the book is interesting to any who, in this day and age, still insist on caring about Lawrence, so that what Frieda Lawrence calls, in a brief foreword, the "love" and "truth" in him may arouse a similar "love" and "truth" in others. To these followers of the Lawrence cult, Professor Tedlock's study is no doubt a valuable help. The style is readable.

No criticism of Mr. Humphries' review (or of Professor Tedlock's book or of D. H. Lawrence) is implied, of course, by this "revision." The task of the book reviewer is twofold: to report facts about the book under discussion *and* to express some of his feelings about the book and its subject. Mr. Humphries has, in a brief review, done something of both tasks—more of the former than of the latter.

However, a critical reader should be able to read either Mr. Humphries' review or the "revision" above and derive the basic information that both reviews convey: that Professor Tedlock's book is painstakingly detailed in its examination of the Lawrence manuscripts, that it has a warm attitude toward Lawrence the man as well as toward his works, that it is likely to be useful to admirers of Lawrence, and so forth. In order to develop one's capacity to get at such basic information, regardless of how the writer colors that information, it is suggested that the reader try "revisions" of this kind. Book reviews are especially interesting to revise in this way. Some reviewers will be found to say little about the book and a great deal about their own tastes. Others write almost pure news stories, with little expression of their own likes or dislikes. "Interpretive reporting" of the kind found in *Time* and in many signed news-features in large newspapers—stories that not only tell what happened but also communicate an attitude toward the events or persons involved—is also interesting to revise in the manner suggested.

Revise the following item from *Time* magazine, using the same basic information but with warm approval of Mr. Beck's undertaking:

Man of Peace

Ever since he got around aging Dan Tobin and became the real ruler of the Teamsters Union, Seattle's tough, pale-eyed Dave Beck has been remolding the A.F.L.'s biggest labor group to suit his fancy. Last week in Manhattan, Beck announced what he proposed to do with his juggernaut when he gets it well-streamlined. He was going to start a coast-to-coast organizing roundup that would make other labor-recruiting drives look like ballet tryouts.

Teamsters in all United States cities will simultaneously set out to double the union's membership from 1,000,000 to 2,000,000. They will go after new members in the automotive trades, bakeries, the beverage industry, building and construction, canneries, dairies, the taxicab and short-haul bus fields, general hauling, sales drivers, the produce field, warehouses and drive-away and truck-away enterprises.

With the air of a man about to pluck a ripe plum, Beck also made a soft-voiced announcement of his plans for New York City.

The teamsters, he said, would concentrate on department store warehousemen but would also claim jurisdiction over the big city's
brewery workers.

Beck added blandly that he was a "man of peace" and had no
desire to revert to the "law of the jungle." He did not expect that
other unions would "infringe on our jurisdiction." But he said, "if
a union that should stick to clerks tries to get our warehousemen (a
remark directed at the powerful C.I.O. Amalgamated Clothing
Workers), we'll step in and organize the whole store to protect ourselves."

To start you off, here's how the first sentence might go:

Ever since he succeeded venerable Dan Tobin and became the director of the Teamsters Union, Seattle's rugged, clear-eyed Dave Beck
has been rebuilding the A.F.L.'s largest labor group to meet his
ideals.

IV. Ponder the following quotations and, if the spirit moves you,
write a one-page essay on calling a spade a spade, paying no attention to what the author has already said on the subject in this chapter:

1. Hog . . . sow . . . runt . . . litter . . . pigsty . . . ham . . .
porky . . . sowbelly. All of these have become harsh and derogatory words in America's street-language. Look up their common definitions in any dictionary. . . . The pig has, actually,
been a citizen of what is now the U.S.A. for 417 years. He first
landed in Florida on May 25, 1539, almost a century before the
Pilgrims. He has played a magnificent role in our history since
then. He is still the second largest agricultural industry, from a
standpoint of producer income. He has been a pioneer. He has
helped to win wars. He has pulled us through periods of starvation. He marches placidly off to the stockyards to become 20
varieties of meat, 50 medicines and a couple hundred industrial
products. In return for all this, his name has become a household symbol for gluttony and filth and he and his descendants
are slaves to the price of the corn crop. . . .

That's why I believe you should sit down and consider the
pig's citizenship rights. Stimulate your own curiosity about his
place in our history, his contributions to our living-standard and
the role he should play in our everyday economy. . . .

Then, one afternoon, drop over to the local school and find
out what their attitudes are about pigs and pork. Go right to the
principal or the superintendent of schools on this one. Ask him
what the children are being taught about The Pig in history
classes . . . in English classes . . . in geography and econom-

ics. . . . There should be a twilight for the fat, filthy American hog of the street-language. And there can, and should be, a sunrise for the American pig as he can be . . . clean, shrewd, adaptable and our best source of lean, sweet meat. Down the trails to tomorrow the pigboy should have as much social prestige as the cowboy.　　　—ROBERT WEST HOWARD, address to the Equity Co-operative Livestock Sales Association

2. Forest Lawn is a cemetery in which nobody calls a spade a spade. Here the loss of life is known as "leavetaking," a corpse is "the loved one" or "the revered clay," the dead are merely "out of sight." Here 1,500,000 visitors a year wander, secure in the knowledge that they can avoid seeing a tombstone; graves, marked only with bronze plaques set level with the ground, are clustered in such consoling sites as Sunrise Slope, Slumberland, Resthaven, Sweet Memories, Everlasting Love. Infants are buried in Babyland, which is "shaped like a mother's heart," and Lullabyland; every Christmas toys and tinseled trees are placed upon the graves. All day long, soft symphonic music is broadcast from loudspeakers concealed in the shrubbery; in fact, Novelist Waugh reported hearing recorded bird songs as well as the *Indian Love Call.*　　—*Time*

V. An organization formerly known as the Artificial Limb Manufacturers Association is now known as the American Orthotics and Prosthetics Association. The International Society for the Welfare of Cripples changed its name in 1960 to International Society for the Rehabilitation of the Disabled. The Hospital for the Society for the Relief of the Ruptured and Crippled, New York City, is now called Hospital for Special Surgery. The Hospital for the Crippled and Deformed, in Lincoln, Nebraska, is now the Nebraska Orthopedic Hospital.

The National Society for Crippled Children and Adults (which conducts one of the Easter Seal campaigns) is deeply interested in the words used to designate the "crippled," especially those who may be candidates for rehabilitation programs. It seems that the word "cripple" itself sometimes discourages the individual who applies it to himself from embarking on training for rehabilitation. Are there any better words that can be used? "Disabled"? "Handicapped"? "Exceptional"? "Impaired"? "Deformed"? Any others?

Write a letter to the Society (2023 W. Ogden Avenue, Chicago 12, Illinois) with your recommendations as to terminology. Should the term "crippled" be maintained in use? If not, what other term or terms should be used instead? Give reasons for your answer.

7 The Language
of Social Control

*The effect of a parade of sonorous phrases upon hu-
man conduct has never been adequately studied.*
                                    —THURMAN W. ARNOLD

*Yet the layman errs in his belief that this lack of
precision and finality is to be ascribed to the lawyers.
The truth of the matter is that the popular notion of
the possibilities of legal exactness is based upon a
misconception. The law always has been, is now, and
will ever continue to be, largely vague and variable.
And how could this well be otherwise? The law deals
with human relations in their most complicated aspects. The whole confused, shifting helter-skelter of
life parades before it—more confused than ever, in
our kaleidoscopic age.*   —JEROME FRANK

Making Things Happen

The most interesting and perhaps least understood relationship between words and the world is that between words and future events.
When we say, for example, "Come here!" we are not describing the
extensional world about us, nor are we merely expressing our feelings; we are trying to *make something happen*. What we call "commands," "pleas," "requests," and "orders" are the simplest ways we
have of making things happen by means of words.

There are, however, more roundabout ways. When we say, for
example, "Our candidate is a great American," we are of course
making an enthusiastic purr about him, but we may also be influencing other people to vote for him. Again, when we say, "Our
war against the enemy is God's war. God wills that we must triumph," we are saying something which, though unverifiable, may
influence others to help in the prosecution of the war. Or if we

merely state as a fact, "Milk contains vitamins," we may be influencing others to buy milk.

Consider, too, such a statement as "I'll meet you tomorrow at two o'clock in front of the Palace Theater." Such a statement about *future* events can only be made, it will be observed, in a system in which symbols are independent of things symbolized. The future, like the recorded past, is a specifically human dimension. To a dog, the expression "hamburger *tomorrow*" is meaningless—he will look at you expectantly, hoping for the extensional meaning of the word "hamburger" to be produced *now*. Squirrels, to be sure, store food for "next winter," but the fact that they store food regardless of whether or not their needs are adequately provided for demonstrates that such behavior (usually called "instinctive") is governed neither by symbols nor by other interpreted stimuli. Human beings are unique in their ability to react meaningfully to such expressions as "next Saturday," "on our next wedding anniversary," "twenty years after date I promise to pay," "some day, perhaps five hundred years from now." That is to say, maps can be made, even though the territories they stand for are not yet actualities. Guiding ourselves by means of such maps of territories-to-be, we can impose a certain predictability upon future events.

With words, therefore, we influence and to an enormous extent *control future events*. It is for this reason that writers write; preachers preach; employers, parents, and teachers scold; propagandists send out news releases; statesmen give addresses. All of them, for various reasons, are trying to influence our conduct—sometimes for our good, sometimes for their own. These attempts to control, direct, or influence the future actions of fellow human beings with words may be termed *directive uses of language*.

Now it is obvious that if directive language is going to direct, it cannot be dull or uninteresting. If it is to influence our conduct, it *must* make use of every affective element in language: dramatic variations in tone of voice, rhyme and rhythm, purring and snarling, words with strong affective connotations, endless repetition. If meaningless noises will move the audience, meaningless noises must be made; if facts move them, facts must be given; if noble ideals move them, we must make our proposals appear noble; if they will respond only to fear, we must scare them stiff.

The nature of the affective means used in directive language is limited, of course, by the nature of our aims. If we are trying to direct people to be more kindly toward each other, we obviously do not want to arouse feelings of cruelty or hate. If we are trying to direct people to think and act more intelligently, we obviously should not use subrational appeals. If we are trying to direct people to lead better lives, we use affective appeals that arouse their finest feelings. Included among directive utterances, therefore, are many of the greatest and most treasured works of literature: the Christian and Buddhist scriptures, the writings of Confucius, Milton's *Areopagitica,* and Lincoln's Gettysburg Address.

There are, however, occasions when it is felt that language is not sufficiently affective by itself to produce the results wanted. We supplement directive language, therefore, by *nonverbal affective appeals* of many kinds. We supplement the words "Come here" by gesturing with our hands. Advertisers are not content with saying in words how beautiful their products will make us; they supplement their words by the use of colored inks and by pictures. Newspapers are not content with saying that communism is a menace; they supply political cartoons depicting communists as criminally insane people placing sticks of dynamite under magnificent buildings labeled "American way of life." The affective appeal of sermons and religious exhortations may be supplemented by costumes, incense, processions, choir music, and church bells. A political candidate seeking office reinforces his speech-making with a considerable array of nonverbal affective appeals: brass bands, flags, parades, picnics, barbecues, and free cigars.[1] Often a candidate's smile or, as

---

[1] The following are excerpts from reports of the Republican National Convention of 1948: "There on the stage a gigantic photograph of the candidate, tinted somewhat too vividly, gazed steadily out over the throngs. Around the balcony hung other photographs: the Dewey family playing with their Great Dane; the Deweys at the circus; Dewey on the farm. Dewey infantrymen passed out soft drinks and small favors to gawking visitors and gave every 200th visitor a door prize. William Horne, a Philadelphia bank employee, was clocked in as the 45,000th visitor and got a sterling silver carving aid." *Time* (July 5, 1948). "Over loudspeakers of the Bellevue-Stratford came a constant stream of official exhortations against undue crowding at the entrance to the Dewey headquarters. The warnings were part of the game, but they were also justified. Why wouldn't the Dewey headquarters be jammed when prizes —from chewing gum and pocket combs to silk lingerie and dresses—were being doled out with the largess of a radio quiz show? At one point the Dewey people even staged a fashion show, complete with eight bathing beauties. A bewildered foreign newspaperman asked a fellow-reporter, 'How can I explain to France what this has to do with electing a President?' . . . The Stassen managers appeared to be saving up their circus talent for Convention Hall, where it turned out to be considerable, ranging from an Indian chief in full regalia to a shapely girl in sailor pants who did a nautical rumba on the rostrum." *Nation* (July 3, 1948).

in the case of President Kennedy, his wife's appearance and charm may be a powerful influence upon the voter.

Now, if we want people to do certain things and if we are indifferent as to *why they do them,* then no affective appeals need be excluded. Some political candidates want us to vote for them regardless of our reasons for doing so. Therefore, if we hate the rich, they will snarl at the rich for us; if we dislike strikers, they will snarl at the strikers; if we like clambakes, they will throw clambakes; if the majority of us like hillbilly music, they may say nothing about the problems of government, but travel among their constituencies with hillbilly bands. Again, many business firms want us to buy their products regardless of our reasons for doing so; therefore, if delusions and fantasies will lead us to buy their products, they will seek to produce delusions and fantasies; if we want to be popular with the other sex, they will promise us popularity; if we like pretty girls in bathing suits, they will associate pretty girls in bathing suits with their products, whether they are selling shaving cream, automobiles, summer resorts, ice-cream cones, house paint, or hardware. Only the law keeps them from presenting pretty girls without bathing suits. The records of the Federal Trade Commission, as well as the advertising pages of many magazines, show that some advertisers will stop at practically nothing.

The Promises of Directive Language

Almost all directive utterances say something about the future. They are "maps," either explicitly or by implication, of *"territories" that are to be.* They direct us to do certain things with the stated or implied promise that if we do these things, certain consequences will follow: "If you adhere to the Bill of Rights, your civil rights too will be protected." "If you vote for me, I will have your taxes reduced." "Live according to these religious principles, and you will have peace in your soul." "Read this magazine, and you will keep up with important current events." "Take Lewis's Licorice Liver Pills and enjoy that glorious feeling that goes with regularity." Needless to say, some of these promises are kept, and some are not. Indeed, we encounter promises daily that are obviously incapable of being kept.

There is no sense in objecting as some people do to advertising and political propaganda—the only kind of directives they worry about—on the ground that they are based on "emotional appeals."

Unless directive language has affective power of some kind, it is useless. We do not object to campaigns that tell us, "Give to the Community Chest and enable poor children to enjoy better care," although that is an "emotional appeal." Nor do we resent being reminded of our love of home, friends, and nation when people issue moral or patriotic directives at us. The important question to be asked of any directive utterance is, "Will things happen as promised if I do as I am directed to do? If I accept your philosophy, shall I achieve peace of mind? If I vote for you, will my taxes be reduced? If I use Lifeguard Soap, will my boy friend really come back to me?"

We rightly object to advertisers who make false or misleading claims and to politicians who ignore their promises, although it must be admitted that, in the case of politicians, they are sometimes compelled to make promises that later circumstances prevent them from keeping. Life being as uncertain and as unpredictable as it is, we are constantly trying to find out what is going to happen next, so that we may prepare ourselves. Directive utterances undertake to tell us how we can bring about certain desirable events and how we can avoid undesirable events. If we can rely upon what they tell us about the future, the uncertainties of life are reduced. When, however, directive utterances are of such a character that things do *not* happen as predicted—when, after we have done as we were told, the peace in the soul has not been found, the taxes have not been reduced, the boy friend has not returned, there is disappointment. Such disappointments may be trivial or grave; in any event, they are so common that we do not even bother to complain about some of them. They are, nevertheless, all serious in their implications. *Each of them serves, in greater or lesser degree, to break down that mutual trust that makes cooperation possible and knits people together into a society.*

Every one of us, therefore, who utters directive language, with its concomitant promises, stated or implied, is morally obliged to be as certain as he can, since there is no absolute certainty, that he is arousing no false expectations. Politicians promising the immediate abolition of poverty, national advertisers suggesting that tottering marriages can be restored to bliss by a change in the brand of laundry detergent used in the family, newspapers threatening the collapse of the nation if the party they favor is not elected—all such utterers of nonsense are, for the reasons stated, menaces to the social order. It does not matter much whether such misleading directives are uttered in ignorance and error or with conscious intent to deceive, because the disappointments they cause are all similarly destructive of mutual trust among human beings.

The Foundations of Society

But propaganda, no matter how persuasive, does not create society. We can, if we wish, ignore its directives. We come now to *directive utterances that we cannot ignore if we wish to remain organized in our social groups.*

What we call society is a vast network of mutual agreements. We agree to refrain from murdering our fellow citizens, and they in turn agree to refrain from murdering us; we agree to drive on the right-hand side of the road, and others agree to do the same; we agree to deliver specified goods, and others agree to pay us for them; we agree to observe the rules of an organization, and the organization agrees to let us enjoy its privileges. This complicated network of agreements, into which almost every detail of our lives is woven and upon which most of our expectations in life are based, consists essentially of *statements about future events which we are supposed, with our own efforts, to bring about.* Without such agreements, there would be no such thing as society. We would all be huddling in miserable and lonely caves, not daring to trust anyone. With such agreements, and a will on the part of the vast majority of people to live by them, behavior begins to fall into relatively predictable patterns; cooperation becomes possible; peace and freedom are established.

Therefore, in order that we shall continue to exist as human beings, we *must* impose patterns of behavior on each other. We must make citizens conform to social and civic customs; we must make husbands dutiful to their wives; we must make soldiers courageous, judges just, priests pious, and teachers solicitous for the welfare of their pupils. In early stages of culture the principal means of imposing patterns of behavior was, of course, physical coercion. But such control can also be exercised, as human beings must have discovered extremely early in history, by *words*—that is, by directive language. Therefore, directives about matters which society as a whole regards as essential to its own safety are made especially powerful, so that no individual in that society will fail to be impressed with a sense of his obligations. To make doubly sure, society further reinforces the directives by the assurance that punishment, possibly including imprisonment and death, may be visited upon those who fail to heed the words.

Directives with Collective Sanction

These directive utterances with collective sanction, which try to impose patterns of behavior upon the individual in the interests of the whole group, are among the most interesting of linguistic events. Not only are they usually accompanied by ritual; they are usually the central purpose of ritual. There is probably no kind of utterance that we take more seriously, that affects our lives more deeply, that we quarrel about more bitterly. Constitutions of nations and of organizations, legal contracts, and oaths of office are utterances of this kind; in marriage vows, confirmation exercises, induction ceremonies, and initiations, they are the essential constituent. Those terrifying verbal jungles called *laws* are simply such directives, accumulated, codified, and systematized through the centuries. In its laws, society makes its mightiest collective effort to impose predictability upon human behavior.

Directive utterances made under collective sanction may exhibit any or all of the following features:

1. Such language is almost always phrased in *words that have affective connotations,* so that people will be appropriately impressed and awed. Archaic and obsolete vocabulary or stilted phraseology quite unlike the language of everyday life is employed. For example: "Wilt thou, John, take this woman for thy lawful wedded wife?" "This lease, made this tenth day of July, A.D. One Thousand Nine Hundred and Sixty-three, between Samuel Smith, hereinafter called the Lessor, and Jeremiah Johnson, hereinafter called Lessee, WITNESSETH, that Lessor, in consideration of covenants and agreements hereinafter contained and made on the part of the Lessee, hereby leases to Lessee for a private dwelling, the premises known and described as follows, to wit . . ."

2. Such directive utterances are often accompanied by *appeals to supernatural powers,* who are called upon to help us carry out the vows, or to punish us if we fail to carry them out. An oath, for example, ends with the words, "So help me God." Prayers, incantations, and invocations accompany the utterance of important vows in practically all cultures, from the most primitive to the most civilized. These further serve, of course, to impress our vows on our minds.

3. The *fear of direct punishment* is also invoked. If God does not punish us for failing to carry out our agreements, it is made clear either by statement or implication that our fellow men will. For example, we all realize that we can be imprisoned for desertion, nonsupport, or bigamy; sued for "breach of contract"; "unfrocked" for activities contrary to priestly vows; "cashiered" for "conduct unbecoming an officer"; "impeached" for "betrayal of public trust"; hanged for "treason."

4. The formal and public utterance of the vows may be preceded by *preliminary disciplines* of various kinds: courses of training in the meaning of the vows one is undertaking; fasting and self-mortification, as before entering the priesthood; initiation ceremonies involving physical torture, as before induction into the warrior status among primitive peoples or membership in college fraternities.

5. The utterance of the directive language may be accompanied by other *activities or gestures calculated to impress the occasion on the mind.* For example, everybody in a courtroom stands up when a judge is about to open a court; huge processions and extraordinary costumes accompany coronation ceremonies; academic gowns are worn for commencement exercises; for many weddings, an organist and a soprano are procured and special clothes are worn.

6. The uttering of the vows may be immediately followed by *feasts, dancing, and other joyous manifestations.* Again the purpose seems to be to reinforce still further the effect of the vows. For example, there are wedding parties and receptions, graduation dances, banquets for the induction of officers and, even in the most modest social circles, some form of "celebration" when a member of the family enters into a compact with society. In primitive cultures, initiation ceremonies for chieftains may be followed by feasting and dancing that last for several days or weeks.

7. In cases where the first utterance of the vows is not made a special ceremonial occasion, the effect on the memory is usually achieved by *frequent repetition.* The flag ritual ("I pledge allegiance to the flag of the United States of America . . .") is repeated daily in most schools. Mottoes, which are briefly stated general directives, are repeated frequently; sometimes they are stamped on dishes, sometimes engraved on a warrior's sword, sometimes inscribed in prominent places such as on gates, walls, and doorways, where people can see them and be reminded of their duties.

The common feature of all these activities that accompany directive utterances, as well as of the affective elements in the language of directive utterances, is the deep effect they have on the memory. Every kind of sensory impression from the severe pain of initiation rites to the pleasures of banqueting, music, splendid clothing, and ornamental surroundings may be employed; every emotion from the fear of divine punishment to pride in being made the object of special public attention may be aroused. This is done in order that the individual who enters into his compact with society—that is, the individual who commits himself to the "map" of the not-yet-existent "territory"—shall never forget to try to bring that "territory" into existence.

For these reasons, such occasions as when a cadet receives his commission, when a Jewish boy has his *bar mitzvah,* when a priest takes his vows, when a policeman receives his badge, when a foreign-born citizen is sworn in as a citizen of the United States, or when a president takes his oath of office—these are events one never forgets. Even if, later on, a person realizes that he has not fulfilled his vows, he cannot shake off the feeling that he should have done so. All of us, of course, use and respond to these ritual directives. The phrases and speeches to which we respond reveal our deepest religious, patriotic, social, professional, and political allegiances more accurately than do the citizenship papers or membership cards that we may carry in our pockets or the badges that we may wear on our coats. A man who has changed his religion after reaching adulthood will, on hearing the ritual he was accustomed to hearing in childhood, often feel an urge to return to his earlier form of worship. In such ways, then, do human beings use words to reach out into the future and control each other's conduct.

It should be remarked that many of our social directives and many of the rituals with which they are accompanied are antiquated and somewhat insulting to adult minds. Rituals that originated in times when people had to be scared into good behavior are unnecessary to people who already have a sense of social responsibility. For example, a five-minute marriage ceremony performed at the city hall for a mature, responsible couple may "take" much better than a full-dress church ceremony performed for an infantile couple. In spite of the fact that the strength of social directives obviously lies in the willingness, the maturity, and the intelligence of the people to whom the directives are addressed, there is still a widespread tendency to rely upon the efficacy of ceremonies as such. This tendency is due, of course, to a lingering belief in word-magic, the notion that, by *saying* things repeatedly or in specified ceremonial ways, we can cast a spell over the future and force events to turn out the way we said they would. ("There'll always be an England!") An interesting manifestation of this superstitious attitude towards words and rituals is to be found among those members of patriotic societies who seem to believe that the way to educate school children in democracy is to stage bigger and better flag-saluting ceremonies and to treble the occasions for singing "God Bless America."

What Are "Rights"?

What, extensionally, is the meaning of the word "my" in such expressions as "my real estate," "my book," "my automobile"? Certainly the word "my" describes no characteristics of the objects named. A check changes hands and "your" automobile becomes "mine" but no change results in the automobile. What has changed?

The change is, of course, in *our social agreements covering our behavior* toward the automobile. Formerly, when it was "yours," you felt free to use it as you liked, while I did not. Now that it is "mine," I use it freely and you may not. The meaning of "yours" and "mine" lies not in the external world, but in *how we intend to act*. And when society as a whole recognizes my "right of ownership" (by issuing me, for example, a certificate of title), it agrees to protect me in my intentions to use the automobile and to frustrate, by police action if necessary, the intentions of those who may wish to use it without my permission. Society makes this agreement with me in return for my obeying its laws and paying my share of the expenses of government.

Are not, then, all assertions of ownership and statements about "rights" directives? Cannot, "This is *mine*," be translated, "I am going to use this object; you keep your hands off"? Cannot, "Every child has a *right* to an education," be translated, *"Give* every child an education"? And is not the difference between "moral rights" and "legal rights" the difference between agreements which people believe *ought* to be made, and those which, through collective, legislative sanction, *have been* made?

Directives and Disillusionment

A few cautions may be added before we leave the subject of directive language. First, it should be remembered that, since words cannot "say all" about anything, the promises implied in directive language are never more than "outline maps" of "territories-to-be." The future will fill in those outlines, often in unexpected ways. Sometimes the future will bear no relation to our "maps" at all, in spite of all our endeavors to bring about the promised events. We swear always to be good citizens, always to do our duty, and so on, but we never quite succeed in being good citizens *every* day of our lives or in performing *all* our duties. A realization that directives cannot *fully* impose any pattern on the future saves us from having impossible expectations and therefore from suffering needless disappointments.

Secondly, one should distinguish between directive and informative utterances, which often look alike. Such statements as "A boy scout is clean and chivalrous and brave" or "Policemen are defenders of the weak" *set up goals* and do not necessarily describe the present situation. This is extremely important, because all too often people understand such definitions as descriptive and are then shocked and disillusioned when they encounter a boy scout who is not chivalrous or a policeman who is a bully. They decide that they are "through with the boy scouts" or "disgusted with all policemen," which, of course, is nonsense. They have, in effect, inferred an informative statement from what is to be taken only as a very general directive.

A third source of disappointment and disillusionment arising from the improper understanding of directives results from reading into directives promises that they do not make. A common instance is provided by advertisements of the antiseptics and patent medicines which people buy under the impression that the cure or prevention of colds was promised. Because of the rulings of the Federal Trade Commission, the writers of these advertisements carefully avoid saying that their preparations will prevent or cure anything. Instead, they say that they "help reduce the severity of the infection," "help relieve the symptoms of a cold," or "help guard against sniffling and other discomforts." If after reading these advertisements you feel that prevention or cure of colds has been promised, you are exactly the kind of sucker they are looking for. (Of course, if you buy the product knowing clearly what was promised and what was not, that is a different matter.)

Another way of reading into directives things that were not said is by believing promises to be more specific and concrete than they really are. When, for example, a candidate for political office promises to "help the farmer," and you vote for him, and then you discover that he helps the *cotton* farmer without helping the *potato* farmer (and you grow potatoes)—you cannot exactly accuse him of having broken his promise. Or, if another candidate promises to "protect union labor," and you vote for him, and he helps to pass legislation that infuriates the officials of your union (he calls it "legislation to protect union members from their own racketeering leadership")—again you cannot exactly accuse him of having broken his promise, since his action may well have been sincerely in accord with his notion of "helping union labor." The ambiguities of campaign oratory are notorious.

Politicians are often accused of breaking their promises. No doubt many of them do. But it must be remarked that they often do not promise as much as their constituents think they do. The platforms of the major parties are almost always at high levels of abstraction ("they mean all things to all men," as the cynical say), but they are often understood by voters to be more specific and concrete (i.e., at lower levels of abstraction) than they are. If one is "disillusioned" by the acts of a politician, sometimes the politician is to blame, but sometimes the voter is to blame for having had the illusion to start with—or, as we shall say, for having *confused different levels of abstraction*. What is meant by this expression will be more fully explained in ensuing chapters.

APPLICATIONS

I. The following statements, in the contexts in which they are usually found, are directives. Which of these directives have collective sanction and which have not? What rewards (if any) are promised to those who follow the directives, and what punishments (if any) are threatened to those who do not? What is the likelihood, in each case, of the consequences following as promised?

1. And remember, ladies and gentlemen of the radio audience, whenever you say "Blotto Coffee" to your grocer, you are saying "thank you" to us.

   SAMPLE ANALYSIS: This is directive language since it attempts to influence the future behavior of the listener. Happily we are free to disregard this directive since it is in the interests of a business concern and, therefore, does not have collective sanction. There is an implied promise that if the listener will show his gratitude by purchasing Blotto Coffee, the manufacturer will continue to provide him with programs such as precede this announcement. If enough people obey this directive, the likelihood of this promise being kept is quite great.

2. Day-lilies may thrive with neglect, but the little bit of extra attention—letting them grow where they get at least four hours of sunshine a day, giving them some well-balanced fertilizer and watering them more often at flowering time—will pay handsome dividends.
—*Flower Grower: The Home Garden Magazine*

3. We hold these truths to be self-evident, that all men are created equal, that they are endowed by their Creator with certain inalienable Rights, that among these are life, liberty and the pursuit of happiness.
—The Declaration of Independence

4. No Trespassing.

5.
Sonnet 2

When forty winters shall besiege thy brow,
And dig deep trenches in thy beauty's field,
Thy youth's proud livery, so gazed on now,
Will be a tattered weed, of small worth held:
Then being asked where all thy beauty lies,
Where all the treasure of thy lusty days,
To say, within thine own deep-sunken eyes,
Were an all-eating shame and thriftless praise.
How much more praise deserved thy beauty's use,
If thou couldst answer, "This fair child of mine
Shall sum my count, and make my old excuse,"
Proving his beauty by succession thine!
This were to be new made when thou art old,
And see thy blood warm when thou feel'st it cold.
—WILLIAM SHAKESPEARE

6. The French House, under the direction and control of the Department, provides a fine opportunity to gain fluency in the spoken language. French and bilingual members of the staff live at the House and help in directing conversation. Residence in the House is open to women, and both men and women may come there for meals. The House is not run for financial profit and prices are kept as low as possible.

The Department strongly urges students of French to room or board at the House so as to take full advantage of the unusual opportunity for speaking the language in everyday situations and hearing it spoken at a normal conversational tempo.

Applications for room reservations should be made early.
—Catalog of the University of Wisconsin

7.   *To the Virgins to Make Much of Time*

Gather ye rose-buds while ye may,
  Old Time is still a-flying:
And this same flower that smiles today,
  Tomorrow will be dying.

The glorious lamp of heaven, the Sun,
  The higher he's a-getting
The sooner will his race be run,
  And nearer he's to setting.

That age is best which is the first,
  When youth and blood are warmer;
But being spent, the worse, and worst
  Times, still succeed the former.

Then be not coy, but use your time;
  And while ye may, go marry:
For having lost but once your prime,
  You may for ever tarry.

                              —ROBERT HERRICK

8.   *The New Colossus: Inscription for the Statue of Liberty*

Not like the brazen giant of Greek fame,
With conquering limbs astride from land to land
Here at our sea-washed sunset gates shall stand
A mighty woman with a torch, whose fame
Is the imprisoned lightning, and her name
Mother of Exiles. From her beaconhand
Glows world-wide welcome; her mild eyes command
The air-bridged harbour that twin cities frame.
"Keep, ancient lands, your storied pomp," cries she
With silent lips. "Give me your tired, your poor,
Your huddled masses yearning to breathe free.
The wretched refuse of your teeming shore,
Send these, the homeless, the tempest-tost to me,
I lift my lamp beside the golden door!"

                              —EMMA LAZARUS

9. Give your child better grades by Christmas. Start his school year off
right with a Jones Galaxy portable typewriter. For typing improves
grades . . . and report cards prove it. When students start typing
assignments, school work (and grades) start to improve almost immediately. Educators acknowledge it. Classroom tests have proved
it. But for truly first-class work, a student needs a portable that is
easy to type on, easy to learn on . . . a Jones Galaxy.

                              —Advertisement in New York *Times*

II. Study the following statements in relation to the contexts in which they are likely to be found. Which are used principally as directives? Are there any which could hardly ever be used for directive purposes?

1. He is un-American.

> SAMPLE ANALYSIS: Ordinarily this statement is used as a strong judgment—a "snarl-word"—expressing the speaker's dislike of another person's opinions. Such a judgment ordinarily has strong directive implications: "Throw him out," or "Don't vote for him." In special contexts, where speaker and listener have agreed upon an *exact* and *verifiable* meaning of the word "un-American," the statement could be a report. Such contexts are rare.

2. With constabulary duties to be done, to be done,
    A policeman's lot is not a happy one.
    > —W. S. GILBERT

3. Man is born free; and everywhere he is in chains.   —ROUSSEAU

4. Oh, East is East, and West is West, and never the twain shall meet,
   Till Earth and Sky stand presently at God's great Judgment Seat.
   But there is neither East nor West, Border, nor Breed, nor Birth,
   When two strong men stand face to face, though they come from the ends of the earth!
   > —RUDYARD KIPLING, "The Ballad of East and West"

5. The performance will begin at 8:30 sharp.

6. I grow old . . . I grow old . . .
    I shall wear the bottoms of my trousers rolled.
    > —T. S. ELIOT, "The Love Song of J. Alfred Prufrock"

7. "With smoker after smoker who has tried different cigarettes—and compared them for mildness, coolness and flavor—Mammals are the 'choice of experience.' "

8. In human speech, different sounds have different meanings. To study this coordination of certain sounds with certain meanings is to study language. This coordination makes it possible for man to interact with great precision. When we tell someone, for instance, the address of a house he has never seen, we are doing something which no animal can do.   —LEONARD BLOOMFIELD, *Language*

9. Go, then, our rash sister! afar and aloof,
    Run wild in the sunshine away from our roof;
    But when your heart aches and your feet have grown sore,
    Remember the pathway that leads to our door!
    > —OLIVER WENDELL HOLMES, "Brother Jonathan's Lament for Sister Caroline," Address to the Confederacy, 1860

10. Some of the follies we commit because of false maps in our heads are so commonplace that we do not even think of them as remarkable. There are those who protect themselves from accidents by carrying a rabbit's foot. Some refuse to sleep on the thirteenth floor of hotels. —S. I. HAYAKAWA, *Language in Thought and Action*

III. Write the copy, draw (or describe) the illustrations you may need, and lay out a campaign (dinners, appointing of committees, personal solicitations, etc.) for a local fund-raising drive on behalf of the Red Cross, the Community Chest, or some such organization. Try sincerely to use appeals that will alter people's behavior: in this case, cause them to contribute where they might otherwise not. Can one go too far in using affective appeals for even such worthy causes? If so, what determines the limits within which one should stay?

IV. "Ownership" is defined in this chapter as a set of directive agreements, recognized by society, as to who may enjoy the use of what things. But the freedom to use and enjoy what is "mine" is limited according to the kind of property; e.g., I may drive "my" automobile only if it is duly registered with the state and if I have a driver's license. What are the differences in the extensional meanings of the word "my" in the following expressions?

my electric iron	*my* house
my real estate lot	*my* hotel room
my shares of General Motors stock	*my* original Rembrandt

V. In an earlier chapter it was stated that "The writer of a dictionary is a historian, not a lawgiver." Having covered seven chapters of this book, you should by now be inclined to question many things, including such a statement as that above. For instance, to what extent is any historian also one who *directs* our thought and future action by what he chooses to record? That is, the historian must choose *not to record* certain things. By recording what he does, he places upon what he records a significance that he does not place upon what he does not record. To what degree is his choice of material directive? Write five hundred words on "History as Directive."

VI. Here are several books that are relevant to the subject matter of this chapter. Write a critique of one or more of these books, paying special attention to their directives, explicit and implied:

The Informed Heart (1960), by Bruno Bettelheim. An eminent psychologist derives a pattern for survival from his experiences at Dachau and Buchenwald. After examining Nazi methods in these concentration camps, the author explains the conditions that made living possible and applies the techniques of resistance to living in today's mass society.

Law and the Modern Mind (1930), by Jerome Frank. A fascinating study of the semantics of law by one who was a pioneer in applying psychological and psychoanalytic ideas to the examination of what goes on in the minds of lawyers and judges.

Survival Through Design (1954), by Richard Neutra. A famous architect sees design as both the coordinating factor in architecture and man's only defense against the hostile environment that he must face in the future.

The Folklore of Capitalism (1938), by Thurman Arnold. This famous and amusing book, by the man who became assistant attorney-general in charge of the Anti-Trust Division in the Roosevelt administration, is a classic in analyzing how certain political and economic directives, rigidly adhered to, prevent societies from understanding and solving their problems.

The contemporary search for practical alternatives to either war or surrender has resulted in a number of books offering directives towards a constructive new foreign policy and a cessation of the armaments race. Among these are *The Peace Race* (1962), by Seymour Melman; *In Place of Folly* (1961), by Norman Cousins; *May Man Prevail?* (1961), by Erich Fromm; *The Limits of Defense* (1962), by Arthur Waskow; *An Alternative to War or Surrender* (1963), by Charles Osgood.

Propaganda is one of the most potent forms of directive, and there are numerous books which analyze some aspect of "thought-control." Leonard Doob's *Public Opinion and Propaganda* (1949) is an authoritative accumulation of facts. Special aspects of the problem of propaganda are treated in such works as *The Strategy of Terror* (1940), by Edmond Taylor; *German Psychological Warfare* (1942), edited by Ladislas Farago; and more recently, such books as Edward Barrett, *Truth Is Our Weapon* (1953); William Sargeant, *Battle for the Mind* (1957); Joost Meerloo, *The Rape of the Mind* (1956); C. John Rogge, *Why Men Confess* (1959); Robert J. Lifton, *Thought Reform* (1961). Vance Packard's *The Hidden Persuaders* (1957) and Martin Mayer's *Madison Avenue, U.S.A.* (1958) are fascinating as studies of the methods of advertising as propaganda.

8   The Language of Affective Communication

What I call the "auditory imagination" is the feeling for syllable and rhythm, penetrating far below the conscious levels of thought and feeling, invigorating every word; sinking to the most primitive and forgotten, returning to the origin and bringing something back, seeking the beginning and the end. It works through meanings, certainly, or not without meanings in the ordinary sense, and fuses the old and obliterated and the trite, the current, and the new and surprising, the most ancient and the most civilized mentality.   —T. S. ELIOT

"What's all this about 'one man, one vote'?" asked the Nottingham miner.
"Why, one bloody man, one bloody vote," Bill replied.
"Well, why the 'ell can't they say so?"
   —HUGH R. WALPOLE

One must know and recognize not merely the direct but the secret power of the word.   —KNUT HAMSUN

The language of reports is instrumental in getting done the work necessary for life, but it does not tell us anything about what life feels like in the living. We can communicate scientific facts to each other without knowing or caring about each other's feelings; but before love, friendship, and community can be established among men so that we *want* to cooperate and become a society, there must be, as we have seen, a flow of sympathy between one man and another. This flow of sympathy is established, of course, by means of the affective uses of language. Most of the time, after all, we are not interested in keeping our feelings out of our discourse, but rather we are eager to express them as fully as we can. Let us examine, then, some more of the ways in which language can be made to work affectively.

Verbal Hypnotism

First, it should be pointed out again that fine-sounding speeches, long words, and the general *air* of saying something important are affective in result, regardless of what is being said. Often when we are hearing or reading impressively worded sermons, speeches, political addresses, essays, or "fine writing," we stop being critical altogether, and simply allow ourselves to feel as excited, sad, joyous, or angry as the author wishes us to feel. Like snakes under the influence of a snake charmer's flute, we are swayed by the musical phrases of the verbal hypnotist. If the author is a man to be trusted, there is no reason why we should not enjoy ourselves in this way now and then. But to listen or read like this habitually is a debilitating habit.

There is a kind of churchgoer who habitually listens in this way, however. He enjoys any sermon, no matter what the moral principles recommended, no matter how poorly organized or developed, no matter how shabby its rhetoric, so long as it is delivered in an impressive tone of voice with proper musical and physical settings. Such listeners are by no means to be found only in churches. The writer has frequently been enraged when, after he has spoken before women's clubs on problems about which he wished to arouse thoughtful discussion, certain ladies have remarked, "That was such a lovely address, professor. You have such a nice voice."

Some people, that is, never listen to *what* is being said, since they are interested only in what might be called the gentle inward massage that the *sound* of words gives them. Just as cats and dogs like to be stroked, so do some human beings like to be verbally stroked at fairly regular intervals; it is a form of rudimentary sensual gratification. Because listeners of this kind are numerous, intellectual shortcomings are rarely a barrier to a successful career in public life, on the stage or the networks, on the lecture platform, or in the ministry.

More Affective Elements

The affective power of repetition of similar sounds, as in catchy titles and slogans, has already been mentioned. Somewhat higher on the scale are repetitions not only of sounds but of grammatical structures, as in:

First in war,
first in peace,
first in the hearts of his countrymen . . .

Government of the people,
　　by the people,
　　for the people . . .

Elements of discourse such as these are, from the point of view of scientific reporting, extraneous; but without them, these phrases would not have impressed people. Lincoln could have signified just as much for informative purposes had he said "government of, by, and for the people," or even more simply, "a people's government." But he was not writing a scientific monograph. He hammers the word "people" at us three times, and with each apparently unnecessary repetition he arouses deeper and more affecting connotations of the word. While this is not the place to discuss in detail the complexities of the affective qualities of language that reside in sound alone, it is important to remember that many of the attractions of literature and oratory have a simple phonetic basis—rhyme, alliteration, assonance, crossed alliteration, and all the subtleties of rhythm. All these sound effects are used to reinforce, wherever possible, the other affective devices.

Another affective device is the *direct address* to the listener or reader, as: "Keep off the grass. This means YOU!" The most painful example of this device is, of course, the spurious friendliness and intimacy with which the announcer of television commercials "personally" addresses each of several million listeners. But direct appeal to an audience is by no means limited to the advertising poster and television announcer. It softens the impersonality of formal speeches, so that when a speaker or writer feels a special urgency about his message, he can hardly help using it. It occurs, therefore, in the finest rhetoric as well as in the simplest. An interesting variant of the "you" device occurs in the college classroom, when the learned professor says, "You will recall what Kropotkin says in his *Mutual Aid: A Factor in Evolution* . . ." although he knows very well that Mr. Merkle, sprawling in his chair at the back of the class, has never even heard of Kropotkin before.

Almost as common as the "you" device is the "we" device. The writer in this case allies the reader with himself, in order to carry the reader along with him in seeing things as he does: *"We* shall now consider next . . ." "Let *us* take, for example . . ." *"Our* duty is to go forward . . ."* This device is particularly common in the politer forms of exhortation used by preachers and teachers, and it is found throughout this book. The "we" device is also often heard in kindergarten and the lower elementary grades, where teachers use it to sugar-coat their disciplinary directives: "Now, Ricky, now, Penny, we don't fight and call each other names here. We'll all say we're sorry and sit down and be friends again, *won't we?"* (Children usually believe that the word "cooperate" means "obey.")

In such rhetorical devices as the *periodic sentence* there is distortion of grammatical order for affective purposes. A periodic sentence is one in which the completion of the thought is, for the sake of the slight dramatic effect that can be produced by keeping the reader in suspense for a while, delayed. Then there are such devices as *antithesis,* in which strongly opposed notions are placed together or even laid side by side in parallel phonetic or grammatical constructions, so that the reader feels the contrast and is stirred by it: "Born a serf, he died a king." "The sweetest songs are those that tell of saddest thought." "The hungry judges soon the sentence sign, / And wretches hang that jurymen may dine."

Metaphor and Simile

As we have seen, words have affective connotations in addition to their informative value, and this accounts for the fact that statements of the kind: "I've been waiting *ages* for you—you're an hour overdue!" "He's got *tons* of money!" "I'm so tired I'm simply *dead!"* —which are nonsensical if interpreted literally—nevertheless "make sense." The inaccuracy or inappropriateness of the informative connotations of our words are often irrelevant from the point of view of affective communication. Therefore we may refer to the moon as "a piece of cheese," "a lady," "a silver ship," "a fragment of angry candy," or anything else, so long as the words arouse the desired feelings toward the moon or toward the whole situation in which the moon appears. This, incidentally, is the reason literature is so difficult to translate from one language to another: a translation that follows informative connotations will often falsify the affective connotations, and vice versa, so that readers who know both the language of the original and the language of the translation are almost sure to be dissatisfied, feeling either that the "spirit of the original has been sacrificed" or else that the translation is "full of inaccuracies."

In translations, a further problem is presented by the fact that a well-understood metaphor in one culture may have entirely different meanings in another part of the world. The United Nations once made a short movie in which an owl was shown, to indicate wisdom. It completely misfired in certain Asiatic countries where the movie was shown, and the footage had to be reshot. Why? Because in those countries it was found that the owl was a traditional image of stupidity and an object of amusement.

During the long time in which *metaphor* and *simile* were regarded as "ornaments" of speech—that is, as if they were like embroidery, which improves the appearance of our linen but adds nothing to its utility—the psychology of such communicative devices was neglected. We tend to assume, in ways that will be discussed more fully in later chapters, that things that create in us the same responses are identical with each other. If, for example, we are revolted by the conduct of an acquaintance at dinner and we have had such a sense of revulsion before only when watching pigs at a trough, our first, unreflecting reaction is naturally to say, "He is a pig." So far as our feelings are concerned, the man and the pig are identical with each other. Again, the soft winds of spring may produce in us agreeable sensations; the soft hands of lovely young girls also produce agreeable sensations; therefore, "Spring has soft hands." This is the basic process by which we arrive at metaphor. Metaphors are not "ornaments of discourse"; they are direct expressions of evaluations and are bound to occur whenever we have strong feelings to express. They are to be found in special abundance, therefore, in all primitive speech, in folk speech, in the speech of the unlearned, in the speech of children, and in the professional argot of theater people, of gangsters, and of those in other lively occupations.

So far as our feelings are concerned, there is no distinction between animate and inanimate objects. Our fright *feels* the same whether it is a creature or object that we fear. Therefore, in the expression of our feelings, a car may "lie down and die," the wind "kisses" our cheeks, the waves are "angry" and "roar" against the cliffs, the roads are icy and "treacherous," the mountains "look down" on the sea, machine guns "spit," revolvers "bark," volcanoes "vomit" fire, and the engine "gobbles" coal. This special kind of metaphor is called *personification* and is ordinarily described in textbooks of rhetoric as "making animate things out of inanimate." It is better understood, however, if we describe it as *a reaction that does not distinguish between the animate and the inanimate.*

Simile

However, even at rudimentary stages of evaluation it becomes apparent that calling a person a pig does not take sufficiently into consideration the differences between the person and the pig. Further reflection compels one to say, in modification of the original statement, "He is *like* a pig." Such an expression is called a *simile* —the pointing out of the similarities in our feelings towards the person and the pig. The simile, then, is something of a compromise stage between the direct, unreflective expression of feeling and the report, but of course closer to the former than the latter.

Adequate recognition has never been given to the fact that what we call slang and vulgarism works on exactly the same principles as poetry does. Slang makes constant use of metaphor and simile: "sticking his neck out," "out like a light," "way out on a limb," "baloney (no matter how thin you slice it)," "punch-drunk," "slick chick," "keep your shirt on," "as phony as a three-dollar bill." Clarence "Pinetop" Smith, one of the founders of the boogie-woogie style of piano-playing, used to admonish his friends: "Take it easy, greasy; there's a long way to slide!"

The imaginative process by which phrases such as these are coined is the same as that by which poets arrive at poetry. In poetry, there is the same love of seeing things in scientifically outrageous but emotionally expressive language:

The hunchèd camels of the night
Trouble the bright
And silver waters of the moon.
　　　　—FRANCIS THOMPSON

The snow doesn't give a soft white
damn Whom it touches.
　　　　—E. E. CUMMINGS

　　　　. . . the leaves dead
Are driven, like ghosts from an enchanter fleeing,
Yellow, and black, and pale, and hectic red,
Pestilence-stricken multitudes.
　　　　—PERCY BYSSHE SHELLEY

Sweet are the uses of adversity,
Which like the toad, ugly and venomous,
Wears yet a precious jewel in his head;
And this our life, exempt from public haunt,
Finds tongues in trees, books in the running brooks,
Sermons in stones, and good in everything.
                                        —WILLIAM SHAKESPEARE

I saw Eternity the other night
Like a great ring of pure and endless light.
                                        —HENRY VAUGHAN

What is called slang, therefore, might well be regarded as the poetry
of everyday life, since it performs much the same function as poetry;
that is, it vividly expresses people's feelings about life and about the
things they encounter in life.

Dead Metaphor

Metaphor, simile, and personification are among the most useful
communicative devices we have, because by their quick affective
power they often make unnecessary the inventing of new words for
new things or new feelings. They are so commonly used for this
purpose, indeed, that we resort to them constantly without realizing
that we are doing so. For example, when we talk about the "head"
of a cane, the "face" of a cliff, the "bowels" of a volcano, the "arm"
of the sea, the "hands" of a watch, the "branches" of a river or an
insurance company, we are using metaphor. A salesman "covers" an
area; an engine "knocks"; people pass "rubber" checks which
"bounce"; a theory is "built up" and then "knocked down"; a government "drains" the taxpayers, and corporations "milk" the consumers. Even in so unpoetical a source as the financial page of a
newspaper, metaphors are to be found: stock is "watered," shares
are "liquidated," prices are "slashed" or "stepped up," markets are
"flooded," the exchange is "bullish"; in spite of government efforts
to "hamstring" business and "strangle" enterprise, there are sometimes "melons" to be "sliced"; although this is—but here we leave
the financial page—"pure gravy" for some, others are left "holding
the bag." The "rings" both of "political rings" and "hydrocarbon
rings" are metaphorical, as are the "chains" in "chain stores" and
"chain reactions."

Metaphors are so useful that they often pass into the language as
part of its regular vocabulary. Metaphor is probably the most impor-

tant of all the means by which language develops, changes, grows, and adapts itself to our changing needs. Sometimes, however, metaphors get overworked—"ball-and-chain" (wife), "head-shrinker," "a horse of a different color," "a pretty kettle of fish"—so that they turn into linguistic deadwood (another metaphor!), or *clichés*.[1] When metaphors are successful, they "die"—that is, they become so much a part of our regular language that we cease thinking of them as metaphors at all.

To object to arguments, as is often done, on the ground that they are based on metaphors or on "metaphorical thinking" is rarely just. The question is not whether metaphors are used, but whether the metaphors represent useful similarities.

Allusion

Still another affective device is *allusion*. If we say, for example, standing on a bridge in St. Paul, Minnesota, in the early morning:

> Earth has not anything to show more fair;
> Dull would he be of soul who could pass by
> A sight so touching in its majesty . . .

we are evoking, in the mind of anyone familiar with the poem, such feelings as Wordsworth expressed at the sight of London in the early morning light in September 1802, and we are applying them to St. Paul. Thus, by a kind of implied simile, we can give expression to our feelings. Allusion, then, is an extremely quick way of expressing and also of creating in our hearers shades of feeling. With a biblical allusion ("Hasten ye, O generation of vipers, and pay me heed") we can often arouse reverent or penitential attitudes; with a historical allusion, such as saying that New York is "the modern Babylon," we can say quickly and effectively that we feel New York to be a luxurious and extremely wicked city, doomed to destruction because of its sinfulness; by a literary allusion, we can evoke the exact feelings found in a given story or poem as a way of feeling toward the event before us.

But allusions work as an affective device only when the hearer is familiar with the history, literature, people, or events alluded to. Family jokes (which are allusions to events or memories in the family's experience) have to be explained to outsiders; classical allu-

---

[1] The word "cliché" conceals still another metaphor; see its etymology as given in *Webster's Third New International Dictionary*.

sions in literature have to be explained to people not familiar with the classics. Nevertheless, whenever a group of people—the members of a single family or the members of a whole civilization—have memories and traditions in common, extremely subtle and efficient affective communications become possible through the use of allusion.

The foreigner, however well he may have studied English before coming to America, will fail to detect the sources of the allusions in such expressions as, "He is a regular Lower Slobbovian" or, "He communicates good, like a semanticist should." The number of times we find it necessary to stop and explain things when we converse with foreigners indicates the degree to which we rely upon allusions in everyday discourse.

One of the reasons, therefore, that the young in every culture are made to study the literature and history of their own linguistic or national groups is that they may be able to understand and share in the communications of the group. Those who fail to understand passing allusions to well-known figures in European or American history, to well-known lines in Chaucer, Shakespeare, Milton, Wordsworth, or the King James version of the Bible, or to well-known characters in Dickens, Thackeray, or Mark Twain, may be said to be outsiders to an important part of the traditions of English-speaking people. The study of history and of literature, therefore, is not merely the idle acquisition of social polish, as practical men are fond of believing, but a necessary means both of increasing the efficiency of our communications with others and of increasing our understanding of what others are trying to communicate to us.

Irony, Pathos, and Humor

A somewhat more complex device, upon which much of humor, pathos, and irony depends, is the use of a metaphor, simile, or allusion that is very obviously inappropriate to the subject at hand. The result of the incongruous comparison is a feeling of conflict, a conflict between our more obvious feelings towards that which we are talking about and the feelings aroused by the expression. In such a case, the conflicting feelings resolve themselves into a *third, new feeling*. Let us suppose, returning to our example above, that we are looking at an extremely ugly part of St. Paul, so that our obvious feelings are those of distaste. Then we arouse, with the Wordsworth quotation, the feeling of beauty and majesty. The result is a feeling suggested neither by the sight of the city alone nor by the allusion alone, but one that is a product of the *conflict* of the two—a sharp sense of incongruity that compels us either to laugh or to weep, depending on the rest of the context. There are many complex shades of feeling that can hardly be aroused in any other way. If a village poet is referred to as the "Mudville Milton," for example, the conflict between the inglorious connotations of "Mudville" and the glorious connotations of "Milton" produces an effect of the ludicrous, so that the poet is exposed to contempt (although, if Craigenputtock can produce a Carlyle, there is no reason that Mudville should not produce a Milton). The rather complex device that we have been discussing may be represented graphically by a diagram borrowed from mathematics:

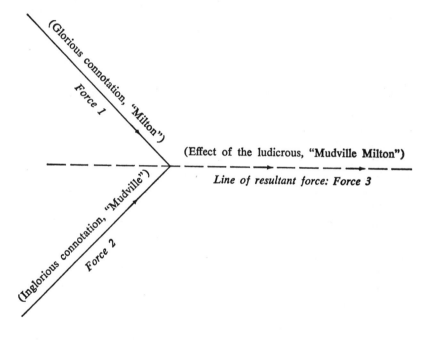

(Glorious connotation, "Milton")
Force 1

(Effect of the ludicrous, "Mudville Milton")

Line of resultant force: Force 3

(Inglorious connotation, "Mudville")
Force 2

The Affectiveness of Facts

The following account of an automobile accident is quoted from the Chicago *Sun-Times:*

> One [victim], Alex Kuzma, 63, of 808 North Maplewood Avenue, was hit with such impact that his right forearm was carried off on the car of the hit-run motorist who struck him. Kuzma was struck Sunday as he crossed Chicago Avenue at Campbell Avenue. Witnesses

saw the car slow down, douse its headlights and speed away. After searching futilely for the dead man's missing arm, police expressed belief it must have lodged in some section of the speeding auto.

There are few readers who will not have some kind of affective reaction to this story—at least a mild horror at the gruesomeness of the accident and some indignation at the driver who failed to stop after striking someone. Facts themselves, *especially at lower levels of abstraction,* can be affective without the use of special literary devices to make them more so.

There is, however, one important difference between the affectiveness of facts and the other affective elements in language. In the latter, the writer or speaker is expressing his own feelings; in the former, he is "suppressing his feelings"—that is to say, stating things in a way that would be verifiable by all observers, regardless of one's feelings.

Often, as in the example given, a report with accurately stated facts is more affective in result than outright and explicit judgments. By bringing the report down to even lower levels of abstraction—describing the blood on the victim's face and torn clothing, the torn ligaments hanging out of the remaining stump of his arm, and so on—one can make it even more affective. Instead of telling the reader, "It was a ghastly accident!" *we can make the reader say it for himself.* The reader is, so to speak, *made to participate in the communicative act by being left to draw his own conclusions.* A skillful writer is often, therefore, one who is especially expert at selecting the facts that are sure to move his readers in the desired ways. We are more likely to be convinced by such descriptive and factual writing than by a series of explicit judgments, because the writer does not ask us to take his word for it that the accident was ghastly. Such a conclusion becomes, in a sense, our own discovery rather than his.

Levels of Writing

Reliance upon the affectiveness of facts—that is, reliance upon the reader's ability to arrive at the judgment we want him to arrive at—varies considerably, of course, with the audience and with the subject being treated.

In this light, it is interesting to compare magazines and stories at different levels: the "pulp" and "confession" magazines, the "slicks" (*Ladies' Home Journal, Cosmopolitan, McCall's, Saturday Evening*

Post, and so on), and the "quality" magazines (*Harper's,* the *Atlantic,* the *New Yorker, Contact,* for example). In the magazines of mass appeal, the writers rarely rely on the reader's ability to arrive at his own conclusions. In order to save any possible strain on the reader's intelligence, the writers *make the judgments for us.* The "slicks" do this less than the "pulps," while in the "quality" group, the tendency is to rely a great deal on the reader: to give no judgments at all when the facts "speak for themselves," or to give enough facts with every judgment so that the reader is free to make a different judgment if he so wishes.

The following passages from *True Confessions* give an example of judgments made for the reader so that he doesn't have to figure them out for himself:

Telling Mrs. Peters and Mrs. Jenks, watching grief engulf them, was nightmare enough, but telling Edie was worst of all. She just stood there in frozen silence, her eyes wide with horror and disbelief, her face getting whiter and whiter.

"I did everything possible to save them!" I cried. "It was an accident—an unpreventable accident!"

But Edie's eyes were bitterly accusing as she choked, *"Accident!* If you hadn't insisted on taking them, there would have been no accident!" Tears streamed down her ravaged face and her voice rose hysterically. "I never want to see you again as long as I live! You—*you murderer!"* she screamed.

I stared at her for what seemed a lifetime of horror before I turned and fled, a million shrieking demons screaming in my ear, *She's right! You're a murderer! Murderer!*

The coroner's verdict called the boat's overloading "a tragic error of judgment." . . . But nothing could lighten that feeling of guilt in my heart or remove the sound of Edie's voice screaming, "Murderer!" It rang in my ears day and night, making work impossible—sleep even more impossible. Until I sought forgetfulness in the only way I could find it—by getting blind drunk and staying that way.

I was lurching through the door of a cheap bar weeks later when . . .

* * *

Jim was big and strong with huge shoulders and a great shock of yellow hair. Just looking at him made me excited and breathless. His great laugh could stir me to laughter. The touch of his hand filled me with a sweet, frightening delight. The day he invited me to the senior prom I thought I'd die of happiness.

Then I told Mother. I can still see her thin, fine-featured face pinched as if with frost. There was cold retreat in her eyes, and the wry smile on her lips made my heart turn over. . . .

The prose style of Ernest Hemingway is perhaps the classic example of the opposite technique—a highly sophisticated one, needless to say—of stating externally observable facts in the form of bare reports and of letting the reported facts have their impact on the reader. The following passage is the famous ending of *A Farewell to Arms:*

> I went into the room and stayed with Catherine until she died. She was unconscious all the time, and it did not take her very long to die.
>
> Outside the room, in the hall, I spoke to the doctor, "Is there anything I can do tonight?"
>
> "No. There is nothing to do. Can I take you to your hotel?"
>
> "No, thank you. I am going to stay here a while."
>
> "I know there is nothing to say. I cannot tell you—"
>
> "No," I said. "There's nothing to say."
>
> "Good-night," he said. "I cannot take you to your hotel?"
>
> "No, thank you."
>
> "It was the only thing to do," he said. "The operation proved—"
>
> "I do not want to talk about it," I said.
>
> "I would like to take you to your hotel."
>
> "No, thank you."
>
> He went down the hall. I went to the door of the room.
>
> "You can't come in now," one of the nurses said.
>
> "Yes I can," I said.
>
> "You can't come in yet."
>
> "You get out," I said. "The other one too."
>
> But after I had got them out and shut the door and turned off the light it wasn't any good. It was like saying good-by to a statue. After a while I went out and left the hospital and walked back to the hotel in the rain.

What Literature Is For

From what has been said, our first and most obvious conclusion is that since the expression of individual feelings is central to literature, affective elements are of the utmost importance in all literary writing. In the evaluation of a novel, poem, play, or short story, as well as in the evaluation of sermons, moral exhortations, political speeches, and directive utterances generally, the usefulness of the given piece of writing as a "map" of actual "territories" is often secondary—sometimes quite irrelevant. If this were not the case, *Gulliver's*

Travels, Alice in Wonderland, The Scarlet Letter, or Emerson's Essays would have no excuse for existence.

Secondly, when we say that a given piece of affective writing is true, we do not mean "scientifically true." We may merely mean that we agree with the sentiment; we may also mean that we believe that an attitude has been accurately expressed; again, we may mean that the attitudes evoked seem such as will lead us to better social or personal conduct.

The word "true" has many meanings. People who feel that science and literature or science and religion are in necessary conflict do so because they habitually think in opposites of black and white, true and false, good and evil. To such people, if science is "true," then literature or religion is nonsense; if literature or religion is "true," science is merely "pretentious ignorance." What should be understood when people tell us that certain statements are "scientifically true" is that they are useful and verifiable formulations, suitable for the purposes of organized cooperative workmanship. What should be understood when people tell us that the plays of Shakespeare or the poems of Milton or Dante are "eternally true" is that they produce in us attitudes toward our fellow men, an understanding of ourselves, or feelings of deep moral obligation that are valuable to humanity under any conceivable circumstances.

Thirdly, let us consider an important shortcoming of the language of reports and of scientific writing. John Smith in love with Mary is not William Brown in love with Jane; William Brown in love with Jane is not Henry Jones in love with Anne; Henry Jones in love with Anne is not Robert Browning in love with Elizabeth Barrett. Each of these situations is unique; no two loves are exactly alike—in fact, no love even between the same people is *exactly* the same from day to day. Science, seeking as always laws of the widest possible applicability and the greatest possible generality, would abstract from these situations *only what they have in common.* But each of these lovers is conscious only of the *uniqueness* of his own feelings: each feels, as we all know, that he is the first one in the world ever to have so loved. Literature creates the sense of what life feels like in the living.

How is that sense of difference conveyed? It is here that affective uses of language play their most important part. The infinity of differences in our feelings towards all the many experiences that we undergo are too subtle to be reported; they must be expressed. And we express them by the complicated manipulation of tones of voice, of rhythms, of connotations, of affective facts, of metaphors, of allusions, of every affective device of language at our command.

Frequently the feelings to be expressed are so subtle or complex that a few lines of prose or verse are not enough to convey them. It is sometimes necessary, therefore, for authors to write entire books, carrying their readers through numbers of scenes, situations, and adventures, pushing their sympathies now this way and now that, arousing in turn their fighting spirit, their tenderness, their sense of tragedy, their laughter, their superstitiousness, their cupidity, their sensuousness, their piety. Sometimes it is only in such ways that the *exact* feelings an author wants to express can be recreated in his readers. This, then, is the reason that novels, poems, dramas, stories, allegories, and parables exist: to convey such propositions as "Life is tragic" or "Susanna is beautiful," not by telling us so, but by putting us through a whole series of experiences that make us feel toward life or toward Susanna as the author did. *Literature is the most exact expression of feelings, while science is the most exact kind of reporting.* Poetry, which condenses all the affective resources of language into patterns of infinite rhythmical subtlety, may be said to be *the language of expression at its highest degree of efficiency.*

Symbolic Experience

In a very real sense, then, people who have read good literature have lived more than people who cannot or will not read. To have read *Gulliver's Travels* is to have had the experience, with Jonathan Swift, of turning sick at one's stomach at the conduct of the human race; to read *Huckleberry Finn* is to feel what it is like to drift down the Mississippi River on a raft; to have read Byron is to have suffered with him his rebellions and neuroses and to have enjoyed with him his nose-thumbing at society; to have read *Native Son* is to know how it feels to be frustrated in the particular way in which many Negroes in Chicago are frustrated. This is the great task that affective communication performs: it enables us to feel how others felt about life, even if they lived thousands of miles away and centuries ago. It is not true that we have only one life to live; if we can read, we can live as many more lives and as many kinds of lives as we wish.

Here, the reader may object by asking, are we not twisting language somewhat to talk about "living" other lives than one's own? In one sense, the objection is correct; two different meanings of the word "live" are involved in the expressions "living one's own life" and "living other people's lives in books." Human life, however, is "lived" at more than one level; we inhabit both the extensional world and the world of words (and other symbols). "Living other people's lives in books" means, as we shall use the expression here, *symbolic experience*—sometimes called "vicarious experience."

In the enjoyment and contemplation of a work of literary or dramatic art—a novel, a play, a moving picture—*we find our deepest enjoyment when the leading characters in the story to some degree symbolize ourselves.* Jessie Jenkins at the movie, watching Elizabeth Taylor being kissed by a handsome man, sighs as contentedly as if she herself were being kissed—and *symbolically,* she is. In other words, she identifies herself with Elizabeth Taylor and her role in the story. Kirk Douglas fighting a villain is watched by thousands of men who clench their hands as if *they* were doing the fighting—which they are, *symbolically.* As we identify ourselves with the people in the story, the dramatist or the novelist puts us through *organized sequences of symbolic experiences.*

The differences between actual and symbolic experiences are great—one is not scarred by watching a moving-picture battle, nor is one nourished by watching people in a play having dinner. Furthermore, actual experiences come to us in highly disorganized fashion: meals, arguments with the landlady, visits to the doctor about one's fallen arches, and so on, interrupt the splendid course of romance. The novelist, however, *abstracts* only the events relevant to his story and then *organizes* them into a meaningful sequence. This business of abstracting (selecting) events and organizing them so that they bear some meaningful relationship to each other and to the central theme of a novel or play constitutes the storyteller's art. Plot construction, development of character, narrative structure, climax, denouement, and all the other things one talks about in technical literary criticism have reference to this organizing of symbolic experiences so that the whole complex of symbolic experiences (i.e., the finished story or play) will have the desired impact on the reader.

All literary and dramatic enjoyment, whether of nursery tales in childhood or of moving pictures later on or of "great literature," appears to involve to some degree the reader's imaginative identification of himself with the roles portrayed and his projection of himself into the situations described in the story.[2] Whether a reader is able

[2] At what age does the capacity for imaginative identification of oneself with the roles portrayed in a story begin? The writer would suggest, on the

to identify himself with the characters of a story depends both on the maturity of the story and the maturity of the reader. If a mature reader finds difficulty identifying himself with the hero of a cowboy story, it is because he finds the hero too simple-minded a character to serve as an acceptable symbol for himself, and the villains and the events too improbable to serve as symbols for his own enemies and his own problems.

However, the simple-mindedness of the people and the improbability of the events of cowboy and western movies contribute much to their popularity on television. We live in a complex civilization, in which the vast majority of us lead peaceful, unaggressive lives. When we are troubled by problems—when sales fall off or profits decline or our jobs are threatened or shipments do not arrive on time or customers complain—many, many things may be to blame: manufacturers, middlemen, the stock market, the labor unions, high taxes, high rentals, the railroads, the government, local zoning regulations, or the problems of communication inevitable in large and complex societies. There is as a rule no single villain or group of villains, no one agency, that can be the object of our wrath when things go wrong. Hence, the world of the television western is comforting to come home to when the day's work is done: the "good guys" (in white hats) and the "bad guys" (in black hats) are clearly distinguishable, and all troubles are dissolved in a happy ending when the "bad guys" are defeated or dead after a heroic gun-fight. (Pictures in which the "good guys" wear black hats are known as "adult westerns.")

One of the reasons for calling some people immature is that they are incapable of confronting defeat, tragedy, or unpleasantness of any kind. Such persons usually cannot endure an "unhappy ending" *even in a set of symbolic experiences.* Hence the widespread passion for happy endings in popular literature, so that even stories about unhappy events have to be made, in the end, to "come out all right." The immature constantly need to be reassured that everything will always come out all right.

Readers who mature as they grow older, however, steadily increase the depth and range and subtlety of their symbolic experiences. Under the guidance of skilled writers who have accurately observed the world and have been able to organize their observations

basis of very limited observation, that it begins around the age of two or earlier. An interesting test case is to read the story of the Three Bears to a very small child to see when he begins to identify himself with Baby Bear.

in significant ways, the mature reader may symbolically experience murder, guilt, religious exaltation, bankruptcy, the loss of friends, the discovery of gold mines or new philosophical principles, or the sense of desolation following a locust invasion in North Dakota. Each new symbolic experience means the enrichment of his insight into people and events.

As we progress in our reading, our consciousness widens. Gradually, the "maps" which we have inside our heads become fuller, more accurate, pictures of the actual "territories" of human character and behavior under many different conditions and in many different times. Gradually, too, our increased insight gives us sympathy with our fellow human beings everywhere. The kings of Egypt, the Tibetan priest behind his ceremonial mask, the Roman political exile, and the embittered Harlem youth are presented to us by the novelist, the poet, and the playwright, at levels of vivid and intimate description, so that we learn how they lived, what they worried about, and how they felt. When the lives of other people, of whatever time and place, are examined in this way, we discover to our amazement that they are all people. This discovery is the basis of all civilized human relationships. If we remain uncivilized—whether in community, industrial, national, or international relationships—it is largely because most of us have not yet made this discovery. Literature is one of the important instruments to that end.

Science and Literature

By means of scientific communication, with its international systems of weights and measures, international systems of botanical and zoological nomenclature, international mathematical symbols, we are enabled to exchange information with each other, pool our observations, and acquire collective control over our environment. By means of affective communication—by conversation and gesture when we can see each other, but by literature and other arts when we cannot—we come to understand each other, to cease being brutishly suspicious of each other, and gradually to realize the profound community that exists between us and our fellow men. Science, in short, makes us able to cooperate; the arts enlarge our sympathies so that we become willing to cooperate.

APPLICATIONS

I. All literary criticism that tries to find out what exactly an author is saying presupposes, of course, knowledge of principles such as those discussed in this chapter. Their real application can only be in abundant and careful reading and in the development of taste through *consciousness of what is going on* in every piece of literature one reads, whether it be a magazine serial, a Katherine Mansfield short story, or an Elizabethan play.

A useful practice, even for an experienced reader, is to take short passages of prose and verse—especially passages he has long been familiar with—and to find out by careful analysis (a) what the author is trying to communicate; (b) what affective elements help him to convey his meaning; (c) what elements, if any, obscure his communication; (d) how successful, on the whole, the author is in conveying his ideas and feelings to the reader; and (e) how appropriate his metaphors are to the various subjects he is dealing with. The following passages may serve as materials for this kind of analysis:

1. It was a crisp and spicy morning in early October. The lilacs and laburnums, lit with the glory fires of autumn, hung burning and flashing in the upper air, a fairy bridge provided by kind Nature for the wingless wild things that have their home in the tree tops and would visit together; the larch and the pomegranate flung their purple and yellow flames in brilliant broad splashes along the slanting sweep of the woodland; the sensuous fragrance of innumerable deciduous flowers rose upon the swooning atmosphere; far in the empty sky a solitary oesophagus slept upon motionless wing; everywhere brooded stillness, serenity, and the peace of God.
   —SAMUEL L. CLEMENS, "A Double-Barreled Detective Story"

2. At the mid hour of night, when stars are weeping, I fly
   To the lone vale we loved when life shone warm in thine eye;
   And I think oft, if spirits can steal from the regions of air
   To revisit past scenes of delight, thou wilt come to me there,
   And tell me our love is remembered, even in the sky.

   Then I sing the wild song 'twas once such a pleasure to hear,
   When our voices, commingling, breathed like one on the ear;
   And as echo far off through the vale my sad orison rolls,
   I think, O my love, 'tis thy voice from the Kingdom of Souls
   Faintly answering still the notes that once were so dear.
   —THOMAS MOORE, "At the Mid Hour of Night"

3. PARIS—Dive as deep as you like into that closet full of last winter's moth-proofed clothes and you will find little to resemble the over-stretched and well-swaddled silhouette now centered on the Paris fashion stage. The emerging blueprint sketched by top couturiers creates an elongated woman, drawn out like a winter's night. Her clothes are fitted to the body, but they skip the curves in a general mood of austerity, backed by a preference for the more melancholic colors and an absence of distracting detail.

Outdoors, she is covered in more layers than an onion. So little of the face is visible that a new heavy-handed way with make-up makes eyes larger than ever. Sketched in black pencil and haloed in green mascara, they require half an hour of skilled attention and seven successive applications of color. They emerge, framed between a small hat clamped down to the hairline (and sometimes covered by a hood) and a tall collar rising into the chin.

Necks vanish inside a soft ring of fur, or a stole as narrow as a stocking. Shoulders are shrugged under cocoon capes or coachman capelets. At the other end of the line, charming little bootees with Edwardian overtones climb up to the calf, to afford similar pro-tection.   —Fashion page of the San Francisco *Sunday Chronicle*

4. There is probably one purpose, and only one, for which the use of force by a government is beneficent, and that is to diminish the total amount of force in the world. It is clear, for example, that the legal prohibition of murder diminishes the total amount of violence in the world. And no one would maintain that parents should have un-limited freedom to ill-treat their children. So long as some men wish to do violence to others, there cannot be complete liberty, for either the wish to do violence must be restrained, or the victims must be left to suffer. For this reason, although individuals and societies should have the utmost freedom as regards their own affairs, they ought not to have complete freedom as regards their dealings with others. To give freedom to the strong to oppress the weak is not the way to secure the greatest possible amount of freedom in the world. This is the basis of the socialist revolt against the kind of freedom which used to be advocated by laissez-faire economists.
     —BERTRAND RUSSELL, *Political Ideals* *

5.   O say, can you see, by the dawn's early light,
          What so proudly we hailed at the twilight's last gleaming?
     Whose broad stripes and bright stars, through the perilous fight,
          O'er the ramparts we watched, were so gallantly streaming!

* From *Political Ideals* by Bertrand Russell, copyright, 1917, by the Cen-tury Company. Reprinted by permission of Appleton-Century-Crofts, Inc.

And the rockets' red glare, the bombs bursting in air,
Gave proof through the night that our flag was still there:
  O say, does that star-spangled banner yet wave
  O'er the land of the free and the home of the brave?

—FRANCIS SCOTT KEY

6. No one can understand conservatism who supposes that a "conservative" is just a man on the side of riches, power, sophistication. Rather, the conservative is the realist, taking ever the side of all that is real, abiding, basic, fundamental—taking the side of the stars and the seas; of the forests of redwood that have gathered strength and wisdom through the centuries; of the multiplication table that even John Dewey cannot change; of the inexorable spectrum of color and the inevitable octaves of the musical scale that were, before the beginning of time, exactly what they will be after the end of time; of the Taj Mahal and the Parthenon and the cathedral of Chartres; of Aeschylus and Dante and Bach and Rembrandt; of the elemental human spirit in its grief and in its glory.

The conservative is a man who distrusts the flicker of time because he trusts the Eternity that ever invades time to make it live. And the world's death—in the first Christmas and today—lies in the fickle temporality that shuns the Eternity that alone is the life of time.   —E. MERRILL ROOT, "Flicker of Time"

7.
    If there were dreams to sell
    What would you buy?
    Some cost a passing bell;
    Some a light sigh
    That shakes from Life's fresh crown
    Only a rose-leaf down.
    If there were dreams to sell,
    Merry and sad to tell,
    And the crier rung the bell,
    What would you buy?

    A cottage lone and still,
    With bowers nigh,
    Shadowy, my woes to still,
    Until I die.
    Such pearl from Life's fresh crown
    Fain would I shake me down.
    Were dreams to have at will,
    This best would heal my ill,
    This would I buy.

—THOMAS LOVELL BEDDOES, "Dream Pedlary"

8. We must learn to reawaken and keep ourselves awake, not by mechanical aids, but by an infinite expectation of the dawn, which does not forsake us in our soundest sleep. I know of no more encouraging fact than the unquestionable ability of man to elevate his life by a conscious endeavor. It is something to be able to paint a particular picture, or to carve a statue, and so to make a few objects beautiful; but it is far more glorious to carve and paint the very atmosphere and medium through which we look, which morally we can do. To affect the quality of the day, that is the highest of arts.

—HENRY DAVID THOREAU, *Walden*

II. The opening of a story, poem, essay, or book has special significance in setting the point of view, establishing the mood, gaining the reader's attention and interest. What can be inferred about the author's purpose from these beginnings?

1. I got another barber that comes over from Carterville and helps me out Saturdays, but the rest of the time I can get along all right alone. You can see for yourself that this ain't no New York City and besides that, most of the boys works all day and don't have no leisure to drop in here and get themselves prettied up.

   You're a newcomer, ain't you? I thought I hadn't seen you round before. I hope you like it good enough to stay. As I say, we ain't no New York City or Chicago, but we have pretty good times. Not as good, though, since Jim Kendall got killed. When he was alive, him and Hod Meyers used to keep this town in an uproar. I bet they was more laughin' done here than any town its size in America. . . . —RING LARDNER, "Haircut"

2. But do not let us quarrel any more,
   No, my Lucrezia; bear with me for once:
   Sit down and all shall happen as you wish.
   You turn your face, but does it bring your heart?
   I'll work then for your friend's friend, never fear,
   Treat his own subject after his own way,
   Fix his own time, accept, too, his own price,
   And shut the money into this small hand
   When next it takes mine. . . .

   —ROBERT BROWNING, "Andrea del Sarto"

3. Rosalie Lyons pushed open the door wearily and walked into the little room they had given her, up above the kitchen. She could hear the pounding of the jukebox coming through the walls from down below. The Flamingo was really swinging tonight, she thought. Every table was filled. And she was so goddamn tired. She hadn't realized

that it could be so exhausting, just waiting on tables. Her body ached.
Her legs throbbed. And her chest was aching, too. She could feel the
exhaustion right through her full breasts.

—DON ELLIOT, "Roadhouse Girl"

4. The Chevalier Tannhauser, having lighted off his horse, stood doubt-
fully for a moment beneath the ombre gateway of the mysterious
hill, troubled with an exquisite fear lest a day's travel should have
too cruelly undone the labored niceness of his dress. His hand, slim
and gracious as La Marquise du Deffand's in the drawing by Car-
montelle, played nervously about the gold hair that fell upon his
shoulders like a finely-curled peruke, and from point to point of a
precise toilet the fingers wandered, quelling the little mutinies of
cravat and ruffle.   —AUBREY BEARDSLEY, "Under the Hill"

5.   Since I am coming to that holy room,
            Where with Thy choir of saints for evermore
            I shall be made Thy music; as I come
            I tune the instrument here at the door,
            And what I must do then, think here before.
                —JOHN DONNE, "Hymn to God"

6.   "Is there anybody there?" said the Traveler,
                Knocking on the moonlit door;
            And his horse in the silence champed the grasses
                Of the forest's ferny floor:
            And a bird flew up out of the turret,
                Above the Traveler's head:
            And he smote upon the door again a second time;
                "Is there anybody there?" he said.
                —WALTER DE LA MARE, "The Listeners"

7. I have often noticed on my trips up to the city that people have
recut their clothes to follow the fashion. On my last trip, however,
it seemed to me that people had remodeled their ideas too—taken in
their convictions a little at the waist, shortened the sleeves of their
resolve, and fitted themselves out in a new intellectual ensemble
copied from a smart design of the very latest page of history. It
seemed to me they had strung along with Paris a little too long.
    I confess to a disturbed stomach. . . .
                —E. B. WHITE, "One Man's Meat"

8. What is the province of psychology? I suggest the word *curing*. But
what kind of curing? I do not want to be cured of my habit of
choosing the colors orange and black; nor do I want to be cured of
smoking; nor of my liking for a bottle of beer. No teacher has the
right to cure a child of making noises on a drum. The only curing
that should be practiced is the curing of unhappiness.

The difficult child is the child who is unhappy. He is at war with himself; and in consequence, he is at war with the world.

The difficult adult is in the same boat. No happy man ever disturbed a meeting, or preached a war, or lynched a Negro. No happy woman ever nagged her husband or her children. No happy man ever committed a murder or a theft. No happy employer ever frightened his employees.

All crimes, all hatreds, all wars can be reduced to unhappiness. This book is an attempt to show how unhappiness arises, how it ruins human lives, and how children can be reared so that much of this unhappiness will never arise.

More than that, this book is the story of a place—Summerhill— where children's unhappiness is cured and, more important, where children are reared in happiness.

—A. S. NEILL, *Summerhill: A Radical Approach to Child Rearing*

III. There are two kinds of identification which a reader may make with characters in a story. First, he may recognize in the story-character a more or less realistic representation of himself. (For example, the story-character is shown misunderstood by his parents, while the reader, because of the vividness of the narrative, recognizes his own experiences in those of the story-character.) Secondly, the reader may find, by identifying himself with the story-character, the fulfillment of his own desires. (For example, the reader may be poor, not very handsome, and not popular with girls, but he may find symbolic satisfaction in identifying himself with a story-character who is represented as rich, handsome, and madly sought after by hundreds of beautiful women.) It is not easy to draw hard-and-fast lines between these two kinds of identification, but basically the former kind (which we may call "identification by self-recognition") rests upon the *similarity* of the reader's experiences with those of the story-character, while the latter kind ("identification for wish-fulfillment") rests upon the *dissimilarity* between the reader's dull life and the story-character's interesting life. Many (perhaps most) stories engage (or seek to engage) the reader's identification by *both* means.

Study carefully a story in a love-story, confession, or male adventure magazine or a television western, analyzing plot and characterization to see in what ways and to what degree "identification by self-recognition" and "identification for wish-fulfillment" are produced in the reader by the author. Do *not* begin this analysis with literature of greater sophistication or higher literary quality, since the mechanisms are most clearly and simply revealed in fiction addressed to an unsophisticated audience.

IV. The above exercise rests on the assumption that the reader, not being a pulp magazine fan, will have performed his analysis "from the outside," as one whose own emotions were not involved in the story analyzed. Next, the same task of analysis may be performed with a story, novel, or play which the reader has found interesting and absorbing. The reader might ask himself such questions as these: "What *in me* responded to what elements in the story? What does my enthusiasm for this story reveal about the story and about myself? Ten years from now, is it likely that I shall be sufficiently like my present self to continue to be moved and delighted by this story?"

V. A collection of articles under the title, *Mass Culture,* edited by Bernard Rosenberg and David Manning White (1957), is a treasury of studies of wish-fulfillment in popular culture, the best area of course to study this phenomenon. We see our national types in movies, comic books, cartoon strips, soap operas, popular songs, and advertising. Take one section of this book, read the four or five articles in that area, and write a 500-word critique adding observations of your own. Related material is to be found in Hortense Powdermaker's *Hollywood, the Dream Factory* (1950); see also Martha Wolfenstein and Nathan Leites, *Movies: A Psychological Study* (1950).

VI. Read the following selection carefully. Then read *all* the fiction in any *one* issue of a mass-circulation magazine addressed either to women or to mixed audiences. Then write a 700-word essay about the fiction in that issue in the light of what Marya Mannes has said.

I was talking shop with a fiction writer who had just sold a short story to a Canadian publication after the American mass weekly that normally bought her work had reluctantly turned it down. "It was quite a happy story," she said, "but there was a mention of death in it, and the editors said that their policy was not to present death to their readers in any form." . . .

This started us off quite naturally on taboos, the "hidden censorship" that we agreed existed to a fantastic degree in the mass-circulation media of the country. I told her of the short story I had almost sold to a women's magazine. The editors praised it highly, but wondered if I would make a few changes. In the story a man of thirty-five and a woman of twenty-nine were in love. Would I change their ages to, say, thirty for the man and twenty-four for the woman, as readers were not interested in love over thirty.

Secondly, the hero of my story was a Czech refugee who was teaching his particular branch of science in a Midwestern university. The editors would like me to make him a Midwestern American instead—possibly a doctor; they preferred not to have the romantic interest foreign. . . .

There were other, more obvious taboos. Disparity in the ages of a couple in love was wholly undesirable. You might just conceivably mate a man of forty with a girl of twenty-five, but you'd have to think up some compellingly virtuous reasons. You could never, but never, write of a woman of forty in a happy relationship with a man of thirty-five. . . .

Another writer, a man, reminded us that in a mass-circulation magazine a girl could be attractive only in currently acceptable ways. You could make her nose short but not long; you could not make her teeth irregular; you certainly could not make her plump, however delightful she might be in other ways. You could not at any time question certain artificialities resulting from cosmetic means, or, on the other hand, praise a girl who dispensed with them. . . .

We agreed, from the pooling of our fictional experiences, that you could never speak ill of a doctor or a banker, although you could make a scientist, a writer, or a musician unsympathetic. If a woman had a career, she could not be happy in it, and would ultimately sacrifice it for split-level security. No mother could express relief at the absence of her children. No characters, in any story, could discuss abstract ideas or important current matters, with the exception of floods and hurricanes. . . .

> —MARYA MANNES, "The Case of the Orange
> Orange," in the *Reporter*

9 Art and Tension

But my position is this: that if we try to discover what the poem is doing for the poet, we may discover a set of generalizations as to what poems do for everybody. —KENNETH BURKE

A well-chosen anthology [of verse] is a complete dispensary of medicine for the more common mental disorders, and may be used as much for prevention as cure. —ROBERT GRAVES

Bearing the Unbearable

Animals know their environment by direct experience only; man crystallizes his knowledge and his feelings in phonetic symbolic representations; by written symbols he accumulates knowledge and passes it on to further generations of men. Animals feed themselves where they find food, but man, coordinating his efforts with the efforts of others by linguistic means, feeds himself abundantly and with food prepared by a hundred hands and brought great distances. Animals exercise but limited control over each other, but man, again by employing symbols, establishes laws and ethical systems, which are linguistic means of imposing order and predictability upon human conduct. Acquiring knowledge, securing food, establishing social order—these activities make sense to the biologist because they contribute to survival. For human beings, each of these activities involves a symbolic dimension—a dimension of which lower animals have no inkling.

Let us attempt to state the functions of literature in scientifically verifiable terms—in other words, in terms of biological "survival value." Granted that this is a difficult task in the present state of psychological knowledge, it is necessary that we try to do so, since most explanations of the necessity or value of literature (or the other arts) take the form of purr-words—which are really no explanations at all. For example, Wordsworth speaks of poetry as "the breath and finer spirit of all knowledge"; Coleridge speaks of it as "the best words in the best order." The explanations of literature given by many teachers and critics follow a similar purr-word pattern, usually reducible to "You should read great literature because it is very, very great." If we are to give a scientific account of the functions of literature, we shall have to do better than that.

Having included under the term "literature" all the affective uses of language, we are helped in our inquiry by recent psychological and psychiatric investigations, as well as by the insights of critics and students of literature. These sources indicate that, from the point of view of the utterer, one of the most important functions of the utterance is the relieving of *tensions*. We have all known the relief that comes from uttering a long and resounding series of impolite vocables under the stress of great irritation. The same releasing of psychological tensions—Aristotle called it *catharsis*—appears to be effected at all levels of affective utterance, if we are to believe what writers themselves have said about the creative process. The novel, the drama, the poem, like the oath or the expletive, arise, at least in part, out of internal necessity when the organism experiences a serious tension, whether resulting from joy, grief, disturbance, or frustration. And as a result of the utterances made, the tension is, to a greater or lesser degree—perhaps only momentarily— mitigated.

A frustrated or unhappy animal can do relatively little about its tensions.[1] A human being, however, with an extra dimension (the world of symbols) to move around in, not only undergoes experience, but also *symbolizes his experience to himself*. Our states of tension—especially the unhappy tensions—*become tolerable* as we manage to *state what is wrong—to get it said*—whether to a sympathetic friend, or on paper to a hypothetical sympathetic reader, or even to oneself.[2] If our symbolizations are adequate and sufficiently

[1] See the account of "substitutive, or symbolic" behavior among cats under conditions of experimentally induced neurosis in Jules Masserman's *Behavior and Neurosis* (1943). It can hardly be denied, in the face of Dr. Masserman's evidence, that an extremely rudimentary form of what might be called "pre-poetic" behavior, analogous to the treasuring of a lock of a loved one's hair, is to be found even among cats. The cats, when hungry, fondle the pushbutton that *used to* trip a mechanism that brought them food, although they appear to know (since they no longer move to the food box after touching the button) that it no longer works.

[2] An indication of the importance of "getting it said" is given in the research of Charles W. Slack of the Harvard Psychological Clinic. Dr. Slack "hired," at modest hourly wages, unemployed young men hanging around street corners in Cambridge. He asked them to be "research consultants" to help inquire into the question of "how guys foul up." Their task was to talk

skillful, our tensions are brought *symbolically under control*. To achieve this control, we may employ what Kenneth Burke has called "symbolic strategies"—that is, ways of reclassifying our experiences so that they are "encompassed" and easier to bear.[3] Whether by processes of "pouring out our hearts" or by "symbolic strategies" or by other means, we may employ symbolizations as mechanisms of relief when the pressures of a situation become intolerable.

As we all know, language is social, and for every speaker there may be hearers. An utterance that relieves a tension for the speaker can relieve a similar tension, should one happen to exist, in the hearer. And because human experience remains fairly constant, this process is possible even when speaker and hearer are separated by centuries or by different cultures. The symbolic manipulation by which John Donne "encompassed" his feelings of guilt in one of his Holy Sonnets enables us too, at another time and under another set of circumstances, to encompass our feelings of guilt about, in all probability, a different set of sins.

William Ernest Henley confronted the fact of his chronic invalidism—he had been ill since childhood and had spent long periods of his life in hospitals—by stating, in his well-known poem "Invictus," his refusal to be defeated:

> Out of the night that covers me,
>   Black as the pit from pole to pole,
> I thank whatever gods may be
>   For my unconquerable soul.
>
> In the fell clutch of circumstance
>   I have not winced nor cried aloud.
> Under the bludgeonings of chance
>   My head is bloody, but unbowed.
>
> Beyond this place of wrath and tears
>   Looms but the horror of the shade,
> And yet the menace of the years
>   Finds, and shall find me, unafraid.

into tape-recorders about themselves and their problems. A dramatic improvement in behavior was shown by almost all the boys who took part in the project: they got jobs and held them; the number of arrests among them dropped by half.

[3] See Kenneth Burke, *Philosophy of Literary Form* (1941). An infielder for the Chicago White Sox some years ago made four errors in four consecutive chances. Naturally, he found his performance difficult to face. His "symbolic strategy" was reported by a Chicago *Times* writer who quoted the infielder as saying, "Anyway, I bet it's a *record!*"

> It matters **not how** strait the gate,
> How charged with punishments the scroll,
> I am the master of my fate:
> I am the captain of my soul.

How, at a different time and under different circumstances, other people can use Henley's utterance to take arms against a different sea of troubles is shown by the fact that this poem is one of the favorite poems of American Negroes and is sometimes recited or sung chorally by Negro organizations. The extra meaning of the word "black" in the second line when the poem is said by Negroes makes it perhaps an even more pointed utterance for the Negro reader than it was for the original author. Indeed, the entire poem takes on different meanings depending on what a reader, putting himself into the role of the speaker of the poem, projects into the words "the night that covers me." [4]

Poetry has often been spoken of as an aid to sanity. Kenneth Burke calls it "equipment for living." It would appear that we can take these statements seriously and work out their implications in many directions. What are, for example, some of the kinds of symbolic manipulation by which we attempt to equip ourselves in the face of the constant succession of difficulties and tensions, great and small, that confront us day by day? Of course, the stimulus of social tension is not necessary for all literature, but unquestionably it is often a significant spur to creation.

Some "Symbolic Strategies"

First of all, of course, there is what is called literary "escape"—a tremendous source of literature, poetry, drama, comic strips, and other forms of affective communication. Edgar Rice Burroughs, confined to a sickbed, symbolically traipsed through the jungle, in the person of Tarzan, in a series of breath-taking and triumphant

[4] Anyone saying, as the present writer does, that a poem may mean different things to different people, lays himself open to the charge that his relativistic position makes it impossible "to distinguish between right and wrong readings of a poem." It is perhaps necessary, therefore, to clarify what is asserted here: saying that a poem may have different meanings for different people is *not* the same as saying that a poem can mean anything at all.

Incidentally, another example of a poem acquiring a changed meaning in a changed context is provided by the Freedom Riders who "sat in" and refused to budge from segregated premises. They responded to threats with the old hymn, "We shall not be, we shall not be moved," endowing the words with a meaning not found when sung in church.

adventures—and by means of this symbolic compensation made his sickbed endurable. At the same time he made life endurable for millions of undersized, frustrated, and feeble people. One may not think much of the author and the readers of the Tarzan stories; still, it is to be emphasized that in order to derive what relief they offer from pain or boredom, it takes, both in the telling and in the reading of such stories, the symbolic process, and hence a *human* nervous system.

Let us take another example of symbolic strategy. When a disgruntled employee calls his employer a "half-pint Hitler," is he not using a "strategy" which, by means of introducing his employer (a petty tyrant) into a perspective which includes Hitler (a great tyrant), symbolically reduces his employer to what Kenneth Burke calls manageable proportions? And did not Dante likewise, unable to punish his enemies as they deserved to be punished, symbolically put them in their places in the most uncomfortable quarters in Hell? There is a world of difference between the completeness and adequacy of such a simple epithet as "half-pint Hitler" and Dante's way of disposing of his enemies—and Dante accomplished many more things in his poem besides symbolically punishing his enemies—but are they not both symbolic manipulations by means of which the utterers derive a measure of relief or relaxation of psychological tensions?

Let us take another example. Upton Sinclair was deeply disturbed by the stockyards as they were in 1906. He could have tried to forget them; he could have buried himself in reading or writing about other things, such as idyllic lands long ago and far away or entirely nonexistent—as do the readers and writers of escape literature. He could have tried, by a different symbolic manipulation, to show that present evil was part of greater good "in God's omniscient plan." This has been the strategy of many religions as well as of many authors. Still another possibility would have been actually to reform conditions at the stockyards so that he could contemplate them with equanimity—but he would have had to be an important official in a packing company or in the government to initiate a change in conditions. What he did, therefore, was to *socialize his discontent*—pass it on to others—on the very good theory that if enough people felt angry or disgusted with the situation, they could collectively change the stockyards in such a way that one could adjust oneself to them. Sinclair's novel, *The Jungle,* upset so many people that it led to a federal investigation of the meat industry and to the enactment of legislation controlling some of its practices.

As is now well known, when tensions are experienced constantly, and permitted to accumulate, they may lead to more or less serious psychological maladjustment. Adjustment, as modern psychology sees the process, is no static condition of unreflective bliss that comes from neither knowing nor caring what is wrong with the world. It is a dynamic, day-to-day, moment-to-moment process, and it involves changing the environment to suit one's personality as much as it involves adapting one's feelings to existing conditions. The greater resources one has for achieving and maintaining adjustment, the more successful will the process be. Literature appears to be one of the available resources.

Both the production and enjoyment of literature, then, being human symbolic devices employed in the day-to-day process of equipping ourselves for living, appear to be extensions of our adjustment mechanism beyond those provided for us by that part of our biological equipment which we have in common with lower animals. If a man were to spend years of his life trying to discover the chemical constituency of salt water without bothering to find out what has already been said on the subject in any elementary chemistry book, we should say that he was making very imperfect use of the resources which our symbolic systems have made available to us. Similarly, can it not be said that people, worrying themselves sick over their individual frustrations, constantly suffering from petty irritations and hypertensions, are making extremely imperfect use of the available human resources of adjustment when they fail to strengthen and quiet themselves through contact with literature and the other arts?

What all this boils down to, then, is that poetry (along with the other arts), whether it be good or bad and at whatever level of crudity or refinement, exists to fulfill a necessary biological function for a symbol-using class of life, that of *helping us to maintain psychological health and equilibrium.*

"Equipment for Living"

Psychiatrists recognize no distinct classes of the "sane" and the "unsane." Sanity is a matter of degree, and "sane" people are all capable of becoming more sane, or less, according to the experiences they encounter and the strength and flexibility of the internal equipment with which they meet them. Even as one's physical health has to be maintained by food and exercise, it would appear that one's psychological health too has to be maintained in the very course of living by "nourishment" at the level of affective symbols: literature that introduces us to new sources of delight; literature that makes us feel that we are not alone in our misery; literature that shows us our own problems in a new light; literature that suggests new possibilities to us and opens new areas of possible experience; literature that offers us a variety of "symbolic strategies" by means of which we can "encompass" our situations.

But there are certain kinds of literature, like certain kinds of processed food, which look very much like nourishment but contain none of the essential vitamin ingredients, so that great quantities can be consumed without affecting one's spiritual undernourishment.[5] (One could mean by "essential vitamin ingredients" in this context, "maps" of actual "territories" of human experience, directives that are both realistic and helpful, and so on.) Certain kinds of popular fiction claim to throw light on given problems in life—stories with such titles as "The Office Wife—Was She Playing Fair?"—but, like patent medicines, these offer apparent soothing to surface symptoms, and ignore underlying causes. Other kinds of fiction, like drugs and liquor, offer escape from pain, and again leave causes untouched, so that the more of them you take the more you need. Fantasy-living—which is one of the important characteristics of schizophrenia—can be aggravated by the consumption of too much of this narcotic literature. Still other kinds of fiction, movies, television programs, and the like, give a false, prettified picture of the world—a world that can be adjusted to *without effort*. But readers who adjust themselves to this unreal world naturally become progressively less adjusted to the world as it is. Such "adjustment to unreality" must lead to an enormous amount of disappointment and heartbreak among the young and unsophisticated, when they discover that the world is not as it was depicted in romantic tales.

On the other hand, it will not do to apply too crudely the principle of literature as an aid to sanity. Some might be tempted to say that, if literature is an instrument for maintaining sanity, the writings of many not-too-sane geniuses will have to be thrown out as unhealthy. It would seem, on the contrary, that the symbolic strategies devised by extremely tortured people like Dostoyevsky or Donne or Shelley for the encompassing of their situations are valu-

[5] Wendell Johnson of the University of Iowa refers to television-viewing, reading the Sunday papers, and similar diversions as "semantic thumb-sucking": you go through the motions of getting nourishment without getting any.

able in the extreme. They mixed themselves powerful medicines against their ills, and their medicines not only help us to encompass whatever similar tortures we may be suffering from, but may serve also as antitoxins for future sufferings.

Furthermore, when a work of literature is said to be "permanent," "lasting," or "great," does it not mean that the symbolic strategy by which the author encompassed his disturbance (achieved his equilibrium) works for other people troubled by other disturbances at other times and places? Is it possible, for example, to read Sinclair's strategic handling of the Chicago stockyards without awareness that it applies more or less adequately to other people's disturbances about factory conditions in Turin, or Manchester, or Kobe, or Montreal? And if it applies especially well to, say, Detroit, does not the Detroiter regard Sinclair's book as having lasting value? And if, under changing conditions, there are no longer social situations which arouse similar tensions, or if the strategies seem no longer adequate, do we not consider the author to be "dated," if not "dead"? [6] But if an author has adequately dealt with tensions that people in all times and under all conditions appear to experience, do we not call his writings "universal" and "undying"?

The relationship between literature and life is a subject about which little is known scientifically at the present time. Nevertheless, in an unorganized way, we all feel that we know something about that relationship, since we have all felt the effects of some kind of literature at some time in our lives. Most of us have felt, even if we have not been able to prove, that harmful consequences can arise from the consumption of such literary fare as is offered in many movies, in popular magazines, and in the so-called comic books.

[6] *The Jungle* is, in the writer's opinion, very much dated in most respects, although still powerful in some. Working people in the United States (and in many other parts of the world as well) are simply not treated as badly as they are in this novel, partly because of unionization, of course, and also partly because of advances in technology and a more highly developed public conscience. But ever since its publication in 1906, it has been widely read by working classes all over the world: few American books have been translated into so many languages.

The symbolic strategies of works of great literary art, unlike those of *The Jungle,* are usually too complex and subtle for such a rough analysis as has been attempted here. *The Jungle* has been chosen for discussion because books like this, which are far from being great masterpieces and yet give a great deal of profoundly felt insight into segments of human experience, are especially helpful in the understanding of the theories of literature proposed in this chapter. The strategies, being not too subtle, can be clearly seen and described.

But the imperfection of our scientific knowledge is revealed by the fact that, when there is widespread argument as to whether or not comic books should be banned, equally imposing authorities on both sides are able to "prove" their cases; some say that comic books stimulate children's imaginations in unhealthy ways and lead them into crime, while others say that the crimes are committed by psychopathic children who would have committed them anyway, and that comic books, by offering to normal children a symbolic release of their aggressive tendencies, actually help to calm them down. It appears to be anybody's guess.

Because no one yet has answers to such questions, it would seem to be extremely desirable for students of literature and of psychology to work together. If they do, perhaps they will some day be able to state, in the interests of everyday sanity, what kinds of literature contribute to maturity and what kinds help to keep us permanently infantile and immature in our evaluations.

Art as Order

At least one other important element enters into our pleasure both in the writing and reading of literature—but about this there is still less available scientific knowledge. It pertains to what are called the artistic or esthetic values of a work of the imagination.

In Chapter 8, we spoke of the relationships, for example in a novel, of the incidents and characters to each other—that is, the meaningful arrangement of experiences that makes a novel different from a jumbled narrative. Before we speak of a narrative as a "novel" and therefore as a "work of art," we must be satisfied that, regardless of whether or not we could "live the story" through imaginative identification with the characters, the incidents are arranged in some kind of *order*. Even when we don't happen to like the story, if we find a complex, but discernible and interesting, order to the incidents in a novel, we are able to say, "It certainly is beautifully put together." Indeed, sometimes the internal order and neat relationships of the parts to each other in a novel may be so impressive that we enjoy it in spite of a lack of sympathy with the kinds of incidents or people portrayed. Why is order interesting almost of itself?

The writer would suggest that if an answer is found to this question, it will have to be found in terms of human symbolic processes and the fact that symbols of symbols, symbols of symbols of symbols, and so on, can be manufactured indefinitely by the human nervous system. This fact, already explained in Chapter 2 (and to be explained further in Chapter 10), can be given a special application that may enable us to understand the functions of literature.

Animals, as we have remarked, live in the extensional world—they have no symbolic world to speak of. There would seem to be no more "order" in an animal's existence than the order of physical events as they impinge on its life. Man, however, both *lives* (at the extensional level) and *talks about his life to himself* (at the symbolic level, either with words or, in the case of painters and musicians and dancers, with nonverbal symbols). A human being is not satisfied simply to know his way around extensionally; he can hardly help talking to himself about what he has seen and felt and done.

The data of experience, when talked about, are full of contradictions. Mrs. Robinson loves her children, but ruins them through misdirected love; the illiterate peasants of a Chinese village show greater social and personal wisdom than the educated people of great cities; people say crime doesn't pay, but in some cases it pays extremely well; a young man who is by temperament a scholar and a poet feels compelled to commit a political murder; a faithful wife of twenty years deserts her husband for no apparent reason; a ne'er-do-well acts courageously in a dangerous situation—these and a thousand other contradictions confront us in the course of our lives. Unordered, and bearing no relationship to each other, our statements about experience are not only disconnected, but they are difficult to use.

Insofar as we are aware of these contradictions, this disorder among our statements is itself a source of tension. Such contradictions provide us with no guide to action; hence they leave us with the tensions of indecision and bewilderment. These tensions are not resolved until we have, *by talking to ourselves about our talking* (symbolizing our symbols), "fitted things together," so that, as we say, things don't seem to be "meaningless" any more. Religions, philosophies, science, and art are equally, and through different methods, ways of resolving the tensions produced by the contradictory data of experience by talking about our talking, then talking about our talking about our talking, and so on, until some kind of *order* has been established among the data.

Talking about things, talking about talking, talking about talking about talking, etc., represent what we shall call talking at different *levels of abstraction.* The imposition of order upon our pictures of the world is, it appears, what we mean by "understanding." When we say that a scientist "understands" something, does it not mean that he has ordered his observations at the objective, descriptive, and higher inferential levels of abstraction into a workable system in which all levels are related to other levels in terms of a few powerful generalizations? When a great religious leader or philosopher is said to "understand" life, does it not mean that he has also ordered his observations into a set of attitudes, often crystallized into exceedingly general and powerful directives? And when a novelist is said to "understand" the life of any segment of humanity (or humanity as a whole), has he not also ordered his observations at many different levels of abstraction—the particular and concrete, the general, and the more general? (Fuller explanation of "levels of abstraction" will be found in Chapter 10, to follow.) However, the novelist presents that order not in a scientific, ethical, or philosophical system of highly abstract generalizations, but in a set of symbolic experiences at the descriptive level of affective reports, involving the reader's feelings through the mechanism of identification. And these symbolic experiences, in the work of any competent novelist, are woven together to frame a consistent set of attitudes, whether of scorn, or compassion, or admiration of courage, or sympathy with the downtrodden, or a sense of futility, depending on his outlook.

Some of the ways of organizing a set of experiences for literary purposes are purely mechanical and external: these are the "rules" governing the proper construction of the novel, the play, the short story, the sonnet, and so on. But more important are the ways of organization suggested by the materials of the literary work—the experiences which the writer wishes to organize. When the materials of a story do not fit into the conventional pattern of a novel, the novelist may create a new organization altogether, more suited to the presentation of his experiences than the conventional patterns. In such a case, critics speak of the materials as "creating their own form." In such a case, too, the order may seem like disorder at first—one thinks of Laurence Sterne's *Tristram Shandy* and James Joyce's *Ulysses*—because the principles of organization, being new, have to be discovered in the course of reading. The reason a poem, novel, or play assumes the shape it ultimately does is the concern of the technical literary critic. He studies the interplay of external and internal demands which finally shape the materials into a "work of art."

To symbolize one's experiences adequately and then to order them into a coherent whole constitute an integrative act. The great novelist or dramatist or poet is one who has successfully integrated and given coherence to vast areas of human experience. Literary greatness requires, therefore, great extensional awareness of the range of human experience as well as great powers of ordering that experience meaningfully. This is why the discipline of the creative artist is endless: there is always more to learn, both about human experience (which is the material to be ordered) and about the techniques of his craft (which are the means of ordering).

From the point of view of the reader, the fact that language is social is again of central importance. The ordering of experiences and attitudes accomplished linguistically by the writer produces, in the reader, some ordering of his own experiences and attitudes. The reader becomes, as a result of this ordering, somewhat better organized himself. That's what art is for.

APPLICATIONS

I. Compare (or contrast) the ideas presented in the following excerpts with the point of view expressed in this chapter. This material may provide the basis for your own paper on the subject, "What Is Art For?" Shorter papers, which carefully distinguish between one of the excerpts and the author's point of view, are also appropriate.

1. The end of writing is to instruct; the end of poetry is to instruct by pleasing. —SAMUEL JOHNSON, *Preface to Shakespeare*

2. Disease . . . First of all it is a question of who is sick, who is insane, who is epileptic or paralytic: an average dolt, whose disease, of course, lacks all intellectual and cultural aspects—or a Nietzsche, a Dostoyevsky. In their cases, the disease bears fruits that are more important and more beneficial to life and to its development than any medically approved normality. The truth is that life has never been able to do without the morbid, and probably no adage is more insane than the one which says that "only disease can come from the diseased." Life is not prudish, and it is probably safe to say that life prefers creative, genius-bestowing disease a thousand times over to prosaic health; prefers disease, surmounting obstacles proudly on horseback, boldly leaping from peak to peak, to lounging, pedestrian healthfulness. Life is not finical and never thinks of making a moral distinction between health and infirmity. It seizes the bold

product of disease, consumes and digests it, and as soon as it is assimilated, it is health. An entire horde, a generation of open-minded, healthy lads pounces upon the work of diseased genius, genialized by disease, admires and praises it, raises it to the skies, perpetuates it, transmutes it, and bequeaths it to civilization, which does not live on the home-baked bread of health alone. They all swear by the name of the great invalid, thanks to whose madness they no longer need to be mad. Their healthfulness feeds upon his madness, and in them he will become healthy.

—THOMAS MANN, "Dostoyevsky—*in Moderation*"

3. A great work of art is like a dream; for all its apparent obviousness it does not explain itself and is never unequivocal. A dream never says: "You ought," or: "This is the truth." It presents an image in much the same way as nature allows a plant to grow, and we must draw our own conclusions. If a person has a nightmare, it means either that he is too much given to fear, or else that he is too exempt from it; and if he dreams of the old wise man it may mean that he is too pedagogical, as also that he stands in need of a teacher. In a subtle way both meanings come to the same thing, as we perceive when we are able to let the work of art act upon us as it acted upon the artist. To grasp its meaning, we must allow it to shape us as it once shaped him. Then we understand the nature of his experience. We see that he has drawn upon the healing and redeeming forces of the collective psyche that underlies consciousness with its isolation and its painful errors; that he has penetrated to that matrix of life in which all men are embedded, which imparts a common rhythm to all human existence, and allows the individual to communicate his feeling and his striving to mankind as a whole.

The secret of artistic creation and of the effectiveness of art is to be found in a return to the state of *participation mystique*—to that level of experience at which it is man who lives, and not the individual, and at which the weal or woe of the single human being does not count, but only human existence. This is why every great work of art is objective and impersonal, but none the less profoundly moves us each and all. And this is also why the personal life of the poet cannot be held essential to his art—but at most a help or a hindrance to his creative task. He may go the way of a Philistine, a good citizen, a neurotic, a fool or a criminal. His personal career may be inevitable and interesting, but it does not explain the poet.

—CARL JUNG, *Modern Man in Search of a Soul*

4. A classic is a work which gives pleasure to the minority which is intensely and permanently interested in literature. It lives on because the minority, eager to renew the sensation of pleasure, is eternally curious and is therefore engaged in an eternal process of

rediscovery. A classic does not survive for any ethical reason. It does not survive because it conforms to certain canons, or because neglect would kill it. It survives because it is a source of pleasure and because the passionate few can no more neglect it than a bee can neglect a flower. The passionate few do not read "the right things" because they are right. That is to put the cart before the horse. "The right things" are the right things solely because the passionate few *like* reading them. . . .

Nobody at all is quite in a position to choose with certainty among modern works. To sift the wheat from the chaff is a process that takes an exceedingly long time. Modern works have to pass before the bar of the taste of successive generations; whereas, with classics, which have been through the ordeal, almost the reverse is the case. *Your taste has to pass before the bar of the classics.* That is the point. If you differ with a classic, it is you who are wrong, and not the book. If you differ with a modern work, you may be wrong or you may be right, but no judge is authoritative to decide. Your taste is unformed. It needs guidance and it needs authoritative guidance. —ARNOLD BENNETT, *Literary Taste: How To Form It*

5. The view that the mental experience of the reader is the poem itself leads to the absurd conclusion that a poem is non-existent unless experienced and that it is re-created in every experience. There thus would not be one *Divine Comedy* but as many Divine Comedies as there are and were and will be readers. We end in complete skepticism and anarchy and arrive at the vicious maxim of *De gustibus non est disputandum.* If we should take this view seriously, it would be impossible to explain why one experience of a poem by one reader should be better than the experience of any other reader and why it is possible to correct the interpretation of another reader. It would mean the definite end of all teaching of literature which aims at enhancing the understanding and appreciation of a text. . . .

The psychology of the reader, however interesting in itself or useful for pedagogical purposes, will always remain outside the object of literary study—the concrete work of art—and is unable to deal with the question of the structure and value of the work of art.
    —RENE WELLEK and AUSTIN WARREN, *Theory of Literature*

6. The business of art is to reveal the relation between man and his circumambient universe, at the living moment. As mankind is always struggling in the toils of old relationships, art is always ahead of the "times," which themselves are always far in the rear of the living moment.

When van Gogh paints sunflowers, he reveals, or achieves, the vivid relation between himself, as man, and the sunflower, as sunflower, at that quick moment of time. His painting does not represent the sunflower itself. We shall never know what the sunflower is. And the camera will *visualize* the sunflower far more perfectly than van Gogh can.

The vision on the canvas is a third thing, utterly intangible and inexplicable, the offspring of the sunflower itself and van Gogh himself. The vision on the canvas is for ever incommensurable with the canvas, or the paint, or van Gogh as a human organism, or the sunflower as a botanical organism. You cannot weigh nor measure nor even describe the vision on the canvas. . . .

It is a revelation of the perfected relation, at a certain moment, between a man and a sunflower. . . . And this perfected relation between man and his circumambient universe is life itself, for mankind. . . . Man and the sunflower both pass away from the moment, in the process of forming a new relationship. The relation between all things changes from day to day, in a subtle stealth of change. Hence art, which reveals or attains to another perfect relationship, will be for ever new.

If we think about it, we find that our life *consists in* this achieving of a pure relationship between ourselves and the living universe about us. This is how I "save my soul" by accomplishing a pure relationship between me and another person, me and other people, me and a nation, me and a race of men, me and animals, me and the trees or flowers, me and the earth, me and the skies and sun and stars, me and the moon: an infinity of pure relations, big and little. . . . This, if we knew it, is our life and our eternity: the subtle, perfected relation between me and my whole circumambient universe. . . .

Now here we see the beauty and the great value of the novel. Philosophy, religion, science, they are all of them busy nailing things down, to get a stable equilibrium. Religion, with its nailed down One God . . . ; philosophy, with its fixed ideas; science with its 'laws': they, all of them, all the time, want to nail us on some tree or other.

But the novel, no. The novel is the highest example of subtle interrelatedness that man has discovered. . . .

—D. H. LAWRENCE, "Morality and the Novel," *Phoenix*

II. In the light of the last two paragraphs under "Equipment for Living," page 151, comment on the following, either by writing a short essay (200 words), or by reading the passages aloud to a small group of friends or a class as a starting point for discussion and the comparison of views:

NEW YORK, Mar. 29—It doesn't matter that the TV drama comes to a wholesome, moralistic end—that virtue triumphs. The child may see and recognize the moral. But the damage is done by the very fact that he is sitting, in a comfortable environment, watching criminals or simply bad guys at work.

This combination—of the comfortable environment and the cruel action—will, over a period of time, break down the conscience of the child. And a firm conscience is what parents are constantly trying to instill in a child. . . .

This is the opinion of British Professor H. J. Eysenck at the Institute of Psychiatry, University of London. He believes that parents, in punishing kiddies for being naughty and rewarding them for goodness, build up the conditioned responses known as conscience. If this theory is true, then violence seen on TV can decondition those consciences which parents have taken so much time to build up. . . .

Thus a child who is warm and relaxed with a cup of cocoa in hand, perhaps, looks upon a fist-fight or a murder. He finds it not unpleasant. His conscience becomes gradually desensitized. . . . In fact, since the television screen reaches youth en masse . . . a whole nation of youth could be rid of that most necessary, highly uncomfortable thing called conscience.   —Associated Press

Garishly presented in clashing colors and cheaply printed in forty-eight pages of paper-bound pulp with even more garish covers, what recourse there is in comic-books to the printed word is, totally, language violence: full capitals throughout, bold-face accents liberally besprinkled, and exclamation points galore; with illiterate little cartouches, where no conversation is thought necessary, saying Pow, Zow, and Whammo! to indicate the administration of violence, while the victims respond with Awrrk, Aagh, Aieee, Ooof, and Uggh.

The price being only ten cents apiece and the distribution national, every American child can and does read from ten to a dozen of these pamphlets monthly, an unknown number of times, and then trades them off for others. If there is only one violent picture per page—and there are usually more—this represents a minimum supply, to every child old enough to look at pictures, of three hundred scenes of beating, shooting, strangling, torture, and blood per month, or ten a day if he reads each comic-book only once. . . . With rare exceptions, every child in America . . . six years old . . . has by now absorbed an absolute minimum of eighteen thousand pictorial beatings, shootings, stranglings, blood-puddles, and torturings-to-death, from comic (ha-ha) books alone, identifying himself— unless he is a complete masochist—with the heroic beater, shooter, strangler, bloodletter, and/or torturer in each case. With repetition like that, you can teach a child anything. . . . At the moment it is being used to teach him—and in no quiet professorial tone, but rather in flaming color and superheated dialogue—that violence is heroic, and murder a red-hot thrill.

—G. LEGMAN, *Love and Death*

III. In light of what has been said in this chapter, study the following poems to see:

a. What tensions of his own the author seems to be trying to resolve (biographical information about the poet may be used here);

b. what symbolic strategies he employs;

c. whether these strategies might be applicable to other people and other situations (cite examples);

d. to what extent the author has succeeded in ordering his experiences into a coherent, meaningful whole;

e. what affective devices the poet has used to bring about the creation of a coherent, meaningful whole (see Chapter 8).

1.   *Death, Be Not Proud*

Death, be not proud, though some have callèd thee
Mighty and dreadful, for thou art not so,
For those whom thou think'st thou dost overthrow
Die not, poor Death, nor yet canst thou kill me.
From rest and sleep, which but thy picture be,
Much pleasure, then from thee much more must flow;
And soonest our best men with thee do go—
Rest of their bones and souls' delivery!
Thou'rt slave to fate, chance, kings and desperate men,
And dost with poison, war, and sickness dwell,
And poppy or charms can make us sleep as well,
And better than thy stroke; why swell'st thou then?
One short sleep past, we wake eternally,
And death shall be no more: Death, thou shalt die!

—JOHN DONNE

2.   *The Snare*

I hear a sudden cry of pain!
There is a rabbit in a snare;
Now I hear the cry again,
But I cannot tell from where.

But I cannot tell from where
He is calling out for aid!
Crying on the frightened air,
Making everything afraid!

Making everything afraid!
Wrinkling up his little face!
As he cries again for aid;
—And I cannot find the place!

And I cannot find the place
Where his paw is in the snare!
Little One! Oh, Little One!
I am searching everywhere!
—JAMES STEPHENS

3. *Ozymandias*

I met a traveler from an antique land
Who said: Two vast and trunkless legs of stone
Stand in the desert. Near them, on the sand,
Half sunk, a shattered visage lies, whose frown,
And wrinkled lip, and sneer of cold command,
Tell that its sculptor well those passions read
Which yet survive, (stamped on these lifeless things),
The hand that mocked them and the heart that fed;
And on the pedestal these words appear:
"My name is Ozymandias, king of kings;
Look on my works, ye Mighty, and despair!"
Nothing beside remains. Round the decay
Of that colossal wreck, boundless and bare,
The lone and level sands stretch far away.
—PERCY BYSSHE SHELLEY

4. *Milton*

And did those feet in ancient time
     Walk upon England's mountains green?
And was the holy Lamb of God
     On England's pleasant pastures seen?

And did the Countenance Divine
     Shine forth upon our clouded hills?
And was Jerusalem builded here
     Among these dark Satanic Mills?

Bring me my bow of burning gold!
     Bring me my arrows of desire!
Bring me my spear! O clouds, unfold!
     Bring me my chariot of fire!

I will not cease from mental fight,
     Nor shall my sword sleep in my hand,

Till we have built Jerusalem
In England's green and pleasant land.

—WILLIAM BLAKE

5. *Say Not the Struggle Nought Availeth*

Say not the struggle nought availeth,
    The labor and the wounds are vain,
The enemy faints not, nor faileth,
    And as things have been they remain.

If hopes were dupes, fears may be liars;
    It may be, in yon smoke concealed,
Your comrades chase e'en now the fliers,
    And, but for you, possess the field.

For while the tired waves, vainly breaking,
    Seem here no painful inch to gain,
Far back, through creeks and inlets making,
    Comes silent, flooding in, the main,

And not by eastern windows only,
    When daylight comes, comes in the light,
In front, the sun climbs slow, how slowly,
    But westward, look, the land is bright.

—ARTHUR HUGH CLOUGH

6. *Composed Upon Westminster Bridge*

Earth has not anything to show more fair:
Dull would he be of soul who could pass by
A sight so touching in its majesty:
This City now doth, like a garment, wear
The beauty of the morning; silent, bare,
Ships, towers, domes, theatres, and temples lie
Open unto the fields, and to the sky;
All bright and glittering in the smokeless air.
Never did sun so beautifully steep
In his first splendor, valley, rock, or hill;
Ne'er saw I, never felt, a calm so deep!
The river glideth at his own sweet will:
Dear God! the very houses seem asleep;
And all that mighty heart is lying still!

—WILLIAM WORDSWORTH

7. *When I Consider How My Light Is Spent*

When I consider how my light is spent
Ere half my days in this dark world and wide,

And that one talent which is death to hide
Lodged with me useless, though my soul more bent
To serve therewith my Maker, and present
My true account, lest He returning chide,
"Doth God exact day-labor, light denied?"
I fondly ask. But Patience, to prevent
That murmur, soon replies, "God doth not need
Either man's work or his own gifts. Who best
Bear His mild yoke, they serve Him best. His state
Is kingly: thousands at His bidding speed,
And post o'er land and ocean without rest;
They also serve who only stand and wait."

—JOHN MILTON

8. *Salutation*

O generation of the thoroughly smug
    and thoroughly uncomfortable,
I have seen fishermen picnicking in the sun,
I have seen them with untidy families,
I have seen their smiles full of teeth
    and heard ungainly laughter.
And I am happier than you are,
And they were happier than I am;
And the fish swim in the lake
    and do not even own clothing.

—EZRA POUND

9. *Naming of Parts*

Today we have naming of parts. Yesterday,
We had daily cleaning. And tomorrow morning
We shall have what to do after firing. But today,
Today we have naming of parts. Japonica
Glistens like coral in all of the neighboring gardens,
    And today we have naming of parts.

This is the lower sling swivel. And this
Is the upper sling swivel, whose use you will see
When you are given your slings. And this is the piling swivel,
Which in your case you have not got. The branches
Hold in the gardens their silent, eloquent gestures,
    Which in our case we have not got.

This is the safety-catch, which is always released
With an easy flick of the thumb. And please do not let me
See anyone using his finger. You can do it quite easy

If you have any strength in your thumb. The blossoms
Are fragile and motionless, never letting anyone see
   Any of them using their finger.

And this you can see is the bolt. The purpose of this
Is to open the breech, as you see. We can slide it
Rapidly backwards and forwards; we call this
Easing the spring. And rapidly backwards and forwards
The early bees are assaulting and fumbling the flowers:
   They call it easing the Spring.

They call it easing the Spring: it is perfectly easy
If you have any strength in your thumb: like the bolt,
And the breech, and the cocking-piece, and the point of balance,
Which in our case we have not got; and the almond-blossom
Silent in all of the gardens and the bees going backwards and for-
   wards,
   For today we have naming of parts.

                                  —HENRY REED

IV. Read, ponder, and digest:

1.   "Terence, this is stupid stuff:
                You eat your victuals fast enough;
                There can't be much amiss, 'tis clear,
                To see the rate you drink your beer.
                But oh, good Lord, the verse you make,
                It gives a chap the belly-ache.
                The cow, the old cow, she is dead;
                It sleeps well, the horned head:
                We poor lads, 'tis our turn now
                To hear such tunes as killed the cow.
                Pretty friendship 'tis to rhyme
                Your friends to death before their time
                Moping melancholy mad:
                Come, pipe a tune to dance to, lad."

                Why, if 'tis dancing you would be,
                There's brisker pipes than poetry.
                Say, for what were hop-yards meant,
                Or why was Burton built on Trent?
                Oh many a peer of England brews
                Livelier liquor than the Muse,
                And malt does more than Milton can
                To justify God's ways to man.

Ale, man, ale's the stuff to drink
For fellows whom it hurts to think:
Look into the pewter pot
To see the world as the world's not.
And faith, 'tis pleasant till 'tis past:
The mischief is that 'twill not last.
Oh I have been to Ludlow fair
And left my necktie God knows where,
And carried half way home, or near,
Pints and quarts of Ludlow beer:
Then the world seemed none so bad,
And I myself a sterling lad;
And down in lovely muck I've lain,
Happy till I woke again.
Then I saw the morning sky:
Heigho, the tale was all a lie;
The world, it was the old world yet,
I was I, my things were wet,
And nothing now remained to do
But begin the game anew.

Therefore, since the world has still
Much good, but much less good than ill,
And while the sun and moon endure
Luck's a chance, but trouble's sure,
I'd face it as a wise man would,
And train for ill and not for good.
'Tis true, the stuff I bring for sale
Is not so brisk a brew as ale:
Out of a stem that scored the hand
I wrung it in a weary land.
But take it: if the smack is sour,
The better for the embittered hour;
It should do good to heart and head
When your soul is in my soul's stead;
And I will friend you, if I may
In the dark and cloudy day.

There was a king reigned in the East:
There, when kings will sit to feast,
They get their fill before they think
With poisoned meat and poisoned drink.
He gathered all that springs to birth
From the many-venomed earth;
First a little, thence to more,
He sampled all her killing store;

And easy, smiling, seasoned sound,
Sate the king when healths went round.
They put arsenic in his meat
And stared aghast to watch him eat;
They poured strychnine in his cup
And shook to see him drink it up:
They shook, they stared as white's their shirt:
Them it was their poison hurt.
—I tell the tale that I heard told.
Mithridates, he died old.

—A. E. HOUSMAN

2. The worst *does* sometimes happen. As men we have to count on that possibility, have to arm ourselves against it, and above all we have to realize that since absurdities necessarily occur, and nowadays manifest themselves with more and more forcefulness, we can prevent ourselves from being destroyed by them and can make ourselves relatively comfortable upon this earth only if we humbly include these absurdities in our thinking, reckon with the inevitable fractures and distortions of human reason when it attempts honestly to deal with reality.   —FRIEDRICH DUERRENMATT, *The Pledge*

BOOK TWO Language and Thought

BOOK TWO

Language and Thought

He [the student of politics] must also be on his guard against the old words, for the words persist when the reality that lay behind them has changed. It is inherent in our intellectual activity that we seek to imprison reality in our description of it. Soon, long before we realize it, it is we who become the prisoners of the description. From that point on, our ideas degenerate into a kind of folklore which we pass to each other, fondly thinking we are still talking of the reality around us.

Thus we talk of free enterprise, of capitalist society, of the rights of free association, of parliamentary government, as though all of these words stand for the same things they formerly did. Social institutions are what they do, not necessarily what we say they do. It is the verb that matters, not the noun.

If this is not understood, we become symbol worshipers. The categories we once evolved and which were the tools we used in our intercourse with reality become hopelessly blunted. In these circumstances the social and political realities we are supposed to be grappling with change and reshape themselves independently of the collective impact of our ideas. We become the creature and no longer the partner of social realities. As we fumble with outworn categories our political vitality is sucked away and we stumble from one situation to another, without chart, without compass, and with the steering-wheel lashed to a course we are no longer following.

This is the real point of danger for a political party and for the leaders and thinkers who inspire it. For if they are out of touch with reality, the masses are not. —ANEURIN BEVAN, *In Place of Fear*

Foreword

The Story of A-town and B-ville:
Second Semantic Parable

Once upon a time, said the Professor, there were two small communities, spiritually as well as geographically situated at a considerable distance from each other. They had, however, these problems in common: both were hard hit by a recession, so that in each of the towns there were about one hundred heads of families unemployed.

The city fathers of A-town, the first community, were substantial and sound-thinking businessmen. The unemployed tried hard, as unemployed people usually do, to find jobs; but the situation did not improve. The city fathers had been brought up to believe that there is always enough work for everyone, if you only look for it hard enough. Comforting themselves with this doctrine, the city fathers could have shrugged their shoulders and turned their backs on the problem, except for the fact that they were genuinely kindhearted men. They could not bear to see the unemployed men and their wives and children starving. In order to prevent hardship, they felt that they had to provide these people with some means of sustenance. Their principles told them, nevertheless, that if people were given something for nothing, it would demoralize their character. Naturally this made the city fathers even more unhappy, because they were faced with the horrible choice of (1) letting the unemployed starve, or (2) destroying their moral character.

The solution they finally hit upon, after much debate and soul-searching, was this. They decided to give the unemployed families "relief payments" of two hundred dollars a month. (They considered using the English term "dole," but with their characteristic American penchant for euphemism, they decided on the less offensive term.) To make sure that the unemployed would not take their unearned payments too much for granted, however, they decided that the "relief" was to be accompanied by a moral lesson; to wit: the obtaining of the assistance would be made so difficult, humiliating, and disagreeable that there would be no temptation for anyone to

■ 171

go through the process unless it was absolutely necessary; the moral disapproval of the community would be turned upon the recipients of the money at all times in such a way that they would try hard to get "off relief" and "regain their self-respect." Some even proposed that people on relief be denied the vote, so that the moral lesson would be more deeply impressed upon them. Others suggested that their names be published at regular intervals in the newspapers. The city fathers had enough faith in the goodness of human nature to expect that the recipients would be grateful, since they were getting something for nothing, something which they hadn't worked for.

When the plan was put into operation, however, the recipients of the relief checks proved to be an ungrateful, ugly bunch. They seemed to resent the cross-examinations and inspections at the hands of the "relief investigators," who, they said, took advantage of a man's misery to snoop into every detail of his private life. In spite of uplifting editorials in A-town *Tribune* telling them how grateful they ought to be, the recipients of the relief refused to learn any moral lessons, declaring that they were "just as good as anybody else." When, for example, they permitted themselves the rare luxury of a movie or an evening of bingo, their neighbors looked at them sourly as if to say, "I work hard and pay my taxes just in order to support loafers like you in idleness and pleasure." This attitude, which was fairly characteristic of those members of the community who still had jobs, further embittered the relief recipients, so that they showed even less gratitude as time went on and were constantly on the lookout for insults, real or imaginary, from people who might think that they weren't as good as anybody else. A number of them took to moping all day long; one or two even committed suicide. Others, feeling that they had failed to provide, found it hard to look their wives and children in the face. Children whose parents were "on relief" felt inferior to classmates whose parents were not "public charges." Some of these children developed inferiority complexes which affected not only their grades at school, but their careers after graduation. Finally, several relief recipients felt they could stand their loss of self-respect no longer and decided, after many efforts to gain honest jobs, that they would earn money by their own efforts even if they had to rob. They did so and were caught and sent to the state penitentiary.

The depression, therefore, hit A-town very hard. The relief policy had averted starvation, no doubt, but suicide, personal quarrels, unhappy homes, the weakening of social organizations, the maladjustment of children, and, finally, crime, had resulted. The town was divided in two, the "haves" and the "have-nots," so that there was class hatred. People shook their heads sadly and declared that it all went to prove over again what they had known from the beginning, that giving people something for nothing inevitably demoralizes their character. The citizens of A-town gloomily waited for prosperity to return, with less and less hope as time went on.

The story of the other community, B-ville, was entirely different. B-ville was a relatively isolated town, too far out of the way to be reached by Rotary Club speakers and other dispensers of conventional wisdom. One of the aldermen, however, who was something of an economist, explained to his fellow aldermen that unemployment, like sickness, accident, fire, tornado, or death, hits unexpectedly in modern society, irrespective of the victim's merits or deserts. He went on to say that B-ville's homes, parks, streets, industries, and everything else B-ville was proud of, had been built in part by the work of these same people who were now unemployed. He then proposed to apply a principle of insurance: If the work these unemployed people had previously done for the community could be regarded as a form of "premium" paid to the community against a time of misfortune, payments now made to them to prevent their starvation could be regarded as "insurance claims." He therefore proposed that all men of good repute who had worked in the community in some line of useful endeavor, whether as machinists, clerks, or bank managers, be regarded as "citizen policyholders," having "claims" against the city in the case of unemployment for two hundred dollars a month until such time as they might again be employed. Naturally, he had to talk very slowly and patiently, since the idea was entirely new to his fellow aldermen. But he described his plan as a "straight business proposition," and finally they were persuaded. They worked out in detail, to everyone's satisfaction, the conditions under which citizens should be regarded as policyholders in the city's social insurance plan, and decided to give checks for two hundred dollars a month to the heads of each of B-ville's indigent families.

B-ville's "claim adjusters," whose duty it was to investigate the claims of the citizen "policyholders," had a much better time than A-town's "relief investigators." While the latter had been resentfully regarded as snoopers, the former, having no moral lesson to teach but simply a business transaction to carry out, treated their clients with businesslike courtesy and got the same amount of information as the relief investigators had, with considerably less difficulty. There were no hard feelings. It further happened, fortunately, that news of B-ville's plans reached a liberal newspaper editor in the big city at the other end of the state. This writer described the plan in a leading feature story headed "B-VILLE LOOKS AHEAD. Adventure in Social Pioneering Launched by Upper Valley Community." As a result of this publicity, inquiries about the plan began to come to the city hall even before the first checks were mailed out. This led, naturally, to a considerable feeling of pride on the part of the aldermen, who, being boosters, felt that this was a wonderful opportunity to put B-ville on the map.

Accordingly, the aldermen decided that instead of simply mailing out the checks as they had originally intended, they would publicly present the first checks at a monster civic ceremony. They invited the governor of the state, who was glad to come to bolster his none-too-enthusiastic support in that locality, the president of the state university, the senator from their district, and other functionaries. They decorated the National Guard armory with flags and got out the American Legion Fife and Drum Corps, the Boy Scouts, and other civic organizations. At the big celebration, each family to receive a "social insurance check" was marched up to the platform to receive it, and the governor and the mayor shook hands with each of them as they came trooping up in their best clothes. Fine speeches were made; there was much cheering and shouting; pictures of the event showing the recipients of the checks shaking hands with the mayor, and the governor patting the heads of the children, were published not only in the local papers but also in several metropolitan picture sections.

Every recipient of these insurance checks had a feeling, therefore, that he had been personally honored, that he lived in a wonderful little town, and that he could face his unemployment with greater courage and assurance, since his community was back of him. The men and women found themselves being kidded in a friendly way by their acquaintances for having been "up there with the big shots," shaking hands with the governor, and so on. The children at school found themselves envied for having had their pictures in the papers. All in all, B-ville's unemployed did not commit suicide, were not haunted by a sense of failure, did not turn to crime, did not manifest personal maladjustments, did not develop class hatred, as the result of their two hundred dollars a month. . . .

* * *

At the conclusion of the Professor's story, the discussion began:

"That just goes to show," said the Advertising Man, who was known among his friends as a realistic thinker, "what good promotional work can do. B-ville's city council had real advertising sense, and that civic ceremony was a masterpiece . . . made everyone happy . . . put over the scheme in a big way. Reminds me of the way we do things in our business: as soon as we called horse-mackerel tuna-fish, we developed a big market for it. I suppose if you called relief 'insurance,' you could actually get people to like it, couldn't you?"

"What do you mean, 'calling' it insurance?" asked the Social Worker. "B-ville's scheme wasn't relief at all. It *was* insurance."

"Good grief, man! Do you realize what you're saying?" cried the Advertising Man in surprise. "Are you implying that those people had any *right* to that money? All I said was that it's a good idea to *disguise* relief as insurance if it's going to make people any happier. But it's still relief, no matter what you *call* it. It's all right to kid the public along to reduce discontent, but we don't need to kid ourselves as well!"

"But they *do* have a right to that money! They're not getting something for nothing. It's insurance. They did something for the community, and that's their prem—"

"Say, are you crazy?"

"Who's crazy?"

"You're crazy. Relief is relief, isn't it? If you'd only call things by their right names. . . ."

"But, confound it, insurance is insurance, isn't it?"

P.S. Those who have concluded that the point of the story is that the Social Worker and the Advertising Man were "only arguing about different names for the same thing," are asked to reread the story and explain what they mean by (1) "only" and (2) "the same thing."

10　How We Know
What We Know

*The crucial point to be considered in a study of
language behavior is the relationship between language and reality, between words and not-words.
Except as we understand this relationship, we run
the grave risk of straining the delicate connection
between words and facts, of permitting our words
to go wild, and so of creating for ourselves fabrications of fantasy and delusion.*—WENDELL JOHNSON

Bessie, the Cow

The universe is in a perpetual state of flux. The stars are growing,
cooling, exploding. The earth itself is not unchanging; mountains
are being worn away, rivers are altering their channels, valleys are
deepening. All life is also a process of change, through birth, growth,
decay, and death. Even what we used to call "inert matter"—chairs
and tables and stones—is not inert, as we now know, for, at the
submicroscopic level, it is a whirl of electrons. If a table looks today
very much as it did yesterday or as it did a hundred years ago, it is
not because it has not changed, but because the changes have been
too minute for our coarse perceptions. To modern science there is
no "solid matter." If matter looks "solid" to us, it does so only because its motion is too rapid or too minute to be felt. It is "solid"
only in the sense that a rapidly rotating color chart is "white" or a
rapidly spinning top is "standing still." Our senses are extremely
limited, so that we constantly have to use instruments, such as micro-
scopes, telescopes, speedometers, stethoscopes, and seismographs, to
detect and record occurrences which our senses are not able to record directly. The way in which we happen to see and feel things
is the result of the peculiarities of our nervous systems. There are
"sights" we cannot see, and, as even children know today with their
high-frequency dog whistles, "sounds" that we cannot hear. It is

absurd, therefore, to imagine that we ever perceive anything "as it really is."

Inadequate as our senses are, with the help of instruments they tell us a great deal. The discovery of microörganisms with the use of the microscope has given us a measure of control over bacteria; we cannot see, hear, or feel electromagnetic waves, but we can create and transform them to useful purpose. Most of our conquest of the external world, in engineering, in chemistry, and in medicine, is due to our use of mechanical contrivances of one kind or another to increase the capacity of our nervous systems. In modern life, our unaided senses are not half enough to get us about in the world. We cannot even obey speed laws or compute our gas and electric bills without mechanical aids to perception.

To return, then, to the relations between words and what they stand for, let us say that there is before us "Bessie," a cow. Bessie is a living organism, constantly changing, constantly ingesting food and air, transforming it, getting rid of it again. Her blood is circulating, her nerves are sending messages. Viewed microscopically, she is a mass of variegated corpuscles, cells, and bacterial organisms; viewed from the point of view of modern physics, she is a perpetual dance of electrons. What she is in her entirety, we can never know; even if we could at any precise moment say what she was, at the next moment she would have changed enough so that our description would no longer be accurate. It is impossible to say completely what Bessie or anything else really *is*. Bessie is not a static "object," but a dynamic process.

The Bessie that we experience, however, is something else again. We experience only a small fraction of the total Bessie: the lights and shadows of her exterior, her motions, her general configuration, the noises she makes, and the sensations she presents to our sense of touch. *And because of our previous experience, we observe resemblances in her to certain other animals to which, in the past, we have applied the word "cow."*

The Process of Abstracting

The "object" of our experience, then, is not the "thing in itself," but *an interaction between our nervous systems (with all their imperfections) and something outside them.* Bessie is unique—there is nothing else in the universe exactly like her in all respects. But we automatically *abstract* or select from the process-Bessie those features of hers in which she resembles other animals of like shape, functions, and habits, and we *classify* her as "cow."

When we say, then, that "Bessie is a cow," we are only noting the process-Bessie's resemblances to other "cows" and *ignoring differences*. What is more, we are leaping a huge chasm: from the dynamic process-Bessie, a whirl of electro-chemico-neural eventfulness, to a relatively static "idea," "concept," or *word,* "cow." In this connection, the reader is referred to the diagram entitled "The Abstraction Ladder," which he will find on page 179.

As the diagram illustrates, the "object" we see is an abstraction of the lowest level; but it is still an abstraction, since it leaves out characteristics of the process that is the real Bessie. The *word* "Bessie" (cow_1) is the lowest *verbal* level of abstraction, leaving out further characteristics—the differences between Bessie yesterday and Bessie today, between Bessie today and Bessie tomorrow—and selecting only the similarities. The word "cow" selects only the similarities between Bessie (cow_1), Daisy (cow_2), Rosie (cow_3), and so on, and therefore leaves out still more about Bessie. The word "livestock" selects or abstracts only the features that Bessie has in common with pigs, chickens, goats, and sheep. The term "farm asset" abstracts only the features Bessie has in common with barns, fences, livestock, furniture, generating plants, and tractors, and is therefore on a very high level of abstraction.

Our concern here with the process of abstracting may seem strange since the study of language is all too often restricted to matters of pronunciation, spelling, vocabulary, grammar, and sentence structure. The methods by which composition and oratory are taught in old-fashioned school systems seem to be largely responsible for this widespread notion that the way to study words is to concentrate one's attention exclusively on words.

But as we know from everyday experience, learning language is not simply a matter of learning words; it is a matter of correctly relating our words to the things and happenings for which they stand. We learn the language of baseball by playing or watching the game *and studying what goes on*. It is not enough for a child to learn to *say* "cookie" or "dog"; he must be able to use these words in their proper relationship to nonverbal cookies and non-

[1] The "Abstraction Ladder" is based on "The Structural Differential," a diagram originated by Alfred Korzybski to explain the process of abstracting. For a fuller explanation both of the diagram and of the process it illustrates, see his *Science and Sanity: An Introduction to Non-Aristotelian Systems and General Semantics* (1933), especially Chapter 25.

ABSTRACTION LADDER

Start reading from the bottom *UP*

8. "wealth"

8. The word "wealth" is at an extremely high level of abstraction, omitting *almost* all reference to the characteristics of Bessie.

7. "asset"

7. When Bessie is referred to as an "asset," still more of her characteristics are left out.

6. "farm assets"

6. When Bessie is included among "farm assets," reference is made only to what she has in common with all other salable items on the farm.

5. "livestock"

5. When Bessie is referred to as "livestock," only those characteristics she has in common with pigs, chickens, goats, etc., are referred to.

4. "cow"

4. The word "cow" stands for the characteristics we have abstracted as common to cow_1, cow_2, cow_3 . . . cow_n. Characteristics peculiar to specific cows are left out.

3. "Bessie"

3. The word "Bessie" (cow_1) is the *name* we give to the object of perception of level 2. The name *is not* the object; it merely *stands for* the object and omits reference to many of the characteristics of the object.

2.

2. The cow we perceive is not the word, but the object of experience, that which our nervous system abstracts (selects) from the totality that constitutes the process-cow. Many of the characteristics of the process-cow are left out.

1. The cow known to science ultimately consists of atoms, electrons, etc., according to present-day scientific inference. Characteristics (represented by circles) are infinite at this level and ever-changing. This is the *process level.*

verbal dogs before we can grant that he is learning the language. As Wendell Johnson has said, "The study of language begins properly with a study of what language is about."

Once we begin to concern ourselves with what language is about, we are at once thrown into a consideration of how the human nervous system works. When we call Beau (the Boston terrier), Pedro (the chihuahua), Snuffles (the English bulldog), and Shane (the Irish wolfhound)—creatures that differ greatly in size, shape, appearance, and behavior—by the same name, "dog," our nervous system has obviously gone to work *abstracting* what is common to them all, ignoring for the time being the differences among them.

Why We Must Abstract

This process of abstracting, of leaving characteristics out, is an indispensable convenience. To illustrate by still another example, suppose that we live in an isolated village of four families, each owning a house. A's house is referred to as *maga;* B's house is *biyo;* C's is *kata,* and D's is *pelel.* This is quite satisfactory for ordinary purposes of communication in the village, unless a discussion arises about building a new house—a spare one, let us say. We cannot refer to the projected house by any one of the four words we have for the existing houses, since each of these has too specific a meaning. We must find a *general* term, at a higher level of abstraction, that means "something that has certain characteristics in common with *maga, biyo, kata,* and *pelel,* and yet is not A's, B's, C's, or D's." Since this is much too complicated to say each time, an *abbreviation* must be invented. So we choose the noise, *house.* Out of such needs do our words come—they are a form of shorthand. The invention of a new abstraction is a great step forward, since it *makes discussion possible*—as, in this case, not only the discussion of a fifth house, but of all future houses we may build or see in our travels or dream about.

A producer of educational films once remarked to the writer that it is impossible to make a shot of "work." You can shoot Joe hoeing potatoes, Frank greasing a car, Bill spraying paint on a barn, but never just "work." "Work," too, is a shorthand term, standing, at a higher level of abstraction, for a characteristic that a multitude of activities, from dishwashing to navigation to running an advertising agency to governing a nation, have in common. The special meaning that "work" has in physics is also clearly derived from abstracting the common characteristics of many different kinds of work. ("A transference of energy from one body to another, resulting in the motion or displacement of the body acted upon, in the direction of the acting force and against resistance." Funk and Wagnalls' *Standard College Dictionary*.)

The indispensability of this process of abstracting can again be illustrated by what we do when we "calculate." The word "calculate" originates from the Latin word *calculus,* meaning "pebble," and derives its present meaning from such ancient practices as putting a pebble into a box for each sheep as it left the fold, so that one could tell, by checking the sheep returning at night against the pebbles, whether any had been lost. Primitive as this example of calculation is, it will serve to show why mathematics works. Each pebble is, in this example, an abstraction representing the "oneness" of each sheep—its numerical value. And because we are abstracting from extensional events on clearly understood and uniform principles, the numerical facts about the pebbles are also, barring unforeseen circumstances, numerical facts about the sheep. Our x's and y's and other mathematical symbols are abstractions made from numerical abstractions, and are therefore abstractions of still higher level. And they are useful in predicting occurrences and in getting work done because, since they are abstractions properly and uniformly made from starting points in the extensional world, the relations revealed by the symbols will be, again barring unforeseen circumstances, relations existing in the extensional world.

On Definitions

Definitions, contrary to popular opinion, tell us nothing about things. They only describe people's linguistic habits; that is, they tell us what noises people make under what conditions. Definitions should be understood as *statements about language.*

> *House.* This word, at the next higher level of abstraction, can be substituted for the more cumbersome expression, "Something that has characteristics in common with Bill's bungalow, Jordan's cottage, Mrs. Smith's guest home, Dr. Jones's mansion. . . ."
>
> *Red.* A feature that rubies, roses, ripe tomatoes, robins' breasts, uncooked beef, and lipsticks have in common is abstracted, and this word expresses that abstraction.
>
> *Kangaroo.* Where the biologist would say "herbivorous mammal, a marsupial of the family Macropodidae," ordinary people say "kangaroo."

Now it will be observed that while the definitions of "house" and "red" given here point *down* the abstraction ladder (see the charts) to *lower* levels of abstraction, the definition of "kangaroo" remains at the same level. That is to say, in the case of "house," we could if necessary go and *look* at Bill's bungalow, Jordan's cottage, Mrs. Smith's guest home, and Dr. Jones's mansion, and figure out for ourselves what features they seem to have in common; in this way, we might begin to understand under what conditions to use the word "house." But all we know about "kangaroo" from the above is that where some people say one thing, other people say another. That is, when we stay at the *same* level of abstraction in giving a definition, we do not give any information, unless, of course, the listener or reader is already sufficiently familiar with the defining words to work himself down the abstraction ladder. Dictionaries, in order to save space, have to assume in many cases such familiarity with the language on the part of the reader. But where the assumption is unwarranted, definitions at the same level of abstraction are worse than useless. Looking up "indifference" in some cheap pocket dictionaries, we find it defined as "apathy"; we look up "apathy" and find it defined as "indifference."

Even more useless, however, are the definitions that go *up* the abstraction ladder to higher levels of abstraction—the kind most of us tend to make automatically. Try the following experiment on an unsuspecting friend:

"What is meant by the word *red?*"
"It's a color."
"What's a *color?*"
"Why, it's a quality things have."
"What's a *quality?*"
"Say, what are you trying to do, anyway?"

You have pushed him into the clouds. He is lost.

If, on the other hand, we habitually go *down* the abstraction ladder to *lower* levels of abstraction when we are asked the meaning of a word, we are less likely to get lost in verbal mazes; we will tend to "have our feet on the ground" and know what we are talking about. This habit displays itself in an answer such as this:

"What is meant by the word *red?*"
"Well, the next time you see some cars stopped at an intersection, look at the traffic light facing them. Also, you might go to the fire department and see how their trucks are painted."

"Let's Define Our Terms"

An extremely widespread instance of an unrealistic (and ultimately superstitious) attitude toward definitions is found in the common academic prescription, "Let's define our terms so that we shall all know what we are talking about." As we have already seen in Chapter 4, the fact that a golfer, for example, cannot define golfing terms is no indication that he cannot understand and use them. Conversely, the fact that a man can define a large number of words is no guarantee that he knows what objects or operations they stand for in concrete situations. Having defined a word, people often believe that some kind of understanding has been established, ignoring the fact that the words in the definition often conceal even more serious confusions and ambiguities than the word defined. If we happen to discover this fact and try to remedy matters by defining the defining words, and then, finding ourselves still confused, we go on to define the words in the definitions of the defining words, and so on, we quickly find ourselves in a hopeless snarl. The only way to avoid this snarl is to keep definitions to a minimum and to point to extensional levels wherever necessary; in writing and speaking, this means giving specific examples of what we are talking about.

Operational Definitions

Another way to keep extensional levels in mind, when definitions are called for, is to use what physicist P. W. Bridgman called "operational definitions." As he says,

> To find the length of an object, we have to perform certain physical operations. The concept of length is therefore fixed when the operations by which length is measured are fixed. . . . In general, we mean by any concept nothing more than a set of operations; *the concept is synonymous with the corresponding set of operations.*[2]

The operational definition, then, as Anatol Rapoport explains, is one that tells you *"what to do* and *what to observe* in order to bring the thing defined or its effects within the range of one's experience." He gives the following simple example of how to define "weight": go to a railroad station or drugstore, look for a scale, stand on it, put in a penny, read the number at which the pointer comes to rest. *That* is your weight. But supposing different scales give different

[2] *The Logic of Modern Physics* (1927), p. 5.

readings? Then your weight can be said to be within the range of, say, 140 to 145 pounds. With more accurate scales you might get closer readings, such as 142 pounds plus-or-minus one. But there is no "property" called weight that exists apart from the operations measuring it. As Rapoport says, "If the only way we can be aware of the amount of weight is by means of the scale, then the very definition of weight has to be in terms of the scale."[3]

Such, then, is the scientific, or "operational," point of view towards definition—one that attempts rigidly to exclude non-extensional, non-sense statements. We can extend this idea from science to the problems of everyday life and thought. Just as there is no such thing as "length" apart from the operations by which length is measured, just as there is no "weight" apart from the operations by which weight is determined, there is likewise no "democracy" apart from the sum-total of democratic *practices,* such as universal franchise, freedom of speech, equality before the law, and so on. Similarly, there is no such thing as "brotherhood" apart from brotherly behavior, nor "charity" apart from charitable actions.

The operational point of view does much to keep our words meaningful. When people say things like, "Let's have no more of *progressive* methods in our schools," "Let's get back to *sound business principles* in running our county government," "Let's try to do the *Christian* thing," "Let's put father back as head of the family," we are entitled to ask, "what do you mean—*extensionally speaking?* To ask this question often—of ourselves as well as of others—is to do our bit towards reducing the vast amount of non-sense that is written, spoken, and shouted in this incredibly garrulous world.

The best examples in everyday life of operational definitions are to be found in cookbooks, which describe the *operations* by means of which the entity defined may be extensionally experienced. Thus: *"Steak Diane.* Slice tenderloin beef very thin and give it a few whacks with a meat mallet to flatten it even more; sprinkle with salt and pepper to taste. Have your pan very hot. . . ." (*The Sunset Cook Book.*) Writers and speakers would do well to study cookbooks occasionally to increase the clarity and verifiability of their utterances.

Chasing Oneself in Verbal Circles

In other words, the kind of "thinking" we must be extremely wary of is that which *never* leaves the higher verbal levels of abstraction,

[3] *Operational Philosophy* (1953), p. 25.

the kind that never points *down* the abstraction ladder to lower levels of abstraction and from there to the extensional world:

"What do you mean by *democracy?*"

"Democracy means the preservation of human rights."

"What do you mean by *rights?*"

"By rights I mean those privileges God grants to all of us—I mean man's inherent privileges."

"Such as?"

"Liberty, for example."

"What do you mean by *liberty?*"

"Religious and political freedom."

"And what does that mean?"

"Religious and political freedom is what we enjoy under a democracy."

Of course it is possible to talk meaningfully about democracy, as Jefferson and Lincoln have done, as Frederick Jackson Turner does in *The Frontier in American History* (1950), as Karl R. Popper does in *The Open Society and Its Enemies* (1950), as T. V. Smith and Eduard Lindeman do in *The Democratic Way of Life* (1939)—to name only the first examples that come to mind. The trouble with speakers who never leave the higher levels of abstraction is not only that their audiences fail to notice when they are saying something and when they are not; but also that they themselves lose their ability to discriminate. Never coming down to earth, they frequently chase themselves around in verbal circles, unaware that they are making meaningless noises.

This is by no means to say that we must never make extensionally meaningless noises. When we use directive language, when we talk about the future, when we utter ritual language or engage in social conversation, we often make utterances that have no extensional verifiability. It must not be overlooked that our highest ratiocinative and imaginative powers are derived from the fact that symbols *are* independent of things symbolized, so that we are free not only to go quickly from low to extremely high levels of abstraction (from "canned peas" to "groceries" to "commodities" to "national wealth") and to manipulate symbols even when the things they stand for cannot be so manipulated ("If all the freight cars in the country were hooked up to each other in one long line . . ."), but we are also free to manufacture symbols at will even if they stand only for abstractions made from other abstractions and not for anything in the extensional world. Mathematicians, for example, often play with symbols that have no extensional content, just to find out what can be done with them; this is called "pure mathematics." And pure mathematics is far from being a useless pastime, because mathematical systems that are elaborated with no extensional applications in mind often prove to be applicable later in useful and unforeseen ways. But when mathematicians deal with extensionally meaningless symbols, they usually know what they are doing. *We* likewise must know what we are doing.

Nevertheless, all of us (including mathematicians), when we speak the language of everyday life, often make meaningless noises without knowing that we are doing so. We have already seen what confusions this can lead to. The fundamental purpose of the abstraction ladder, as shown in both this chapter and the next, is to make us aware of the process of abstracting.

The Distrust of Abstractions

We may, using our abstraction ladder, allocate statements as well as words to differing levels of abstraction. "Mrs. Levin makes good potato pancakes" may be regarded as a statement at a fairly low level of abstraction, although, to be sure, it leaves out many elements, such as (1) the meaning of "goodness" in potato pancakes, and (2) the infrequent occasions when her pancakes fail to turn out well. "Mrs. Levin is a good cook," is a statement at a higher level of abstraction, covering Mrs. Levin's skill not only with potato pancakes, but also with roasts, pickles, noodles, strudels, and so on, nevertheless omitting *specific* mention of what she can accomplish. "Chicago women are good cooks," is a statement at a still higher level of abstraction; it can be made (if at all) only from observation of the cooking of a statistically significant number of Chicago women. "The culinary art has reached a high state in America," would be a still more highly abstract statement and, if made at all, would have to be based not only on observation of the Mrs. Levins of Chicago, New York, San Francisco, Denver, Albuquerque, and Chattanooga, but also on observation of the quality of meals served in hotels and restaurants, the quality of training in high school and college departments of home economics, the quality of writings on culinary art in American books and magazines, and many other relevant factors.

Unfortunately, though understandably, there is a tendency in our times to speak with contempt of "mere abstractions." The ability to climb to higher and higher levels of abstraction is a distinctively human trait, without which none of our philosophical or scientific insights would be possible. In order to have a science of chemistry, one *has* to be able to think of "H_2O," leaving out of consideration for the time being the wetness of water, the hardness of ice, the pearliness of dew, and the other extensional characteristics of H_2O at the objective level. In order to have a study called "ethics," one has to be able to think of what elements in ethical behavior have in common under different conditions and in different civilizations; one has to abstract that which is common to the behavior of the ethical carpenter, the ethical politician, the ethical businessman, and the ethical soldier—and that which is common to the laws of conduct of the Buddhist, the Orthodox Jew, the Confucian, and the Christian. Thinking that is most abstract can also be that which is most generally useful. The famous injunction of Jesus, "And as ye would that men should do to you, do ye also to them likewise," is, from this point of view, a brilliant generalization of more particular directives—a generalization at so high a level of abstraction that it appears to be applicable to all men in all cultures.

But high-level abstractions acquire a bad reputation because they are so often used, consciously or unconsciously, to confuse and befuddle people. A grab among competing powers for oil resources may be spoken of as "protecting the integrity of small nations." (Remember Japan's "Greater East Asia Co-prosperity Sphere"?) An unwillingness to pay social security taxes may be spoken of as "maintaining the system of free enterprise." Depriving the Negro of his vote in violation of the Constitution of the United States may be spoken of as "preserving states' rights." The consequence of this free, and often irresponsible, use of high-level abstractions in public controversy and special pleading is that a significant portion of the population has grown cynical about *all* abstractions.

But, as the abstraction ladder has shown, *all we know are abstractions.* What you know about the chair you are sitting in is an abstraction from the totality of that chair. When you eat white bread, you cannot tell by the taste whether or not it has been "enriched by vitamin B" as it says on the wrapper; you simply have to trust that the process (from which the words "vitamin B" are abstracted) is actually there. What you know about your wife—even if she has been your wife for thirty years—is again an abstraction. Distrusting all abstractions simply does not make sense.

The test of abstractions then is not whether they are "high-" or "low-level" abstractions, but *whether they are referrable to lower levels.* If one makes a statement about "culinary arts in America," one should be able to refer the statement down the abstraction ladder to particulars of American restaurants, American domestic science, American techniques of food preservation, down to Mrs. Levin in her kitchen. If one makes a statement about "civil rights in Wisconsin," one should know something about national, state, and local statutes; one should also know something about the behavior of policemen, magistrates, judges, academic authorities, hotel managers, and the general public in Wisconsin, all of whose acts and whose decisions affect that minimum of decent treatment in the courts, in politics, and in society that we call "civil rights." A preacher, a professor, a journalist, or politician whose high-level abstractions can systematically and surely be referred to lower-level abstractions is not only talking, he is saying something. As *Time* would say, no windbag, he.

"Dead-Level Abstracting"

Professor Wendell Johnson of the University of Iowa, in his *People in Quandaries* (1946), discusses a linguistic phenomenon which he calls "dead-level abstracting." Some people, it appears, remain more or less permanently stuck at certain levels of the abstraction ladder, some on the lower levels, some on the very high levels. There are those, for example, who go in for "persistent low-level abstracting":

> Probably all of us know certain people who seem able to talk on and on without ever drawing any very general conclusions. For example, there is the back-fence chatter that is made up of he said and then I said and then she said and I said and then he said, far into the afternoon, ending with, "Well, that's *just* what I told him!" Letters describing vacation trips frequently illustrate this sort of language, detailing places seen, times of arrival and departure, the foods eaten and the prices paid, whether the beds were hard or soft, etc.

A similar inability to get to higher levels of abstraction characterizes certain types of mental patients who suffer, as Johnson says, "a general blocking of the abstracting process." They go on indefinitely, reciting insignificant facts, never able to pull them together to frame a generalization that would give a meaning to the facts.

Other speakers remain stuck at higher levels of abstraction, with little or no contact with lower levels. Such language remains permanently in the clouds. As Johnson says:

It is characterized especially by vagueness, ambiguity, even utter meaninglessness. Simply by saving various circulars, brochures, free copies of "new thought" magazines, etc. . . . it is possible to accumulate in a short time quite a sizable file of illustrative material. Much more, of course, is to be found on library shelves, on newsstands, and in radio programs. Everyday conversation, classroom lectures, political speeches, commencement addresses, and various kinds of group forums and round-table discussions provide a further abundant source of *words cut loose from their moorings.* [Italics supplied.]

(The writer once heard of a course in esthetics given at a large Middle Western university in which an entire semester was devoted to Art and Beauty and the principles underlying them, and during which the professor, even when asked by students, persistently declined to name specific paintings, symphonies, sculptures, or objects of beauty to which his principles might apply. "We are interested," he would say, "in principles, not in particulars.")

There are psychiatric implications to dead-level abstracting on higher levels, too, because when maps proliferate wildly without any reference to a territory, the result can only be delusion. But whether at higher or lower levels, dead-level abstracting is, as Johnson says, always dull:

The low-level speaker frustrates you because he leaves you with no directions as to what to do with the basketful of information he has given you. The high-level speaker frustrates you because he simply doesn't tell you what he is talking about. . . . Being thus frustrated, and being further blocked because the rules of courtesy (or of attendance at class lectures) require that one remain quietly seated until the speaker has finished, there is little for one to do but daydream, doodle, or simply fall asleep.

It is obvious, then, that interesting speech and interesting writing, as well as clear thinking and psychological well-being, require the constant interplay of higher- and lower-level abstractions, and the constant interplay of the verbal levels with the nonverbal ("object") levels. In science, this interplay goes on constantly, hypotheses being checked against observations, predictions against extensional results. (Scientific *writing,* however, as exemplified in technical journals, offers some appalling examples of *almost* dead-level abstracting—which is the reason so much of it is hard to read. Nevertheless, the interplay between verbal and nonverbal experimental levels does continue, or else we would not have science.)

The work of good novelists and poets also represents this constant interplay between higher and lower levels of abstraction. A "significant" novelist or poet is one whose message has a high level of *general* usefulness in providing insight into life; but he gives his generalizations an impact and a persuasiveness through his ability to observe and describe actual social situations and states of mind. A memorable literary character, such as Sinclair Lewis' George F. Babbitt, has *descriptive* validity (at a low level of abstraction) as the picture of an individual, as well as a *general* validity as a picture of a "typical" American businessman of his time. The great political leader is also one in whom there is interplay between higher and lower levels of abstraction. The ward heeler knows politics only at lower levels of abstraction: what promises or what acts will cause what people to vote as desired; his loyalties are not to principles (high-level abstractions) but to persons (e.g., political bosses) and immediate advantages (low-level abstractions). The so-called impractical political theorist knows the high-level abstractions ("democracy," "civil rights," "social justice") but is not well enough acquainted with facts at lower levels of abstraction to get himself elected county register of deeds. But the political leaders to whom states and nations remain permanently grateful are those who were able, somehow or other, to achieve simultaneously higher-level aims ("freedom," "national unity," "justice") *and* lower-level aims ("better prices for potato farmers," "higher wages for textile workers," "judicial reform," "soil conservation").

The interesting writer, the informative speaker, the accurate thinker, and the sane individual, operate on all levels of the abstraction ladder, moving quickly and gracefully and in orderly fashion from higher to lower, from lower to higher—with minds as lithe and deft and beautiful as monkeys in a tree.

APPLICATIONS

I. Starting with the one at the lowest level of abstraction, arrange the following statements in order of increasing abstraction.

1. I like motoring better than flying.
2. I like Rambler cars.
3. I like American cars better than English cars.
4. I like my Rambler Classic four-door sedan.
5. I like travel.

1. Joe keeps all our household appliances in working condition.

2. Joe is a mechanical genius.

3. Joe is very handy with tools.

4. Joe is a 100 percent real American boy.

5. Yesterday Joe replaced a burned-out condenser in the radio.

6. Joe is an awfully useful person to have around.

7. Joe keeps that radio in working condition.

II. In the light of this chapter—especially of the discussion of "operational definitions"—apply the following terms to events in the extensional world; that is, go down the abstraction ladder and tell "what to do and what to observe in order to bring the thing defined or its effects within the range of one's experience." If you can translate the illustrative quotations accompanying the words into operational definitions, do so. If not, please so state, then make up your own operational definitions.

1. ART: as in, *"Art* is a spiritual necessity for all men."

2. TELEVISION: as in, *"Television* is a means of presenting the American public with the chance to elevate itself beyond the mundane, and to experience the liberation of the mind and heart."

3. RACE: as in, "We are members of the master *race."*

4. PHILOSOPHY: as in, "There are more things in Heaven and earth, Horatio,/Than are dreamt of in your *philosophy."*
   —*Hamlet,* Act I, Sc. 5, ll. 166–67

5. LIBERAL: as in, "The *Liberal* is hotly (though sometimes fitfully) compassionate toward people in the abstract and in the mass; his essential respect goes to the Common People."
   —WILLIAM S. WHITE, *Harper's*

6. CONSERVATIVE: as in, "The *Conservative* is warmly, and unalterably, compassionate to the individual; his essential respect goes not so much to mankind as to Man." —*Ibid.*

7. THE BATTLE OF GETTYSBURG: as in, "The *Battle of Gettysburg* was fought near Gettysburg, Pennsylvania, during the Civil War."

8. HONOR: as in, "Rightly to be great/Is not to stir without great argument,/But greatly to find quarrel in a straw/When *honor's* at the stake." —*Hamlet,* Act IV, Sc. 4, ll. 53–56.
   (Note: Does the play itself provide a context in which the terms used to define "honor" are themselves operationally defined? If you suspect that Shakespeare may have been naive about "honor," see *King Henry the Fourth: Part One,* Act V, Sc. 1, ll. 127–43.)

9. SPORTSMANSHIP: as in, "Gene Fullmer was guilty of poor *sportsmanship* in the twelfth round of the fight."

10. FREEDOM: as in, "Land where my fathers died,/Land of the pilgrims' pride,/From every mountainside,/Let *freedom* ring."

11. NUCLEAR DETERRENT: as in, "We must keep our *nuclear deterrent* in readiness if we wish to preserve peace."

12. REASON: as in, "*Reason* is substance, as well as infinite power, its own infinite material underlying all the natural and spiritual life; as also the infinite form, that which sets the material in motion. *Reason* is the substance from which all things derive their being."
    —GEORG WILHELM FRIEDRICH HEGEL

III. Analyze the following passages in terms of levels of abstraction:

1. A *phobia* is a recurrent and persistent fear of a particular object or situation which in "objective" reality presents no actual danger to the subject—although (cf. Case 1) in his unconsciously equated experience the patient may conceive the symbolized danger to be overwhelming. Phobias, indeed, are originally derived from situation-related fears, and differ from the latter only in their "rationality," symbolic spread, and generalization to remote aspects of the situation. For instance, fear of a rampant tiger is directly understandable, but it is justifiable to c nsider abnormal the reactions of a severely ailurophobic patient who exhibits fear within a mile of a well-protected zoo, cannot bear the approach of a kitten, and experiences anxiety when any animal of the genus *Felis* is shown on a motion picture screen. In neither the "normal" or "abnormal" instance, be it noted, need the fear be based on a direct experience with the "object" feared, although in both the tiger is, of course, symbolically equated with physical danger. The difference lies in this: that the phobia, unlike the fear, is based on no rational conscious reasons whatever, but springs from experiences deeply repressed and not necessarily related to a direct attack by a big or little cat at any time in the patient's life. To illustrate:
    Case 7: An₁ e A——, an eighteen-year-old girl was brought to the psychiatric out-patient clinic by her . . .
    —JULES MASSERMAN, *Principles of Dynamic Psychiatry*

    SAMPLE ANALYSIS: The author starts with a definition of phobia that names the general conditions under which a fear may be called a phobia. The second sentence is also general and adds information about the origin of a phobia and shows how it differs from "situation-related fears." So far the author seems to be writing at a high level of abstraction without much progress up or down the abstraction ladder. The third sentence goes, however, down the abstraction ladder to a specific example, capable of being visualized by the reader ("rampant tiger") and also gives examples of specific situations (zoo, kitten, moving pictures) where fear may be termed a phobia. After more general explanations, there is a case history of a specific patient, Anne A——, reporting facts at still lower (descriptive) levels of abstraction. Whether or not other scientists agree with Dr. Masserman in calling this case a phobia, we at least know that, when *he* uses the word, this is the kind of case *he* is talking about. So far as relationships between higher and lower levels of abstraction are concerned, this passage is a good extensionally-directed definition of phobia.

2. A function . . . is a table giving the relation between two variable quantities, where a change in one implies some change in the other. The cost of a quantity of meat is a function of its weight; the speed of a train, a function of the quantity of coal consumed; the amount of perspiration given off, a function of the temperature. In each of these illustrations, a change in the second variable: weight, quantity of coal consumed, and temperature, is correlated with a change in the first variable: cost, speed, and volume of perspiration. The symbolism of mathematics permits functional relationships to be simply and concisely expressed. Thus $y = x$, $y = x^2$, $y = \sin x$, $y = \operatorname{csch} x$, $y = e^x$ are examples of functions.

—EDWARD KASNER and J. R. NEWMAN,
Mathematics and the Imagination

3. HAYWARD, Ira N, Prof Eng, Utah SU, Logan, Utah
   HAYWARD, Wayne, Prof Eng, Pennsylvania SC, Indiana, Pa
   HAZARD, Clifton E, Instr Eng, U of Cincinnati, Cincinnati 21, Ohio
   HAZARD, Forrest E, Asst Prof Eng, Wayne STC, Wayne, Neb
   HAZELRIGG, Charles T, Assoc Prof & Chm Eng, Centre C, Danville, Ky
   HAZELRIG, Matthew S, Jr, Asst Prof Eng, Fenn C, Cleveland 15, Ohio
   HAZELTON, Richard M, Asst Prof Eng, Washington U, St Louis 30, Mo
   —Directory of the Modern Language Association of America

4. "Very well," I said, "tell me what you think of recurrence. . . . Do we live only this once and then disappear, or does everything repeat and repeat itself, perhaps an endless number of times, only we do not know and do not remember it?"

   "This idea of repetition," said G[urdjieff], "is not the full and absolute truth, but it is the nearest possible approximation of the truth. In this case truth cannot be expressed in words. But what you say is very near to it. And if you understand why I do not speak of this, you will be still nearer to it. What is the use of a man knowing about recurrence if he is not conscious of it and if he himself does not change? One can say even that if a man does not change, repetition does not exist for him. If you tell him about repetition, it will only increase his sleep. Why should he make any efforts today when there is so much time and so many possibilities ahead—the whole of eternity? Why should he bother today? This is exactly why the system [Gurdjieff's system of thought] does not say anything about repetition and takes only this one life which we know. The system has neither meaning nor sense without striving for self-change. And work on self-change must begin today, immediately. All laws can be seen in one life. Knowledge about the repetition of lives will add nothing for a man if he does not see how everything repeats itself in one life, that is, in this life, and if he does not strive to change himself in order to escape this repetition. But if he changes something essential in himself, that is, if he attains something, this cannot be lost."

—P. D. OUSPENSKY, *In Search of the Miraculous*

5. And Shem lived after he begat Arphaxad five hundred years, and begat sons and daughters.

And Arphaxad lived five and thirty years, and begat Salah;

And Arphaxad lived after he begat Salah four hundred and three years, and begat sons and daughters.

And Salah lived thirty years, and begat Eber.

And Salah lived after he begat Eber four hundred and three years, and begat sons and daughters.

And Eber lived four and thirty years, and begat Peleg. . . .

—Genesis, 11:11–18

6. Educators have done a good deal less than they might reasonably have been expected to do in explaining to young people the nature, the limitations, the huge potentialities for evil as well as for good, of that greatest of all human inventions, language. Children should be taught that words are indispensable but also can be fatal—the only begetters of civilization, all science, all consistency of high purpose, all angelic goodness, and the only begetters at the same time of all superstition, all collective madness and stupidity, all worse-than-bestial diabolism, all the historical succession of crimes in the name of God, King, Nation, Party, Dogma.

Never before, thanks to the techniques of mass communication, have so many listeners been so completely at the mercy of so few speakers. Never have misused words—those hideously efficient tools of all the tyrants, war-mongers, persecutors, and heresy-hunters—been so widely and so disastrously influential as they are today. Generals, clergymen, advertisers, and the rulers of totalitarian states —all have good reasons for disliking the idea of universal education in the rational use of language. To the military, clerical, propagandist, and authoritarian mind such training seems (and rightly seems) profoundly subversive.

To those who think that liberty is a good thing . . . a thorough education in the nature of language, in its uses and abuses, seems indispensable. Whether in fact the mounting pressures of overpopulation and overorganization in a world still enthusiastically dedicated to nationalistic idolatry will permit this kind of subversive linguistic education to be adopted by even the more democratic nations remains to be seen.

—ALDOUS HUXLEY, "Education on the Nonverbal Level,"
Perspective, September 1962

7.   Let Observation, with extensive view,
        Survey mankind, from China to Peru;
        Remark each anxious toil, each eager strife,
        And watch the busy scenes of crowded life;
        Then say how hope and fear, desire and hate
        O'erspread with snares the clouded maze of fate,
        Where wavering man, betray'd by vent'rous pride
        To tread the dreary paths without a guide,
        As treach'rous phantoms in the mist delude,
        Shuns fancied ills, or chases airy good;
        How rarely Reason guides the stubborn choice,
        Rules the bold hand or prompts the suppliant voice;
        How nations sink, by darling schemes oppress'd,
        When Vengeance listens to the fool's request.
        —SAMUEL JOHNSON, *Vanity of Human Wishes*

8.   The last pose flickered, failed. The screen's dead white
        Glared in a sudden flooding of harsh light
        Stabbing the eyes; and as I stumbled out
        The curtain rose. A fat girl with a pout
        And legs like hams, began to sing "His Mother."
        Gusts of bad air rose in a choking smother;
        Smoke, the wet steam of clothes, the stench of plush,
        Powder, cheap perfume, mingled in a rush.
        I stepped into the lobby—and stood still
        Struck dumb by sudden beauty, body and will.
        Cleanness and rapture—excellence made plain—
        The storming, thrashing arrows of the rain!
        —STEPHEN VINCENT BENÉT,*
        Rain after a Vaudeville Show

9. PRESIDENT EISENHOWER: . . . I'd like to point out that all of the political moves, all of the educational moves you make, must be supported by trade. We must have better trade. We must have better trade because it is through trade that all of us are going to achieve better standards. And I know this is one subject that is dear to your heart, and it's one I think we should all think about very thoroughly.

MR. MACMILLAN: Well, Mr. President, you, we both believe the same thing, I think, that these problems in the world can only be solved by the expanding of the wealth and trade of the world. Of course, we are up against quite a lot of pressures, you are and I am. And it isn't always easy to say, it isn't always too easy to do. Yet I think we've done pretty well. And it's a great satisfaction to us to feel that the enormous increase of trade between Britain and the United States [*sic*]. You helped us very much with the heavy engineering. I wish you could do something for us on wool textiles but perhaps you'll be able to do that. . . .

PRESIDENT EISENHOWER: Let me tell you this: we are concerned about it. I mean we want to see it just as strong as you want to see it. I'd like to point out that supporting this kind of thing is the necessity for broadening our contacts in the world, particularly—not only among ourselves—but particularly with the Iron Curtain countries. I believe we've got to have better exchange of ideas, of the products and the conclusions of scientific people; we have got to have more in books; but above all, the people. I like to believe that the people, in the long run, are going to do more to promote peace than our government. Indeed, I think that people want peace so much that one of these days governments better get out of their way and let 'em have it. . . .

—Eisenhower-Macmillan television discussion, "Issues Confronting the West," September 1, 1959

10. The thing that has made the glory of English literature is description simple concentrated description not of what happened nor what is thought or what is dreamed but what exists and so makes the life the island life the daily island life. It is natural that an island life should be that. What could interest an island as much as the daily the completely daily island life. . . .

Then there is the poetry that too comes out of a daily island life, because granted that a daily island life is what it is and the English daily island life has always been completely what it is, it is necessary that poetry is not what they lose or what they feel but is the things with which they are shut up, that is shut in, in the daily the simply daily island life. And so the poetry of England is so much what it is, it is the poetry of the things with which any of them are

shut in in their daily, completely daily island life. It makes very
beautiful poetry because anything shut in with you can sing. . . .
It is easy to know all that.

—GERTRUDE STEIN, *Lectures in America*

11. If one listens to the two sides of the long-playing record that Jerry
Newman issued on his Esoteric label, one hears Charlie Christian
in all his glory. These sides were originally tape recordings made by
Jerry at jam sessions in Minton's Playhouse. . . . The recording
was made in May 1941; it was made because Jerry . . . knew
[Charlie] was a musician whose every moment counted. Here, playing
with some of the first musicians to make the move from swing to
bop, Charlie plays rhapsodic chorus after chorus, threading his way
through such familiar chords and melodic lines as those of "Stompin'
at the Savoy" to give shape to a whole new conception of music.
The beat never stops; its steady pulsation is elaborated, complicated,
simplified. The sound never loses beauty or flourish; the harpsi-
chord-like texture of Charlie's guitar is produced in arpeggios, trills,
cascades, clusters, in phrases sometimes of tumultuous power, sometimes of elegant restraint. The recording shows clearly what Charlie
did for the electric guitar. . . . Charle changed the playing technique of the guitar and structured for it a dramatic role in jazz which
[other guitarists] had never dreamed of. . . . So effectively did he
transform the guitar from a rhythmic servant into an eloquent master that today very few bands, big or small, can find guitarists good
enough for their needs—and after Christian a bad one would be
unthinkable.   —BARRY ULANOV, *A History of Jazz in America*

12.   Behold, a sower went forth to sow;
    And when he sowed, some seeds fell by the wayside, and the fowls
came and devoured them up:
    Some fell upon stony places, where they had not much earth: and
forthwith they sprung up, because they had no deepness of earth:
    And when the sun was up, they were scorched; and because they
had no root, they withered away.
    And some fell among thorns; and the thorns sprung up, and choked
them:
    But other fell into good ground, and brought forth fruit, some an
hundredfold, some sixtyfold, some thirtyfold.
    Who hath ears to hear, let him hear.   —Matthew, 13:3–9

IV. Alfred Korzybski in *Science and Sanity* (1933) points out
that consciousness of abstracting enables us, among other things, to
become aware of what happens when we go from low to higher levels
of abstraction with a single term. For example, to worry about worry
or to fear fear may lead to morbid responses but, with another group

of words, the higher level of abstraction reverses or annuls the lower-level effects as in "hatred of hatred." Consider the responses that are likely to be the outcome when you

1. are curious about curiosity;
2. doubt your doubts;
3. are nervous about your nervousness;
4. reason about reasoning;
5. try to know about knowing;
6. are impatient with your impatience;
7. are intolerant of intolerance;
8. are in love with love.

V. Consciousness of abstracting must be permanent or habitual if we are to avoid errors of evaluation.

We know that every word is an abstraction, but we forget. We know that every word is a class word that abstracts (takes away from the whole object named) only the similarities of the class to which the object is ascribed and leaves out all the differences. But we forget.

BESS SONDEL, *The Humanity of Words*

Write a three hundred-word paper in which you recall illustrations of such forgetting in your own experience. What were the practical consequences of this forgetting?

11 The Little Man Who Wasn't There

> As I was going up the stair
> I met a man who wasn't there.
> He wasn't there again to-day.
> I wish, I wish he'd stay away.
>
> HUGHES MEARNS

> *Everybody is familiar with the fact that the ordinary man does not see things as they are, but only sees certain fixed types. . . . Mr. Walter Sickert is in the habit of telling his pupils that they are unable to draw any individual arm because they think of it as an arm; and because they think of it as an **arm** they think they know what it ought to be.*
>
> —T. E. HULME

How Not To Start a Car

The following newspaper story is presented in the hope that the reader will find it as instructive (and as depressing) as the writer did:

> More than one motorist has secretly wished he could do what Samuel Rios, 30, was accused of doing yesterday. Driving at 12:30 A.M. through Williamsburg, he swung around a corner and accidentally sideswiped a sedan parked at the curb in front of 141 Hopkins Street. Furious, police charged, Rios stopped, took the jack handle from his car trunk, and slam-banged the offending obstacle from windshield to tail-lights. —New York *Post*

Let us examine the mechanism of this man's reaction. He got angry at the parked car just as he might have gotten angry at a person, horse, or mule that got in his way. He thereupon proceeded to "teach" that a car a "lesson." Although the reaction was unreflecting and automatic, it is nevertheless a complicated one, since it in-

■ 199

volves (1) his making up an abstraction about the car (which is seen as maliciously obstructive) and then (2) his reacting to his own abstraction rather than to the actual car itself.

People in primitive societies often act in similar ways. When crops fail or rocks fall upon them, they make a deal with—offer sacrifices to—the "spirits" of vegetation or of the rocks, in order to obtain better treatment from them in the future. We too have certain reactions of similar kinds: sometimes, tripping over a chair, we kick it and call it names; some people, indeed, when they fail to get letters, get angry at the postman. In all such behavior, we *confuse* the abstraction which is *inside* our heads with that which is *outside*, and act as if the abstraction *were* the event in the outside world. We create in our heads an imaginary chair that maliciously trips us and then "punish" the extensional chair that bears ill will to nobody; we create an imaginary, inferential postman who is "holding back our mail" and then we bawl out the extensional postman who would gladly bring us letters if he had any to bring.

It is in these terms that Sigmund Freud sought to explain the origin of religion: our primitive ancestors, frightened by natural events they could not understand, projected their fears and anxieties upon the world, personalized them into a malevolent Being, and then tried to propitiate this Being through sacrifices of one kind or another. They mistook their abstractions for reality.

Confusion of Levels of Abstraction

In a wider sense, however, we are confusing levels of abstraction—confusing what is inside our heads with what is outside—all the time. For example, we talk about the yellowness of a pencil as if the yellowness were a "property" of the pencil and not a product, as we have seen, of the *interaction* of something outside our skins with our nervous systems. We confuse, that is to say, the two lowest levels of the abstraction ladder (see p. 179) and treat them as one. Properly speaking, we should not say, "The pencil is yellow," which is a statement that places the yellowness in the pencil; we should say instead, "That which has an effect on me which leads me to say 'pencil' also has an effect on me which leads me to say 'yellow.' " We don't have to be that precise, of course, in the language of everyday life, but it should be observed that the latter statement takes into consideration the part our nervous systems play in creating whatever pictures of reality we may have in our heads, while the former statement does not.

Now this habit of confusing what is inside our skins and what is outside is essentially a relic of prescientific patterns of thinking. The more advanced civilization becomes, the more conscious we must be that our nervous systems *automatically leave out characteristics* of the events before us. If we are not aware of characteristics left out, if we are not conscious of the process of abstracting, we make *seeing and believing a single process.* If, for example, you react to the twenty-second rattlesnake you have seen in your life as if it were identical with the abstraction you have in your head as the result of the last twenty-one rattlesnakes you have seen, you may not be far out in your reactions. But civilized life provides our nervous systems with more complicated problems than rattlesnakes to deal with.

There is a case cited by Korzybski in *Science and Sanity* of a man who suffered from hay fever whenever there were roses in the room. In an experiment, a bunch of roses was produced unexpectedly in front of him, and he immediately had a violent attack of hay fever, despite the fact that the "roses" in this case were *made of paper.* That is, his nervous system saw-and-believed in one operation.

But words, as we have seen by means of the abstraction ladder, are still higher levels of abstraction than the "objects" of experience. The more words at extremely high levels of abstraction we have, then, the more conscious we must be of this process of abstracting. For example, the word "rattlesnake" leaves out every important feature of the actual rattlesnake. But if the word is vividly remembered as part of a whole complex of terrifying experiences with an actual rattlesnake, the word itself is capable of arousing the same feelings as an actual rattlesnake. There are people, therefore, who turn pale at the *word.*

A once popular musical comedy (*High-Button Shoes*) contains a routine in which a comedian gets an attack of sneezing at the mention of the words "fresh country air" and "ragweed." The fact that this theme of reacting to words as things is extremely common in the humor of comic strips, movies, and radio demonstrates, I believe, not only that such reactions are widespread, but also that most people in the audience have enough of a tendency in this direction to recognize in the comedy characterization *an exaggeration of their own reactions.*

Confusion of Levels of Abstraction ■ 201

Professor Leo Hamalian adds the following anecdote:

Another interesting example of reactions to words took place when I was officer in charge of a group of men preparing a ship for embarkation at Port Newark. When we finished our work, we were told to go below and stay there until the following morning, when we could expect to be miles at sea. We did so, and the next morning a number of the men declared that the ship's motion was making them seasick. They vomited and showed all the symptoms. I decided to go above for some fresh air. When I got to the deck, I saw that we were still tied up at our berth in Port Newark!

This, then, is the origin of word-magic. The word "rattlesnake" and the actual creature are felt to be *one and the same thing,* because they arouse the same reactions. This sounds like nonsense, of course, and it is nonsense. But from the point of view of a pre-scientific logic, it has its justification. As Lévy-Bruhl explains in his *How Natives Think* (1926), primitive "logic" works on such a principle. The creature frightens us; the word frightens us; therefore the creature and the word are "the same"—not actually the same, perhaps, but there is a "mystic connection" between the two. This sense of "mystic connection" is Lévy-Bruhl's term for what we have called "necessary connection" in our discussion in Chapter 2 of naïve attitudes towards symbols. As a consequence of this naïveté, "mystical power" is attributed to words. There come to be "fearful words," "forbidden words," "unspeakable words"—words taking on the characteristics of the things they stand for. The word "grammarian" once referred to a person who had magical power—one who was versed in "gramarye" and therefore could manipulate to advantage the mystical power of words.

The feeling that a repetition of the right *words* will somehow or other bring about the desired *events* remains with us, in spite of the pride we take in our allegedly advanced scientific culture. In the 1930's, politicians and business leaders and newspapers repeated, like an incantation, the words, "Prosperity is just around the corner!" Cheering squads at football games urge their teams to "Go! Go! Go!" reiterating the word as if it had magical power. In craps, the dice-thrower will call for "Little Ada from Decatur," and if he rolls a seven before an eight, he attributes his failure to "the wrong kind of call." Crapshooters are especially given to talking to their dice in order to influence outcomes; in this they behave very much like commentators on the stock market. The very intensity with which a player will hiss, "Snake eyes! you son-of-a-bitch!" reveals the degree to which he believes in the power of his words over the dice.

However, the commonest form of this confusion of levels of abstraction is illustrated by our reacting to the "conservative" to whom we are just being introduced ("I want you to meet Mr. Lee Buck, who is active in our new conservative movement on campus") as if he were identical with the abstraction "conservative" inside our heads. "If he is a conservative, he is OK"—or "he is a Bircher"— we are likely to say, confusing the extensional conservative with our abstraction, "conservative," which is the product not only of the previous "conservatives" we have met, but also of all that we have been *told* about "conservatives."

"Jews"

To make the principles clearer, we shall use an example that is loaded with prejudices for many people: "Mr. Miller is a *Jew.*" On hearing this, some "Christians" have marked hostile reactions instantaneously; they will, for example, put themselves on guard against Mr. Miller's expected sharp financial practices. That is to say, a "Christian" of this kind confuses his high-level abstraction, "Jew," with the extensional Mr. Miller and behaves towards Mr. Miller as if he were identical with that abstraction. (See the abstraction ladder, p. 179.) "Jew" is only *one* of thousands upon thousands of abstractions which may be applied to Mr. Miller, to whom such terms as "left-hander," "parent," "amateur golfer," "history teacher," "teetotaler," "Bostonian," and so on may possibly be equally applied. But the prejudiced person is unaware of all but the one abstraction—perhaps in most contexts the least relevant one—"Jew."

Moreover, the word "Jew" is perhaps one of the most sloppily constructed abstractions in the language—that is, one of the most difficult to refer systematically down the abstraction ladder to lower levels. Does "Jew" refer to a race, a religion, a nationality, a physical type, a state of mind, a caste? If not these, what? Major conferences and conventions of American Jews in recent years have included sessions on the question, "What is a Jew?" The prime minister of Israel and most members of his cabinet do not set foot in a synagogue except on special state occasions. Are they Jews? What about the fanatical Neturai Karta sect of Jerusalem, who in addition to three regular daily services also hold a midnight prayer and vigil for the coming of the Messiah—and refuse to recognize the

Jewish state or to bear arms for it? The government of Israel, confronted with a flood of "Jewish" refugees from many parts of Europe, the Middle East, and Asia, was compelled long ago to give up the attempt to define a "Jew"; the rule now is that *anyone who calls himself a "Jew" is a Jew*—an operational definition that is difficult to improve upon.

Now it happens that the word "Jew" has powerful affective connotations in Christian culture as the result of a number of historical accidents associating "Jews" with money. These affective connotations create such expressions as, "He *jewed* me out of ten dollars," "I *jewed* down the price." In parts of rural America where itinerant Jewish peddlers used to roam, some mothers disciplined their children with, "If you don't behave, I'll sell you to the old Jew man."

Let us return to our hypothetical Mr. Miller, who has been introduced as a "Jew." To a person for whom these affective connotations are very much alive, and who habitually confuses what is inside his head with what is outside, Mr. Miller is a man "not to be trusted." If Mr. Miller succeeds in business, that "proves" that "Jews are smart"; if Mr. Johansen succeeds in business, it only proves that Mr. Johansen is smart. If Mr. Miller fails in business, it is alleged that he nevertheless has "money salted away somewhere." If Mr. Miller is strange or foreign in his habits, that "proves" that "Jews don't assimilate." If he is thoroughly American—i.e., indistinguishable from other natives—he is "trying to pass himself off as one of us." If Mr. Miller fails to give to charity, that is because "Jews are tight"; if he gives generously, he is "trying to buy his way into society." If Mr. Miller lives in the Jewish section of town, that is because "Jews are so clannish"; if he moves to a locality where there are no other Jews, that is because "they try to horn in everywhere." In short, Mr. Miller is automatically condemned, no matter who he is or what he does.

But Mr. Miller may be, for all we know, rich or poor, a wife-beater or a saint, a stamp collector or a violinist, a farmer or a physicist, a lens grinder or an orchestra leader. If, as the result of our automatic reactions, we put ourselves on guard about our *money* immediately upon meeting Mr. Miller, we may offend a man from whom we might have profited financially, morally, or spiritually, or we may fail to notice his attempts to run off with our wife—that is, we shall act with complete inappropriateness to the *actual* situation at hand. Mr. Miller is not identical with our notion of "Jew," *what-*

ever our notion of "Jew" may be. The "Jew," created by intensional definition of the *word, simply is not there.*

Indeed, to say that some people are blinded by prejudice seems to be more than a metaphor. Ralph Ellison calls his central character, a Negro, "The Invisible Man," in his novel of that name. This is to suggest that most white people, on encountering a Negro, see only the abstraction "Negro" that they carry in their heads; busy with this "little man that isn't there," they never notice the actual Negro individual.

Something similar may be said about the typical Western attitude towards the "Arab." Many people would be surprised to know that not all Arabs are Moslems (there are thousands of Christian Arabs living in Lebanon and Syria), that the Arabs of Syria hate the Arabs of Egypt, that the Arabs of Lebanon want little to do with the Arabs of Syria or Iraq, and that not infrequently Arabs are tall, blond, and blue-eyed. The term "Arab" as it is often used by the Westerner must be regarded as brother to the term "Jew" as it is used by the prejudiced or the ignorant. This does not mean that the term "Arab" should be discarded; it should be used more accurately. According to Edward Atiyah, an expert on the Arab world, the term may have three meanings. (1) It may designate the nomadic people who inhabit the Jordanian, Arabian, Syrian, and North African deserts, known as the *Bedu* or *Bedouin.* (2) It may designate the people of the Arabian peninsula (often referred to as "the Arabians"), both the nomads and the city-dwellers; in this sense, the word denotes an ethnic group—the present-day Saudis, Yemenites, Kuwaitis, and other descendants of the original Arab homeland. (3) Finally, the word "Arab" may mean a culture group—a *bloc* of Arab-speaking communities stretching continuously from the Persian Gulf in the east to the Atlantic in the west. In this vast area, the proportion of nomads to sedentary population is very small, the majority of people being *fellahin* (farmers) and inhabitants of the ancient and famous cities—Aleppo, Damascus, Beirut, Latakia, Cairo, Alexandria, Baghdad, Jerusalem, Tunis, Algiers—once the centers of world civilization. Hence, if we wish to speak with some precision and without giving offense to a group of people whose importance in the world is growing daily, we should learn at least to distinguish among these different abstractions and to avoid applying the word "Arab" as if it corresponded to the stereotype many of us know from adventure movies about the Foreign Legion.

John Doe, the "Criminal"

Another instance of the confusion of levels of abstraction is to be found in cases like this: Let us say that a man, John Doe, is introduced as one "who has just been released after three years in the penitentiary." This statement is already on a fairly high level of abstraction, but it is nevertheless a *report*. From this point, however, many people *immediately and unconsciously* climb to still higher levels of abstraction: "John Doe is an *ex-convict* . . . he's a criminal!" But the word "criminal" is not only on a much higher level of abstraction than "the man who spent three years in the penitentiary," but it is also, as we have seen before in Chapter 3, a *judgment*, with the implied prediction, "He has committed a crime in the past and will probably commit more crimes in future." The result is that when John Doe applies for a job and is forced to state that he has spent three years in the penitentiary, prospective employers, automatically confusing levels of abstraction, may say, *without bothering to learn any more about him,* "You can't expect me to give jobs to criminals!"

John Doe, for all we know from the report, may have undergone a complete reformation or, for that matter, may have been unjustly imprisoned in the first place; nevertheless, he may wander in vain, looking for a job. If, in desperation, he finally says to himself, "If everybody is going to treat me like a criminal, I might as well become one," and goes out and commits a robbery, the blame can hardly be said to be entirely his.

The reader is familiar with the way in which rumor grows as it spreads. Much of the exaggeration is again due to this tendency on the part of some people to climb to higher levels of abstraction— from reports to inferences to judgments—and then to confuse the levels. According to this kind of "reasoning":

> *Report.* "Mary Smith didn't get in until three last Saturday night."
> *Inference.* "I bet she was out tearing around!"
> *Judgment.* "She's nothing but a tramp. I never did like her looks. I knew it the moment I first laid eyes on her."

Basing our actions towards our fellow human beings on such hastily abstracted judgments, it is no wonder that we frequently make life miserable not only for others, but for ourselves.

As a final example of this type of confusion, *notice the difference between what happens when a man says to himself, "I have failed three times," and what happens when he says, "I am a failure!"*

Consciousness of abstracting prepares us in advance for the fact that (1) things that look alike may *not* be alike; (2) things that have the same name are *not* necessarily the same; and (3) judgments which may be based on reports are *not* reports. In short, it prevents us from acting like fools. Without consciousness of abstracting—or rather, without the habit of *delaying reactions,* which is the product of a deep awareness that seeing is not believing—we are completely unprepared for the differences between roses and paper roses, between the intensional "Jew" and the extensional Mr. Miller, between the intensional "criminal" and the extensional John Doe.

Such delayed reactions are a sign of adulthood. It happens, however, that as the result of miseducation, bad training, frightening experiences in childhood, traditional beliefs, propaganda, and other influences in our lives, all of us have what might be termed "areas of insanity" or, perhaps better, "areas of infantilism," in which we are at the mercy of ingrained, inappropriate semantic reactions. Some people, as the result of childhood experience, cannot help being frightened by the mere sight of a policeman—any policeman; the terrifying "policeman" inside their heads "is" the extensional policeman outside, who probably has no designs that anyone could regard as terrifying. Some people turn pale at the sight of a spider—any spider—even a nice, harmless one safely enclosed in a bottle. Some people automatically become hostile at the *words* "un-American," "communist," "conservative," "liberal," and "welfare."

Dr. G. Brock Chisholm, former director general of the World Health Organization (1948–53) and president of the World Federation for Mental Health, has commented eloquently on the tyranny of prejudice-laden words:

> The power these words have over much of the race is astonishing. They . . . are the chains that bind man to his miserable past and his discouraging present. They are the premises which were incorporated . . . when each human was too young and dependent to defend himself by using his intelligence. We find that rarely is it possible to discuss intelligently, without striking prejudices which have been inculcated in childhood, such ordinary commonplace subjects as health, clothes, Negroes, politics, patriotism, conscience, Jews, superstitions, war and peace, money, sex, property, marriage, religions, some diseases, India, wage scales, socialism, communism, trade unions, political parties, and so on through a long list which varies from place to place, time to time, and family to family. Very

few people can think clearly and honestly about many of these things; and yet these, and such as these, are the things which make up the life of man and which, misunderstood, mishandled, and fought over, have caused most of the fear and misery of the world.[1]

Dr. Chisholm does not mean, of course, that we must not learn from our elders. We learn two kinds of things from those who teach us: (1) a body of ideas and beliefs, and (2) a *way of holding them.* If our ideas and beliefs are held with consciousness of abstracting, they can be changed if found to be inadequate or erroneous. But if they are held without consciousness of abstracting—if our mental maps are believed *to be* the territory—they are prejudices. As teachers and parents, we cannot help passing on to the young a certain amount of misinformation and error, however hard we may try not to. But if we also teach them to be habitually conscious of the process of abstraction, we give them the means with which to free themselves from whatever erroneous notions we may have taught them. Our educational efforts will then not "bind them to a miserable past," but enable them to grow with advancing years and experience.

The picture of reality created inside our heads by the lack of consciousness of abstracting is not a "map" of any existing "territory." It is a delusional world. In this never-never land, all "Jews" are out to cheat you; all "capitalists" are overfed tyrants, smoking expensive cigars and gnashing their teeth at labor unions. In this world, too, all snakes are poisonous, all widows and orphans are meritorious, automobiles can be disciplined by being beaten with a tire-iron, and every stranger with a foreign accent is a communist spy. Some of the people who spend too much of their time in such delusional worlds eventually get locked up but, needless to say, there are many still at large.

How do we reduce such areas of infantilism in our thought? One way is to know deeply that there is no "necessary connection" between words and what they stand for. For this reason, the study of a foreign language is always good for us, even if it has no other uses. Other ways have already been suggested: to be aware of the process of abstracting and *to realize fully that words never "say all" about anything.* The abstraction ladder—an adaptation of a diagram originated by Alfred Korzybski to illustrate visually the relationship between words, "objects," and events—is designed to help us understand and remain conscious of the process of abstracting.

[1] "Can Man Survive?" *ETC.,* IV (1947), p. 107.

I. It was suggested at the end of Chapter 2 that examples of language in action be collected in a scrapbook or on filing cards. Enough general principles of the relationship between language and behavior have now been presented to expand the collection to include illustrations of many different linguistic principles. The following sample headings will suggest some of the clippings and quotations one might look for:

Straight reports.
Stories featuring inferences, with full awareness that they are inferences.
Stories featuring inferences in such a way that they may be mistaken for reports.
Reacting to judgments as if they were reports.
Shifts of meaning resulting from changes in context.
Snarl-words and purr-words mistaken for reports.
Slanting.
Quarrels over nonsense questions.
Social conversation.
Over-reacting to affective connotations of words.
Directives mistaken for reports.
Disillusionment caused by directives imperfectly understood.
Dead-level abstracting.
Meaningless use of high-level abstractions.
Higher- and lower-level abstractions properly related.
Seeing-and-believing.
The little man who wasn't there.

Other headings will occur to the reader as he reviews the chapters to follow. The study of the relationships between language and behavior is one that can be pursued at any time anywhere—in an office, at school, at church, behind (or in front of) a hosiery counter, at parties, at meetings, in all one's reading, and in the course of intimate family or personal relationships. Even a desultory collection of examples of language-in-action, if carefully noted and pasted down and pondered over, will help the reader understand what the writer of this book is saying *and why he wants to say it*. Collectors of such examples will no doubt find reasons for wishing to refine, expand, or correct some of the statements made in this book. Further progress in the scientific study of the relationships between language and behavior depends upon such corrections and improvements of the present generalizations. The reader's cooperation is earnestly invited.

II. People sometimes talk about punishing children who use dirty language by washing out their mouths with soap. Is this ever actually done? Comment on the semantic reactions or thought processes involved among those who use this method of control over their children's language.

III. In Jonathan Swift's *Gulliver's Travels,* the academicians of Lagado, perhaps as aware as the semanticists of the pitfalls of language, communicate as follows:

> An expedient was therefore offered, that since words are only names for things, it would be more convenient for all men to carry about them such things as were necessary to express the particular business they are to discourse on. . . . I have often beheld two of those sages almost sinking under the weight of their packs, like pedlars among us; who when they met in the streets would lay down their loads, open their sacks, and hold conversation. . . . Another great advantage proposed by this invention was that it would serve as an universal language to be understood in all civilized nations.

Before dismissing the scheme of the Lagadoan philosophers with a laugh, try to think of situations in which it is advantageous to communication to exhibit objects instead of talking. Having done this, can you state, using the formulations about levels of abstraction in this and the previous chapter, what is basically wrong with the philosophers' scheme?

IV. The following is an excerpt from John Kenneth Galbraith's essay, "The Age of the Wordfact." Ignoring the bias that leads Mr. Galbraith to select examples of this phenomenon from a Republican rather than a Democratic administration, write a paper of 500 words about "wordfact," providing examples from your own experience or reading.

> In June of 1960 President Eisenhower returned from a trip to the Pacific which would seem, superficially, to have been an unparalleled disaster of its kind. Japan, which was the principal object of this tour, had been beset by violent riots over the visit, and in the end it had been forced to urge him not to come. With the aid of his press secretary, however, the President was able to report on his return that his trip had been a success. . . .
> The wordfact makes words a precise substitute for reality. This is an enormous convenience. It means that to say that something

exists is a substitute for its existence. And to say that something will happen is as good as having it happen. . . .

Lest any of this seem farfetched . . . let us remind ourselves of some of the achievements of wordfact in these last years. . . . By a bold use of wordfact, we were long able to convert South American dictators into bulwarks of the free world. . . . Though farmers have been leaving their farms at an unprecedented rate, the forces making for this migration have been favorably described by the Secretary of Agriculture in a book with the agreeable title *Freedom to Farm*. . . . [I]n the days immediately following the last flight of the U-2, by the massive use of wordfact all of the relevant circumstances were changed. Flying planes over other countries became a kind of fifth freedom. . . . The flights were then suspended, and this became an act of wise restraint. . . .

Such is the service of wordfact in transforming misfortune into fortune. —*Atlantic*

V. Define each of the following terms.

vampire	criminal	obscenity
flying saucer	political pressure	Thursday
radioactivity	folk music	semantics

For each word, try one or all of the following kinds of definition. (If further clarification of the task is needed, see Anatol Rapoport, *Science and the Goals of Man* [1950], Chapter 7.):

1. Definition by synonym: "*Attain* means to achieve."

2. Definition by classification and differentiation (Aristotelian definition): "*Autocracy* is a form of government in which power is held by one person."

3. Definition by enumerating words to which the defined word refers collectively: "*Spices* are cinnamon, cloves, ginger, and such."

4. Extensional definition: definition by pointing to, or exhibiting, that which is defined (see Chapter 4).

Indicate which of the foregoing terms are *not* capable of being defined operationally.

VI. Reading about, discussing, and writing papers on racial and religious prejudice are clearly pertinent to this chapter. Anti-Semitic literature is abundant and has been so for hundreds of years, although in the United States today practically none of it appears under the imprint of well-known and reputable publishing houses. A curious example is *The Iron Curtain Over America* (1951) by John Beaty, which not only blames all of America's troubles (two world wars and everything that has happened since) on the Jews, but also accuses them of withholding the truth from the public through control of the publishing houses, newspapers, and other media. Those who have never done so should, at least once in their lives, expose themselves to the furious anti-Semitic writings of Adolf Hitler (Norman H. Baynes, ed., *The Speeches of Adolf Hitler*, 2 vols., 1942) and his colleagues of the Third Reich. The story of Hitler's attempt to destroy the Jews completely must never be forgotten as an example of how far racial madness can be carried. See William Shirer, *The Rise and Fall of the Third Reich* (1960) and Gerald Reitlinger, *The Final Solution: The Attempt to Exterminate the Jews of Europe, 1939–1945* (1953).

Of the hundreds of books on racial prejudice, the following should be of special interest to students of semantics:

Harold Isaacs, *Scratches on Our Minds: American Images of China and India* (1958). This fascinating book shows how movies, comic strips, travelogues, and fictional stereotypes create our images of the people of China and India. Today, when our relations with the people of the world are undergoing great changes, it is especially important that we correct our mistaken notions.

Morton Grodzins' *Americans Betrayed: Politics and the Japanese Evacuation* (1949). This volume is especially important for its revelation of the part played by pressure groups, political leaders, and newspapers in creating the atmosphere for placing both citizen and alien Japanese-Americans of the West Coast in concentration camps during World War II.

Harry and David Rosen, *But Not Next Door* (1962). This is an extremely extensional report of what happened to a private development of family houses in Deerfield, Illinois, when it was learned that Negro families were going to have homes there. Based on interviews, newspaper stories, and court records, the book uses three fictionalized families to illustrate the feelings and actions of the town's citizens. Despite avowals of the absence of racial feelings, the town did not permit the development to become a reality.

Julia Abrahamson, *A Neighborhood Finds Itself* (1959), and Herbert A. Thelen, *The Dynamics of Groups at Work* (1954). Both these books emerge from the experience of the authors in a community movement in the Hyde Park-Kenwood district of Chicago. Neighborhood blight was combatted and urban renewal was set in motion by establishing, among other things, communication among neighbors, especially whites and Negroes—communication that went far towards allaying the anxieties each group had about the other. Mrs. Abrahamson's book emphasizes the story; Dr. Thelen's emphasis is on the theoretical implications of the experience, as his title indicates.

12 Classification

Giving Things Names

The figure below shows eight objects, let us say animals, four large and four small, a different four with round heads and another four with square heads, and still another four with curly tails and another four with straight tails. These animals, let us say, are scampering about your village, but since at first they are of no importance to you, you ignore them. You do not even give them a name.

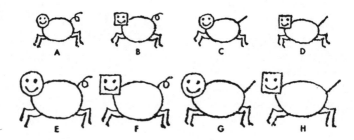

One day, however, you discover that the little ones eat up your grain, while the big ones do not. A differentiation sets itself up, and abstracting the common characteristics of A, B, C, and D, you decide to call these *gogo;* E, F, G, and H you decide to call *gigi.* You chase away the *gogo,* but leave the *gigi* alone. Your neighbor, however, has had a different experience; he finds that those with square heads bite, while those with round heads do not. Abstracting the common characteristics of B, D, F, and H, he calls them *daba,* and A, C, E, and G he calls *dobo.* Still another neighbor discovers, on the other hand, that those with curly tails kill snakes, while those with straight tails do not. He differentiates them, abstracting still another set of common characteristics: A, B, E, and F are *busa,* while C, D, G, and H are *busana.*

Now imagine that the three of your are together when E runs by. You say, "There goes the *gigi*"; your first neighbor says, "There goes the *dobo*"; your other neighbor says, "There goes the *busa.*" Here immediately a great controversy arises. What is it really, a *gigi,* a *dobo,* or a *busa?* What is its *right name?* You are quarreling violently when along comes a fourth person from another village who calls it a *muglock,* an edible animal, as opposed to *uglock,* an inedible animal—which doesn't help matters a bit.

Of course, the question, "What is it *really?* What is its *right name?*" is a nonsense question. By a nonsense question is meant one that is not capable of being answered. Things can have "right names" only if there is a necessary connection between symbols and things symbolized, and we have seen that there is not. That is to say, in the light of your interest in protecting your grain, it may be necessary for you to distinguish the animal E as a *gigi;* your neighbor, who doesn't like to be bitten, finds it practical to distinguish it as a *dobo;* your other neighbor, who likes to see snakes killed, distinguishes it as a *busa.* What we call things and where we draw the line between one class of things and another depend upon the interests we have and the purposes of the classification. For example, animals are classified in one way by the meat industry, in a different way by the leather industry, in another different way by the fur industry, and in a still different way by the biologist. None of these classification is any more final than any of the others; each of them is useful for its purpose.

This holds, of course, for everything we perceive. A table "is" a table to us, because we can understand its relationship to our conduct and interests; we eat at it, work on it, lay things on it.

But to a person living in a culture where no tables are used, it may be a very big stool, a small platform, or a meaningless structure. If our culture and upbringing were different, that is to say, our world would not even look the same to us.

Many of us, for example, cannot distinguish between pickerel, pike, salmon, smelts, perch, crappies, halibut, and mackerel; we say that they are "just fish, and I don't like fish." To a seafood connoisseur, however, these distinctions are real, since they mean the difference to him between one kind of good meal, a very different kind of good meal, or a poor meal. To a zoologist, even finer distinctions become of great importance, since he has other and more general ends in view. When we hear the statement, then, "This fish is a specimen of the pompano, *Trachinotus carolinus*," we accept this as being "true," even if we don't care, not because that is its "right name," but because that is how it is *classified* in the most complete and most general system of classification which people most deeply interested in fish have evolved.

When we name something, then, we are classifying. *The individual object or event we are naming, of course, has no name and belongs to no class until we put it in one.* To illustrate again, suppose that we were to give the *extensional* meaning of the word "Korean." We would have to point to all "Koreans" living at a particular moment and say, "The word 'Korean' denotes at the present moment these persons: $A_1, A_2, A_3 \ldots A_n$." Now, let us say, a child, whom we shall designate as Z, is born among these "Koreans." *The extensional meaning of the word "Korean," determined prior to the existence of Z, does not include Z.* Z is a new individual belonging to no classification, since all classifications were made without taking Z into account. Why, then, is Z also a "Korean"? *Because we say so.* And, saying so—fixing the classification—we have determined to a considerable extent future attitudes toward Z. For example, Z will always have certain rights in Korea; he will always be regarded in other nations as an "alien" and will be subject to laws applicable to "aliens."

In matters of "race" and "nationality," the way in which classifications work is especially apparent. For example, the present writer is by birth a "Canadian," by "race" a "Japanese," and is now an "American." Although he was legally admitted to the United States on a Canadian passport as a "non-quota immigrant," he was unable to apply for American citizenship until after 1952. According to American immigration law (since 1952 as well as before), a Canadian entering the United States as a permanent resident has no trouble getting in, unless he happens to be of Oriental extraction, in which case his "nationality" becomes irrelevant and he is classified by "race." If the quota for his "race"—for example, Japanese—is filled (and it usually is), and if he cannot get himself classified as a non-quota immigrant, he is not able to get in at all. Are all these classifications "real"? Of course they are, and *the effect that each of them has upon what he may and may not do constitutes their "reality."*

The writer has spent his entire life, except for short visits abroad, in Canada and the United States. He speaks Japanese haltingly, with a child's vocabulary and an American accent; he does not read or write it. Nevertheless, because classifications seem to have a kind of hypnotic power over some people, he is occasionally credited with (or accused of) having an "Oriental mind." Since Buddha, Confucius, General Tojo, Mao Tse-tung, Pandit Nehru, Syngman Rhee, and the proprietor of the Golden Pheasant Chop Suey House all have "Oriental minds," it is difficult to know whether to feel complimented or insulted.

When is a person a "Negro"? By the definition accepted in the United States, any person with even a small amount of "Negro blood"—that is, whose parents or ancestors were classified as "Negroes"—is a "Negro." *It would be exactly as justifiable to say that any person with even a small amount of "white blood" is "white."* Why do they say one rather than the other? Because the former system of classification *suits the purposes of those making the classification.* Classification is not a matter of identifying "essences," as is widely believed. It is simply a reflection of social convenience and necessity—and different necessities are always producing different classifications.

There are few complexities about classifications at the level of dogs and cats, knives and forks, cigarettes and candy, but when it comes to classifications at high levels of abstraction—for example, those describing conduct, social institutions, philosophical and moral problems—serious difficulties occur. When one person kills another, is it an act of murder, an act of temporary insanity, an act of homicide, an accident, or an act of heroism? As soon as the process of classification is completed, our attitudes and our conduct are to a considerable degree determined. We hang the murderer, we lock up the insane man, we free the victim of circumstances, we pin a medal on the hero.

The Blocked Mind

Unfortunately, people are not always aware of the way in which they arrive at their classifications. Unaware of those characteristics of the extensional Mr. Miller not covered by classifying him as "a Jew," and attributing to Mr. Miller all the characteristics *suggested* by the affective connotations of the term with which he has been classified, they pass final judgment on Mr. Miller by saying, "Well, a Jew's a Jew. There's no getting around that!"

We need not concern ourselves here with the injustices done to "Jews," "Roman Catholics," "Republicans," "red-heads," "chorus girls," "sailors," "brass-hats," "Southerners," "Yankees," "school teachers," "government regulations," "socialistic proposals," and so on, by such hasty judgments or, as it is better to call them, fixed reactions. "Hasty judgments" suggests that such errors can be avoided by thinking more slowly; this, of course, is not the case, for some people think very slowly with no better results. What we are concerned with is the way in which we block the development of our own minds by such automatic reactions.

To continue with our example of the people who say, "A Jew's a Jew. There's no getting around that!"—they are, as we have seen, confusing the denoted, extensional Jew with the fictitious "Jew" inside their heads. Such persons, the reader will have observed, can usually be made to admit, on being reminded of certain "Jews" whom they admire—perhaps Albert Einstein, perhaps Associate Justice Arthur Goldberg, perhaps Jascha Heifetz, perhaps Mort Sahl—that "there are exceptions, of course." They have been compelled by experience, that is to say, to take cognizance of at least a few of the multitude of "Jews" who do not fit their preconceptions. At this point, however, they continue triumphantly, "But exceptions only prove the rule!" [1]—which is another way of saying, "Facts don't count."

The writer, who lives in Marin County, California, once attended hearings at the county court house concerning a proposed ordinance to forbid racial discrimination in the rental and sale of housing. (Such discrimination in Marin is chiefly directed against Negroes.) He was impressed by the fact that a large majority of those who rose to speak were in favor of the ordinance; but he was

---

[1] This extraordinarily fatuous saying originally meant, "The exception *tests* the rule"—*Exceptio probat regulam*. This older meaning of the word "prove" survives in such an expression as "automobile proving ground."

also impressed by the number who, though maintaining that they counted Negroes among their best and most admired friends, still spoke heatedly against a law that would, by forbidding racial discrimination in the sale and rental of housing, enable Negroes to live anywhere in the county. Presumably, all the Negroes whom they loved and admired were "exceptions," and the stereotyped "Negro" remained in their heads in spite of their experience.

People like this may be said to be impervious to new information. They continue to vote for their party *label,* no matter what mistakes their party makes. They continue to object to "socialists," no matter what the socialists propose. They continue to regard "mothers" as sacred, no matter which mother. A woman who had been given up both by physicians and psychiatrists as hopelessly insane was being considered by a committee whose task it was to decide whether or not she should be committed to an asylum. One member of the committee doggedly refused to vote for commitment. "Gentlemen," he said in tones of deepest reverence, "you must remember that this woman is, after all, a mother." [2] Similarly such people continue to hate "Protestants," no matter which Protestant. Unaware of characteristics left out in the process of classification, they overlook, when the term "Republican" is applied to the party of Abraham Lincoln, the party of Warren Harding, the party of Herbert Hoover, and the party of Dwight Eisenhower, the rather important differences between them.

Cow₁ Is Not Cow₂

How do we prevent ourselves from getting into such intellectual blind alleys, or, finding we are in one, how do we get out again? One way is to remember that practically all statements in ordinary conversation, debate, and public controversy taking the form, "Republicans are Republicans," "Business is business," "Boys will be boys," "Women drivers are women drivers," and so on, are *not true.* Let us put one of these back into a context in life.

> "I don't think we should go through with this deal, Bill. Is it altogether fair to the railroad company?"
> "Aw, forget it! *Business is business,* after all."

[2] One wonders how this committee member would have felt about Elizabeth Duncan, executed for murder in San Quentin in 1962, whose possessive love of her son led her to hire assassins to kill her pregnant daughter-in-law.

Such an assertion, although it looks like a "simple statement of fact," is not simple and is not a statement of fact. The first "business" *denotes* transaction under discussion; the second "business" invokes the *connotations* of the word. The sentence is a *directive,* saying, "Let us treat this transaction with complete disregard for considerations other than profit, as the word 'business' suggests." Similarly, when a father tries to excuse the mischief done by his sons, he says, "Boys will be boys"; in other words, "Let us regard the actions of my sons with that indulgent amusement customarily extended toward those whom we call 'boys,'" though the angry neighbor will say, of course, "Boys, my eye! They're little hoodlums; that's what they are!" These too are not informative statements but directives, directing us to classify the object or event under discussion in given ways, in order that we may feel or act in the ways suggested by the terms of the classification.

There is a simple technique for preventing such directives from having their harmful effect on our thinking. It is the suggestion made by Korzybski that we add "index numbers" to our terms, thus: $Englishman_1$, $Englishman_2$, $Englishman_3$, . . . ; cow_1, cow_2, cow_3, . . . ; $Frenchman_1$, $Frenchman_2$, $Frenchman_3$, . . . ; $communist_1$, $communist_2$, $communist_3$, . . . The terms of the classification tell us what the individuals in that class have in common; *the index numbers remind us of the characteristics left out.* A rule can then be formulated as a general guide in all our thinking and reading: *Cow_1 is not cow_2; Jew_1 is not Jew_2; $politician_1$ is not $politician_2$, and so on.* This rule, if remembered, prevents us from confusing levels of abstraction and forces us to consider the facts on those occasions when we might otherwise find ourselves leaping to conclusions which we might later have cause to regret.

"Truth"

Most intellectual problems are, ultimately, problems of classification and nomenclature. Some years ago there was a dispute between the American Medical Association and the Antitrust Division of the Department of Justice as to whether the practice of medicine was a "profession" or "trade." The American Medical Association *wanted* immunity from laws prohibiting "restraint of trade"; therefore, it insisted that medicine *is* a "profession." The Antitrust Division *wanted* to stop certain economic practices connected with medicine, and therefore it insisted that medicine *is* a "trade."

Partisans of either side accused the other of perverting the meanings of words and of not being able to understand plain English.

Can farmers operate oil wells and still be "farmers"? In 1947 the attorney general of the state of Kansas sued to dissolve a large agricultural cooperative, Consumers Cooperative Association, charging that the corporation, in owning oil wells, refineries, and pipe-lines, was exceeding the statutory privileges of purchasing cooperatives under the Cooperative Marketing Act, which permits such organizations to "engage in any activity in connection with manufacturing, selling, or supplying to its members machinery, equipment or supplies." The attorney general held that the cooperative, under the Act, could not handle, let alone process and manufacture, general farm supplies, but only those supplies used in the marketing operation. The Kansas Supreme Court decided unanimously in favor of the defendant (CCA). In so deciding, the court held that gasoline and oil *are* "farm supplies," and producing crude oil *is* "part of the business of farming." The decision which thus enlarged the definition of "farming" read,

> This court will take judicial notice of the fact that in the present state of the art of farming, gasoline . . . is one of the costliest items in the production of agricultural commodities. . . . Anyway, gasoline and tractors are here, and this court is not going to say that motor fuel is not a supply necessary to carrying on of farm operations. . . . Indeed it is about as well put as can be on Page 18 of the state's Exhibit C where the defendant (CCA) says: *"Producing crude oil, operating pipe-lines and refineries, are also part of the business of farming. It is merely producing synthetic hay for iron horses. It is 'off-the-farm farming' which the farmer, in concert with his neighbors, is carrying on. . . . Production of power farming equipment, then, is logically an extension of the farmers' own farming operations."* (Italics supplied.)

Is a harmonica player a "musician"? Until 1948, the American Federation of Musicians had ruled that the harmonica was a "toy." Professional harmonica players usually belonged, therefore, to the American Guild of Variety Artists. Even as distinguished a musician as Larry Adler, who has often played the harmonica as a solo instrument with symphony orchestras, was by the union's definition "not a musician." In 1948, however, the AFM, finding that harmonica players were getting popular and competing with members of the union, decided that they were "musicians" after all—a decision that did not sit well with the president of AGVA, who promptly declared jurisdictional war on the AFM.[3]

Thurman Arnold tells of another instance of a problem in classification:

> A plaster company was scraping gypsum from the surface of the ground. If it was a mine, it paid one tax; if a manufacturing company, it paid another. Expert witnesses were called who almost came to blows, such was their disgust at the stupidity of those who could not see that the process was essentially mining, or manufacturing. A great record was built up to be reviewed by the State Supreme Court on this important question of "fact." [4]

Is aspirin a "drug" or not? In some states, it is legally classified as a "drug," and therefore it can be sold only by licensed pharmacists. If people want to be able to buy aspirin in groceries, lunchrooms, and pool halls (as they can in other states), they must have it reclassified as "not a drug."

Is medicine a "profession" or a "trade"? Is the production of crude oil "a part of farming"? Is a harmonica player a "musician"? Is aspirin a "drug"? Such questions are commonly settled by appeals to dictionaries to discover the "real meanings" of the words involved. It is also common practice to consult past legal decisions and all kinds of learned treatises bearing on the subject. The decision finally rests, however, not upon appeals to past authority, but upon *what people want*. If they want the AMA to be immune from antitrust action, they will go to the Supreme Court if necessary to get medicine "defined" as a "profession." If they want the AMA prosecuted, they will get a decision that it is a "trade." (They got, in this case, a decision from the Court that it did not matter whether the practice of medicine was a "trade" or not; what mattered was that the AMA had, as charged, *restrained* the trade of Group Health Association, Inc., a cooperative which procured medical services for its members. The antitrust action was upheld.)

If people want agricultural cooperatives to operate oil wells, they will get the courts to define the activity in such a way as to make it possible. If the public doesn't care, the decision whether a harmonica

---

[3] "The S.F. Police Dept. Bagpipe Band . . . will soon be decked out in the traditional finery of bagpipers. Pan-Am is flying over from Scotland 21 uniforms. . . . The pipers, by the way, don't have to belong to the Musicians Union since the bagpipe is classified as 'an instrument of war.' Has there ever been any doubt?" Herb Caen in the San Francisco *Chronicle*.

[4] *The Folklore of Capitalism* (1938), p. 182.

player is or is not a "musician" will be made by the stronger trade union. The question whether aspirin is or is not a "drug" will be decided neither by finding the dictionary definition of "drug" nor by staring long and hard at an aspirin tablet. It will be decided on the basis of where and under what conditions people want to buy their aspirin.

In any case, society as a whole ultimately gets, on all issues of wide public importance, the classifications it wants, even if it has to wait until all the members of the Supreme Court are dead and an entirely new court is appointed. When the desired decision is handed down, people say, "Truth has triumphed." *In short, society regards as "true" those systems of classification that produce the desired results.*

The scientific test of "truth," like the social test, is strictly practical, except for the fact that the "desired results" are more severely limited. The results desired by society may be irrational, superstitious, selfish, or humane, but the results desired by scientists are only that our systems of classification produce predictable results. Classifications, as amply indicated already, determine our attitudes and behavior toward the object or event classified. When lightning was classified as "evidence of divine wrath," no courses of action other than prayer were suggested to prevent one's being struck by lightning. As soon, however, as it was classified as "electricity," Benjamin Franklin achieved a measure of control over it by his invention of the lightning rod. Certain physical disorders were formerly classified as "demonic possession," and this suggested that we "drive the demons out" by whatever spells or incantations we could think of. The results were uncertain. But when those disorders were classified as "bacillus infections," courses of action were suggested that led to more predictable results.

Science seeks only the *most generally useful* systems of classification; these it regards for the time being, until more useful classifications are invented, as "true."

APPLICATIONS

I. Study carefully a page of jokes in a popular magazine, the script of a variety show, or the text of a comedy, and note the extent to which humor is dependent upon sudden and unexpected *shifts of classification.* For example, a comedy drummer may start beating time on someone's head, thus *reclassifying* a head as a musical instrument. Here are a few examples, starting with some real chestnuts:

1. "I'm sorry," said the dentist. "I can't give you an appointment today. I have eighteen cavities to fill." Then he picked up his golf bag and was gone.   *—Wall Street Journal*

2. "The difference between bop and Dixieland? In bop, they flat their fifths; in Dixieland, we drink them."   —attributed to Eddie Condon

3. Two Hollywood producers were watching the star of a Las Vegas show. "I wonder who made her dress?" said one of them admiringly.

   "It's hard to say," said the other. "Probably the police."

4. PRISON LIBRARIAN: And what would you like to read today?

   PRISONER: Got any escape literature?

5. He looked out of the window and called to his wife, "There goes that woman Bill Jones is in love with."

   She dropped the cup she was drying, hurtled through the door, craned her neck to look. "Where?" she panted.

   "There," he pointed, "that woman at the corner in the tweed coat."

   "You idiot," she said. "That's his wife."

   "Of course," he replied.   *—Wall Street Journal*

6. KHRUSHCHEV (shown in a cartoon handing a Russian general a rocket): Remember, ours are called *factors of peace* and theirs, *instruments of aggression.*   *—Settimana* (Rome)

7. In a small town that was borderland South, three youngsters, two of them white and the third a Negro, burst into the soda fountain, clambered onto the stools, and ordered chocolate milk shakes. The owner, who was behind the counter, took in the situation at a glance. With baseball gloves hanging out of their jeans, the boys had obviously come from the community's newly integrated play program.

   "I'm sorry, boys," the man began in a not unkind but firm tone of voice. "Don't you know we have segregation here?"

   "Sure," answered one of the white boys, "but we've segregated him. He's sitting between us!"   *—Reader's Digest*

8. At a textile machinery plant in Worcester, Teddy [Edward F. Kennedy, campaigning for the U.S. Senate] moved eagerly through the din and smell of hot metal to shake the hands of the men in the foundry. . . . Everything went Teddy's way. At one point, a worker buttonholed him and said, "Teddy, me boy, they say you've never worked a day in your life." After an uneasy pause, the man added: "Let me tell you, you haven't missed a thing."   *—Time*

9. TAXI DRIVER: It's not just the work I enjoy. It's the people I run into. —*Breck's Gold Box*

II. Read carefully and comment on the following:

1. I am writing on behalf of a group of Chinese in the United States who . . . are suffering under a grave injustice. They are those who have overstayed the terms of their admission into the United States but who cannot return to mainland China because they would face physical persecution. . . . More than 500 of them, I understand, are now to be sent to Holland. The basis for this is that they entered the United States on Dutch ships. . . . These Chinese have never been in Holland, but merely shipped on vessels of Dutch registry. The situation is analogous to a Chinese seaman on an American vessel which he deserts in another country. Would the United States at the request of that country agree to the deportation of such a Chinese seaman to the United States?
—Letter from Pearl Buck, New York *Post*

2. WASHINGTON, Aug. 29—The cow became a horse, and now it's quite all right to shoot the beast. It's a tale of mystic India, told in testimony at Senate hearings on the new foreign aid bill. A big wild animal of the antelope family and known as the "Nehil Gae" was causing extensive damage to crops in the field. But the farmers would not harm it because "Nehil Gae" means "Blue Cow," and the cow is sacred to the Hindu. So the Indian Government has changed the name to "Nehil Goa"—which means "Blue Horse." Horses are not sacred, and so now the beast can be killed to protect the crops.
—Associated Press

3. The workings of the retail excise tax would stump many a Phi Beta Kappa man. The drugstore clerk may be pardoned for not knowing, for example, that shampoos advertised for their beautifying qualities are taxable as cosmetics, while those touted for cleaning properties are classed as soaps (provided, of course, they contain the requisite percentage of "saponaceous matter"). Cleanliness being next to godliness, soap is exempt from taxation.
—New York *Times Magazine*

4. The diatoms are not the only wonders offered us by Lake Michigan. There are the flagellates, which present characters of both the animal and the plant world, to such an extent that it is impossible to decide to which of the two great groups in which man has divided the living world these belong. For instance, in comparing a cat and a daisy, it is easy to apply our classification keys and decide which is plant and which is animal. Such keys, however, do not easily apply to this minute organism, for man's methods of classifying

living material were made before he encountered this form of life. Therefore, in observing the specialities of *Euglena viridis,* we find that it contains chlorophyll as do most plants, that it moves about as do most animals (and some plants), and that it feeds at times as an animal does but at other times as a plant, manufacturing its own food with the aid of sunlight.

—*Bulletin* of the Chicago Natural History Museum

5. A Roman Catholic cannot be a Jew, the Israeli Supreme Court ruled last week. Before the court was the case of Father Daniel, a Polish-born Jew who was converted to Catholicism and became a Carmelite friar. He had claimed Israeli citizenship under provisions of the country's Law of Return, which declares: "Every Jew shall be entitled to come to Israel as an immigrant." . . . Said the judge: . . . No one can regard an apostate as belonging to the Jewish people.   —*Time*

6. You begin the interview [with Malcolm X, leader of the Black Muslim movement] by asking why his second name is "X." He grins and replies, "During slavery days black men were given the names of their masters—like the branding of cattle. Smith, Jones, and Williams are not African names; they're Anglo-Saxon names that were forced upon the so-called Negro. Rather than bear the brand of a slave-master, we Muslims change our second names to X—which is the Arabic symbol for the unknown. It removes the white man's stigma."

Why does he use the expression, "so-called Negro"?

"Not content with stripping us of our names," states Malcolm, "the white man, in his evilness, stripped us of our humanity. . . . So the white man made up a special name for his slave-animal— 'Negro.' It's a synthetic name that means low, filthy beast. We want no part of it."   —*Saga*

III. There is a psychological test which can be made the basis for an interesting exercise in one's own home—especially in a home with children. Lay on a table an assortment of objects from all over the house: hammer, screw driver, toy hammer, toy screw driver, pipe, bubble pipe, kitchen equipment, metal spoon, plastic spoon, electrical-equipment parts, scissors, fishing or sports equipment, and so forth, until you have twenty-five or more objects. Ask your friends to divide the objects into two piles, and to do this at least five times, using different systems of classification each time—but don't suggest the systems. Make a note of the systems of classification used and the order in which they come (e.g., painted and unpainted; metal and non-metal; toys and non-toys). Make notes, too, on the points at which people show marked indecision (e.g., do toy hammers belong with tools or non-tools? is an object made of hard molded rubber a plastic or a non-plastic?) and note also what objects seem to remain unclassifiable. When classifications are made that you don't understand, ask about them. If people insist that two categories are not enough and make a third or fourth pile, make a note of the reasoning. Write up the results, drawing any conclusions you can.

Salvatore Russo and Howard Jaques have written a paper, "Semantic Play Therapy," [5] which deals with an emotionally disturbed eleven-year-old boy who "clung so rigidly to his categories that he was enslaved by them. . . . When his stubborn use of categories became frustrating or painful, he . . . resorted to sulking, crying, or temper tantrums." The authors describe the treatment given the boy; it consisted mostly of having him play this sorting game with piles of assorted objects. This paper is instructive to read in connection with the Application above.

IV. Here are some difficult problems in classification:

1. What is likely to be a speaker's intention when he says, "What people ordinarily call rabbits are really hares, and what they call hares are really rabbits"?

2. When a corporation is classified as a "person," what are the characteristics of "persons" (as the word is understood in everyday, non-legal speech) attributed to corporations? What are the characteristics of "persons" left out of consideration in this classification?

3. Under what circumstances are tomatoes classified as a "fruit" and under what circumstances as a "vegetable"? How else can they be classified?

4. When is an athlete an "amateur"? Investigate the rules for determining "amateur standing" in three or four different areas of sport (football, boxing, tennis, polo, and so forth) and the various methods used to give substantial compensation to "amateurs" so as not to jeopardize their "amateur standing." In England, until 1962, a distinction was made between "gentlemen" (amateurs) and "players" (professionals); they dressed in different rooms and ate at different tables, even when playing together on the same cricket teams. Why did the distinction exist, and why was it abolished? Why, in college football, do we not put athletes on a straight, professional, salary basis, or, on the other hand, make the sport "completely amateur," i.e., without material compensation of any kind?

[5] *ETC.*, XIII (1956), pp. 265–71; reprinted in Hayakawa, ed., *Our Language and Our World* (1959), pp. 133–40.

5. Is motherhood an act of God? This question, involving all the profundities of metaphysics, faith, and physiology, might well give pause to anyone, however learned. The answer YES would surely affront countless atheists and agnostics. The answer NO would just as surely anger multitudes of the pious. Yet several men were actually confronted with this question last week and expected to make a public reply.

Actress Helen Hayes, wife of Playwright Charles MacArthur, lately withdrew from the play *Coquette,* then on the road, saying: "I am going to have a baby." Producer Jed Harris ordered the play closed without notice. Five members of the cast at once demanded extra salary, said that Mr. Harris had violated the rules of Actors' Equity Association.

The question depended on the Equity contract clause stating: "The management is not responsible for fire, strikes, or an act of God." Mr. Harris declared the expected MacArthur baby was certainly "an act of God." The protesting actors said it was no such thing.

Equity arbitrators then met, discussed God and his acts. Appalled by the cosmic dimensions of their dilemma, they adjourned, wordless.
—*Time* (1929)

Advise the Equity arbitrators on the course of action most likely to secure general approval.

6. Comment on the following story from the Chicago *Sun-Times:*

WASHINGTON: (UP)—The House voted Monday to make the word "wife" mean "husband" too—sometimes. It passed and sent to the Senate a bill extending to dependent husbands of women veterans the same pay and privileges given to dependent wives of men veterans. It was done by defining the word wife to mean husband, too, when that's necessary.

V. Sweden is said to have the highest suicide rate in the world. But people have pointed out that the rate only appears to be high, because many deaths which are classified in other ways in other countries are *classified* as "suicides" in Sweden. Perhaps some readers will find this question worth looking into: Is there a higher suicide rate in Sweden than elsewhere? What are some of the meanings of the word "suicide"?

(In this connection, Dr. F. G. Crookshank has suggested that a reported increase in the incidence of a given disease, let us say disease X, may mean only that more doctors are giving the *name* X to the ailments their patients are suffering from—so that it is the *diagnosis,* not the disease, that is increasing:

Medical statistics relate to the usage of symbols for general references, whether or not the symbolization is correct and the references adequate, rather than to things, occurrences, or happenings. They have no necessary value, other than as analyses of symbol-frequency, unless the relation of the symbols . . . to the referents be agreed. . . .

See "The Importance of a Theory of Signs and a Critique of Language in the Study of Medicine," Supplement II, in *The Meaning of Meaning,* by C. K. Ogden and I. A. Richards.)

VI. According to at least one author, index numbers are not nearly so important as is claimed in this chapter. Indeed, they are a hindrance to necessary social action. Comment on this criticism, which is vigorously argued in the following passage:

One can imagine a semanticist in Poland, France, Norway, Greece, or any other country occupied by the Nazis. . . . Here, where revolutionary resistance to alien oppression was the only constructive therapy, the treacherous effects of the cult [of semantics] would have been clear. $Nazi_1$ was not the same as $Nazi_2$ or $Nazi_3$, to be sure, but more important for the victims was the functioning of all Nazis in a single pattern of destructive, anti-human behavior. In the coming period, with its sharpened imperialist rivalries so dreadfully jeopardizing our efforts toward world peace, there will no doubt be further destructive group actions which must be countered by positive and heroic struggles toward constructive ends. The alternatives are critical as never before in human history. In these times, harkening to the semantic cult is . . . rendering ourselves completely defenseless while we indulge in private games. For this reason I believe the vogue must not be dismissed as another curious but unimportant preoccupation of quasi-intellectuals. It must be clearly revealed as a menace to the constructive social action so sorely needed today, and vigorously opposed. —MARGARET SCHLAUCH, "The Cult of the Proper Word," *New Masses*

13 The Two-Valued Orientation

*People with college educations, the student said, know
more, and hence are better judges of people. But
aren't you assuming, I asked, that a college education gives not only what we usually call "knowledge"
but also what we usually call "shrewdness" or "wisdom"? Oh, he said, you mean that there isn't any
use in going to college!* —FRANCIS P. CHISHOLM

*Once we have cast another group in the role of the
enemy, we know that they are to be distrusted—that
they are evil incarnate. We then twist all their communications to fit our belief.* —JEROME D. FRANK

In the expression, "We must listen to both sides of every question,"
there is an assumption, frequently unexamined, that every question
has two sides—and only two sides. We tend to think in opposites,
to feel that what is not good must be bad, and that what is not
bad must be good. When children are taught English history, for
example, the first thing they want to know about every ruler is
whether he was a "good king" or a "bad king." Much popular political
thought, like the plots of television westerns, views the world as divided
into "good guys" and "bad guys"—those who believe in "one-hundred-
per-cent Americanism" as opposed to those who harbor "un-American ideas." The same tendency is clearly discernible in those who do
not believe in the existence of "neutralist" nations; any nation that is
not fully committed to "our side" in the cold war is believed to be on
the Russian side. This proneness to divide the world into two opposing
forces—"right" versus "wrong," "good" versus "evil"—and to ignore or deny the existence of any middle ground, may be termed
the *two-valued orientation*.

In a situation of actual physical combat, the two-valued orientation is inevitable—and necessary. Total absorption in the fight re-

duces reality for the time being into two, and only two, objects of concern—myself and the enemy. This narrowed view of the world is accompanied by accelerated heart-beat and circulation, increased muscular tension, and the release by the adrenal glands of hormones into the blood to contract the arteries and thus slow down the flow of blood in case of injury. This ability to direct and mobilize one's entire mental and physical resources in the face of physical danger— which the physiologist Walter B. Cannon described as the "fight or flight" mechanism—has been necessary to survival through most of the long history of the human race, and probably remains so.

However, for the symbol-using class of life at a high level of cultural development, fighting and fleeing, the primitive outlets for fear, hatred, and anger, are not available. Although we may some- times get angry enough at our rivals and enemies to *want* to strike them down, or even to kill them, we have to content ourselves most of the time with *verbal* assaults: calling them names, criticizing them, reporting them to the boss, writing letters of complaint or accusation, outmaneuvering them in social or business competition, or in rare cases instituting lawsuits against them. Words are not blows, name- calling breaks no bones, and even a smashing insult results in no loss of blood. Hence, some individuals—especially those who are quick to lose their tempers and slow to regain them—are in an al- most constant state of overstimulation under the influence of a higher-than-necessary concentration of adrenal hormones in their systems. For such people, the two-valued orientation is a way of life.

The Two-Valued Orientation in Politics

Under a two-party political system such as we have in the United States, there is abundant occasion for uttering two-valued pronounce- ments. The writer has often listened to political speeches carried by sound-trucks in crowded Chicago streets and he has been impressed with the thoroughness with which the Republicans (or Democrats) have been castigated and the Democrats (or Republicans) praised. Not a shadow of faint praise or even of extenuation is offered to the opposing party. When the writer asked a candidate for state repre- sentative why this was so, he was told, "Among our folks, it don't pay to be subtle."

Fortunately, most voters regard this two-valuedness of political debate as "part of the game," especially around election time, so that it does not appear to have uniformly harmful consequences;

overstatements on either side are at least partially canceled out by overstatements on the other. Nevertheless, there remains a portion of the electorate—*and this portion is by no means confined to the uneducated*—who take the two-valued orientation seriously. These are the people (and the newspapers) who speak of their opponents as if they were enemies of the nation rather than fellow-Americans with differing views as to what is good for the nation.

On the whole, however, a two-valued *orientation* in politics is difficult to maintain in a two-party system of government. The parties have to cooperate with each other between elections and therefore have to assume that members of the opposition are something short of fiends in human form. The public, too, in a two-party system, sees that the dire predictions of Republicans regarding the probable results of Democratic rule, and the equally dire predictions of the Democrats regarding Republican rule, are never more than partially fulfilled. Furthermore, criticism of the administration is not only possible, it is energetically encouraged by the opposition. Hence the majority of people can never quite be convinced that one party is "wholly good" and the other "wholly bad."

But when a nation's traditions (or its lack of traditions) permit a political party to feel that it is *so good for the country that no other party has any business existing*—and such a party gets control—there is immediate silencing of opposition. In such a case the party declares its philosophy to be the official philosophy of the nation and its interest to be the interests of the people as a whole. "Whoever is an enemy of the National Socialist party," as the Nazis said, "is an enemy of Germany." Even if you loved Germany greatly, but still didn't agree with the National Socialists as to what was good for Germany, you were liquidated. *Under the one-party system, the two-valued orientation, in its most primitive form, becomes the official national outlook.*

Because the Nazis carried the two-valued orientation to extremes never before reached by a political party—extremes of ridiculousness as well as extremes of barbarity—it is worth while recalling, in the context of semantic study, some of the techniques they used. First of all, the two-valued assumption was explicitly stated over and over again:

> Discussion of matters affecting our existence and that of the nation must cease altogether. Anyone who dares to question the rightness of the National Socialist outlook will be branded as a traitor.
>
> —HERR SAUCKEL, Nazi Governor of Thuringia, June 20, 1933

Everyone in Germany is a National Socialist—the few outside the party are either lunatics or idiots.

> —ADOLF HITLER, at Klagenfurt, Austria, on April 4, 1938.
> Quoted by New York *Times,* April 5, 1938

Everyone not using the greeting "Heil Hitler" or using it only occasionally and unwillingly, shows he is an opponent of the Fuehrer or a pathetic turn-coat . . . The German people's only greeting is "Heil Hitler." Whoever does not use it must recognize that he will be regarded as outside the community of the German nation.

> —Labor Front chiefs in Saxony, December 5, 1937

National Socialists say: Legality is that which does the German people good; illegality is that which harms the German people.

> —DR. FRICK, Minister of the Interior

Anyone or anything that stood in the way of Hitler's wishes was "Jewish," "degenerate," "corrupt," "democratic," "internationalist," and, as a crowning insult, "non-Aryan." On the other hand, everything that Hitler chose to call "Aryan" was by definition noble, virtuous, heroic, and altogether glorious. Courage, self-discipline, honor, beauty, health, and joy were "Aryan." Whatever he called upon people to do, he told them to do "to fulfill their Aryan heritage."

An incredible number of areas were examined in terms of this two-valued orientation: art, books, people, calisthenics, mathematics, physics, dogs, cats, architecture, morals, cookery, religion. If Hitler approved, it was "Aryan"; if he disapproved, it was "non-Aryan" or "Jewish-dominated."

We request that every hen lay 130 to 140 eggs a year. The increase can not be achieved by the bastard hens (non-Aryan) which now populate German farm yards. Slaughter these undesirables and replace them. . . .   —Nazi Party News Agency, April 3, 1937

The rabbit, it is certain, is no German animal, if only for its painful timidity. It is an immigrant who enjoys a guest's privilege. As for the lion, one sees in him indisputably German fundamental characteristics. Thus one could call him a German abroad.

> —GENERAL LUDENDORFF, in *Am Quell Deutscher Kraft*

Proper breathing is a means of acquiring heroic national mentality. The art of breathing was formerly characteristic of true Aryanism and known to all Aryan leaders. . . . Let the people again practice the old Aryan wisdom.

> —Berlin *Weltpolitische Rundschau,* quoted in *The Nation*

Cows or cattle which were bought from Jews directly or indirectly may not be bred with the community bull.

> —Mayor of the Community of Koenigsdorf, Bavaria.
> *Tegernseerzeitung,* Nazi Party organ, October 1, 1935

There is no place for Heinrich Heine in any collection of works of German poets. . . . When we reject Heine, it is not because we consider every line he wrote bad. The decisive factor is that this man was a Jew. Therefore, there is no place for him in German literature.

> —*Schwarze Korps*

Because the Japanese were, before and during World War II, on friendly terms with Hitler's Germany, they were classified as "Aryans." At one point in the war, when Germany was hoping for Mexico as an ally, the German ambassador in Mexico City announced that Mexicans were members of the Nordic race who had emigrated by way of the Bering Straits and come south! But the greatest error in classification that the Nazis made was when they labeled certain theories in physics as "non-Aryan," and deprived of his property, position, and citizenship the originator of those theories, Albert Einstein. Hitler could hardly have guessed then that those same theories would have military consequences beyond his wildest dreams.

The connection between the two-valued orientation and combat is clearly apparent in the history of Nazism. From the moment Hitler achieved power, he told the German people that they were surrounded by enemies. Long before World War II started, the German people were called upon to act as if a war were already in progress. Everyone, including women and children, was pressed into "war" service of one kind or another. In order to keep the combative sense from fizzling out for want of tangible enemies before the start of actual warfare, the people were kept fighting at home against alleged enemies within the gates: principally the Jews, but also anyone else whom the Nazis happened to dislike. Education, too, was made to serve the purposes of war and to create a warlike spirit:

> There is no such thing as knowledge for its own sake. Science can only be the soldierly training of our minds for service to the nation. The university must be a battleground for the organization of the intellect. Heil Adolf Hitler and his eternal Reich!
>
> —Rector of Jena University

The task of universities is not to teach objective science, but the militant, the warlike, the heroic.

—DR. DRIECK, headmaster of the Mannheim public schools [1]

The official National Socialist orientation never permitted a relaxation of the two-valued conviction that nothing is too good for the "good," and nothing is too bad for the "bad," and *that there is no middle ground.* "Whoever is not for us is against us!"

Man's Inhumanity to Man

The cruelties of the Nazi treatment of Jews and other "enemies"— the wholesale executions, the gas chambers, the "scientific" experiments in torture, starvation, and vivisection performed on political prisoners—have often taxed the credulity of the outside world. Stories of Nazi prison camps and death chambers are still regarded in some quarters as wartime anti-Nazi fabrications.

To the student of two-valued orientations, however, these stories are credible. If good is "absolutely good" and evil is "absolutely evil," the logic of a primitive, two-valued orientation demands that "evil" be exterminated by every means available. Murdering Jews becomes, under this orientation, a moral duty—to be carried out systematically and conscientiously. Judging from the evidence produced at the Nuremberg trials as well as at the Eichmann trial, this appears to be how the task was regarded. Nazi prison guards and executioners carried out their ghastly tasks, not in rage or in fiendish glee, but simply as matters of duty. So completely had the abstraction "Jew" blotted out all other perceptions, that killing Jews became pretty much a matter of course. Aldous Huxley has said that it is the function of propaganda to enable people to do in cold blood things that they could otherwise do only in the heat of passion. Two-valued propaganda, seriously believed, has precisely this effect.

The Marxist Two-Valued Orientation

The orientation of Russian communist spokesmen is also notoriously two-valued, the world being divided, in their view, into "peace-loving, progressive, scientific, materialist socialists," like themselves, and

[1] The National Socialist pronouncements quoted in this chapter are from a collection of such utterances by Adolf Hitler and his associates, compiled by Clara Leiser and published under the title *Lunacy Becomes Us* (1939).

"war-mongering, bourgeois, reactionary, idealist, imperialistic capitalists," like us—or anyone else who disagrees with their views. Because the communists are extremely concerned with ideology, there is no talk of "blood," "instinct," and "soul" as there was in Nazi Germany, and much talk about "historical necessity," "the class struggle," "objective reality," and "the nature of capitalist exploitation and colonialism." Nazi Germany offers classic examples of the two-valued orientation in rabble-rousing and popular oratory. Russian communism offers the best examples of the two-valued orientation among social theorists, philosophers, and intellectuals.

Lenin molded the theories of Karl Marx into a political weapon, and the combative fervor of the revolutionist has remained an important ingredient of communist oratory and orientation ever since. Lenin had, as Anatol Rapoport has explained, "an intense compulsion to view each difference of opinion as irreconcilable":

> If someone whom he considered to be in the enemy camp expressed any view acceptable to him, he took great pains to prove that the opponent was either guilty of inconsistency or was muddle-headed, or else (a favorite explanation) was masking his real nature. If someone in his own camp expressed a view unacceptable to him, he again either accused him of muddle-headedness or argued that eventually this view would drive his erring colleague to the complete acceptance of the enemy position. As Lenin wrote, "Enmesh a single claw and the bird is caught. . . . You cannot eliminate one basic assumption, one substantial part of this philosophy of Marxism (it is as if it were a block of steel) without abandoning objective truth, without falling into the arms of bourgeois-reactionary falsehood." [2]

In short, you either agree *completely* with Lenin (or whoever is running the party at the moment) or you are an outcast.

There is a curious preoccupation with *labeling* in Marxist polemics —a need to characterize the ideological position of an individual or a school of thought with an epithet. In analyzing an author's outlook, a philosophical tendency, or a scientific theory, the Marxist critic first of all has to decide "what it *is*." Is it "idealism" or "materialism"? Is it "agnosticism," "bourgeois charlatanism," "empirio-criticism," "fideism," "formalism," "immanentism," or "revisionism"? Is it "Trotskyism," "Kautskyism," "Machism," "Kantianism," or "Berkeleianism"? Is it "Michurinism" or "Weismannism"? Some of these "-isms" are "good," some "bad."

---

[2] "Death of Communication with Russia?" *ETC.*, VIII (1950), p. 89.

When Marxist polemicists decide that something deserves one of the "bad" labels, they let go with both barrels. Thus, B. Bykhovsky, writing in 1947 on "Semantic Philosophy," found it to be "nothing but . . . a neo-nominalism" which is trying to bring back to life a discredited "subjective idealism." Then comes the blast:

> The semantic fad in Anglo-American philosophy is one of the manifestations of the decomposition and decay which characterize the idealist philosophy of the imperialist epoch. . . . The grimaces of the semantic obscurantists, that is, the Walpurgis Night, is celebrated in the darkness which pervades the spiritual life of the modern bourgeoisie. . . . Like all the currents of modern idealist philosophy, semantic idealism is a spiritual weapon of imperialism in its struggle against the progressive ideas of our time. Poisoning the consciousness of the intellectuals with the poison of scepticism, nihilism, and agnosticism, scientific, moral, political, the semanticists are the most vicious enemies of progressive ideas.[3]

The two-valued character of Soviet orientations is ironically illustrated by the career of Stalin. Long idolized as a great leader, the epitome of strength and wisdom and communist virtue (a "good guy"), he was after his death accused of numberless crimes, among them that of building up a "cult of personality" for the sake of personal power and self-aggrandizement. Towns and streets which had been named after him were renamed, and his body was removed from enshrinement and hauled away to be buried in obscurity (a "bad guy"). Apparently official ideology could find no middle ground for him at some point between "great hero" and "great villain."

The present generation in Soviet Russia is not engaged, as an earlier generation was, in the task of building a new social order. The revolution having been won, there is no longer any need for the revolutionary spirit, so that one of the problems for Soviet leadership is the apathy of the public towards yesterday's fighting slogans and

[3] B. Bykhovsky, "The Morass of Modern Bourgeois Philosophy" (trans. Anatol Rapoport), *ETC.*, VI (1948), pp. 13–15. The article appeared originally in the *Bolshevik: A Theoretical Political Journal* (Moscow), August 30, 1947. With the passage of time and the passing of Stalin, a much more temperate view of semantics has emerged from Marxist circles. See *Introduction to Semantics*, by the Polish philosopher Adam Schaff (1962); also G. Brutyan, *Teoria Poznaniya v Obschchei Semantike* [Theory of Cognition in General Semantics] (Erevan: Academy of Sciences of the Armenian S.S.R., 1959). The books by Schaff and Brutyan are discussed by Rapoport in "Two Marxist Critiques of General Semantics," *ETC.*, XVIII (1961), pp. 289–314. The chapter on "General Semantics" from Schaff's book appears in translation in *ETC.*, XIX (1962), pp. 401–18.

fiery polemics. Soviet leaders respond to this apathy by creating crises to keep people united in a common purpose against "threats to peace"—a technique not unknown in other parts of the world. There are indications that more and more young people, instead of being aroused to patriotic fervor by such propaganda, simply get bored.

The official ideology, however, remains as two-valued as ever. The following account of an interview with a Soviet professor of philosophy is given by Maurice Hindus, who has studied the development of the Soviet Union over many years:

"Suppose," I asked, "a student questions the validity of dialectical materialism?"

"You must remember," the professor replied, "that throughout his five years in the university our student takes courses in dialectical materialism and related subjects. Besides, the study of all our courses is permeated with this philosophy. The student cannot possibly question its validity."

"Suppose he disagrees with the professor's position that there is no truth other than what the dialectical materialism he studies reveals to him? In America, students are free to disagree with their professors."

"Then we reason with the student. On the conclusion of a lecture we have from ten to fifteen minutes of questions and the student is free to bring up whatever arguments come to his mind. The professor takes up the arguments one by one and proves them false. . . ."

"Einstein," I said, "was one of the greatest scientists of all time, and so far as I know he never accepted the philosophy of dialectical materialism."

"We have translated the book Einstein wrote with Enfield [Infeld]. We study the book because the authors are great scientists. But we reject their idealistic doctrines."

"Suppose the student sees merit in these doctrines?"

"We argue him out of it."

"But suppose he remains unconvinced?"

"Impossible. We have the question period and we hold seminars and in the end we defeat our ideological enemies."

"But if the student persists in contradicting the professor?"

"It doesn't happen. It cannot happen. Our arguments are incontrovertible."

"And if it were to happen?"

This time the professor replied solemnly: "Then the student would place himself outside our Soviet society." [4]

[4] Maurice Hindus, *House Without a Roof* (1961).

Two-Valued Logic

The term "two-valued orientation" was originated by Alfred Korzybski, whose main concern was with the orientations that determine health or disorder in people's semantic reactions. Although he described the two-valued orientation as characteristic of a primitive or emotionally disturbed outlook, he was not attacking two-valued *logic*. Ordinary logic, such as we use in arithmetic, is strictly two-valued. Within the framework of ordinary arithmetic, two plus two are four. This is the "right" answer, and all other answers are "wrong." Many demonstrations in geometry are based on what is called "indirect proof": in order to prove a statement, you take its opposite and assume it to be "true" until you find in the course of further calculation that it leads to a flat contradiction; such a contradiction proves it to be "false," whereupon the original statement is regarded as "true." This too is an application of two-valued logic. Korzybski had no quarrel with arithmetic or geometry, and neither does the present writer.

Logic is a set of rules governing *consistency in the use of language*. When we are being "logical," our statements are consistent *with each other;* they may be accurate "maps" of real "territories" *or they may not,* but the question whether they are or are not is *outside the province of logic*. Logic is language about language, not language about things or events. The fact that two quarts of marbles plus two quarts of milk do not add up to four quarts of the mixture does not affect the "truth" of the statement, "Two plus two are four," because all that this statement says is that "four" *is the name of* "the sum two and two." Of such a statement as "Two plus two are four," a two-valued question may be asked: "Is it true or false?" —meaning, "Is it or is it not consistent with the rest of our system? If we accept it, shall we be able to talk consistently without eventually contradicting ourselves?" As a set of rules for establishing discourse, a two-valued logic is one of the possible instruments for creating order out of linguistic chaos. It is indispensable, of course, to most of mathematics.

In some areas of discourse and within some special groups of people, it is possible, so to speak, to "police" the language so that it comes to have some of the clarity and freedom from ambiguity enjoyed by mathematics. In such cases, people may agree to call certain animals "cats," certain forms of government "democracy," and a certain gas "helium." They would also have clear agreements as to what *not* to call "cats," "democracy," or "helium." The two-valued rule of traditional (Aristotelian) logic, "A thing is either a cat or not a cat," and the Aristotelian "law of identity," "A cat is a cat," make a great deal of sense when we understand them as *devices for creating and maintaining order in one's vocabulary*. They may be translated, "We must, in order to understand one another, make up our minds whether we are going to call Tabby a 'cat' or 'not a cat.' *And once we have entered into an agreement as to what to call him, let's stick to it.*"

Such agreements do not, of course, *completely* solve the problem of what things to call by what names, nor do they guarantee the certainty of statements logically deduced. In other words, definitions, as stated in Chapter 10, say nothing about things, but only describe (and often prescribe) people's linguistic habits. Even with the strictest of agreements, therefore, as to what to call "cats" and what not to call "cats," whatever we may logically deduce about cats *may* turn out, on extensional examination of Tabby, Cinders, or Fluff, not to be true.

> Cats are creatures that meow.
> Tabby, Cinders, and Fluff are cats.
> Therefore Tabby, Cinders, and Fluff meow.

But what if Fluff has a sore throat and cannot meow? The *intensional* cat (the cat by definition, *whatever* our definition may be, "creatures that meow" *or any other*) IS NOT the *extensional* cat (Fluff, April 16, 2 P.M.). Each cat is different from every other cat; each cat also, like Bessie the Cow, is a *process,* undergoing constant change. Therefore, the only way to guarantee the "truth" of logically deduced statements and to arrive at agreements through logic alone is to talk only about cats-by-definition, and not about actual cats at all. The nice thing about cats-by-definition is that, come hell or high water, they *always* meow (although, to be sure, they only meow-by-definition).

This principle is well understood in mathematics. The mathematical "point" (which "has position but occupies no space") and the mathematical "circle" (which is a "closed figure in which all points are equidistant from the center") exist *only as definitions;* actual points occupy *some* space, and actual circles are never *exactly* circular. Hence, in Einstein's words, "As far as the laws of mathematics refer to reality, they are not certain; and as far as they are certain, they do not refer to reality." Therefore, even in an area such as chemistry, in which the vocabulary is quite strictly "policed," statements logically deduced *still have to be checked* against extensional observation. This is another reason why the rule for extensional orientation—cat_1 is not cat_2—is extremely important. No matter how carefully we have defined the word "cat," and no matter how logically we have reasoned, extensional cats still have to be examined.

The belief that logic will substantially reduce misunderstanding is widely and uncritically held, although, as a matter of common experience, we all know that people who pride themselves on their logic are usually, of all the people we know, the hardest to get along with. Logic can lead to agreement only when, as in mathematics or the sciences, there are *pre-existing,* hard-and-fast agreements as to what words stand for. But among our friends, business associates, and casual acquaintances—some of them Catholic and some Protestant, some of them no-nonsense scientists and some mystics, some sports fans and some interested in nothing but money —only the vaguest of linguistic agreements exist. In ordinary conversation, therefore, we have to learn people's vocabularies in the course of talking with them—which is what all sensible and tactful people do, without even being aware of the process.

On the whole, therefore, except in mathematics and other areas where clear-cut linguistic agreements either exist or can be brought into existence, the assiduous study and practice of traditional, two-valued logic is not recommended.[5] The habitual reliance on two-valued logic *in everyday life* quickly leads to a two-valued orientation—and we have already seen what *that* leads to.

Korzybski was rarely concerned with the specific *content* of people's beliefs—whether people were religious or unreligious, liberal or conservative. He was concerned, rather, with how people held their beliefs and convictions: whether with a two-valued orientation ("I am right and everybody else is wrong") or a multi-valued orientation ("I don't know—let's see"). Korzybski saw the two-valued orientation as an *internalization* of the laws of Aristotelian logic, which say that:

---

[5] It is interesting to note that even in mathematics, stress is laid today on the fact that two-valued logic is only one of many possible systems of logic. The logic of probability, on the basis of which insurance companies quote premiums, bookmakers quote odds, and physicists predict the behavior of neutrons, may be regarded as an infinite-valued logic.

A is A (law of identity);

Everything is either A or not-A (law of the excluded middle);

Nothing is both A and not-A (law of non-contradiction).

He regarded his own system as an internalization of modern, multi-valued and infinite-valued logics. He therefore called general semantics a *"non-Aristotelian* system." This has led some people to believe that Korzybski was fighting Aristotle. He was not. He was simply fighting unsanity, whether individual or national. As for Aristotle, he must have been one of the sanest men of his time; but anyone whose knowledge and thinking are limited to Aristotle's can hardly behave sanely in *our* time.

Defeating One's Own Ends

Action resulting from two-valued orientations notoriously fails to achieve its objectives. The mobs that tried to force dissenting pacifist or religious groups to kiss the flag during World War I did not advance the cause of national defense; they weakened it by creating burning resentments among those minorities. Southern lynch mobs did not solve the Negro problem; they simply made matters worse. What hardens "hardened criminals" is usually the way they are treated by a two-valued society and two-valued policemen. In short, the two-valued orientation increases combativeness but sharply diminishes the ability to evaluate the world accurately. When guided by it for any purpose other than fighting, we practically always achieve results *opposite from* those intended.

Nevertheless, some orators and editorial writers employ the crude, unqualified two-valued orientation with extraordinary frequency, although allegedly in the interests of peace, prosperity, good government, and other laudable aims. Do such writers and speakers use this primitive approach because they know no better? Or are they so contemptuous of their audiences that they feel that "it don't pay to be subtle"? Another possibility is that they are sincere; like some physicians at the mention of "socialized medicine," they cannot help having two-valued reactions when certain hated subjects come into their minds. And still another explanation, less pleasant to think about but in many instances highly probable, is that the two-valued furor is a means of diverting public attention from urgent and practical issues. By making enough of an uproar about "atheism in the state university," "communists on the government payroll," or "who's to blame for the mess in South-East Asia," one can keep people from noticing what is going on in legislative lobbies "crowded," as Winston Churchill once said, "with the touts of protected industries."

APPLICATIONS

I. It is important to distinguish between two-valued *utterances* and the two-valued *orientation*. Nearly everyone makes two-valued statements at one time or another: "There's only one right way to make Yorkshire pudding; people who make it any other way just don't know what Yorkshire pudding is"; "If I can't go to the college I want, I won't go to college at all." At what point can we say that a person's *orientation* (his general approach to issues) is two-valued? Is the author of this book guilty of a two-valued orientation because of the two-valued pronouncements he has made? Go through the book and find as many of these two-valued pronouncements as you can. Do they add up to a two-valued orientation?

Write a paper of about five hundred words describing or giving a "profile" of the two-valued mentality as you see it operate around you in daily life.

II. The two-valued orientation appears in each of the following passages, at higher levels of feeling as well as in crude form, qualified as well as unqualified. Analyze each statement carefully, especially in the light of the questions: "How much confidence can I safely repose in the judgment of the author of this passage? A great deal? None at all? Or is there not enough evidence to be able to say?"

1. It's time we hit the sawdust trail. It's time we revived the idea that there is such a thing as sin. . . . It's time we brought self-discipline back into style. . . . So I suggest:

   Let's look at our educational institutions at the local level, and if Johnny can't read by the time he's ready to get married let's find out why.

   Let's look at the distribution of public largesse, and if, far from alleviating human misery, it is producing the sloth and irresponsibility that intensifies it, let's get it fixed.

   Let's quit being bulldozed and bedazzled by self-appointed longhairs. Let's have the guts to say that a book is dirt if that's what we think of it. . . . And if some beatnik welds together a collection of rusty cogwheels and old corset stays and claims it's a greater sculpture than Michelangelo's "David" let's have the courage to say that it looks like junk and may well be. . . .

I am fed up to here with the medicine men who try to pass off pretense for art and prurience for literature. . . .

In this hour of misbehavior, self-indulgence and self-doubt . . . let there be a fresh breeze of new pride, new idealism, new integrity. —JENKIN LLOYD JONES, address to the American Society of Newspaper Editors

2. In John Milton's *Paradise Lost,* Satan and his following of rebel angels, having been driven out of Heaven, debate whether to hazard another battle for the recovery of Heaven. Moloch speaks:

> My sentence is for open war. Of wiles
> More unexpert, I boast not: them let those
> Contrive who need, or when they need; not now.
> For, while they sit contriving, shall the rest . . .
> Accept this dark opprobrious den of shame,
> The prison of his tyranny who reigns
> By our delay? No! let us rather choose,
> Armed with Hell-flames and fury, all at once
> O'er Heaven's high towers to force resistless way,
> Turning our tortures into horrid arms
> Against the Torturer. . . .
> —*Paradise Lost,* Book II, ll. 51–64

3. Politics, vacillation, the eternal straining after cleverness, a mind, as H. G. Wells observed of the President [Franklin Roosevelt], "appallingly open," open indeed at both ends, through which all sorts of half-baked ideas flow, love of the spectacular, preoccupation with war problems and the affairs of Europe, and only a dim perception of the profound problems of economics and finance that dominate our scene, good intentions mixed with confused ethical concepts— these have brought the President to the tragic point where the only thing that can save his regime is to take the country off into a war hysteria.

Seven years after he took office there are eleven million unemployed, private investment is dead, the farm problem is precisely where he found it. He put through some social reforms that the country was yelling for. But these social reforms have to be almost completely overhauled. As for recovery—the President has not one plan. The cost of all this has been twenty-two billion dollars, all yet to be paid.

If it has all happened that way, it is because Franklin D. Roosevelt is that way.

—JOHN T. FLYNN, *Country Squire in the White House*

4. India's Prime Minister Nehru denies with some rather labored theorizing that his country is neutral. Well, who in this part of the

world thought she was neutral? . . . Nehru says the "neutral" tag reflects a war mentality in those who apply it to India. And he tries to fortify that frail assumption with another one of equal flimsiness. He argues that people think every nation must stand with one of the two great groups of nations which are supposed "to be more or less opposed to each other."

What's wrong with that view? The division between the Red bloc and the free nations is over a great principle. It concerns the liberty, the dignity, of mankind. . . . Yet he says that India should be described as "nonaligned" or "preferably independent." If India's attitude is Nehru's idea of independence, he has a sadly limited grasp of what the word means.   —Editorial in the Arkansas *Democrat*

5.   WE ARE FOR THE STRIKING RAILROAD MEN 100 PER CENT—
     WE ARE FOR A LIVING WAGE AND FAIR WORKING CONDITIONS.

These words on a card in a number of Emporia show windows express a mild opinion of friendly sympathy with the strikers. The cards have been ordered out by the Kansas Industrial Court. The order is an infamous infraction of the right of free press and free speech. Certainly it has not come to such a pass in this country that a man may not say what he thinks about an industrial controversy without disobeying the law.

One of these cards went up in the GAZETTE window today. Instead of 100 per cent, we have started it at 49 per cent. If the strike lasts until tomorrow we shall change the per cent to fifty, and move it up a little every day. As a matter of fact, the GAZETTE does not believe that anyone—not even the GAZETTE—is 100 per cent right. But somewhere between forty-nine and 100 per cent the men are right. And if the Industrial Court desires to make a test case, here it is. This is not a question of whether the men are right or wrong, but a question of the right of an American citizen to say what he pleases about this strike. And if forty-nine per cent sympathy is permissible, in the next fifty days we shall all see where violation of the law begins. The Industrial Court which we have upheld from its conception, and still uphold, will have the nicest little chance to see just where it is lawful for a man to express sympathy with his friends and neighbors, even if in his heart he believes that they have made a mistake in the time of their strike.

Either we have free speech and a free press in this country, or we have not. Now is the time to find out.

—WILLIAM ALLEN WHITE, Editorial in
the Emporia *Gazette* *

* From *Forty Years on Main Street.* Copyright, 1937, by William Allen White. Reprinted by permission of Rinehart & Company, Inc., publishers.

6. I repeat, the conflicts about capitalism (and, really, about everything else as well) come from the two opposite views of the nature of man. The basic question is: Are all men endowed by the Creator with inalienable liberty? Or are all persons controlled, as wind and water are, by forces outside themselves?

If everyone answered that question definitely and positively, for himself, and did all his thinking logically and soundly on the basis of his answer to that question, at least there would be no confusion in human affairs. The lines would be clearly drawn; the enemies would face each other in solid ranks; and the issue could be decided once for all. . . .

Now, from the pagan belief that human beings are not free individuals, straight thinking leads directly to some kind of slavery. For if individuals do not control themselves, something else must control them; and in human society this Controller must have some kind of human form—a Living God, such as the Mikado; an autocrat, such as an Emperor, a King, a Leader, a Dictator; or a group of persons, such as a Ruling Class, a Party, a Parliament, or a Majority. . . .

Whatever may be the political form that is established by the pagan view of man, the economy must always be a controlled economy. Of course, if individuals do not control their own actions, their actions are controlled by forces outside themselves; and since our first necessities are food, clothing and shelter, the major part of human activities will be farming, manufacturing, trading. Controlling anyone means controlling all their economic activities; that is, it means a controlled economy, now called a "planned" economy. In other words, a controlled economy is a tyranny; a tyranny is a controlled economy.

The tyrant may be a Mikado, an Emperor, a King, a Leader, a military dictator, a Ruling Class, a Party, or a Parliament (or Congress). The tyrant may control the economy in a number of ways: feudalism, communism, fascism, syndicalism, international or national socialism. The constant fact is that any controlled economy is some form of tyranny, and in it all men are slaves.

—ROSE WILDER LANE, Pittsburgh *Courier*

7. The WHITE man's present insane refusal to recognize the basic importance of RACE can only result in his own extinction. He is being exploited and his TAX money is used to support and encourage a NEGRO WELFARE STATE, for the benefit of that race, which is rapidly OUT-breeding the WHITES, largely at the Whites' expense. The NEGRO spends HIS money on his own pleasures, pays a minimum tax and does not even support his own ill-gotten children.

HELP!

Our American Birthright,
Christian Heritage and our American
Way of Life need your active DEFENSE.

USE AND DISTRIBUTE
"FIGHT COMMUNISM"
Stamps
200 for $1; 1000 for $2

The use of these stamps is an easy and inexpensive way to STAND UP AND BE COUNTED. Their use injures or embarrasses no one other than tools of those of evil influence, communists, anti-anti-communists, traitors, dual loyalists, fellow travelers, one-worlders, gullible stooges (including educators and churchmen, male and female), "experts" (?), and professional do-gooders. . . .
GET THE U.S. OUT OF THE U.N. AND THE U.N. OUT OF THE U.S.

—Leaflet of the American Birthright Committee,
Los Angeles, California

8. Mississippi is still cut off from the words that stir men's love and compassion and the clarity of their thinking. But this need not be. The conspiracy of silence that once bound the entire South is broken. Southerners by the thousands have taken a stand against segregation as a way of life too injurious, to both Negro and White, to endure. Millions of other Southerners have taken a giant step toward reality by holding to the solid rock of their highest allegiance: to our country and its laws. We are Americans or we are not Americans: there is no halfway station where privileges can be accepted and obligations ignored.

This is where Southerners must begin. It is a good first step, an inevitable first step. —LILLIAN SMITH, *Life*

9. It is in vain, sir, to extenuate the matter. Gentlemen may cry peace, peace, but there is no peace. The war is actually begun. The next gale that sweeps from the north will bring to our ears the clash of resounding arms. Our brethren are already in the field. Why stand we here idle? What is it that gentlemen wish? What would they have? Is life so dear, or peace so sweet, as to be purchased at the price of chains and slavery? Forbid it, Almighty God! I know not what course others may take, but as for me, give me liberty, or give me death! —PATRICK HENRY, at the Second Revolutionary Convention, Richmond, Virginia

III. The following syllogistic advertisement contains a number of logical fallacies. Can you detect them?

Orlon has chic;
Knits have chic;
It follows: knits of orlon have chic to spare!

Although Korzybski called general semantics a "non-Aristotelian system," knowledge of the correct forms of the Aristotelian syllogism sometimes guides the student to more accurate and adequate thinking. For this reason, you may wish to read one or more of the following books. Stuart Chase, who is familiar with both non-Aristotelian semantics and Aristotelian semantics, and who is always an interesting and entertaining writer, provides many useful and amusing examples of errors in the thinking process in his *Guides to Straight Thinking* (1956). Another useful book is Robert H. Thouless' *How to Think Straight* (1950), which is especially good on the subject of the *enthymeme,* or syllogism with one of its propositions missing. See also Richard D. Altick, *Preface to Critical Reading* (1951), and Harold F. Graves and Bernard S. Oldsey, *From Fact to Judgment* (1957).

14 The Multi-Valued Orientation

> *Faith in reason is not only a faith in our own reason but also—and even more—in that of others. Thus a rationalist, even if he believes himself to be intellectually superior to others, will reject all claims to authority since he is aware that, if his intelligence is superior to that of others (which is hard for him to judge), it is so only in so far as he is capable of learning from criticism as well as from his own and other people's mistakes, and that one can learn in this sense only if one takes others and their arguments seriously. Rationalism is therefore bound up with the idea that the other fellow has a right to be heard, and to defend his arguments.*
>
> —KARL R. POPPER

A Matter of Degree

Except in quarrels and violent controversies, the language of everyday life shows what may be termed a multi-valued orientation. We have *scales* of judgment. Instead of "good" and "bad," we have "very bad," "bad," "not bad," "fair," "good," "very good"; we also have mixed judgments: in some respects "good" and in others "bad." Instead of "sane" and "insane," we have "quite sane," "sane enough," "mildly neurotic," "sane on most subjects," "neurotic," "extremely neurotic," and "psychotic." The greater the number of distinctions, the greater becomes the number of courses of action suggested to us. This means that we become increasingly capable of reacting *appropriately* to the many complex situations life presents. The physician does not lump all people together into the two classes of the "healthy" and the "ill." He distinguishes an indefinite number of conditions that may be described as "illness" and has an indefinite number of treatments or combinations of treatments.

The two-valued orientation is an orientation based ultimately, as we have seen, on a single interest. But human beings have many interests: they want to eat, to sleep, to have friends, to publish books, to sell real estate, to build bridges, to listen to music, to maintain peace, to conquer disease. Some of these desires are stronger than others, and life presents a perpetual problem of weighing one set of desires against others and making choices: "I like having the money, but I think I would like having that car even better." "I don't like to stand in line for tickets, but I do want to see that show." "I'd like to fire the strikers, but I think it's more important to obey the labor board." "I'd like to uphold the Constitution, but I don't want to admit Negroes to the University." For weighing the various and complicated desires that civilization gives rise to, an increasingly finely graduated scale of values is necessary, as well as foresight, lest in satisfying one desire we frustrate even more important ones. The ability to see things in terms of more than two values may be referred to as a *multi-valued orientation.*

The Multi-Valued Orientation and Democracy

The multi-valued orientation shows itself, of course, in almost all intelligent or even moderately intelligent public discussion. The editors of responsible papers, such as the New York *Times,* Chicago *Sun-Times,* Milwaukee *Journal,* St. Louis *Post-Dispatch,* Louisville *Courier-Journal*—to name only a few— and the writers for reputable magazines, such as *New Republic, Harper's, Atlantic Monthly, Encounter,* or *Commonweal,* almost invariably avoid the unqualified two-valued orientation. They may condemn communism, but they try to see what makes communists act as they do. They may denounce the actions of a foreign power, but they do not forget the extent to which American actions may have provoked the foreign power into behaving as it did. They may attack a political administration, but they do not forget its positive achievements. It does not matter whether it is from fair-mindedness or timidity that some writers avoid speaking in terms of angels and devils, pure "good" and pure "evil." The important thing is that they do avoid it, and by so doing they keep open the possibility of adjusting differences, reconciling conflicting interests, and arriving at just estimates. There are people who object to this "shilly-shallying" and insist upon an "outright yes or no." They are the Gordian-knot cutters; they may undo the knot, but they ruin the rope.

Indeed, many features of the democratic process presuppose the multi-valued orientation. Even that most ancient of judicial procedures, the trial by jury, restricted to the conclusions "guilty" and "not guilty," is not as two-valued as it looks, since in the very selection of the charge to be brought against the defendant a choice is made among many possibilities, and also, in the jury's verdict as well as in the judge's sentence, guilt is often modified by recognition of "extenuating circumstances." Modern administrative tribunals and boards of mediation, not tied down by the necessity of arriving at clear verdicts of "guilty" and "not guilty," and empowered to issue "consent decrees" and to close agreements between litigants, are even more multi-valued than the trial by jury and therefore, for some purposes, considerably more efficient.

To take another example, very few bills ever pass a democratic parliamentary body in exactly the form in which they were proposed. Opposing parties argue back and forth, make bargains and compromises with each other, and by this process tend to arrive at decisions that are more nearly adjusted to the needs of everyone in the community than the original proposals. The more fully developed a democracy, the more flexible become its orientations, and the more fully does it reconcile the conflicting desires of the people.

Even more multi-valued is the language of science. Instead of saying "hot" and "cold," we give the temperature in *degrees on a fixed and agreed-upon scale:*—20° F., 37° C., and so on. Instead of saying "strong" and "weak," we give strength in *horsepower* or *voltage;* instead of "fast" and "slow," we give speed in miles per hour or feet per second. Instead of being limited to two answers or even to several, we have an infinite number when we use these numerical methods. The language of science, therefore, can be said to offer an *infinite-valued orientation.* Having at its command the means to adjust action in an infinite number of ways according to the exact situation at hand, science travels rapidly and gets things done.

The Pitfalls of Debate

In spite of all that has been said to recommend multi- and infinite-valued orientation, it must not be overlooked that in the *expression of feelings,* the two-valued orientation is almost unavoidable. There is a profound "emotional" truth in the two-valued orientation that accounts for its adoption in strong expressions of feeling, especially those that call for sympathy, pity, or help in a struggle. "Fight polio!" "Down with slums and up with better housing!" "Throw out the crooks! Vote the Reform ticket!" The more spirited the expression, the more sharply will things be dichotomized into the "good" and the "bad."

Where there are expressions of feeling and therefore affective elements in speaking and writing, the two-valued orientation almost always appears. It is hardly possible to express strong feelings or to arouse the interest of an apathetic listener without conveying to some extent this sense of conflict. Everyone who is trying to promote a cause, therefore, shows the two-valued orientation somewhere in the course of his writing. It will be found, however, that the two-valued orientation is *qualified* in all conscientious attempts at presenting what is believed to be truth—qualified sometimes, in the ways explained above, by pointing out what can be said against the "good" and what can be said for the "bad"—qualified at other times by the introduction, elsewhere in the text, of a multi-valued approach to the problems.

The two-valued orientation, in short, can be compared to a paddle, which performs the functions, in primitive methods of navigation, both of starter and steering apparatus. In civilized life the two-valued orientation may be the starter, since it arouses interest with its affective power, but the multi-valued or infinite-valued orientation is the steering apparatus that directs us to our destination.

Although we all like to think of ourselves as rational beings, there are few among us who do not exhibit the two-valued orientation when we are stirred up by controversy. In the course of a debate, if *one* of the debaters has a two-valued orientation which leads him to feel that the Democrats, for example, are "entirely good" and the Republicans "entirely bad," he unconsciously forces his opponent into the position of maintaining that the Democrats are "entirely bad" and the Republicans "entirely good." If we argue with such a person at all, there is hardly any way to escape being put into a position that is as extreme on one side as his is on the other. This fact was well stated by Oliver Wendell Holmes in his *Autocrat of the Breakfast-Table,* where he speaks of the "hydrostatic paradox of controversy":

> Don't you know what that means?—Well, I will tell you. You know that, if you had a bent tube, one arm of which was of the size of a pipestem, and the other big enough to hold the ocean, water would stand at the same height in one as in the other. Controversy equalizes fools and wise men in the same way—*and the fools know it.*

Disputes in which this "equalization" is likely to occur are, of course, a waste of time. The *reductio ad absurdum* of this kind of discussion is often to be found in the high school and college debate, as still practiced in some localities. Since both the "affirmative" and "negative" can do little other than exaggerate their own claims and belittle the claims of the opposition, the net intellectual result of such encounters is usually negligible—unless teachers consciously guide the discussions in the direction of multi-valuedness, and draw attention to the processes of abstraction underlying the question under debate. Parliaments and congresses, it will be observed, do not try to conduct much of their serious discussion on the floor. Speeches are made principally for the constituents back home and not for the other legislators. The main work of government is done in the committee room, where the traditional atmosphere of debate is absent. Freed from the necessity of standing resolutely on "affirmative" and "negative" positions, legislators in committee are able to thresh out problems, investigate facts, and arrive at workable conclusions that represent positions between the possible extremes. It would seem that, in training students to become citizens in a democracy, practice in being members of and testifying before committees of inquiry would be more suitable than debating, after the fashion of medieval schoolmen, for "victory."

In the course of everyday conversation, most of us need to watch for the two-valued orientation in ourselves. In a competitive society, conversation is often a battleground in disguise on which we are constantly (and unconsciously) trying to win victories—showing up the other fellow's errors, exposing his lack of information, confronting him (and all others present) with the superiority of our own erudition and logic. This habit of jousting for status is so deeply ingrained in most of us (especially in professional and university circles) that every meeting of intellectuals and every literary cocktail party is likely to include, as part of the entertainment, some sort of verbal dogfight among those present.[1] Most people in such circles are so accustomed to this jousting that they rarely take offense at the remarks of their opponents. Nevertheless, they waste in argument a good deal of time that might more profitably be spent exchanging information and views. An unconscious assump-

[1] The fame and popularity of Stephen Potter's concept of "one-upmanship" is an amusing commentary on the not-too-well-concealed struggle for status that characterizes our social life. See his *Gamesmanship* (1948) and *Lifemanship* (1951).

tion, convenient for the purposes of those who are looking for occasions to argue and therefore underlying most of this kind of conversation, is that statements are either "true" or "false."

An important way to get the most out of conversation (and out of other forms of communication) is the following *systematic* application of the multi-valued orientation. Instead of assuming a statement to be "true" or "false," one should assume that it has a *truth-value* that stands somewhere *between* 0 and 100 per cent. For example, let us say that we are sympathetic to organized labor, and someone says to us, "Labor unions are rackets." Our immediate temptation is to say, "They are not"—and the battle would be on. But what is the truth-value of the man's statement? It is clearly neither 0 per cent ("No unions are rackets") nor 100 per cent ("All unions are rackets"). Let us then silently grant a *tentative* truth-value of 1 per cent ("One union out of 100 is a racket") and say to him, "Tell me more." If he has no more basis for his remark than the vague memory of something somebody once wrote in a newspaper column, he will fizzle out shortly, so that we need not be bothered with him any more. But if he does have experience with even *one* instance of union racketeering, he is talking about something quite real to him, although he may be vastly overgeneralizing his experience. If we listen sympathetically to his experience, the following are some of the things that may happen:

1. We may learn something we never knew before. We may, without giving up our pro-union sympathies, at least modify them so that they rest upon a clearer recognition of the shortcomings of unions as well as of their advantages.

2. He may moderate his statement with such an admission as, "Of course, I haven't had experience with many unions." Again, if he tries to describe as extensionally as possible his experience with a labor union, he may find that some term other than "racketeering" more accurately fits the facts. In these and other ways, then, he may modify his remarks and make them increasingly acceptable as he proceeds.

3. By inviting him to communicate to us, we establish lines of communication with him. This enables us later to say things to him which he may then be disposed to listen to.

4. Both may profit from the conversation.

To attempt to converse in this way is to make all our social contacts occasions for what we have earlier called "the pooling of knowledge." We can, if we are able to listen as well as to speak, become better informed and wiser as we grow older, instead of being stuck, like some people, with the same little bundle of prejudices at sixty-five that we had at twenty-five.

Statements made in everyday conversation, even if based on slip-shod inferences and hasty overgeneralizations, can usually be found to have *some* modest degree of truth-value. To find the needle of meaning in the haystacks of nonsense that the other fellow is talking is to learn something, even from the apparently prejudiced and uninformed. And if the other fellow is equally patient about looking for the needle of meaning in *our* haystacks of nonsense, he may learn something from us. Ultimately, all civilized life depends upon the willingness on the part of all of us to learn as well as to teach. To delay one's reactions and to be able to say "Tell me more," and then *to listen before reacting*—these are practical applications of some of the theoretical principles with which this book has been concerned: no statements, not even our own, say all about anything; inferences—for example, that the man who made the nasty remarks about unions is a "labor-hating reactionary"—need to be checked before we react to them; a multi-valued orientation is necessary to democratic discussion and to human cooperation.

The Open and Closed Mind

Important insights into the two-valued orientation are to be found in *The Open and Closed Mind* (1960), by Milton Rokeach of Michigan State University. First, Rokeach says, let us divide a communicative event into two elements, the *speaker* and the *statement*. To put matters as simply as possible, the listener may either accept or reject (like or dislike) the speaker; he may likewise accept or reject (agree or disagree with) the statement. Then the following are the possible ways for the listener to react to the communication:

1. he may accept the speaker and accept his statement;
2. he may accept the speaker but reject his statement;
3. he may reject the speaker but accept his statement;
4. he may reject the speaker and reject his statement.

A person with what Rokeach calls a "closed mind" is able to have only reactions (1) and (4): he either accepts the speaker *and* his statement, or rejects the speaker *and* his statement. The person with the "open mind," however, is able to have, in addition to reactions (1) and (4), the more complex reactions (2) and (3): of accepting the speaker but rejecting his statement, or rejecting the speaker but accepting his statement.

The person with the closed mind is apparently one who finds life threatening. If *either* the speaker *or* the statement is unacceptable to him, he rejects *both*. As the reader will recall, according to Anatol Rapoport's account of Lenin's evaluations, this is exactly the orientation Lenin habitually exhibited: an individual on his side who said anything unacceptable to him was shown to be either muddle-headed or "unconsciously" on the enemy side; anyone on the "enemy" side who said anything acceptable to him was also declared to be either muddle-headed or "masking his true nature." In short, the closed mind is definitely two-valued in its orientation: you have to like *everything* about the speaker or *nothing*.

Psychologically, Rokeach says, all human beings are engaged simultaneously in two tasks: (1) they seek to know more about the world, and (2) they wish to protect themselves from the world—especially from information that might prove upsetting. As the need for defense against disturbing information gets stronger, curiosity about the world gets weaker. ("A person will be open to information *insofar as possible,* and will reject it, screen it out, or alter it *insofar as necessary.*")

Rokeach refers to the things you believe in as your "belief system," and to the things you don't believe in as your "disbelief system." (For example, if you are a Catholic, Catholicism is your "belief system," and your "disbelief system" would be Protestantism, Judaism, Buddhism, and so on.) If you are a reasonably secure and well-organized individual, you enjoy your own belief system, but you are also open to information about your disbelief system. (You are able, although Catholic, to take in information about Protestantism, Judaism, Buddhism, and so on, and *to see the differences* among the various bodies of ideas that you *do not* believe in.) *To be open to information about the disbelief system,* says Rokeach, *is to have an open mind.*

However, if you are chronically insecure or anxious or frightened, you cling desperately to your belief system, and you are too busy defending yourself against real or imagined threats to take in information about the disbelief system. That is, if "communism" and "socialism" are both part of your disbelief system, *the more frightened you are, the less you are able to distinguish between them.*

The term "socialism" is used in a variety of ways in a number of contexts. There is the Russian kind of state capitalism organized under the banner of the Union of Soviet *Socialist* Republics. There is "democratic socialism" (Sweden, Britain), with "socialistic" measures (health, welfare, unemployment benefits, and such) instituted through democratic, parliamentary procedures. There are also "socialistic" measures imposed by armed dictatorships with the help of informers and secret police (for example, the collectivization of farms in Russia and China). Then there are all the measures *called* "socialistic" by their opponents: prepaid medical care, the income tax, social security, aid to dependent children, or whatever. The frightened individual's reaction to all of these *different* measures is *to see them as alike:* "One is just as bad as the other—they are all "socialism," which means that they are all "communism." Other disturbing areas are also seen as "communism": the fluoridation of the public water supply, abstract art, or the Negro demand for equal rights. According to Rokeach, *this inability to see the differences among the various thing you do not believe in characterizes the closed mind.*

With such a view, the individual with the closed mind looks around at the world through frightened eyes, and he sees what he calls "communism" making progress everywhere. (He does not observe communist setbacks.) From here it takes only a short inferential step to conclude that all these "communists" are secretly united in a vast conspiracy. Further inferences are made to explain why this "conspiracy" is so "successful." The communists are "fiendishly clever" and "extremely dedicated." Furthermore, it is believed, our own government has been penetrated by "communists," their "dupes," and "sympathizers." Therefore, it is argued, the most urgent task is to expose and drive from office all the "communists" now occupying high places in our society—especially in government and education. "The greatest dangers to America are internal!"

Robert Welch, who said that "Dwight Eisenhower is a dedicated and conscious agent of the Communist conspiracy" and who in his major opus, *The Blue Book of the John Birch Society,* said that President Roosevelt and General George C. Marshall were guilty of "plain unadulterated treason" (p. 99),[2] gives frequent and eloquent expression to this two-valued orientation and its logical consequences.

[2] *The Blue Book* is based, according to its author, on a series of lectures given before eleven men in an Indianapolis hotel on December 8 and 9, 1958. The John Birch Society was founded at that time by Robert Welch and these eleven. The book is privately printed; page references are to the fourth printing, 1961. Welch's comment on President Eisenhower is from his earlier, privately circulated book, *The Politician.*

He says that communists control, or are about to control, all the Moslem nations of the Mediterranean in addition to controlling Eastern Europe. Most of Western Europe is also in communist hands: "Any idea that Norway is not, for all practical purposes, now in Communist hands, or that Iceland and Finland are not completely so, is in my opinion . . . unrealistic" (pp. 18–19). Communists have taken over most of Asia "with the full help of our government, completely misled by Communist influence" (p. 14). Nehru is a communist; so is Nasser. Communists control most of Latin America. They have a "stranglehold on the economic life of Hawaii . . . so great that it constitutes virtual political control" (pp. 20–21). Communists are well entrenched in the State Department; they exercise enormous influence on the press, radio, and television (p. 21). There are "at least thirty huge Communist espionage rings operating in this country today." "Scores of known Communist sympathizers have been restored, by Supreme Court rulings, to their former jobs within our Federal Government" (p. 24).

> The [communist] conspiracy is incredibly well organized. It is so well financed that it has billions of dollars annually just to spend on propaganda. It has the benefit of decades of successful experience. . . . And it is guided by men who had to have supreme cunning and ruthlessness to have achieved their present positions within the conspiracy itself.
>
> This octopus is so large that its tentacles now reach into all of the legislative halls, all of the union labor meetings, a majority of the religious gatherings, and most of the schools *of the whole world*. It has a central nervous system which can make its tentacles in the labor unions of Bolivia, in the farmers' co-operatives of Saskatchewan, in the caucuses of the Social Democrats in West Germany, in the classrooms of the Yale Law School, all retract or reach forward simultaneously. It can make all of these creeping tentacles turn right or left, or a given percentage turn right while the others turn left, at the same time, in accordance with the intentions of a central brain in Moscow or Ust'-Kamenogorsk. The human race has never before faced any such monster of power which is determined to enslave it (pp. 72–73).

A generation ago, when liberals and conservatives alike were deeply (and rightly) concerned with the rising fascism of Germany and Italy, the more doctrinaire liberals (and the communists) saw fascists in almost as many places as Mr. Welch and his friends see communists today. Two-valued orientation, whether of the right or the left, makes raving fools of all who succumb to it.

The writer does not deny the reality of the threat posed by the aggressive and warlike nationalism of the U.S.S.R., nor does he deny that actual communists (members of the Communist Party) and Russian espionage agents and their mistaken American sympathizers entered into conspiracies inimical to the best interests of the United States. He simply wishes to warn against permitting the justifiable concern with genuine communists at home or abroad to spread into a panicky fear of everyone with ideas different from one's own.

APPLICATIONS

I. Giving your reasons in each case, consider the relative advantages of two-valued and multi-valued orientations in the following situations:

1. Arguing for a preference for abstract as against representational art (or *vice versa*).

2. Deciding with other members of the family where the family will spend the summer vacation.

3. Giving a speech urging support of the United Nations.

4. Reaching an agreement with Russia on nuclear-arms inspection.

5. Dealing with the issue of segregation in Southern bus depots and restaurants.

6. Deciding whether to grant free speech to admitted members of the American Nazi party or the American Communist party.

7. Writing a script to be broadcast to the people of an *enemy* nation in time of war.

8. Leading an infantry unit into battle.

9. Getting elected mayor of *your* town or city. (Be careful not to answer on the basis of a generalization about "politics." Be extensional about the *special* conditions that govern election to the office of mayor in *your* home town.)

10. Dealing, as mayor of your town or city, with the problem of traffic congestion on the principal streets.

11. Increasing the efficiency and morale of the department, office, store, or factory unit in which you work.

12. Trying to get parental consent to your marriage to someone outside your religious or racial group.

13. Trying to get your children to eat what you believe to be the proper foods in what you believe to be the proper way.

II. Korzybski argues that Indo-European language structure, with its strong sense of *"is"* and *"is not,"* contributed much to our tendency toward the two-valued orientation. Benjamin Lee Whorf also argues for the recognition of the influence of language upon thought; if you spoke Hopi or Thai, you would have difficulty having the same thoughts that you have in English! (See Korzybski's *Science and Sanity,* especially Chapters 4, 5, and 7; also *The Selected Writings of Benjamin Lee Whorf,* edit. John B. Carroll.)

Stuart Chase, in *Power of Words* (1954), makes the following application of the Korzybski-Whorf theories on the relation between language and thought. Read it carefully and comment, on the basis of whatever you may happen to know or are willing to conjecture about present-day Communist China:

> Linguists have also emphasized that Chinese is a "multi-valued" language, not primarily two-valued like English and Western languages generally. We say that things must be "good" or "bad," "right" or "wrong," "clean" or "dirty," "black" or "white"—ignoring shades of gray. When an economist talks about a middle road between "socialism" and "capitalism," both camps vie in their ferocity to tear him apart. (I have been that unhappy economist.)
>
> Speakers of Chinese set up no such grim dichotomies; they see most situations in shades of gray, and have no difficulty in grasping the significance of a variety of middle roads. As a result, Chinese thought has been traditionally tolerant, not given to the fanatical ideologies of the West. . . . This happy lack of two-valued thinking raises an interesting question. Communism, as formulated by Marx and developed by Lenin, is rigidly two-valued. The heroic worker stands against the wicked capitalist and one or the other must go down. There is no place for shades of gray or for innocent bystanders. Those who are not with us are against us. Which side are you on?
>
> Russian is an Indo-European language, and the two-sided choice is readily accepted by its speakers. The choice is accepted, too, by top leaders of the Chinese Communists today, for they went to Moscow to be indoctrinated, and to learn the Russian language. But four hundred million Chinese have not been to Moscow or learned Russian, or any other Indo-European language, and there is small prospect of their doing so. How, then, can the Chinese people become good ideological Communists, since it is difficult if not impossible for them to take seriously the central dialectic of Marxism? The structure of their language seems to forbid the idea.

III. One of the most effective ways of understanding and applying some of the central ideas in this chapter is to experiment, along with other people who have read it, in seeing how these ideas work.

For example, in a group of people who are familiar with the distinctions made here, choose some controversial subject of genuine interest to the group, such as the censorship of movies or of television, the abolition of college fraternities and sororities, world government, national health insurance by the federal government, pacifism, or the closed shop. Ask two members of the group to present a discussion of the chosen subject with one person persistently maintaining a two-valued orientation on the subject ("All censorship is bad," "The closed shop is undemocratic") and with the other person taking an opposing two-valued orientation.

Then ask two other members of the group to discuss the same subject, again with one of them maintaining a two-valued orientation but this time with the second person using the approach suggested in this chapter ("Tell me more," "Let's see").

The role-playing suggested here need not be lengthy—a three-to five-minute demonstration will usually suffice. A discussion of the demonstration, followed perhaps by another demonstration, will help to get the "feel" of "verbal jousting" as compared with the "systematic application of multi-valued orientation." In general discussion following such a demonstration, let the role-taker who has been most "on the spot" have the first chance to criticize what has been done, then his collaborator, and then those who were present as spectators.

15 Poetry and Advertising

> *I've snuff and tobaccy and excellent jacky;*
> *I've scissors and watches and knives;*
> *I've ribbons and laces to set off the faces*
> *Of pretty young sweethearts and wives.*
> —W. S. GILBERT

> *The advertisement is one of the most interesting and*
> *difficult of modern literary forms.*
> —ALDOUS HUXLEY

The Poet's Function

One does not often mention poetry and advertising in the same breath. Poetry is universally conceded to be the loftiest of the verbal arts. Advertising, on the other hand, is not even an autonomous art; it is but the handmaiden of commerce. Its name carries connotations, often well deserved, of half-truth, deception, and outright fraud; of appeals to vanity, fear, snobbery, and false pride; of radio and television programs hideous with wheedling voices.

There are many more contrasts. The best poetry seems to be fully appreciated only by the few and to be beyond the comprehension of the many. The best advertising, however, is thought about, laughed over, and acted upon by multitudes. Poetry is, in the general apprehension, something special, to be studied in schools, to be enjoyed by cultivated people who have time for that sort of thing, to be read on solemn or momentous occasions. Advertising is part of everyday life.

Nevertheless, poetry and advertising have much in common. To begin with, they both make extensive use of rhyme and rhythm ("What's the word? Thunderbird!"). They both use words chosen for their affective and connotative values rather than for their denotative content ("Take a puff . . . it's springtime! Gray rocks and the fresh green leaves of springtime reflected in a mountain pool. . . . Where else can you find air so refreshing? And where can you find a smoke as refreshing as Salem's?"). William Empson, the English critic, said in his *Seven Types of Ambiguity* that the best poems are ambiguous; they are richest when they have two or three or more levels of meaning at once. Advertising, too, although on a much more primitive level, deliberately exploits ambiguities and plays on words: a vodka is advertised with the slogan, "Leaves you breathless"; an automobile is described as "Hot, Handsome, a Honey to Handle."

But the most important respect in which poetry and advertising resemble each other is that they both strive to give meaning to the data of everyday experience; they both strive to make the objects of experience symbolic of something beyond themselves. Speaking of the untutored, "wild and rude" Peter Bell in the poem of that name, William Wordsworth said:

> A primrose by the river's brim,
> A yellow primrose was to him,
> And it was nothing more.

A poet, however, cannot let a yellow primrose remain merely a yellow primrose; his function is to invest it with meanings. In the poet's eye the primrose comes to symbolize many things: the joy of early spring, his love of his darling Lucy, the benevolence of God, the transitoriness of life, or other things.

Similarly, an advertising writer cannot permit a cake of soap to remain a cake of soap and "nothing more." Whatever the object for sale is, the copywriter, like the poet, must invest it with significance so that it becomes symbolic of something beyond itself—symbolic of domestic happiness (like Van Camp's pork and beans), of aristocratic elegance (like Chanel No. 5), of rugged masculinity (like Marlboros), or of solid, traditional American virtues (like Log Cabin syrup). Whether he writes about toothpaste or tires, convertibles or colas, the task of the copywriter is *the poeticizing of consumer goods.*

Art and Life

All literary and dramatic enjoyment involves to some degree, as stated in Chapter 8, the reader's imaginative identification of himself with the roles portrayed in the story or play, and his projection of himself into the situations described. The same principles hold for poetry and advertising, of course. In reading poetry, we identify ourselves with the characters the poet creates, or with the poet himself. Advertisers also invite us to identify ourselves with the roles they portray. "Put yourself in this picture!" says the advertiser, showing radiant groups of young people drinking Seven Up; families wide-eyed with joy as they try out their new Dodge Dart or sit down to their dinner of fried chicken made with new, improved Mazola; aristocratic gentlemen and sportsmen wearing Hathaway shirts; and the lovely young woman who, having found a toothpaste that cleans her breath while it cleans her teeth, is now a happy bride.

The identification which great poets invite us to make requires of the reader both close attention and imaginative strenuousness; it is not everyone who can empathize with Lucifer in Milton's *Paradise Lost* or with "The Ancient Mariner" of Coleridge. The identifications which advertisers invite us to make are easy and pleasant: most of us would *like* to be as handsome and well-dressed and joyous and radiant as the people in the advertisements. Looking at the four-color picture of the serene mother standing by her Norge washer with spotless children and piles of fluffy towels, the harassed housewife readily dreams herself into the picture and says, *"That's for me!"* According to the advertisements, happiness is always within reach.

In spite of this marked contrast in the demands which poetry and advertising make upon their audiences, both have the common function of entering into our imaginations and shaping those idealizations of ourselves that determine, in large measure, our conduct. "Life," said Oscar Wilde, "is an imitation of art." Insofar as both poetry and advertising exact this tribute of imitation, they are both, in a real sense, "creative." Outsiders to the advertising business are often surprised and sometimes amused to learn that the art and copy departments of advertising agencies are known as "creative departments" and their head is known as "creative director." The more you think about it, the more appropriate the term becomes—whether or not you approve of what is created.

Let us call this use of verbal magic (or verbal skulduggery) for the purpose of giving an imaginative, symbolic, or ideal dimension to life and all that is in it, *poetry*. If we speak separately of what we ordinarily call poetry and advertising, let us speak of the latter as *sponsored poetry,* and of the former as *unsponsored poetry*.

Using our terms in this way, we see that our age is by no means deficient in poetry, if we include under that term the poetry of consumer goods. We have more access to poetry (or perhaps we should say that poetry has more access to us) than people have had at any other time in history. It is not possible to listen to most radio stations for five minutes, or to television stations for ten, without running into a panegyric for a beer, a roll-on deodorant, or a chewing gum. Most American large-circulation magazines are so full of sponsored poetry about breakfast foods, hams, electric appliances, clothing, liquor, and automobiles, and this poetry is so lavishly illustrated by the most expensive processes of color-reproduction and printing in order to attract attention, that reading the articles and stories is like trying to do your algebra homework in Times Square on New Year's Eve.

The Laureate's Task

To say that poetry is sponsored, however, is not to say that it is necessarily bad. Poets have been sponsored in times past, although the conditions of their sponsorship were different. The court poet, or poet laureate, is a typical example of the sponsored poet of a previous age. Such a poet, a paid retainer in the court of an emperor, king, or nobleman, had the task of saying, in odes and epics on suitable occasions, how great and powerful was the ruler who employed him, and how happy the people were under that ruler's benign and just government. Good poet laureates rose above the level of personal flattery of the kings they worked for, and sometimes gave expression to the highest ideals of their times and of their nation. Virgil was poet laureate to the Emperor Augustus. When Virgil wrote *The Aeneid,* according to the *Encyclopaedia Britannica* (11th edition), "The problem before him was to compose a work of art on a large scale, which should represent a great action of the heroic age, and should at the same time embody the most vital ideas and sentiments of the hour—which in substance should glorify Rome and the present ruler of Rome." In brief, Virgil had a sponsor and was working under assignment. Nevertheless, because of the character of Virgil as a poet and as a man, and because of his genuine dedication to his task, the fulfillment of his assignment turned out to be a very great poem indeed—many would say the greatest poem of his age.

Another example of a poet laureate is Alfred, Lord Tennyson, who held that post under Queen Victoria. In 1852 Tennyson was called upon to write a poem on the occasion of the burial of the Duke of Wellington in Westminster Abbey. His task was to express the sentiments of his queen and his nation at the death of a national hero. These opening lines from his "Ode on the Death of the Duke of Wellington" (a poem of over 500 lines) show unmistakably that sponsored art can also be art of a very impressive kind, certainly worthy of attentive study in a course in English literature:

Bury the Great Duke
  With an empire's lamentation,
Let us bury the Great Duke
  To the noise of the mourning of a mighty nation,
Mourning when their leaders fall,
Warriors carry the warrior's pall,
And sorrow darkens hamlet and hall.

Where shall we lay the man whom we deplore?
Here, in streaming London's central roar.
Let the sound of those he wrought for,
And the feet of those he fought for,
Echo round his bones for evermore.

Lead out the pageant: sad and slow,
As fits an universal woe,
Let the long long procession go,
And let the sorrowing crowd about it grow,
And let the mournful martial music blow;
The last great Englishman is low.

It is a curious fact that American advertising has also shown itself capable of performing a poet laureate's function—that of giving expression to a nation's ideals and sentiments on an important public occasion. In 1950 the tomb of the Unknown Soldier of World War II was dedicated in Washington, and at that time the following advertisement appeared in the newspapers of Boston and in national magazines:

He Is the Stranger Who Is My Brother

This is the story of a man I never knew, and yet I know all about him.

He is dead now, and he lies in a tomb of polished marble whose splendor would surprise him. And people come from everywhere to stand here with their heads bowed, their eyes serious, their hearts filled with mourning for this man they never knew.

Because he wore a uniform when he died, they call him the Unknown Soldier. I think he was a good soldier, though fighting was never his business. He was a man of peace, I'm sure, though he never told me.

He was born on a farm in the Dakotas . . . or was it a miner's cottage in Pennsylvania, a tenement in the Bronx, a ranch house in Texas, a duplex apartment on Park Avenue? I can't be sure, as I stand here with my hat in my hand, reverent at the grave of this man I never knew.

Was he a poet, bookkeeper, truck driver, surgeon, lumberjack, errand boy, student? Was he telling a joke, or cursing his sergeant, or writing to his family, when the missile came?

I don't know. For when they picked this man, from among all our nameless dead, he was lying quiet in a closed coffin, and known only to God.

But I do know that he is deserving of honor and respect. For, whoever he may be, I feel sure he must have believed, as I do, in the equality of men, the promise of men, the duty of men to live justly with each other and with themselves.

And that is why I stand here with my hat in my hand, reverent at the grave of the stranger who is my brother, my father, my son, my countryman, my friend. —John Hancock Mutual Life Insurance Company, Boston, Massachusetts

A comparison of this advertisement with Tennyson's "Ode" is instructive. Both express a nation's mourning. Both express, too, something of the spirit of the nations that produced them: Tennyson's poem, the pomp and military pride of the British Empire of the mid-nineteenth century; the insurance company advertisement, the simple, colloquial accents of the democratic America of the mid-twentieth century. The advertisement, necessarily addressed to a wider public than the poem, makes freer use of clichés; the reader trained in literary appreciation would find its language commonplace. Nevertheless, the writer of this advertisement performed on this occasion a laureate's task for a nation that has no poet laureate.

The Problems of the Unsponsored Poet

Let us turn from sponsored poetry to unsponsored poetry—the kind poets write not to satisfy any external demand, but to satisfy themselves. For decades there has been much wringing of the hands at the sad state of modern poetry. Robert Hillyer, a poet himself, in an article on "Modern Poetry vs. the Common Reader" in the *Saturday Review,* speaks of the poets of today as being in a "welter of confusion and frustration." He is distressed by their obscurity of language—"the flight from clarity," as he calls it. He is certain that both the unintelligibility and the tone of despair characteristic of much modern verse are due to the moral defects of the poets themselves. "Their confusion," he writes, "is a sign of artistic effeminacy and egotism."

It is true that many modern poets, from T. S. Eliot to Ezra Pound to Wallace Stevens to Delmore Schwartz to Robert Lowell, are not easy to understand on first reading, or even on second or third reading. But Mr. Hillyer is mistaken, it seems to this writer, in blaming the difficulties of modern poetry on the moral shortcomings of poets. He fails to take into account the *context* in which the unsponsored poet has to write today.

The unsponsored poet of today works in a semantic environment in which almost all the poetry that ordinary people hear and read is the sponsored poetry of consumer goods. Poetic language is used so constantly and relentlessly for the purposes of salesmanship that it has become almost impossible to say anything with enthusiasm or joy or conviction without running into the danger of sounding as if you were selling something. John Keats could write:

> To one who has been long in city pent
> 'Tis very sweet to look into the fair
> And open face of heaven,—to breathe in prayer
> Full in the smile of the blue firmament . . .

Today, anyone writing like this would immediately be suspected of working for the Hawaii Visitors Bureau or for the American Export Line promoting Mediterranean cruises.

Robert Herrick could write without self-consciousness about the beauty of women:

> Whenas in silks my Julia goes,
> Then, then, methinks, how sweetly flows
> The liquefaction of her clothes . . .

And so could William Wordsworth:

> She was a phantom of delight
> When first she gleamed upon my sight;
> A lovely apparition sent
> To be a moment's ornament;
> Her eyes as stars of twilight fair . . .

Today, such lines remind us inevitably of the promises of advertising copy. Herrick's Julia is a testimonial to the effects of wearing Van Raalte lingerie and Hanes' hosiery, while Wordsworth's unnamed beauty obviously exemplifies the results of using Clairol and the new Max Factor eye shadow. Indeed, anyone who is moved to express his thankfulness for the freedoms we enjoy in America will soon begin to sound like an advertisement of the Investor-Owned Electric Light and Power Companies on the necessity of keeping the government out of the utilities business.

The Symbols We Live By

To repeat, advertising is a symbol-manipulating occupation. The symbols of fashion and elegance are used to glamorize clothing and cosmetics. The symbols of youthful gaiety sell soft drinks and candy bars. The symbols of adventure and sportsmanship are used to promote cigarettes and liquor. The symbols of love and delight in one's new baby have been completely appropriated by the sellers of prepared baby foods, canned milk, and diaper services. Advertising is a tremendous creator and devourer of symbols. Even the symbols of patriotism are used for the purposes of salesmanship. There are advertisers who assure us that "It's *American* to want something better," while a beer called "Lucky Lager" advertises with the slogan, "It's *Lucky* if you live in America." Not even the symbols of religion are off limits—Christmas and Easter are so strenuously exploited commercially that they almost lose their religious significance. And there are other examples of the commercial use of religious symbols: A Midwestern flour company, for example, once organized the women's auxiliaries of churches into listener clubs for a quasi-religious program it was sponsoring. The women were urged to save box-tops from the company's cake flour in order to earn furniture and equipment for their churches—with the result that these churches were converted in effect into promotional outlets for that company's cake flour.

The problems of the unsponsored poet in an environment dominated by advertising are therefore difficult. Poets, too, must work with the symbols that exist in the culture, and they must create new ones as well. Almost all the symbols of daily living—especially those symbols that have any connotations of happiness and joy—have been appropriated by the advertisers. If unsponsored poets seem to concern themselves too much with negative moods, such as disillusionment, despair, or cynicism, part of the reason may well be that the positive moods have come to smell too much of salesmanship. Also, the verse of unsponsored poets is often difficult to understand and full of obscure symbolism. For at least a generation there have been no poets—not even Robert Frost or Carl Sandburg—who could communicate with as large a portion of the literate public as Tennyson and Longfellow did in their time. One reason for the obscurity of modern poets may again be that the familiar symbols of courtship, home, mother, nature, and love of country have been so completely appropriated for commercial purposes as to appear unusable to the unsponsored poet. He is practically driven to use obscure symbols out of the Upanishads or Zen Buddhism in his search for something the advertisers have not already used.

Some poets, more aware of the world around them than other poets, have known very clearly who their chief rivals are in the business of manufacturing dreams—and, therefore, patterns of living. E. E. Cummings, in his famous "Poem, or Beauty Hurts Mr. Vinal" (quoted at the end of this chapter), equates advertising with bad poetry. More recently, the so-called "beat" poets have made something of a cult of rejecting the consumer-advertising culture. The definition of a "square" in beat circles is a person who believes the advertisements, and who is therefore caught in the rat-race of late-model cars, wall-to-wall carpeting, installment payments, conformity, and constant financial anxiety. To be "hip" is, among other things, to have ceased believing the ads. "I can do *without* things," cries a newly liberated young lady of Venice, California, quoted by Lawrence Lipton in *The Holy Barbarians*. "God!—do you know what a relief that is?"

Symbols for Our Times

"Poets," said Shelley, "are the unacknowledged legislators of the world." Poets, by creating new ways of feeling and perceiving, help to create the new ways of thinking that bring us to terms with a changing world. Every age finds its appropriate symbols. In medieval times, religious images symbolized what people believed in and lived by: God, the angels, and the saints. In Renaissance times, the prevailing image was that of the human body, which was used in endless ways to symbolize the ideas of an age of humanism.

With what symbols shall the poet bring us to terms with the realities of our own times? In the past few decades whole new areas of thought and exploration have been opened up by the sciences—by electronics, by astrophysics, by microbiology, by photo-elasticity studies, by the study of nucleo-proteins and their role in genetics, by radioactive tracer studies, and by nuclear physics. Every few months a newly born nation seeks membership in the United Nations, and parts of the world that we had never thought about before suddenly become objects of concern. Astronauts shoot through space, so that the limits of the planet we live on are no longer the limits of our exploration. We can, and do, describe these new developments in the language of science, but how are we to take these new and urgent realities into our hearts as well as our minds, unless poets give us new images with which to experience them?

APPLICATIONS

I. To what extent do the following advertisements confirm the writer's assertion that "Whatever the object for sale is, the copywriter, like the poet, must invest it with significance so that it becomes symbolic of something beyond itself"? The relative absence of information and the deluge of affective connotations in advertising is notorious, of course. Nevertheless, it is revealing to analyze closely specimens like the following, separating the verifiable *information about the product* from the *affective and symbolic meanings*. What are the products in these advertisements said to be symbolic of? The reader will find it interesting to place the two kinds of assertions about the product into separate columns:

1. You'll enjoy *different* tomato juice made from *aristocrat* tomatoes.
—Advertisement

SAMPLE ANALYSIS:

Information About Product	Affective and Symbolic Meanings
Tomato juice is made from tomatoes.	Because you have cultivated and discriminating tastes, you will prefer tomato juice made from superior, exclusive tomatoes to that made from common ordinary tomatoes. An average person may not notice the difference, but you will. To drink our tomato juice is to symbolize your own aristocratic taste and aristocratic way of life.

2. Now it's Pepsi—for those who think young! Now parties are more informal, more fun. They reflect the new way of life everyone's leading. It's called thinking young. This is the life for Pepsi—light, bracing, clean-tasting Pepsi. So think young. Say "Pepsi, please!"
—Advertisement

3. *Why the Duke of Montina has consented to link his name with a new vinyl floor.* It is called Montina Vinyl Corlon. It is, of course, a well-bred floor. The Duke insisted. It is in impeccable taste and, at the same time, strikingly interesting. . . . Colors are subtle and flattering, very right with distinguished furnishings. The Duke says,

"Montina is a noble house. Now it is a noble floor. I refused to have my name linked with a cravat or a sandwich, something paltry, as has happened with other noblemen. But Montina—that is different. . . . Montina Corlon is one of the famous ARMSTRONG vinyl floors."　　　　　　　　　　　　　　　　　　　　　　—Advertisement

4. THE EXECUTIVE LOOK . . . *Exemplified by Webster Executive cigars.* It's the look of confidence; the faculty for being decisive, the willingness to delegate, the wisdom to use time well . . . and the ability to enjoy life. It's here in this very important cigar—the new Webster Executive.　　　　　　　　　　　　　　　　　　　—Advertisement

5. Softly . . . softly . . . softly you move to the crib to make certain that all is well with the most precious thing in your life, the most wonderful baby in all the world. Softly, too, the smooth Ocean Brand Sheets welcome you when you return to your own bed. And softly these Ocean Brand Sheets meet your budget requirements. For these are the famous Ocean Combed Percales, latest products of Ocean Brand craftsmanship.　　　　　　　　　　　　—Advertisement

6. IT ISN'T FAIR, BUT IT WORKS! Love is a game to be played with no holds barred. So throw conscience to the winds. Wear Helena Rubinstein's triumphant new fragrance—Vis à Vis (Veez-ah-Vee). You can wear Vis à Vis in so many devilish ways. . . .
　　　　　　　　　　　　　　　　　　　　　　—Advertisement

7. "I'd brought down big cats before, but never with a hypodermic needle," says Don Higley, American friend of Canadian Club. "This was my assignment for an international wild life survey in Tanganyika . . . to anesthetize wild animals with sleep-producing arrows, then attach tags to their ears so that their movements could be traced. I didn't have long to wait for my prey. It was a lion. . . . I crouched. Carefully I aimed my arrow. It flew straight and true . . . a hit!

"The big cat turned, his eyes glaring with hate. . . . Then suddenly he sank to his haunches, his head lolling. . . .

"Later in the day we relaxed at the pool of the Lake Manyara Hotel. We enjoyed everyone's favorite whisky—Canadian Club— and relived the day's experience. . . ."　　　　—Advertisement

8. GREAT JEWEL ROBBERY! CUTEX steals the sparkle of precious gems for your fingertips. Lucky you! Cutex puts a fortune in pearls, amethysts, and rubies at your fingertips. But you don't have to rob a safe to own them. Cutex polish, with its diamond-bright sparkle, is the nearest thing to a precious jewel. . . .　　　　—Advertisement

9. When you first drive up in a Cadillac, even old friends will see you in a new light. This is going to be especially true when you make your initial appearance in a 1963 Cadillac. . . . And when the

inevitable inspection comes, be prepared for "Ohs" and "Ahs" at the craftsmanship, luxury and elegance of the widest choice of personal options in Cadillac history. Isn't there someone you'd like to surprise? Go ahead and do it. Your Cadillac dealer will help stage the scene.   —Advertisement

10. [Under a picture, with an early-American look, of two gentlemen drinking to each other:] Andrew Jackson entertains his friend Martin Van Buren. Andrew Jackson, the great "Hero of the Plain People," enjoyed the pleasant ways of life. To distinguished guests like Martin Van Buren, he proudly displayed his personal liquor chest. Jackson's preference for Old Crow is reported in a 19th Century newspaper. *Taste the Greatness of* OLD CROW—*America's preferred Bourbon.*   —Advertisement

11. AN IMPORTANT MESSAGE by Dr. Frederick Brown Harris, Chaplain of the United States Senate:

"Please Omit Flowers" is a request often issued when arrangements are announced for what is usually called a funeral service. In life's darkest hours, when hearts are torn by poignant grief, when it seems as a dear one goes from our sight and side that life has tumbled in, a strange new directive puts a taboo on the Creator's petaled masterpieces which can say nameless things that no human lips can utter . . . In "Say It With Flowers" there stretch enchanting vistas of sacramental beauty like the glory of a garden or the shimmer of moonlight on a silvery sea.

—Advertisement for the Florists' Telegraph Delivery Service
("in the public interest")

II. The following advertisements do not advertise a specific brand nor a specific store or business enterprise; their purpose is more general. They are intended to change or confirm certain beliefs and attitudes rather than to send the reader out to buy a specific product. What are the beliefs and attitudes these advertisements strive to foster, and do they correspond with your own? Comment on how these advertisements move you—favorably or unfavorably—and why.

1. Ivan Ivanovich has only one automobile dealer that he can go to see—the government. And he goes with his pockets full of rubles and his hat in his hand.

John Smith, U.S.A., sort of takes the car and truck dealers in his town for granted. Seems they've always been there—ever since that shining day when he and Dad and Mom drove that first car home. Drove the long way, smack up Main Street, sitting up tall. Smitty would sure howl to high heaven if he had to pay between three and four times his whole year's pay for a new car that can't hold a candle to any American car mechanically, in comfort, equipment or styling. Ivan does. And wait two years for delivery to boot! Ivan does. And deal with mechanics whose way of checking your anti-freeze is to taste the radiator water. (Guess they haven't invented the hydrometer yet.)

Can't you see Ivan's eyes popping if he walked into Smitty's dealer's showroom? Here's a man, now, who has built his business on the solid rock of fine products. . . . This dealer and John Smith have been friends for a long time. See each other at the PTA and the lodge, the town council and the Little League practice sessions. Smitty's boy is learning to drive in the car the dealer donated to the high-school driving course.

Saw Smitty just this morning. Grinning like a Chessy cat. On his way to pick out the new family bus. According to Smitty, now's the time to buy. . . . See "Automobile Row" . . . the industry's spectacular array of new cars . . . in the January 3rd issue of the *Saturday Evening Post,* the nation's year-round new-car showroom. Then see your car or truck dealer. He'll greet you with a big smile and the best value in your whole ever-lovin' lifetime!

—Advertisement in the *Saturday Evening Post*

2. This is the time of year when Americans traditionally observe a day of thanksgiving for their blessings. It is good that we should do this.

But is it not also fitting that on this day—so reminiscent of our origins—we should be mindful of our heritage and the trust it imposes on us. The price the Pilgrims paid for survival. The bloody feet at Valley Forge. The thunder at the Alamo, Gettysburg, the Argonne, Midway, Bastogne and Pork Chop Hill.

Of the people we are and must continue to be. The people who fathered Washington, Jefferson, Franklin, Lincoln and Lee. The people who first united a continent with roads and railroads, produced the steamship, the telephone, the airplane and the greatest economy the world has ever known.

Yes, let us remember who we are. For a little pride is the wellspring of courage. Let us endure unflinchingly whatever sacrifices we are called upon to make to defend our free institutions from the night of communism, which is bent on undermining our faith in ourselves. Let us rely not only on the gold in our vaults, but the iron in our blood. And let us cling like ivy to the faith of our fathers until, in God's good time, all men are free.

—Advertisement sponsored by the Savings and Loan Foundation,
Washington, D.C.

3. Sometimes a danger is hard to recognize even though a warning lamp is lighted.

The loss of freedom is one such danger. And the steady growth of government-in-business is one such danger signal.

In the last 30 years the federal government has come to own many thousands of businesses, from cement mixing plants to ice cream factories. In the field of electricity alone it now has an investment of 5½ billion dollars in power plants and lines. And advocates of government-in-business press constantly for more.

When government owns business it has in its hands both political *and* economic powers—the means of controlling goods and jobs. In such a state it can become difficult indeed for individuals to keep their basic freedoms.

Is this a risk you want to take?

—Advertisement of Investor-Owned Light and Power Companies

III. The following poem has as its subject matter a nationally advertised product. It is, however, an unsponsored poem by an unsponsored poet. Compare this poem with advertisements for the same product, such as you can find in any popular magazine. How does the poem differ from the advertisements? Can you account for the differences?

Buick

As a sloop with a sweep of immaculate wing on her delicate spine
And a keel as steel as a root that holds in the sea as she leans,
Leaning and laughing, my warm-hearted beauty, you ride, you ride,
You tack on the curves with parabola speed and a kiss of goodbye,
Like a thoroughbred sloop, my new high-spirited spirit, my kiss.

As my foot suggests that you leap in the air with your hips of a girl,
My finger that praises your wheel and announces your voices of song,
Flouncing your skirts, you blueness of joy, you flirt of politeness,
You leap, you intelligence, essence of wheelness with silvery nose,
And your platinum clocks of excitement stir like the hairs of a fern.

But how alien you are from the booming belts of your birth and the smoke
Where you turned on the stinging lathes of Detroit and Lansing at night
And shrieked at the torch in your secret parts and the amorous tests,
But now with your eyes that enter the future of roads you forget;
You are all instinct with your phosphorous glow and your streaking hair.

And now when we stop it is not as the bird from the shell that I leave

Or the leathery pilot who steps from his bird with a sneer of delight,
And not as the ignorant beast do you squat and watch me depart,
But with exquisite breathing you smile, with satisfaction of love,
And I touch you again as you tick in the silence and settle in sleep.

—KARL SHAPIRO

IV. Read, ponder, and digest:

Poem, or Beauty Hurts Mr. Vinal

take it from me kiddo
believe me
my country, 'tis of

you, land of the Cluett
Shirt Boston Garter and Spearmint
Girl With The Wrigley Eyes (of you
land of the Arrow Ide
and Earl &
Wilson
Collars) of you i
sing: land of Abraham Lincoln and Lydia E. Pinkham,
land above all of Just Add Hot Water And Serve—
from every B.V.D.

let freedom ring

amen. i do however protest, anent the un
-spontaneous and otherwise scented merde which
greets one (Everywhere Why) as divine poesy per
that and this radically defunct periodical. i would

suggest that certain ideas gestures
rhymes, like Gillette Razor Blades
having been used and reused
to the mystical moment of dullness emphatically are
Not To Be Resharpened. (Case in point

if we are to believe these gently O sweetly
melancholy trillers amid the thrillers
these crepuscular violinists among my and your
skyscrapers—Helen & Cleopatra were Just Too Lovely,
The Snail's On The Thorn enter Morn and God's
In His andsoforth

do you get me?) according
to such supposedly indigenous
throstles Art is O World O Life
a formula: example, Turn Your Shirttails Into
Drawers and If It Isn't An Eastman It Isn't A

Kodak therefore my friends let
us now sing each and all fortissimo A-
mer

i

ca, I
love,
You. And there're a
hun-dred-mil-lion-oth-ers, like
all of you successfully if
delicately gelded (or spaded)
gentlemen (and ladies)—pretty

littleliverpill-
hearted-Nujolneeding-There's-A-Reason
americans (who tensetendoned and with
upward vacant eyes, painfully
perpetually crouched, quivering, upon the
sternly allotted sandpile
—how silently
emit a tiny violetflavoured nuisance: Odor?

ono.
comes out like a ribbon lies flat on the brush

—E. E. CUMMINGS

16   The Dime in the Juke-Box

> *The habit of common and continuous speech is a symptom of mental deficiency.*   —WALTER BAGEHOT

> *The tongue is the most mobile structure of the human body.*   —WENDELL JOHNSON

Many a practical-minded lecturer and clergyman has no doubt discovered for himself the principle that when someone in the audience asks a question you cannot answer, the thing to do is to make an appropriate-*sounding* set of noises, and few people will notice that the question has not been answered. Words are used sometimes intentionally, often unintentionally, as smoke screens for ignorance and the absence of ideas.

At one time when the then governor of Wisconsin forced the resignation of the then president of the state university, the merits and demerits of the case were heatedly debated in newspapers throughout the state. The writer was an extension lecturer for the University of Wisconsin at the time and often encountered acquaintances and strangers who asked, "Say, doc, what's going on down there in Madison? It's all politics, isn't it?" The writer never found out what anybody meant by "It's all politics," but in order to save trouble he usually answered, "Yes, I suppose it is." Thereupon the questioner would look pleased with himself and say, "That's what I thought!" In short, "politics" was the appropriate-sounding word in this context. The question at the heart of the controversy—namely, whether the governor had *abused his political powers* or had *carried out his political duty*—was never asked and never answered.

Intensional Orientation

In previous chapters, we have analyzed particular kinds of misevaluation. All of these can now be summed up under one term: *intensional orientation*—the habit of guiding ourselves by *words alone,* rather than by the facts to which words should guide us.

We all tend to assume, when professors, writers, politicians, or other apparently responsible individuals open their mouths, that they are saying something meaningful. When we open our own mouths, we are even more likely to make that assumption. As Wendell Johnson says, "Every man is his most interested and affected listener." The result of such indiscriminate lumping together of sense and nonsense is that "maps" pile up independently of "territory." And, in the course of a lifetime, we may pile up entire systems of meaningless noises, placidly unaware that they bear no relationship to reality whatever.

Intensional orientation may be regarded as a general term covering the multitude of more specific errors already pointed out: (1) the unawareness of contexts; (2) the tendency toward automatic reactions; (3) the confusion of levels of abstraction (confusing what is inside one's head with what is outside); (4) the consciousness of similarities, but not of differences; (5) the habit of being content to explain words by means of definitions, that is, more words. When we are intensionally oriented, "capitalists," "bureaucrats," and "labor bosses" *are* what we *say* they are. People in communist countries *must* be unhappy because they are ruled by communists. (The intensional communist meanwhile believes that people in capitalist countries *must* be unhappy because they are ruled by "imperialist warmongers.") Atheists *must* be immoral because if people do not fear God they have "no reason to behave themselves." Politicians *must* be untrustworthy because all they do is "play politics."

Ororverbalization

Let us take a term, such as "churchgoer," which *denotes* Smith$_1$, Smith$_2$, Smith$_3$ . . . , who attend divine services with moderate regularity. Note that the *denotation* says nothing about the "churchgoer's" character. It simply says that he goes to church. The *intensional* meanings or *connotations* of the term, however, are quite a different matter. "Churchgoer" *suggests* "good Christian"; "good Christian" *suggests* fidelity to wife and home, kindness to children, honesty in business, sobriety of living habits, and a whole range of admirable qualities. These suggestions further *suggest,* by two-valued orientation, that non-churchgoers are likely not to have these qualities.

If our intensional orientations are serious, therefore, we can manufacture verbally a whole system of values—a whole system for the classification of mankind into sheep and goats—out of the con-

notations, informative and affective, of the term "churchgoer." That
is to say, once the term is given, we can, by proceeding from connotation to connotation, keep going indefinitely. A map is independent of territory, so that we can keep on adding mountains and
rivers after we have drawn in all the mountains and rivers that
actually exist in the territory. Once we get started, we can spin out
whole essays, sermons, books, and even philosophical systems on
the basis of the word "churchgoer"—without paying a particle of
further attention to churchgoer$_1$, churchgoer$_2$, churchgoer$_3$. . . .

There is no way of stopping this process by which free associations, one word "implying" another, can be made to go on and on.
That is why, of course, there are so many people in the world whom
one calls windbags. That is why many orators, newspaper columnists,
commencement-day speakers, politicians, and high-school elocution-
ists can speak at a moment's notice on any subject whatever. Indeed,
a great many of the "personality development" and "dynamic salesmanship" courses offered commercially, and some English and speech
courses in our schools, are merely training in this very technique—
how to keep on talking importantly when one hasn't a thing to say.

The kind of associative "thinking" we have been discussing,
which is the product of intensional orientation, is called *circular* because, since all the possible conclusions are contained in the connotations of the word to start with, we are bound, no matter how hard
or how long we "think," to come back to our starting point. Indeed,
we can hardly be said ever to leave our starting point. Of course, as
soon as we are face to face with a fact, we are compelled to shut up,
or start over again somewhere else. That is why it is so rude in certain
kinds of meetings and conversations to bring up any facts. They spoil
everybody's good time.[1]

Now let us say that while churchgoers$_{1, 2, 3, \text{etc.}}$ prove to be the
fine people that we (intensionally) expect them to be, churchgoer$_{17}$
is discovered to be unfaithful to his wife and dishonest in his trustee-
ship of other people's funds. Some people find such a case completely
bewildering: how *can* a man be a churchgoer and such a rascal at
the same time? Unable to separate the intensional from the extensional "churchgoer," such people are forced to one of three conclusions, all absurd:

[1] "When Harold Stassen in a 'Forum of the Air' radio debate charged that
no great advance like penicillin had ever come from a country with a medical-
insurance plan, Oscar Ewing quietly pointed out that penicillin came from
England." *New Republic.*

1. "This is an exceptional case"—meaning, "I'm not changing my mind about churchgoers, who are *always* good people no matter how many exceptions you can find."

2. "He isn't *really* that bad. He *can't* be!"—that is, denying the facts in order to escape the necessity of accounting for them.

3. "A man can't believe *anything* any more. I'll never trust another churchgoer as long as I live."

An unfounded complacency, which can so easily be followed by "disillusionment," is perhaps the most serious consequence of intensional orientation. And, as we have seen, we all have intensional orientation regarding some subjects. In the 1930's the federal government, confronted by mass unemployment, created the Works Progress Administration, an agency which hired men and women and thought up public projects for them to work on. These WPA jobs were described scornfully by opponents of the administration as "made work," to be distinguished from "real work" such as private industry was at that time failing to provide. It became a matter of pious faith on the part of these critics of the administration to believe that "WPA workers don't ever *really* work." The capacity for verbal autointoxication being as great as it is in some people, many of the believers in this faith were able to drive daily past gangs of WPA workers sweating over the construction of roads and bridges and still to declare quite honestly, "I've never yet seen a WPA worker do any work!" Another instance of this same self-induced blindness is to be found in widespread attitudes toward "women drivers." Many men encounter hundreds of cars daily that are expertly driven by women; yet they declare, again quite honestly, "I never saw a woman yet who could *really* drive a car." By *definition,* driving is a "man's job"; women are "timid," "nervous," "easily frightened," and therefore they "can't drive." If the critics happen to know women who have driven successfully for years, they maintain that those women "have just been lucky," or that "they don't drive like women." [2]

The important fact to be noticed about such attitudes towards "churchgoers," "WPA workers," and "women drivers" is that we should never have made such mistakes nor so blinded ourselves if we had never heard anything about them beforehand. Such attitudes

[2] As is well known now, the statistics of insurance companies indicate clearly that women have much better safety records than men do. Nor do insurance companies raise their rates for families with daughters of driving age, as they do for families with sons of driving age.

are not the product of ignorance; genuine ignorance doesn't have attitudes. They are the result of false knowledge—false knowledge that robs us of whatever good sense we were born with. As we have already seen, part of this false knowledge we make up for ourselves with our confusions of levels of abstraction and other evaluative errors described in earlier chapters. However, a great deal of it is *manufactured* simply through our universal habit of *talking too much.*

Many people, indeed, move in a perpetual vicious circle. Because of intensional orientation, they are oververbalized; by oververbalization, they strengthen their intensional orientation. Such people burst into speech as automatically as juke boxes; a dime in the slot, and they're off. With habits of this kind, it is possible for us to *talk ourselves into un-sane attitudes,* not only towards "women drivers," "Jews," "capitalists," "bankers," and "labor unions," but also towards our personal problems: "mother," "relatives," "money," "popularity," "success," "failure"—and, most of all, towards "love" and "sex."

Advertising and Intensional Orientation

Among the forces in our present culture contributing to intensional orientation, advertising must be counted as one of the most important. The fundamental purpose of advertising—the announcing of products, prices, new inventions, or special sales—is not to be quarreled with; such announcements deliver needed information, which we are glad to get. But in national advertising directed to the consumer, the techniques of persuasion are rarely informative. As stated in the previous chapter on "Poetry and Advertising," the main endeavor is to "poeticize" or glamorize the objects you wish to sell by giving them brand names and investing those names with all sorts of desirable affective connotations suggestive of health, wealth, popularity with the other sex, social prominence, domestic bliss, fashion, and elegance. The process is one of creating intensional orientations toward brand names:

> If you want love interest to thrive, then try this dainty way. . . . For this way is glamorous! It's feminine! It's alluring! . . . Instinctively, you prefer this costly perfume of Verona Soap. . . . It's a fragrance men love. Massage each tiny ripple of your body daily with this delicate, cleansing lather. . . . Thrill as your senses are kissed by Verona's exquisite perfume. Be radiant.

Advertisers further promote intensional habits of mind by playing on words: the "extras" of skill and strength that enable champions to win games are equated with the "extras" of quality that certain products are claimed to have; the "protective blending" that harmonizes wild animals with their environment and makes them invisible to their enemies is equated with the "protective blending" of whiskies.

There is another subtle way in which advertising promotes intensional habits: through the practice of making slogans out of commonplace facts, advertisers make the facts appear to be unique to particular products. Rosser Reeves, head of Ted Bates and Company advertising agency, cites with admiration a number of phenomenally successful campaigns using this technique—the parenthetical comments are his own: "OUR BOTTLES ARE WASHED WITH LIVE STEAM" ("His client protested that every other brewery did the same"); "IT'S TOASTED" ("So, indeed, is every other cigarette"); "GETS RID OF FILM ON TEETH" ("So, indeed, does every other toothpaste"); "STOPS HALITOSIS" ("Dozens of mouth-washes stop halitosis"); "STOPS B.O." ("All soaps stop body odor").[3] The skill that advertisers and propagandists often display in this kind of slanting reminds us of William Blake's famous warning:

> A truth that's told with bad intent
> Beats all the lies you can invent.

When advertising by verbal hypnotism succeeds in producing these intensional orientations, the act of washing with Verona Soap becomes, in our minds, a thrilling experience indeed. Brushing our teeth with Colgate toothpaste becomes a dramatic and timely warding off of terrible personal calamities, like getting fired or losing one's girl friend. The smoking of Marlboros becomes an assertion of masculinity (instead of a possible invitation to lung cancer)—making one a rugged, outdoor, he-man type, like a telephone lineman or a paratrooper—even though in actuality one may be simply a clerk at a necktie counter. The taking of unnecessary (and even dangerous) laxatives becomes "following the advice of a world-renowned Viennese specialist." We are sold daydreams with every bottle of mouthwash and delusions of grandeur with every package of breakfast food.

Advertising, then, has become in large part the art of overcoming us with pleasurable affective connotations. When the consumer demands that, as a step towards guiding himself by facts rather than

[3] Rosser Reeves, *Reality in Advertising* (1961), pp. 55–57.

by affective connotations of brand names, certain products be re-quired by law to have informative labels and verifiable government grading, the advertising industry raises a hue-and-cry about "gov-ernment interference with business." [4] This is the sort of argument presented against grade-labeling *in spite of the fact that businessmen, both retailers and wholesalers, rely extensively on grading according to federally established standards when they do their own purchasing.*

In other words, many advertisers *prefer* that we be governed by automatic reactions to brand names rather than by thoughtful con-sideration of the facts about their products. An important reason for this preference lies in the mechanics of present-day retail distribution. Most of the buying of groceries, for example, is done at supermarkets, where the housewife must make choices among huge and dazzling displays of packaged merchandise, with no clerk to explain to her the advantages of one choice over another. Therefore, to use the termi-nology of the trade, she must be "pre-sold" *before* she gets to the market—and this is done by getting her to remember, through tire-less reiteration on radio and television commercials, a brand name, and by investing that name with nothing but pleasant connotations.

Thoughtful purchasing is the last thing many merchandisers want. Once the customer is hooked on a brand name, all sorts of tricks can be played on him (or her). A currently widespread practice is to reduce the contents of a package without reducing its size or price; many items traditionally bought in one-pound and half-pound pack-ages now come in such sizes as 15 oz., 14½ oz., 7 oz., and 6¾ oz. These figures are usually printed in tiny letters on the package in places where they are least likely to be seen. For the unwary house-wife, the costs of "brand loyalty" can be high. [5]

[4] For example, a pamphlet called "Your Bread and Butter: A Salesman's Handbook on the Subject of Brand Names," prepared by "Brand Names Re-search Foundation" (no address given), undertakes to explain "What's Be-hind All the Smoke" of the consumer movement which, for many years, has demanded grade-labeling of consumer goods. Most of the members of women's organizations in the consumer movement, the pamphlet says, are "honestly concerned with solving the perennial problems of common sense buying," but a "vocal minority" of "self-appointed champions of the consumer" are the "spokesmen." This minority, it is explained, "want to standardize most con-sumer goods, to eliminate advertising and competing brands, to see govern-ment controls extended over production, distribution and profits. They be-lieve in a planned economy, with a government brain trust doing all the planning."

[5] Not all proprietors of brand names do this sort of thing, of course. The following comments from readers published in *Consumer Reports* give the other side of the picture: "It has always impressed me how the *Wheatena*

Within recent years, the advertising of brand names has climbed to a higher level of abstraction. In addition to the advertising of specific products by their brand name, there is now *advertising of advertising*. As the pamphlet of the Brand Names Research Foundation urges, "So it's up to you as a salesman for a brand name to keep pushing not only YOUR BRAND, but brands in general. *Get on the Brand Wagon!*" A whisky advertisement says: "AMERICA IS NAMES . . . Seattle, Chicago, Kansas City . . . Elm Street, North Main, Times Square . . . Wrigley, Kellogg, Squibb, Ipana . . . Heinz, Calvert . . . Goodrich . . . Chevrolet. Names [the American has] always known . . . names of things he's bought and used . . . believed in. . . . Yes, America is names. *Good* names. Familiar names that inspire confidence. . . . For America *is* names . . . *good* names for good things to have. . . ." This sort of advertising of advertising has become increasingly common. The assumption is dinned into us that if a brand name even *sounds* familiar, the product it stands for must be good. ("The best in the land if you buy by brand.") *A graver example of systematic public miseducation can hardly be imagined. Intensional orientation is elevated to a guiding principle in the life of the consumer.*

Sometimes it seems as if the conflict between the aims of the advertiser and those of the educator is irreconcilable. When the teacher of home economics says, "Buy wisely," she means careful and reflective purchasing in the light of one's real needs and of accurate information about the product. When the advertiser says, "Buy wisely," he often means, "Buy our brand, regardless of your special situation or special needs, because DUZ DOES EVERYTHING!" The teacher's job is to encourage intellectual and moral self-discipline. The job of the advertiser often seems to be to encourage thoughtlessness ("impulse buying") and self-indulgence, even at the cost of life-long bondage to finance companies.

However, the writer is far from certain that the conflict between the aims of the advertiser and the educator is inevitable. It is inevitable *if* advertising cannot perform its functions *except* through the promotion of mistaken reactions to words and other symbols. Because advertising is both so powerful and so widespread, it in-

---

cooked-cereal boxes are filled so close to the top that they can hardly be opened without running over. What a happy experience to encounter in today's world of commerce." "I am happy to call attention to the *Hi Ho* crackers package. A one-pound size, so designated in large type on the front and back, was a welcome relief."

fluences more than our choice of products; it also influences our patterns of evaluation. It can either increase or decrease the degree of sanity with which people respond to words. Thus, if advertising is informative, witty, educational, and imaginative, it can perform its necessary commercial function and contribute to our pleasure in life without making us slaves to the tyranny of affective words. If, however, products are sold largely by manipulating affective connotations—*"pin-point* carbonation," *"activated* chlorophyll," *"dual-filter* Tareytons," "contains *RD-119,"* *"tired blood"*—the influence of advertising is to deepen the already grave intensional orientations widely prevalent in the public. The schizophrenic is one who attributes a greater reality to words, fantasies, daydreams, and "private worlds" than to the actualities around him. Surely it is possible for advertising to perform its functions without aggravating our all-too-prevalent verbomania! Or is it?

Higher Education, Learned Jargon, and Babuism

Education of the wrong kind also contributes tremendously to our intensional orientations. Some people look upon education largely as a matter of acquiring a learned vocabulary (including terms like "intensional orientation") *without* a corresponding concern (and sometimes with no concern at all) for *what the vocabulary stands for.*

In the course of getting an education, students have to read many difficult books. Some of these books, the student feels, are much more difficult to read than they need to be, because of the addiction of many scholars to extremely difficult terminology. Students, like other people, often ask why all books cannot be written more simply.

There are of course two answers to this question. The first is that some books are difficult because the ideas they deal with are difficult. An advanced work in chemistry or economics is difficult to one who knows no chemistry or economics for the simple reason that such a work presupposes on the part of the reader a background of previous study.

But there is another reason why books may be difficult. A learned vocabulary has two functions: first, it has the *communicative function* of giving expression to ideas—including important, difficult, or recondite ideas; secondly, it has a *social function* of conferring prestige upon its users and arousing respect and awe among those who do not understand it. ("Gosh, he must be smart. I can't understand a word he says!") It can be stated as a general rule that *whenever the social function of a learned vocabulary becomes more important to its users than its communicative function, communication suffers and jargon proliferates.*[6] This rule may be illustrated by a passage from a recent issue of the *American Journal of Sociology:*

> In any formal organization, the goals as reflected in the system of functional differentiation result in a distinctive pattern of role differentiation. In turn, role differentiation, whether viewed hierarchically or horizontally, leads to what Mannheim called "perspectivistic thinking," namely, incumbency in a particular status induces a corresponding set of perceptions, attitudes and values. In an organization, as in society as a whole, status occupants tend to develop a commitment to subunit goals and tasks—a commitment that may be dysfunctional from the viewpoint of the total organizational goals. In other words, "perspectivistic thinking" may interfere with the coordination of effort toward the accomplishment of total organizational goals, thus generating organizational pressures to insure adequate levels of performance.

In this passage the author is merely saying (1) that in any formal organization, different people have different tasks; (2) that people sometimes get engrossed in their own special tasks to a degree that interferes with the goals of the organization as a whole; and therefore (3) that the organization has to put pressures on them to get the over-all job done. What is clear from this passage (the *only* thing that is clear) is that the author's concern with his professional standing as a sociologist has almost completely submerged his concern with communicating his ideas. Thus, students are compelled in their studies to read, in addition to material that is intrinsically difficult, material that is made unnecessarily difficult by jargon.

This sociological passage, however, has at least the merit of possessing a discoverable meaning. There are some readings a college student encounters for which even this much cannot be said with certainty. For example:

> The being that exists is man. Man alone exists. Rocks are, but they do not exist. Trees are, but they do not exist. Horses are, but they do not exist. Angels are, but they do not exist. God is, but he does not exist. The proposition "man alone exists" does not mean by any means that man alone is a real being while all other beings are unreal and mere appearances or human ideas. The proposition "man exists"

[6] The word "jargon" is used here, as it is defined in *Webster's Third New International Dictionary*, to mean "pretentious or unnecessarily obscure and esoteric terminology."

means: man is that being whose Being is distinguished by the open-standing standing-in in the unconcealedness of Being, from Being, in Being. The existential nature of man is the reason why man can represent beings as such, and why he can be conscious of them. All consciousness presupposes ecstatically understood existence as the *essentia* of man—*essentia* meaning that as which man is present insofar as he is man. But consciousness does not itself create the openness of beings, nor is it consciousness that makes it possible for man to stand open for beings. Whither and whence and in what free dimension could the intentionality of consciousness move, if instancy were not the essence of man in the first instance? [7]

The foregoing are only samples of the many kinds of abstract prose that the student—especially the college and university student—encounters daily in his studies. Sometimes his professor, who presumably understands the readings he assigns, lectures at equally high levels of abstraction, so that the student is never quite sure, from the beginning of the course to the end, what it is all about. What is the effect upon students of readings and lectures of this kind? Obviously, the student is left with the impression that simplicity and clarity of style will get him nowhere in intellectual life, and that even a simple idea (or no idea at all) will gain academic respectability if it is phrased in a sufficiently abstract and incomprehensible vocabulary.

The British in India used to have a derogatory term for the pretentious and often comically inappropriate English used by poorly trained Indian clerks and civil servants: they called it "babu English." [8] The term is admittedly offensive, and the writer uses it only because it contains an idea for which there is no other term. Abandoning its original application, then, let us use "babu English," or "babuism," as a general term to mean *discourse in which the speaker (or writer) throws around learned words he does not understand in order to create a favorable impression.* Babuism probably has existed and will continue to exist in every culture in which there is a learned class of magicians, shamans, priests, teachers, and other professional verbalizers with big vocabularies. Babuism results whenever people

[7] Martin Heidegger, "The Way Back into the Ground of Metaphysics," in *Existentialism from Dostoevsky to Sartre,* trans. and ed. Walter Kaufmann (1957), pp. 214–15.

[8] "Babu" (or "baboo") is defined in the Funk and Wagnalls *New Standard Dictionary* as "1. A Hindu gentleman: a polite term of address, equivalent to *sir* or *Mr.* 2. In India, a native merchant or clerk who can write English. 3. A native of India with a smattering of English education: a derogatory term. . . . babuism."

who are not learned try to confer upon themselves by purely verbal means the *social* advantages of being considered learned.

Elsewhere in this volume, much has been said of the common tendency to confuse symbols with the things they stand for. The student may do the same: he may confuse symbols of learning (such as an abstract and difficult vocabulary) with learning itself. Not being able to understand the books he is reading, and blaming himself for his failure to understand, he conscientiously applies himself again and again to his assignments until he is familiar with the *vocabulary* of the course—a vocabulary that cannot help becoming a "babu English," since he still does not know what it is all about. If he is verbally clever, he will be able to parrot enough of this vocabulary in his final term paper to make it sound extremely plausible. The teacher reading the paper will also not be too sure what it is all about, but he will recognize the vocabulary as his own and so will give it a passing grade.

Thus the student, by learning to speak and write several kinds of babu—literary babu, psychological babu, educational babu, philosophical babu, the babu of art criticism, etc.—will eventually get his bachelor's degree. Perhaps he will go on to graduate school and get his Ph.D. Then he will teach it to others.

Thus does intensional orientation, like Ol' Man River, keep a-rollin' along.

APPLICATIONS

I. Because this chapter is open to misinterpretations, perhaps it will be helpful to the reader to check the following statements as "true" or "false"—"true" meaning that the assertion is one that *the writer makes in this chapter,* "false" meaning that the assertion is one that he *does not make.**

1. "Intensional orientation" means that the speaker is full of good intentions.

2. People in communist countries are unhappy because they are ruled by communists.

3. In order to be popular and make friends, it is important to be able to converse freely and easily on any subject.

4. You are always better off buying well-known, brand-name merchandise.

* Answers on p. 294.

5. Brand-name advertising should be prohibited by law and all goods should be government-graded.

6. Churchgoers are not to be trusted with other people's wives or money.

7. The aims of advertising and the aims of education are incompatible.

8. The passage from the *American Journal of Sociology* is an example of "babuism."

9. "Babu English" is high-falutin' language that is difficult for the average person to understand.

10. The passage quoted from Heidegger is an example of "babuism."

II. The trade magazine *Advertising Age* reprinted the following "correction" advertisement from a Chicago newspaper and commented that it was "undoubtedly the correction to end all corrections." It reads:

> Recently we advertised lots for sale in California City, California. We indicated this property is "In Greater Los Angeles"; "Commuting Distance Los Angeles"; "Already a Large Community"; "Parks, Schools, Churches Provided For"; "Running Water, Paved Streets Already In." An illustrated lake was captioned, "Isabella Lake near California City."
>
> The development is located 115 miles from Los Angeles; 40 homes have been completed. Parks, schools, churches have not been provided for. Land has been dedicated for such use. Water and paved streets are not already in this tract. They are guaranteed as provided by California law. The lake illustration should not have been used since we have been informed the only mapped lake in California named "Isabella Lake" is not "near California City."
>
> We regret these errors and pledge they will not occur again.

Glaring misrepresentations such as those which necessitated this correction are no longer common in national advertising in reputable magazines. However, a subtler kind of misleading copy is extremely common, namely, *copy that seems to give information but does not.* One example of this is what might be called the "uncomparative comparative," in which tires may be said to last "twenty percent longer" —but there is no answer to the question, "longer than what?" Similarly for the "quicker acting" headache remedy and the "faster drying" hair-set.

Another kind of statement that seems to give information but does not is that which says, for example, that a given cold remedy contains "not one, not two, not three, but FOUR precious ingredients so valuable in relieving the miseries of a cold that doctors prescribe them." A cosmetic is said to "texturize as it cleanses," whatever that may mean. The naming of mysterious-sounding ingredients is still another example ("contains IRIUM!" "enriched with new, patented *Formula X-11!*"). If we call a statement that gives verifiable facts "information," statements of the foregoing kind may be called "anti-information."

Collect examples of *anti-information* for your scrapbook. Here is a sample to add to your collection:

> For the woman who could weep because her skin beauty is drying out. . . . If time is showing too soon on your face . . . if you've tried creams and moisturizers with only fleeting results . . . you'll want to know *why:*
>
> You see, after 25, the skin that needs moisture *most* can hold it *least*. Some formulas do little more than sit *on* your skin; keep it smooth and moist for a while. But moisture, alas, evaporates, and back come the lines and dryness. And the despair! But "Moon Drops" four moisturizing formulas work in their own scientific way to help store up and hold natural moisture *inside,* to help *keep* your skin misty-moist. And, like plumping up a pillow, this inner moisture fills out little lines! With "Moon Drops" Moisture Treatment, there need never be a dry spell for your skin . . . "MOON DROPS" Moisture Treatment by REVLON.

III. Translate the following sentences into academic jargon:

1. Like father, like son.

   > SAMPLE TRANSLATION: It can be asserted as a generally tenable hypothesis that the male offspring of a given individual male parent is likely closely to resemble that parent in external appearance, in attitudinal set, in characterological configuration, in patterns of behavior, or in all four of these dimensions of personality structure.

2. The race is not always to the swift.
3. She goes to church only in order to show off her clothes.
4. Little fishy in the brook; baby catch him with a hook.

IV. Some of the following passages show a marked intensional orientation (a tendency to be carried away by words—one's own or another's), while some clearly show an extensional orientation (a concern with the nonverbal things or events for which words stand). Study these passages to decide which are predominantly intensional and which are predominantly extensional—and state your reasons for your conclusion in each case:

1. Probably the greatest American speech of our century was Gen. Douglas MacArthur's address to Congress on his return from Korea. Search all others, read this masterpiece, and you will recall what I mean. Many men are full of good language. . . . But a truly great speech requires not only superb language but great wisdom and great truth at a great moment from the heart of a great man. . . .

   Gen. MacArthur wrote this speech flying in the "Bataan" from San Francisco to Washington . . . and in longhand, much as Lincoln reportedly wrote the Gettysburg Address on an envelope aboard the train carrying it to immortality. He could compose it because he understood it. He spoke the truth because he knew it. . . . This speaker's great calling was liberty. Events full of terror and sorrow were at hand. Here was the needed reminder to his countrymen that the people who were in this war all the way were our men who ennoble the high, sharp Korean walls and live on Heartbreak Ridge every day. And die.

   Here was prophecy as revealing as a beacon light. . . . Here was hope: the dedication that we will live in a world where those of us who are Americans can be proud. . . . Here was history tolling like an old and important bell: the mighty warning that mighty America, once having entered this major war, must not let it end in impasse. . . .

   It was all spoken in less than 30 minutes and in 3074 words.
   —HENRY J. TAYLOR, San Francisco *News*

2. What indeed are faculties? We talk of faculties as if they were distinct, things separable; as if a man had intellect, imagination, fancy, etc. as he has hands, feet and arms. That is a capital error. Then again, we hear of a man's "intellectual nature," and of his "moral nature," as if these again were divisible, and existed apart. Necessities of language do not perhaps prescribe such forms of utterance; we must speak, I am aware, in that way, if we are to speak at all. *But words ought not to harden into things for us.* It seems to me, our apprehension of this matter is, for most part, radically falsified thereby. We ought to know withal, and to keep forever in mind, that these divisions are at bottom but *names;* that man's spiritual nature, the vital Force which dwells in him, is essentially one and indivisible; that what we call imagination, fancy, understanding, and so forth, are but different figures of the same Power of Insight, all indissolubly connected with each other, physiognomically related; that if we knew one of them, we might know all of them.
   —THOMAS CARLYLE, *Heroes and Hero Worship*

3. My Great Books class recently spent two hours in trying to come to an agreement on what "peace" really is. At the beginning of the class, all the members were confident that they knew what the word meant—at the end, nobody was quite sure. Is peace merely the absence of armed conflict? If so, slavery would be peace. Is it the absence of "physical" conflict? Then what about psychological warfare, which subjugates a people without firing a shot?

Is it possible to have peace without justice? Without government? Without love? Without religion? Can nations which respect no common authority really have peace between them, or simply an uneasy truce? Is the jungle in a state of peace when the animals are not fighting, or is it always in a state of potential warfare? . . .

—SIDNEY J. HARRIS, Chicago *Daily News*

4. I wanted to have the correct English word for "fleuve." . . . "River" means "rivière," and anyone who has sense knows that a "rivière" and "fleuve" are two entirely different things. . . . I looked into my dictionary. To my great surprise, "fleuve" was translated by "river." . . . Only one English word, "river," to translate both "rivière" and "fleuve." What a discovery! I had a vague suspicion that English was a very poor language compared to French. . . . Even in such simple tasks as naming the natural objects, English was short of words. . . .

A little later I had to translate English into French. The word "giggle" was in the sentence. . . . The French term was "ricaner." You see, for every English word, we have at least one French word—clear, precise, picturesque. Further down came "titter." . . . "Titter" and "giggle" had one translation in French: "ricaner." . . . In another context was the word "chuckle." . . . How do we say that in French? Well, well! I could hardly believe it: "ricaner" is the only word we have. The score was turning against us. I was disturbed.

My feeling of French superiority received a crushing blow when I eventually looked for the French translation of "to sneer." Little did I expect that once again I would find the ubiquitous "ricaner." . . .

The moral of the story is that I don't see the same things, I don't observe the same events when I change my English for my French thinking tool. Changing my language changes me as an observer. It changes my world at the same time. I cannot dissociate my senses and my brain from the tool I am using.

—J. SAMUEL BOIS, *Explorations in Awareness*

5. THE QUESTION MAN: *What annoys you most about women drivers?* (Asked at 7th and Mission Sts.) FRANK RUGGIERO, mailman: The worst thing about women drivers is that they are unpredictable.

When a woman gives a hand signal the only thing you can be sure of is that the window is open. . . . RAUL CHALCO, trucker: The majority of them are too nervous. They make too many sudden stops. They let their eyes wander from the road. If there is another female in the car the gabbing is more important than the driving. LEONARD PRZYBYLYSKI, shipping clerk: . . . She seems to be always in a hurry. Spends an hour making herself up and then wants to break the sound barrier to get where she's going. ADOLPH EICHENBAUM, retired investor: They either don't know the laws or else they are just plain inconsiderate. . . . JAMES LOUGHREY, mold loftsman: Of one thing you can be sure—a woman backing up is utterly confused. For some reason shifting into reverse makes her go to pieces. BILL GUALTIERI, order clerk: Women can't adapt to an unusual situation. They panic. . . . BOB SEVERIDA, coffee-brewer engineer: They hate to give up a lane. They get in it and it's their very own. . . . She thinks the rear view mirror is there so she can pat her hair.

—San Francisco *Chronicle*

6. Education implies teaching. Teaching implies knowledge. Knowledge is truth. The truth is everywhere the same. Hence education should be everywhere the same.

   —ROBERT M. HUTCHINS, *The Higher Education in America*

7. I asked professors who teach the meaning of life to tell me what is happiness.

   And I went to famous executives who boss the work of thousands of men.

   They all shook their heads and gave me a smile as though I was trying to fool with them.

   And then one Sunday afternoon I wandered out along the Desplaines River

   And I saw a crowd of Hungarians under the trees with their women and children and a keg of beer and an accordion.

   —CARL SANDBURG

Answer to Application I: All the statements are "false."

17 Rats and Men

Reactors that produce, say, five million kilowatts of electricity are too large to be accepted by our present economic and political units. The scale of the new energy source determined by the logic of economics and of the inherent nature of the technology is larger than the scale determined by our traditionally fragmented political and economic structures. But it is not only nuclear energy in its peaceful aspects that makes our divided world obsolete. As John von Neumann pointed out some ten years ago, the H-bomb and the ICBM also make geographic boundaries obsolete. The imperative toward unification resulting from the intrinsic massiveness of modern technology is not confined to nuclear energy. Our communications systems, our transportation systems, the possibility of using superconducting cable for transmission of electricity, all these and many other new technologies point strongly to the mismatch between the size of our political or economic units and the size of our technologies. I think all of us who are involved in these new technologies can only hope that before they destroy us, our political instruments will accommodate to the logic of massiveness, and that the major fruit of the new technologies will be a unified and peaceful world.

—ALVIN M. WEINBERG

"Insoluble" Problems

Professor N. R. F. Maier of the University of Michigan performed a series of experiments several years ago in which "neurosis" is induced in rats. The rats are first trained to jump off the edge of a platform at one of two doors. If the rat jumps to the right, the door holds fast, and it bumps its nose and falls into a net; if it jumps to the left, the door opens, and the rat finds a dish of food. When the rats are well trained to this reaction, the situation is changed. The food is put behind the other door, so that in order to get their reward they now have to jump to the right instead of to the left. (Other changes, such as marking the two doors in different ways, may also be introduced by the experimenter.) If the rat fails to figure out the new system, so that each time it jumps it never knows whether it is going to get food or bump its nose, it finally gives up and refuses to jump at all. At this stage, Dr. Maier says, "Many rats prefer to starve rather than make a choice."

Next, the rats are forced to make a choice, being driven to it by blasts of air or an electric shock. "Animals which are induced to respond in the insoluble problem situation," says Dr. Maier, "settle down to a specific reaction (such as jumping *solely* at the left-hand door) which they continue to execute regardless of consequences. . . . The response chosen under these conditions becomes fixated. . . . Once the fixation appears, the animal is incapable of learning an adaptive response in this situation." When a reaction to the left-hand door is thus fixated, *the right-hand door may be left open so that the food is plainly visible.* Yet the rat, when pushed, *continues to jump to the left,* becoming more panicky each time. When the experimenter persists in forcing the rat to make choices, it may go into convulsions, racing around wildly, injuring its claws, bumping into chairs and tables, then going into a state of violent trembling, until it falls into a coma. In this passive state, it refuses to eat, refuses to take any interest in anything: it can be rolled up into a ball or suspended in the air by its legs—the rat has ceased to care what happens to it. It has had a "nervous breakdown." [1]

It is the "insolubility" of the rat's problem that leads to its nervous breakdown, and, as Dr. Maier shows in his studies of disturbed children and adults, rats and human beings seem to go through pretty much the same stages. First, they are trained to make habitually a given choice when confronted by a given problem; secondly, they get a terrible shock when they find that the conditions have changed and that the choice doesn't produce the expected results; third, whether through shock, anxiety, or frustration, they may fixate on the original choice and continue to make that choice regardless of

[1] Norman R. F. Maier, *Frustration: The Study of Behavior Without a Goal* (1949). See especially Chapter 2, "Experimental Evidence of Abnormal Behavior Reactions," and Chapter 6, "Comparison of Motivational and Frustration-Induced Behavior Problems in Children."

consequences; fourth, they sullenly refuse to act at all; fifth, when by external compulsion they are forced to make a choice, they again make the one they were originally trained to make—and again get a bump on the nose; finally, even *with the goal visible in front of them,* to be attained simply by making a different choice, they go crazy out of frustration. They tear around wildly; they sulk in corners and refuse to eat; bitter, cynical, disillusioned, they cease to care what happens to them.

Is this an exaggerated picture? It hardly seems so. The pattern recurs throughout human life, from the small tragedies of the home to the world-shaking tragedies among nations. In order to cure her husband's faults, a wife may nag him. His faults get worse, so she nags him some more. Naturally his faults get worse still—and she nags him even more. Governed, like the rat, by a fixated reaction to the problem of her husband's faults, she can meet it only in one way. The longer she continues, the worse it gets, until they are both nervous wrecks.

Again, white people in a northern city, deploring the illiteracy and high crime rate among Negroes, segregate them, persecute them (it is well known that the police are almost always tougher on Negro suspects than on whites), and deny them opportunities for employment and advancement. The denial of opportunity perpetuates the illiteracy and the high crime rate, which in turn perpetuate the segregation, persecution, and denial of opportunity. The search for a way to break up this vicious circle taxes the best minds among those interested in orderly social change: city councilmen, educators, urban planners, Negro organizations, as well as state governments and federal authorities.

To cite another example, students trying to express themselves in writing may write poorly. In order to improve their writing, says the English teacher, I must teach them the fundamentals of grammar, spelling, and punctuation. By thus placing excessive emphasis on grammar and mechanics while ignoring the students' ideas, the teacher quickly destroys student interest in writing. That interest destroyed, the students write even more poorly. Thereupon the teacher redoubles his dose of grammar and mechanics. The students become increasingly bored and rebellious. Such students fill the ranks of "remedial English" classes in high school and college.

Again, a nation, believing that the only way to secure peace and dignity is through armed strength, may embark on a huge armaments program. The program arouses the fears of neighboring nations, so that they too increase their armaments to match those of the first nation. Anxiety and tension increase. It is clear, the first nation declares, that we shall continue to feel anxious about our national security so long as we are not adequately prepared for all emergencies; we must therefore *double* our armaments. This naturally makes the neighboring nations even more anxious, so that they too double their armaments. Anxiety and tension increase even more. It is clear, the first nation declares, that our mistake has been to underestimate our defense needs. This time we must be *sure* to be sufficiently armed to preserve peace. We must *triple* our armaments. . . .[2]

Of course these instances are oversimplified, but it is often because of vicious circles of this kind that we are unable to get at or do anything about the conditions that lead to disaster. The pattern is frequently recognizable; the goal may be in sight, attainable by a mere change in methods. Nevertheless, governed by fixated reactions, the rat "cannot" get food, the wife "cannot" cure her husband's faults, Negroes will have to wait two or three generations "until the time is ripe" for social change, and we "cannot afford" to stop devising and manufacturing weapons so deadly that they cannot be used without destroying civilization itself.

There is, however, an important difference between the insolubility of the rat's problems and the insolubility of human problems. Dr. Maier's rats were driven to their nervous breakdowns by problems more complicated than would naturally occur in a rat's environment. But human breakdowns are ordinarily caused by problems that human beings themselves have created: problems of religious and ethical belief; problems of money and credit and mortgages and trust funds and stock-market fluctuations; problems of man-made custom and etiquette and social organization and law.

Rats can hardly be blamed for not being able to solve problems set for them by Dr. Maier; there are limits to a rat's powers of ab-

---

[2] "Let us represent the explosive power of a World War II blockbuster by a one-foot ruler. On this scale the bomb that demolished Hiroshima would be represented by the height of the Empire State Building, and a 20-megaton weapon by the height of the orbit of Sputnik I." Since Harrison Brown and James Real wrote these words in their pamphlet, *Community of Fear* (1960), Khrushchev's government has claimed a 100-megaton bomb! At the meeting of the American Association for the Advancement of Science in December 1960, Dr. Ralph E. Lapp estimated that the United States had then a bomb stockpile equal to 50,000 bombs of the Hiroshima type, and that in another three years would add the equivalent of another 30,000 Hiroshima-type bombs. All this means, of course, that the U.S.S.R. is also stockpiling atomic and thermonuclear weapons at as nearly as possible the same rate.

straction. But there are no known limits to the human capacity to abstract and organize and make use of abstractions. Hence, if human beings find problems insoluble because of fixated reactions— if they are frustrated because they can respond in only one way, regardless of context or circumstances, to certain symbolically defined situations—they are functioning at less than full human capacity. They can be said, in Korzybski's suggestive phrase, to be "copying animals" in their reactions. Wendell Johnson summarized this idea aptly when he said, "To a mouse, cheese is cheese; that's why mousetraps work." How do these fixations occur in human beings?

Cultural Lag

A basic reason for such "insoluble" problems in society is what might be called "institutional inertia." An "institution," as the word is used in sociology, is "an organized pattern of group behavior, well-established and accepted as a fundamental part of a culture" (*American College Dictionary*). Human beings are so constituted that they inevitably organize their energies and activities into patterns of behavior more or less uniform throughout a social group. People who are identified with institutions therefore have their own way of looking at things: people in a communist (or capitalist) society accept and perpetuate communist (or capitalist) habits of economic behavior; the soldier looks at the world through a soldier's eyes and abstracts from it what a soldier has been trained to abstract; the banker and the union official and the stockbroker similarly abstract in accordance with their special training. And through long habituation to a professional or institutional way of looking at the world, each tends to believe that his abstractions of reality—his maps of the territory—*are* reality: defense *is* defense; deficit *is* deficit; a scab *is* a scab; a blue-chip *is* a blue-chip.

Hence we have the peculiar fact that, once people become accustomed to institutions, they eventually get to feeling that their particular institutions represent the *only right and proper* way of doing things. The institution of human slavery, like the caste system in India, was claimed by its defenders to be "divinely ordained," and attacks upon the institution were regarded as attacks upon natural law, reason, and the will of God. Those who had contrary institutions, on the other hand, regarded their system of free labor as "divinely ordained," and slavery as contrary to natural law, reason, and the will of God. In a similar way today, those who believe in corporate capitalist enterprise regard their way of organizing the distribution of goods as the *only proper way;* while communists adhere to their way with the same passionate conviction. This loyalty to one's own institutions is understandable: almost everyone in any culture feels that his institutions are the very foundations of reasonable living. A challenge to those institutions is almost inevitably felt to be a threat to *all* orderly existence.

Consequently, social institutions tend to change slowly—and, most importantly—they tend to continue to exist long after the necessity for their existence has disappeared, and sometimes even when their continued existence becomes a nuisance and a danger. This is not to say, of course, that *all* contemporary institutions are obsolete. Many institutions are changing rapidly enough to keep up with changes in conditions. Many, however, are not. The continued existence of obsolete institutional habits and forms (like the systems of county government in many states of the Union, geographically arranged to suit the needs of a horse-drawn rural population) is called by sociologists "cultural lag." In everyday language, "cultural lag" is summed up in a peculiarly appropriate expression, "horse-and-buggy" ways.

The Fear of Change

The pressing problems of our world are then problems of cultural lag—problems arising from trying to organize a jet-propelled, supersonic, electronic, and atomic world with horse-and-buggy institutions. The rate of technological advancement for almost two hundred years now has been greater than the rate of the change of our social institutions and their accompanying loyalties and ideologies; and the disparity between the two rates is increasing rather than decreasing. Consequently, in every contemporary culture which has felt the impact of technology, people are questioning the appropriateness of nineteenth-century (eighteenth-century, medieval, or Stone Age) institutions to twentieth-century conditions. They are progressively more alarmed at the dangers arising from old-fashioned nationalism in a world that has become, technologically, one world; they are increasingly anxious over the possibility of attaining a sane world economic order with the instruments of nineteenth-century capitalism (or of nineteenth-century socialism). Wherever technologies are producing changes not adequately matched by changes in social institutions, there are people under strain and tension.

Some, of course, meet these strains and tensions in the only sensible way possible: they strive to change or abandon outmoded institutions and to bring into being new institutions or newer forms of old institutions. Changes in educational practice, in governmental organization, in the responsibilities of trades unions, in the structure of corporations, in the techniques of librarianship, in the marketing of agricultural commodities, and so on, go on all the time because extensional people are constantly striving to bring institutions into closer relationship with reality. An especially successful example of institutional adaptation is the Federal Deposit Insurance Corporation. Prior to 1934, bank failures resulted in the partial or total loss of the savings of depositors; panics, once started, were almost impossible to control. Since the setting up of FDIC, however, panics have disappeared. Bank failures are extremely rare, and even when they occur, depositors do not lose their money. American people now take the stability of their banks for granted, with a serenity that could hardly have been imagined before 1934. A more recent example of successful institutional adaptation in response to new problems is the Peace Corps—an ingenious combination of elements drawn from the military, the Civilian Conservation Corps of Depression days, the Salvation Army, and the missionary organizations of Christian churches. The Common Market is a triumphant example in Europe of what can be done by extensionally minded people when they are really determined to modify ancient social institutions and practices in favor of a more workable economic order.

Some people, however, seeing the need for changes, agitate for cures which, on examination, appear to be no better than the ailment; still others agitate for changes that cannot possibly be brought about. In some of the most important areas of human life—especially in our ideas about international relations and in the closely related problem of an equitable world economic order—areas in which our failure to find solutions threatens the future of civilization itself—we are, all over the world, in a state of cultural lag.

What causes this cultural lag? In the case of many groups, the cause is obviously ignorance. Some people manifestly don't know the score, so far as the realities of the modern world are concerned. Their "maps" represent "territories" that have long since passed out of existence. In other cases, the lag is due to fixed economic or political interests. Many individuals enjoy power and prestige within the framework of outmoded institutions—and with institutional inertia to support them, it is not hard for them to believe that their familiar institutions are beautiful and wonderful things. Indeed, there is little doubt that the desire of the wealthy and powerful to keep their wealth and power is a major reason for cultural lag in any society. Threatened with social change, they often act in such narrowly short-sighted and selfish ways that, like the Bourbons, they seem willing to destroy both the civilization they live in and themselves in grim, pigheaded attempts to hang on to their prerogatives.

But wealth and power are not in themselves guarantees either of social irresponsibility or of stupidity, and the existence of a powerful wealthy class in a culture is not in itself a guarantee that there will be cultural lag. At least some of the rich and powerful have known how to yield gracefully to institutional adjustments—sometimes they have even helped to introduce them—and by so doing they have maintained their favored position and have saved both society and themselves from the disasters that attend complete social disruption. When this happens, cultural lag is kept small enough to be manageable. In some Latin American countries today, there is a touch-and-go race going on between social reform and revolution, the outcome depending largely on the willingness of the privileged class to accept and adjust to change.

But even when the rich and powerful are shortsighted and irresponsible, they must have support among those who are neither rich nor powerful in order to be able to hold back necessary institutional adjustments. To comprehend cultural lag, then, we must account not only for the shortsightedness of tne powerful but also for the shortsightedness of the ordinary citizen who supports policies that are contrary to his own interests. In addition to institutional inertia (which is a tremendous force for keeping people busy doing things they should have stopped doing long ago), it appears that fear is another major force influencing both rulers and the ruled in the direction of institutional rigidity. Perhaps the ultimate strength of cultural lag comes from those persons in all walks of life whom change has made afraid.

The Revision of Group Habits

Whether the cultural lag arises from inertia, from shortsighted selfishness, from fear of change, or from a combination of these and other reasons, it is clear that the solution of social problems is basically a matter of adapting institutional habits to new conditions.

Perhaps the most dramatic thing about human behavior is how

many problems which are "insoluble" for institutional reasons are promptly solved the moment a war breaks out. War is an institution the demands of which, at least in modern culture, take precedence over almost all other demands. Before World War II, it would have been "impossible" to send the slum children of London to the country for the sake of their health. But when the air raids on London began, the evacuation of all the children took place over a weekend. Institutionally minded men, before the war, demonstrated time and again that it was "impossible" for either Germany or Japan to fight without an adequate gold supply. Nevertheless, Germany and Japan did manage to put up quite a fight in spite of the predictions of extremely reputable editorialists and economists. At Sydenham, England, and at Biarritz, France, the American government put together, almost overnight after the war closed, two great universities for GI's in Europe. Textbooks and equipment were flown over, luxurious quarters were provided for the thousands of students, and distinguished professors from the leading universities of America were hired at handsome salaries in order to provide, for a very short time, an educational Utopia for war-wearied American soldiers. In ordinary times, is there any conceivable way in which a similar university could be set up, say, in Mississippi, the state which, since it has the least per capita to spend on education, would be in greatest need of such a school? One of the lessons of war is that institutions, while powerful and long-lasting, are often not insuperably rigid *if the emergency is great enough.*

The problem, then, the world over, is to learn that the emergency is serious enough—in international affairs, in race relations, in the world population explosion, and in many other areas—to require modifying or abandoning some of our institutions. And the problem for us as citizens, once we understand the emergency, is how we can contrive ways of adjusting our thinking and acting so that institutional adjustments may be made both realistically and rapidly, with a minimum of human suffering and a maximum of general benefit.

The Extensional Approach

Every widely debated public issue—proposed changes in labor laws, proposed changes in the methods of distributing medical care, proposals for unifying the armed services under a single command, proposals to set up new ways of settling disputes between nations—

is, then, a discussion of institutional adaptation. If we persist in discussing our social problems in terms of "justice" *versus* "injustice,"
"natural law, reason, and the will of God" *versus* "the forces of
anarchy and chaos," reactions of fear and anger become general on
both sides—and fear and anger paralyze the mind and make intelligent decision impossible. The escape from this two-valued debate
lies in thinking about social problems as problems of institutional
adaptation. Once we begin to do so, our questions with respect to
hotly debated social issues begin automatically to become more extensional. We cease to ask whether a proposed institutional change
is "right" or "wrong," "progressive" or "reactionary." We begin to
ask instead, "What will be the results? Who would benefit, and by
how much? Who would be harmed, and to what degree? What safe-
guards does the proposal contain to prevent further harm? Are people actually ready for such a measure? What will be the effect on
prices, on the labor supply, on public health, or whatever? And who
says so, on the basis of what kind of research and what kind of expert knowledge?" From extensional answers to such extensionally
directed questions, decisions begin to flow. The decisions that flow
from extensional information are neither "left-wing" nor "right-wing."
They are simply the sensible things to do under the circumstances.

Here, let us say, is a proposed municipal ordinance to permit
trucks to pass over Oak Street bridge. Backing the measure are the
trucklines, which will save much time and money if the measure is
passed. If our discussion of the proposal is reasonably extensional,
our questions about it will be of the following kind: "Will the bridge
structure stand the additional load? What will be the effect on traffic
flow on Oak Street and streets approaching it? Is there danger of an
increase in street accidents? Will the beauty of the city be adversely
affected? What will be the effect on residences or businesses on and
near Oak Street?" When such questions have been answered by
persons of known ability in making accurate predictions in their several fields of knowledge, every voter has the materials with which
to decide the question for himself according to his own interests and
values, whether he is concerned with the safety of his children walk-
ing to school, with the beauty of the city, with trucking profits, with
the effect on the tax rate, or whatever. Each voter's decision, made
against a background of responsibly made predictions, will have some
kind of reasonable relationship to his real desires.

Let us further suppose, however, that the measure is advantageous to practically no one in town *except* the trucklines. Then, if

the trucklines want the measure passed, they may try to *prevent* the public from discussing the issue extensionally. The technique (familiar in the discussion of legislation affecting railroads, insurance, housing, medical care, and so on) is immediately to move the discussion to higher levels of abstraction and to talk about "unreasonable restraints on business," and the need to protect "free enterprise" and "the American way" against harassment by "politicians," "officeholders," and "petty bureaucrats." By systematic confusion of levels of abstraction, the "freedom" of trucklines to operate over Oak Street bridge is made to appear one with the freedom fought and bled for at Valley Forge.

The tragedy is not only that many of us are innocent enough to be deceived by this sort of talk; a deeper tragedy is that in many communities the newspapers provide us with almost no extensional materials for discussion. Partly because many newspapers have largely given up their news function in favor of entertainment, and partly because the sensational, two-valued utterances of extreme partisans make livelier stories than the testimony of extensionally minded experts, newspapers in some communities are scanty sources of information on important public issues.[3] And television, often governed by the whims of sponsors who are quick to cancel a news commentator's contract at the first hint of controversy, is often as empty of extensional content as the newspapers are.

Then, under present circumstances, the tenor of discussion (and therefore of public opinion) being what it is, what are the chances for institutional adaptation with respect to some of our most pressing problems? The replacement of maladjustments by new maladjustments and the continuation of old maladjustments under new names are about as near as we can get to correcting cultural lag.

The End of the Road

When, as the result of protracted debate of a futile kind, years pass without the successful accomplishment of institutional adjustments, cultural lag widens. As social dislocations grow more serious, fear and confusion spread. As fear and confusion spread, societies, like individuals, grow increasingly disturbed at their failure to solve their problems. Lacking the knowledge or the confidence to try new patterns of behavior and at the same time panicky with the knowledge

[3] See Lester Markel, "The Real Sins of the Press," *Harper's* (December 1962).

that their traditional methods no longer work, societies often appear to behave, to a greater or lesser degree, like Dr. Maier's rats, who, "induced to respond in the insoluble problem situation, settle down to a specific reaction which they continue to make regardless of circumstances. . . . The response under these conditions becomes fixated. . . . Once the fixation appears, the animal is incapable of learning an adaptive response in this situation." Thus do societies, as they have so often done in the past and continue to do today, fixate on *one* solution to their most pressing problem: the *only* way to appease the angry gods is to throw *still more* babies to the crocodiles; the *only* way to protect the social order is to detect and hunt down *still more* witches; the *only* way to insure prosperity is to reduce federal expenditures; and the *only* way to insure peace is to have *still greater* armaments. (The last two beliefs are, of course, held simultaneously.)

Such are the mental blockages—such are the patterns of repetitious behavior—that prevent us from meeting our "insoluble" problems with the only approach which can ever help us solve them: the extensional approach—for we cannot distribute goods, feed people, or establish cooperation with our neighbors by intensional definitions and high-level abstractions. What is done in the extensional world must be done by extensional means, no matter who does it. If we as citizens of a democracy are going to carry our share in the important decisions about the things that concern us so greatly, such as the problems of peace and a just world economic order, we must prepare ourselves to do so by coming down out of the clouds of high-level abstractions and learning to consider the problems of the world, whether at local, state, national, or international levels, as extensionally as we now consider the problems of getting food, clothing, and shelter.

If, however, we cling to our fixations and our intensional orientations, and the belligerent, two-valued sense of "I am right and you are wrong" which they produce, we have little before us but a fate similar to that of Dr. Maier's rat. We shall remain pathologically incapable of changing our ways of behavior, and there will be nothing for us to do but, like the rat, to try the same wrong solutions over and over again. After prolonged repetition of such futile conduct, would it be remarkable if we found ourselves finally in a condition of political "nervous breakdown"—sick of trying, disillusioned with the processes of democracy, and willing to permit dictators to dangle us upside down by our tails?

The Scientific Attitude

The most striking characteristic of science has been its continued success in the solving of "insoluble" problems. It was once considered "impossible" to devise means of traveling over twenty miles an hour, but now we have attained speeds of over 18,000 miles an hour. It was "impossible" for man to fly—people "proved" it again and again—but now we fly across oceans as a matter of everyday routine. The writer was told repeatedly during the course of his education that the release of atomic energy was merely a *theoretical* possibility—of course, they would never actually *do* it. The scientist may almost be called the professional accomplisher of the "impossible." He does this because, as a scientist, he is extensionally oriented. He may be, and often is, intensionally oriented toward what he calls "nonscientific" subjects; therefore, the physical scientist talking about social or political problems or about love and marriage is often no more sensible than the rest of us.

As we have seen, scientists have special ways of talking about the phenomena they deal with, special "maps" to describe the "territories" with which they are concerned. On the basis of these maps, they make predictions; when things turn out as predicted, they regard their maps as "true." If, however, things do not turn out as predicted, they *discard* their maps and make new ones; that is, they act on *new sets of hypotheses* that suggest *new courses of action.*[4] Again they check their map with the territory. If the new one does not check, they cheerfully discard it and make still more hypotheses, until they find some that *work*. These they regard as "true," but "true" *only for the time being.* When, later on, they find new situations in which the "working" hypotheses no longer work, they are again ready to discard them, to reexamine the extensional world, and to make still more new maps that again suggest new courses of action.

When scientists work with a minimum of interference from financial or political influences—when, that is, they are free to pool their knowledge with their co-workers all over the world and to check the accuracy of one another's maps by observations independently made and freely exchanged—they make rapid progress. Highly multi-valued and extensional in their orientations, they are troubled less

4 Alfred North Whitehead, in *Science and the Modern World,* says that it is not unusual for a scientist to *rejoice* when he is proved wrong; that all human progress has depended on "new questions" rather than on "new answers" to the "old questions."

than other men by fixed dogmas and nonsense questions. In a way that is paradoxical in terms of traditional orientations but quite understandable in terms of the new, the conversations and writings of scientific people are full of admissions of ignorance and declarations of partial knowledge. Expressions like the following appear with impressive frequency in the conversation of nuclear physicists with whom the writer has been acquainted: "According to Henderson's last paper—although there may be still later findings not yet published. . . ." "No one knows exactly what happens, but our guess is that it's something like this. . . ." "What I tell you is probably wrong, but it's the only plausible theory we've been able to construct. . . ." It has been said that knowledge is power, but *effective knowledge is that which includes knowledge of the limitations of one's knowledge.*

The last thing a scientist would do is cling to a map because he inherited it from his grandfather or because it was used by George Washington or Abraham Lincoln. By intensional orientation, "If it was good enough for Washington and Lincoln, it's good enough for me." By extensional orientation, *we don't know until we have checked.*

The Left-Hand Door Again

Notice the differences between the technological, scientific attitudes that we have toward some things and the intensional attitudes we have toward others. When we are having a car repaired, we think in terms of mechanisms. We do not ask: "Is the remedy you suggest consistent with the principles of thermodynamics? What would Faraday or Newton have done under similar circumstances? Are you sure that the remedy you suggest does not represent a degenerative, defeatist tendency in the technological traditions of our nation? What would happen if we did this to *every* car? What has Aristotle to say on this?" These are nonsense questions. We only ask, "What will be the *results?*"

But a different thing happens when we are trying to have society repaired. Few people have a sense of societies as mechanisms—as collections of going institutions. Accustomed to thinking of social problems in terms of simple moral indignation, we denounce the wickedness of labor unions (or of capitalists), we denounce the wickedness of those who clamor for Negro rights (or of those who persecute Negroes), we denounce Russia (or, if we are Russians, we denounce "American imperialism"). In so doing, we miss entirely the basic requirement of "mapping" social problems, namely, the initial task of describing the *established patterns of group behavior* (i.e., the institutions) that constitute a society and create its social problems. Indignant at the wickedness of those with whom we disagree, we do not ask of a proposed institutional change what the results will be. We are usually more interested in "punishing the wicked" than in determining the results. And suggested social remedies are almost always discussed in the light of questions to which verifiable answers cannot be given: "Are your proposals consistent with sound economic policy? Do they accord with the principles of true liberalism (or true conservatism)? What would Alexander Hamilton, Thomas Jefferson, or Abraham Lincoln have said? Would it be a step in the direction of communism or fascism? What would happen if everybody followed your scheme? Why don't you read Aristotle?" And we spend so much time discussing nonsense questions that often we never get around to finding out exactly what the results of proposed actions would be.

During the course of our weary struggles with such nonsense questions, someone or other is sure to come along with a campaign to tell us, "Let's get *back* to normalcy. . . . Let's stick to the good *old-fashioned, tried-and-true* principles. . . . Let's *return* to *sound* economics and *sound* finance. . . . America must get *back* to this. . . . America must get *back* to that. . . ." Most of such appeals are, of course, merely invitations to take another jump at the left-hand door—in other words, INVITATIONS TO CONTINUE DRIVING OURSELVES CRAZY. In our confusion we accept those invitations—with the same old results.

APPLICATIONS

I. Taking some community you know well, jot down some of its problems of cultural lag other than those mentioned in this chapter. What sort of questions would an extensionally oriented person be likely to ask if called upon to help solve one of these problems? What resource groups or persons would he be likely to consult?

II. Two friends of yours, both strongly opinionated but not at all well informed, one vigorously in favor of and the other vigorously opposed to "socialized medicine" (whatever either of them might mean by the term), are coming to your house tonight to spend the evening in conversation. Prepare some remarks you can throw into the discussion and some questions you can ask that might help make them see the problem of medical-care distribution as a problem of institutional adjustment (of course, you will avoid using such fancy terms) and that might therefore help them keep the discussion at more extensional levels than would otherwise be the case. Warning: Do not start out by making them define "socialized medicine" (see pp.181–86).

III. Scientists have been successful in the laboratory in part because they are "highly multi-valued and extensional in their orientations" and "troubled less than any other men by fixed dogmas." In trying to solve the problems of desegregated schooling in the South, should the federal government be two-valued or multi-valued in its attitude? What would be the advantage of each approach? Should the government be two-valued in some places (where there is hard-backed resistance to the law) and multi-valued in others (where desegregation is proceeding peacefully)? If the government were to suit its attitude to the place, would this be an instance of the multi-valued orientation that works so well for the scientist?

IV. Imagine that an election is about to take place. Four candidates are running. You believe that all four have the best interests of the country sincerely at heart; they all believe in social justice and the realization of democratic ideals, although they differ as to the means of achieving these ideals. Imagine, too, that you plan to vote neither as a "liberal" nor as a "conservative"; you simply want to vote for the candidate who, because he is realistic and extensional, is most likely to be able to recognize the actualities of the situation before him, and is therefore most likely to be able to work effectively towards his ideals.

Here are passages from the speeches of the four candidates. On the basis of these passages (please do not use other evidence), indicate the order of your preference among these candidates and give reasons for your choices. (Try not to be influenced by the names of the candidates!)

Candidate 1

Socialism is thus for me not merely an economic doctrine which I favor; it is a vital creed which I hold with all my head and heart. I work for Indian independence because the nationalist in me cannot tolerate alien domination; I work for it even more because for me it is the inevitable step to social and economic change. I should like the Congress to become a socialist organization and to join hands with the other forces in the world who are working for the new civilization. But I realize that the majority in the Congress, as it is constituted today, may not be prepared to go thus far. We are a nationalist organization, and we think and work on the nationalist plane. . . .

Much as I wish for the advancement of socialism in this country, I have no desire to force the issue in the Congress and thereby create difficulties in the way of our struggle for independence. I shall co-operate gladly and with all the strength in me with all those who work for independence even though they do not agree with the socialist solution. But I shall do so stating my position frankly and hoping in course of time to convert the Congress and the country to it, for only thus can I see it achieving independence. It should surely be possible for all of us who believe in independence to join our ranks together even though we might differ on the social issue. . . .

How does socialism fit in with the present ideology of the Congress? I do not think it does. . . .

—JAWAHARLAL NEHRU, presidential address,
Indian National Congress, Lucknow, April 1936

Candidate 2

I believe that communism should be taught in the educational system, but I believe it should be taught with a moral directive, in the same way that a medical student is taught that cancer is evil, that tuberculosis is evil, and education about them is directed to their elimination and defeat. I think the teaching of communism without a moral directive can be very dangerous. Teaching it with a moral directive should emphasize the basic foundations of American civilization, revealing the enemy threatening their destruction, the erroneous beliefs leading the communists to undertake the destruction of freedom, the methods by which they propose to destroy, and what must be done to defeat them. If it is presented without moral direction, it appears simply as an alternative economic system with certain superior virtues. This has frequently been done in the past and instead of opposing communism, it tends to recruit to communism.

I believe there is a great problem before the American people: to provide education with a moral dynamic that reveals communism as a rationale of murder and lying and the destruction of freedom. It is totally immoral, and mental and emotional barriers against it should be erected in the minds of the young.

—DR. FREDERICK SCHWARZ in testimony before the House
Committee on Un-American Activities, May 29, 1957

Candidate 3

The pointing up of racial conflicts and injustices is important in a study of both the position of the Negro and the state of American culture. But the frictions are a healthy sign. They indicate a many-sided contact between the two races. The frictions are an evidence of the fact that the Negro and white man live in the same community and quarrel over the same values. As long as the two races are striving and disagreeing over the manifold issues of living in the same culture, then it means that they are engaged in the painful process of accommodation to each other and to the world. The real danger would be if the Negro managed to live in a vacuum where there was no friction between him and his white neighbors; then there would be real danger of the developing of a perpetual caste system. . . . It is desirable that nothing should remain static until the issues over which the friction arises have themselves ceased to trouble either the white or the blacks. To want peace when the contrasts are so great is to dream of an unreal world. To expect either the white or the Negro community to show neither anger nor hate, neither fear nor violence, when their values are challenged and their aspirations are frustrated is to ask for the impossible. . . . [Friction] shows that the evils complained of are alive, troublesome, and impelling. They force men to do something about them. They will do many wrong things about them, but, by the same token, many right ones.

—FRANK TANNENBAUM, "An American Dilemma,"
Political Science Quarterly, September 1944

Candidate 4

Some men look at constitutions with sanctimonious reverence and deem them like the ark of the convenant, too sacred to be touched. They ascribe to the men of the preceding age a wisdom more than human, and suppose what they did to be beyond amendment. . . . I am certainly not an advocate for frequent and untried changes in laws and constitutions. . . . But I know also that laws and institutions must go hand in hand with the progress of the human mind. . . . As new discoveries are made, new truths disclosed, and manners and opinions change with the change of circumstances, institutions must advance also, and keep pace with the times. We might as well require a man to wear still the coat which fitted him when a boy, as civilized society to remain ever under the regimen of their barbarous ancestors. . . . Each generation . . . has the right to choose for itself the form of government it believes the most promotive of its own happiness.   —THOMAS JEFFERSON

V. Read, ponder, and digest:

Triolet

TO AN INDOLENT STUDENT
IN A CLASS IN GENERAL SEMANTICS

To a mouse, cheese is cheese; that's why mousetraps work.
—WENDELL JOHNSON, *People in Quandaries*

To a rodent, cheese is cheese;
    That's why mousetraps work.
No date or index, if you please,
To a rodent, cheese *is* cheese
Without semantic subtleties
    (Listen, you mouse-brained jerk!).
To a rodent, cheese is cheese;
    That's why mousetraps. (Work!)
        —S. I. HAYAKAWA

18 Towards Order Within and Without

> *But I say unto you, That every idle word that men shall speak, they shall give account thereof in the day of judgment. For by thy words thou shalt be justified, and by thy words thou shalt be condemned.*
> —Matthew 12:36–37

Rules for Extensional Orientation

Just as a mechanic carries around a pair of pliers and a screw driver for use in an emergency—just as we all carry around in our heads tables of multiplication for daily use—so can we all carry in our heads convenient rules for extensional orientation. These rules need not be complicated; a short, rough-and-ready set of formulas will do. Their principal function will be to prevent us from going round in circles of intensional thinking, to prevent automatic reactions, to prevent us from trying to answer unanswerable questions, to prevent us from repeating old mistakes endlessly. They will *not* magically show us what better solutions are possible, but they will *start us looking* for courses of action that are better than the old ones. The following rules, then, are a brief summary of the parts of the book that directly apply to problems of evaluation. These rules should be memorized.

1. A map is NOT the territory it stands for; words are NOT things.

   A map does not represent ALL of a territory; words never say ALL about anything.

   Maps of maps, maps of maps of maps, and so on, can be made indefinitely, with or without relationship to a territory. (Chapters 2 and 10.)

2. The meanings of words are NOT in the words; they are in US. (Chapters 2 and 11.)

3. Contexts determine meaning (Chapter 4):

I like fish. (Cooked, edible fish.)
He caught a fish. (Live fish.)
You poor fish! (Not fish at all.)
To fish for compliments. (To seek.)

4. Beware of the word "is," which, when not used simply as an auxiliary verb ("he is coming"), can crystallize misevaluations:

The grass *is* green. (But what about the part our nervous system plays? Chapters 10 and 11.)

Mr. Miller *is* a Jew. (Beware of confusing levels of abstraction. Chapters 11 and 12.)

Business *is* business. (This is a directive, not to be mistaken for a statement of fact. Chapter 7.)

A thing *is* what it *is*. (Unless this is understood as a rule of language, there is danger of ignoring alternative ways of classifying, as well as of ignoring the fact that everything is in process of change. Chapters 10, 12, 13, and 17.)

5. Don't try to cross bridges that aren't built yet. Distinguish between directive and informative statements. (Chapter 7.)

6. Distinguish at least four senses of the word "true":

Some mushrooms are poisonous. (If we call this "true," we mean that it is a *report that can be and has been verified*. Chapter 3.)

Sally is the sweetest girl in the world. (If we call this "true," we mean that *we feel the same way* towards Sally. Chapters 6 and 8.)

All men are created equal. (If we call this "true," we mean that this is *a directive which we believe should be obeyed*. Chapter 7.)

$(x + y)^2 = x^2 + 2xy + y^2$. (If we call this "true," we mean that this statement is *consistent with the system of statements possible to be made in the language called algebra*. Chapter 14.)

7. When tempted to "fight fire with fire," remember that the fire department usually uses water. (Chapter 14.)

8. The two-valued orientation is the *starter, not the steering apparatus*. (Chapter 14.)

9. Beware of definitions, which are words about words. Think with examples rather than definitions wherever possible. (Chapter 10.)

10. Use *index numbers* and *dates* as reminders that *no word ever has exactly the same meaning twice*.

Cow_1 is *not* cow_2, cow_2 is *not* cow_3, . . .
$Smith_{1963}$ is *not* $Smith_{1964}$, $Smith_{1965}$ is *not* $Smith_{1970}$, . . .

If these rules are too much to remember, the reader is asked to memorize *at least* this much:

Cow_1 is not cow_2, cow_2 is not cow_3, . . .

This is the simplest and most general of the rules for extensional orientation. The word "cow" gives us the intensional meanings, informative and affective; it calls up in our minds the features that this "cow" has *in common* with other "cows." The index number, however, reminds us that this one is *different;* it reminds us that "cow" does *not* tell us "all about" the event; it reminds us of the *characteristics left out* in the process of abstracting; it prevents us from equating the word with the thing, that is, from confusing the abstraction "cow" with the extensional cow.

Symptoms of Disorder

Not to observe, consciously or unconsciously, such principles of interpretation is to think and react in primitive and infantile ways. There are a number of ways in which we can detect unhealthy reactions in ourselves. One of the most obvious symptoms is sudden displays of temper. When blood pressure rises, when quarrels become excited and feverish, and when arguments end up in snarling and name-calling, there is a misevaluation somewhere in the background.

Another obvious symptom is worry—when we keep going round and round in circles. "I love her. . . . I love her. . . . If I could only forget that she is a *waitress!*" But $waitress_1$ is not $waitress_2$. "Gosh, what a terrible governor we've got! . . . We thought he was a businessman, but he proves to be only a *politician.*" But $politician_1$ is not $politician_2$. As soon as we break these circles and think about *facts* instead of *words,* new light is thrown on our problems.

Still another symptom of unhealthy reactions is a tendency to be oversensitive, easily hurt, and quick to resent insults. The infantile mind, equating words with things, regards unkind words as unkind acts. Attributing to harmless sets of noises a power of injuring, such a person is "insulted" when those noises are uttered at him. So-called "gentlemen" in semisavage and infantile societies used to dignify reactions of this kind into "codes of honor." By "honor," they meant extreme readiness to pull out swords or pistols whenever they imagined that they had been "insulted." Naturally, they killed each other off much faster than was necessary, illustrating again a principle often implied in this book: the lower the boiling point, the higher the mortality rate.

It has already been pointed out that the tendency to talk too much and too readily is an unhealthy sign. We should also be wary of "thinking too much." It is a mistake to believe that productive thinkers necessarily "think harder" than people who never get anywhere. They only think more efficiently. "Thinking too much" often means that somewhere in the back of our minds there is a "certainty"—an "incontrovertible fact," an "unalterable law," an "eternal principle"—some statement which we believe "says all" about something. Life, however, is constantly throwing into the face of our "incontrovertible certainties" facts that do not fit our preconceptions: "Politicians" who *aren't* corrupt, "friends" who *aren't* faithful, "benevolent societies" that *aren't* benevolent. Refusing to give up our sense of "certainty" and yet unable to deny the facts that do not fit, we are forced to "think and think and think." And, as we have seen before, there are only two ways out of such dilemmas: first, to deny the facts altogether, and secondly, to reverse the principle altogether, so that we go from *"All* insurance companies are reliable" to *"No* insurance companies are reliable." Hence such infantile reactions as, "I'll *never* trust another woman!" "Don't *ever* say politics to me again!" "I'm through with lawyers for good!" "Men are all alike, the heels!"

The mature mind, on the other hand, knows that words never say all about anything, and such a mind is therefore *adjusted to uncertainty*. In driving a car, for example, we never know what is going to happen next; no matter how often we have gone over the same road, we never find *exactly* the same traffic conditions. Nevertheless, a competent driver travels over all kinds of roads, even at high speeds, without either fear or nervousness. As driver, he is *adjusted to uncertainty*—the unexpected blowout or the sudden hazard—and *he does not feel insecure.*

Similarly, the intellectually mature person does not "know all about" anything. And this does not make him insecure, because he knows that the only kind of security life offers is the *dynamic security that comes from within: the security derived from infinite flexibility of mind—from an infinite-valued orientation.*

"Knowing all" about this, "knowing all" about that, we have only ourselves to blame when we find certain problems "insoluble." With some working knowledge of how language acts, in ourselves and others, we save both time and effort; we prevent ourselves from running around in verbal squirrel cages. With an extensional orientation, we are adjusted to the inevitable uncertainties of all our science and wisdom. And whatever other problems the world thrusts upon us, we at least escape those of our own making.

The Lost Children

Then there are the unhappy people who *don't* know "all about this" or "all about that," and *wish they did.* Being in a more or less chronic state of anxiety about not knowing all the answers, they are always looking for "the answer" that will forever still their anxieties. They drift from one church, political party, or "new thought" movement to another; they may drift from one psychiatrist to another if they are educated, or from one fortuneteller to another if they are not. Occasionally such people happen upon fortunetellers, political leaders, or systems of thought that hit them just right. Thereupon they are suddenly overwhelmed with relief and joy. Feeling that they have found *the* answer to all their problems, they become passionately devoted to spreading the news to everyone they know.

A major source both of the excessive anxiety which such people feel and of their excessive enthusiasm when they do find their problems "solved" has been described by psychiatrists. An adult—an emotionally mature person—is independent, able to work out his own answers to problems, and able to realize that there is no one answer to everything. If, however, we have not been brought up to be independent—if, for example, we were deprived of love and care at an age when we needed love and care, or if we had parents who did too much for us through excessive and misdirected love— we grow up physically mature but emotionally immature. No matter what our age, we continue to need a *parent-symbol:* some figure of comforting authority to whom we can turn for "all the answers." If we are so troubled, we will successively seek one parent-symbol after another, when we can no longer depend on our own parents— sometimes a kindly teacher, sometimes an authoritative and impressive clergyman, sometimes a fatherly employer, sometimes a political leader.

From our point of view as students of human linguistic behavior, the verbal aspects of this search for a parent-symbol deserve attention. Those who, for one reason or another, are unable to accept a priest, teacher, or political leader as a parent-symbol, may find a parent-symbol in a *big, systematic collection of words*—for example, a huge and difficult-to-understand philosophical work, a politico-economic philosophy, a system of "new thought," or the Hundred Great Books. "Here, here," they cry, "are all the answers in one place!" Finding "all the answers" in such collections of words is a sophisticated and, in our culture, a respectable form of both emotional immaturity and what we have earlier called naïveté regarding the symbolic process. It is emotional immaturity because it involves the giving up of independent thought in favor of dependence on a (verbal) parent-symbol. It is nevertheless respectable, because those who manifest their immaturity in this way acquire, in doing so, an impressively complicated and abstract vocabulary which they exhibit on all possible occasions—and our culture respects the fluent talker, especially one who talks at high levels of abstraction. This dependence on verbal parent-symbols is also naïve because it assumes what we have already seen to be an impossible assumption, namely, that a verbal "map" can "say all" about the "territory" of experience.

This is not to say, of course, that an enthusiasm for a "great book," or for a hundred of them, is necessarily a symptom of immaturity. However, there is a world of difference between the enthusiasm of the emotionally immature and that of the mature. An immature person, discovering a new intellectual system or philosophy that somehow meets his needs, tends to adopt it uncritically, to repeat endlessly the verbal formulas with which he has been provided, and *to resent any imputation that anything more needs to be discovered.* The mature reader, on the other hand, pleased and excited as he may be by the "great book" he has found, is *eager to test it.* Are these new and exciting principles or human insights as general as they appear to be? Are they true in many different cultural or historical contexts? Do they need correction or revision or refinement? How do the principles or attitudes apply in specific cases and under different conditions? As he asks himself these and other questions, he may find that his newly discovered system is quite as important as he originally thought it to be, but, along with his increased sense of power, he also gets a deep sense of *how much more there is to be learned.*

Indeed, the better and more widely useful a new philosophical or scientific synthesis is, the greater will be the number of fresh problems raised. The answers given to perplexing questions by Darwin in his *Origin of Species* did not stop biological inquiry; they gave biology the greatest spurt to fresh inquiry in modern times. The answers given by Freud to psychological questions did not stop psychology; they opened up whole new areas of investigation.[1] "Great books" are those which open great new questions. Great books are misread if their effect is to stop investigation.

In other words, the wiser people become, whether in science, religion, politics, or art, the less dogmatic they become. Apparently, the better we know the territory of human experience, the more aware we are of the limitations of the verbal maps we can make of it. We have earlier (Chapter 11) called this awareness of the limitations of maps "consciousness of abstracting." The mature person retains "consciousness of abstracting" even with respect to philosophies or systems of thought about which he feels the greatest enthusiasm.

"Know Thyself"

Another area in which "consciousness of abstracting" is necessary is in *what we say to ourselves about ourselves*. We are all a great deal more complex than Bessie the Cow, and even more than Bessie, we are constantly undergoing change. Furthermore, we all describe ourselves to ourselves in some kind of language (or other abstractions, like "mental pictures," "idealizations," or "images"). These descriptions of ourselves are more or less clearly formulated: "I am the home-loving type," "I am beautiful," "I am hopelessly unattractive," "I believe in efficiency," "I am kind-hearted," "I can't understand mathematics," "I have a natural talent for music," "I'm not that kind of a girl," "I am not a snob," "I am a friend of the downtrodden," and so on. All such statements are *more or less* accurate "maps" of that "territory" which is ourselves. Some people make better maps of themselves than others. If a person makes a reasonably good map of himself, we say that he "knows himself"— that he accurately assesses his strengths and his limitations, his emotional powers and his emotional needs. The psychologist Carl R. Rogers refers to this "map" we make of ourselves as the "self-concept," which, according to his terminology, may be "realistic"

[1] The communist use of the writings of Marx appears to the writer to be a misreading of books which were in their time important contributions to social science. The communists have treated all deviations from Marx (or at least deviations from their interpretations of Marx) as attacks upon "Truth," and they seem thereby to have rendered the progress of social science in the Soviet Union almost impossible. See Anatol Rapoport, "Dialectical Materialism and General Semantics," *ETC.,* V (1948), pp. 81–104.

or "unrealistic." What we do, how we dress, what manners or mannerisms we affect, what tasks we undertake and what tasks we decline, what kind of society we seek, and so on, are determined not so much by our *actual* powers and limitations as by what we *believe to be* our powers and limitations—i.e., by our "self-concepts." [2]

All that has previously been said in this book about maps and territories applies with special relevance to our "self-concepts." A map *is not* the territory: one's self-concept *is not* one's self. A map represents *not all* of the territory: one's self-concept *omits* an enormous amount of one's actual self—we never know ourselves *completely*. We can make maps of maps of maps, and so on: we can describe ourselves to ourselves, and then make about ourselves *any number of inferences and generalizations at higher levels of abstraction*.

The pitfalls of map-territory relationships therefore threaten the adequacy of our evaluations of ourselves just as much as they threaten the adequacy of our evaluations of other people and of external events. Indeed, as is suggested in the famous Socratic injunction, "Know thyself," it is more than probable that our wisdom in evaluating other people and external events rests largely upon our wisdom in evaluating ourselves. What kinds of "maps," then, do we make of ourselves?

Some people obviously have extremely unrealistic self-concepts. The person who says, "I have the ability to act as general manager" and accepts such a job, and then turns out not to have the ability, seriously disappoints himself and others. If another person says, "I'm not any good" and takes himself seriously when he says this, he may dissipate his talents, his opportunities, his entire life. The not uncommon sight of the middle-aged woman who dresses and acts like an eighteen-year-old is another instance of a person who lives in terms of an extremely *unrealistic* self-concept.

Students in school often defeat themselves by saying, "I'm not good at mathematics," or "I just *can't* learn to spell." They will be poor at mathematics or spelling not because of lack of ability, but because their self-concepts prevent them from tackling mathematics and spelling with any hope of victory.

[2] See Carl R. Rogers, *Client-Centered Therapy* (1951) and *On Becoming a Person* (1961); also Prescott Lecky, *Self-Consistency: A Theory of Personality* (1945); Gardner Murphy, *Personality: A Biosocial Approach to Origins and Structure* (1947); Donald Snugg and Arthur Combs, *Individual Behavior* (1949).

Furthermore, there are those who do not seem to realize that their self-concepts do *not* include *all* the relevant facts about themselves. As psychiatrists have shown us time and again, we all have a way of concealing from others and from ourselves our deeper reasons for doing things; instead, we offer, in justification of our acts, more or less elaborate rationalizations. Let us suppose, for example, that a critic has given as his reason for attacking a book its "shoddy argument and bad prose style." Let us suppose, furthermore, that his deeper reasons are entirely different, reasons such as professional jealousy, fear of the book's upsetting ideas, or a personal quarrel with the author ten years earlier. If the reviewer believes that his self-concept "says all" about himself, his picture of himself as "one who believes in rigorous logic and high standards of prose style" becomes to him a complete and adequate account of why he dislikes the book. In other words, the most common effect of not knowing that one's self-concept does not "say all" about one's self is *the tendency on the part of many people to believe their own rationalizations.* Some persons, indeed, believe their "self-concepts" so completely and sincerely—that is, they surround themselves with such airtight rationalizations—that they become incapable of any genuine self-knowledge.

Self-knowledge, of course, is often disturbing: statements of the kind "My real reason for not liking this book is that I'm jealous of the author," "The reason I am not getting ahead is that I am less intelligent than my colleagues," and so on, are extremely difficult to face if we are emotionally insecure. Therefore, we often *need* to believe our rationalizations: "The book is shoddy in its arguments," "The reason I am not getting ahead is that my colleagues are conspiring against me." If the need to believe in these inaccurate maps is strong enough, we can shut our eyes to any amount of evidence that contradicts them.

How do we prevent ourselves from getting into this emotional predicament? Those who are already in it can probably be helped only by a professionally trained counselor or a psychiatrist. But for the rest of us, there remain the day-to-day problems of action and decision; the more realistic our self-concepts are, the more likelihood there is of fruitful action and sane decision. Can we do anything to achieve a greater realism about ourselves? It is important that we do, because those who cannot be realistic about themselves are as a rule also incapable of being realistic about their relations with other people.

Reports and Judgments

In at least one respect, people who are capable of some degree of self-insight can do for themselves what psychological counselors and many psychiatrists do. As we have seen, we manufacture false self-concepts because truer statements are unbearable. The reason they are unbearable is often that they involve the uncritical acceptance from our environment (from what our friends and neighbors say, or what we think they are saying) of *other people's judgments*. Using the word "judgment" here as we have used it in Chapter 3, notice the difference between "I am a service-station attendant" (which is a report) and "I am *only* a service-station attendant" (which involves a judgment, implying that I ought to be something different and that it is disgraceful that I am what I am).

One of the most important aspects of a psychiatrist's or counselor's assistance is the fact that he *does not pass any judgments on us*. When the patient admits that he is "only" a service-station attendant, or that ten years ago he lost his grocery store through bankruptcy, the counselor indicates by word or by manner that, while he understands the patient's feelings of shame or guilt or embarrassment, he does not condemn him for being what he is or for having done what he has done. In other words, he helps the patient change the *judgment*, "I am *only* a service-station attendant and *therefore not much good*," into the *report*, "I am a service-station attendant." [3] The judgment, "I am a *bankrupt* and a *failure*," is changed into "Ten years ago I lost my grocery store through bankruptcy." As a result of the accepting attitude of the psychiatrist or counselor, the patient is better able to accept himself.

The fact that we permit other people's judgments (and what we believe to be their judgments) to influence us unduly is one of the commonest reasons for feelings of inferiority and guilt and insecurity. If a man, saying to himself, "I am a Negro," simultaneously accepts the judgment of certain white people on Negroes, he will find it very hard to be a Negro, and may spend the rest of his life being jumpy and defensive and miserable. If a man makes a hundred dollars a week and accepts the real or imagined judgment of others that if he were any good he would be making two hundred, he will find it difficult to face the fact of making a hundred. The training

---

[3] The writer once had a fireman as a student in a graduate class. Several weeks elapsed before he could say in class, "I am a fireman," and contribute to the discussion from his own unique experiences.

suggested in Chapter 3 of *writing reports from which judgments are excluded* may be applied to writing *about ourselves*. Such self-descriptions are an especially helpful technique in arriving at more realistic self-concepts.

We should, in performing this exercise, put down facts about ourselves—especially the facts about which we feel some shame or embarrassment—and then ask with respect to each fact such questions as these: "Is it necessary to pass judgment at all on this fact?" "Who passes judgment on this fact, anyway, and should I also do so?" "Are no other judgments possible?" "What does an unfavorable judgment on one of my actions *in the past* prove about what I am *today?*" Reports of the following kind may lead to such reevaluations as are indicated in the parentheses:

> I am a service-station attendant. (Some people think it is somehow inferior to be a service-station attendant. Do *I* have to think so, too?)
>
> I went through bankruptcy. (But that was ten years ago! I've had a lot more business experience since then. Who knows what will happen if I start again—in a different line of business? in a different location?)
>
> I cracked up on the battlefield. (Who says I shouldn't have cracked up? Were they in Korea? Did they have to go through what I did? I was psychologically wounded in battle; others were physically wounded. Why don't they give Purple Hearts to psychiatric casualties?)
>
> I am a housewife. (Well?)

Naturally, if one's rationalizations are deeply rooted, this technique is difficult to practice. For example:

> My real reason for disliking this book is professional jealousy. (Oh, no! The author's arguments *are* shoddy and his style *is* awful!)

But as we grow increasingly extensional about our own feelings— as we grow in our ability to accept ourselves, so that we are able to confront *without judgments of good or bad* such reports as, "I am below average in height," "I am not athletic," "I am the child of divorced parents," "My sister gets better grades than I do," "I never went to college," and so on—we progressively have less and less need to deceive ourselves. *In self-knowledge as in science, the conquest of little areas leads progressively to the conquest of larger and more difficult areas.* As our self-concepts grow more realistic, our actions and decisions become progressively wiser, since they are based on a more accurate "mapping" of that complex territory of our own personalities.

Institutionalized Attitudes

Another way in which we can increase our extensional awareness of ourselves is by distinguishing between attitudes *institutionally* arrived at and attitudes *extensionally* arrived at. As we have seen in Chapter 17, we are all members of institutions, and as members of institutions we incorporate into ourselves certain institutionally demanded attitudes. If we are Democrats, we are expected to support all Democratic candidates. If we belong to an employers' association, our fellow members may expect us to be hostile to all labor unions. If we are Montagues, we are expected to be hostile to the Capulets.

A source of widespread misevaluation implicit in such institutionalized attitudes is that each of them involves a generalization at a high level of abstraction, while actual Democratic candidates, labor unions, and Capulets exist at the level of extensional fact. Many persons are, through emotional insecurity as well as through lack of an extensional orientation, unable to depart from institutionally expected attitudes. Seeking security by adopting the "official" point of view prevalent in the institutions of which they are members, they become excessively conventional and excessively given to commonplace ideas and emotions. They feel what they are expected to feel by their political party, their church, their social group, or their family; they think what they are expected to think. They find it both easier and safer not to examine too extensionally any *specific* Democratic candidate, any *specific* labor union, any *specific* Capulet, because extensional examination of any one of these *might* lead to an evaluation different from the institutionally accepted point of view.

But to have nothing but institutionalized attitudes is eventually to have no personality of one's own, and therefore to have nothing original or creative to contribute to the institutions of which one is a member. Furthermore, there is the danger to one's personal adjustment implicit in continually living by high-level generalizations and repressing (or avoiding) extensional evaluations.

The rule already suggested for the avoidance of excessively intensional attitudes is helpful for the avoidance of excessively conventional, institutionalized attitudes, because intensional attitudes are often the result of the uncritical acceptance of institutional dogmas. With the application of the cow_1 is not cow_2 rule, we begin to *look* in order to find out if $Democrat_1$ differs in any important respects from $Democrat_2$, if labor $union_1$ differs from labor $union_2$, if $Capulet_1$ differs from $Capulet_2$. As the result of such extensional examination we may find that the original institutional attitudes were the correct ones after all; or we may find it necessary, as Romeo and Juliet did, to depart from them.[4] But whatever conclusions we may arrive at, the important thing is that they will be our own—the result of *our own* extensional examination of the events or objects to be evaluated.

People who are not accustomed to distinguishing between attitudes institutionally arrived at and those extensionally arrived at are capable of real self-deception. In a real sense, they don't know which of their opinions are simply parrot-like repetitions of institutional opinions, and which are the result of their own experience and their own thinking. Lacking that self-insight, they are unable to arrive at realistic self-concepts; they are unable to map accurately the territory of their own feelings and attitudes.

Reading Towards Sanity

A few words, finally, need to be said on the subject of reading as an aid to extensional orientation. Studying books sometimes has the effect of producing excessive intensional orientation; this is especially true in literary study, for example, when the study of words— novels, plays, poems, essays—becomes an end in itself. When the study of literature is undertaken, however, not as an end in itself, but as a guide to life, its effect is extensional in the best sense.

Literature works by intensional means; that is, by the manipulation of the informative and affective connotations of words. By these means, it not only calls our attention to facts not previously noticed, but it also is capable of arousing feelings not previously experienced. These new feelings in turn call our attention to still more facts not previously noticed. Both the new feelings and the new facts, therefore, upset our intensional orientations, so that our blindness is little by little removed.

The extensionally oriented person, as has been repeatedly said, is governed not by words only, but by the facts to which the words

---

[4] Of course, Romeo and Juliet were not always as extensional as they might have been. Had they not been prone to confusing inferences with facts, they might both have lived a little longer.

have guided him. But supposing there were no words to guide us? Should we be able to guide ourselves to those facts? The answer is, in the vast majority of cases, no. To begin with, our nervous systems are extremely imperfect, and we see things only in terms of our training and interests. If our interests are limited, we see extremely little; a man looking for cigarette butts in the street sees little else of the world passing by. Furthermore, as everyone knows, when we travel, meet interesting people, or have adventures before we are old enough to appreciate such experiences, we often feel that we might just as well not have had them. Experience itself is an extremely imperfect teacher. Experience does not tell us what it is we are experiencing. Things simply happen. And if we do not know *what to look for* in our experience, the happenings often have no significance to us whatever.

Many people put a great deal of stock in experience as such; they tend automatically to respect the person who has "done things." "I don't want to sit around reading books," they say; "I want to get out and do things! I want to travel! I want to have experiences!" But often the experiences they go out and get do them no good whatever. They go to London, and all they remember is their hotel and the American Express Company office; they go to Mexico and remember only their gastro-intestinal difficulties. The result is that some people who have never traveled know more about the world than some people who have. We all tend to go around the world with our eyes shut unless someone opens them for us.

And this eye-opening, then, is the tremendous function that language, in both its scientific and its affective uses, performs. In the light of abstract scientific generalizations, "trivial" facts lose their triviality. When we have studied, for example, surface tension, the alighting of a dragonfly on a pool of water is a subject for thought and explanation. Those who have never read Wordsworth have missed something of the English lake country, even if they have lived there all their lives; to those who have read Faulkner, a trip through Mississippi is a doubly meaningful experience. In the light of the subtleties of feeling aroused in us by literature and poetry and drama, every human experience is filled with rich relationships and significances.

The communications we receive from others, insofar as they do not simply retrace our old patterns of feeling and tell us things we already know, increase the efficiency of our nervous systems. Poets, as well as scientists, have aptly been called "the window washers of the mind"; without their communications to widen our interests and increase the sensitivity of our perceptions, we could very well remain as blind as puppies.

Language, as has been repeatedly emphasized in these pages, is social. Reading or listening, writing or talking, we are constantly involved in the processes of social interaction made possible by language. Sometimes, as we have seen, the result of that social interaction is the sharing of knowledge, the enrichment of sympathies and insight, and the establishing of human cooperation. But at other times, the social interaction does not come out so well: every exchange of remarks, as between two drunks at a bar or between two hostile delegates at the United Nations Security Council, leads progressively to the conviction on the part of each that it is impossible to cooperate with the other.

We come back, then, to the judgments explicitly announced at the beginning of this book—the ethical judgments on which the argument has been based throughout—that widespread intraspecific cooperation through the use of language is the fundamental mechanism of human survival, and that, when the use of language results, as it so often does, in the creation or aggravation of disagreements and conflicts, there is something wrong with the speaker, the listener, or both. Sometimes, as we have seen, this "something wrong" is the result of ignorance of the territory which leads to the making of inaccurate maps; sometimes it is the result, through faulty evaluative habits, of refusing to look at the territory but insisting on talking anyway; sometimes it is the result of imperfections in language itself, imperfections which neither speaker nor listener have taken the trouble to examine; often it is the result of using language not as an instrument of social cohesion, but as a weapon. The purpose of this book has been to lay before the reader some of the ways in which, whether as speakers or listeners, we may use or be used by the mechanisms of linguistic communication. What the reader may wish to do with these mechanisms is up to him.

POSTSCRIPT

Although the principles which have been explained throughout this book have as their purpose the establishment of agreement and the avoidance of conflict, some people may be tempted to use them as weapons with which to stir up arguments, as clubs with which to beat people over the head: "The trouble with you, Joe, is that you've got a bad case of two-valued orientation," "For God's sake, Mabel, stop being so intensional!" Those who use the formulations of this book in this way may be said to have understood the book but dimly.

Selected Bibliography

* Arnold, Thurman W. *The Symbols of Government.* New Haven, Conn.: Yale University Press, 1935.

* ————. *The Folklore of Capitalism.* New Haven, Conn.: Yale University Press, 1937.

* Ayer, A. J. *Language, Truth and Logic.* New York: Oxford University Press, 1936.

Barnlund, Dean C., and Franklyn S. Haiman. *The Dynamics of Discussion.* Boston: Houghton Mifflin, 1960.

Bell, Eric Temple. *The Search for Truth.* New York: Reynal and Hitchcock, 1934.

* Benedict, Ruth. *Patterns of Culture.* Boston: Houghton Mifflin, 1934.

Bentley, Arthur F. *Linguistic Analysis of Mathematics.* Bloomington, Ind.: The Principia Press, 1932.

Berrien, F. K., and Wendell H. Bash. *Human Relations: Comments and Cases.* New York: Harper, 1957.

Bloomfield, Leonard. *Language.* New York: Henry Holt, 1933.

Bois, J. Samuel. *Explorations in Awareness.* New York: Harper, 1957.

* Bridgman, P. W. *The Logic of Modern Physics.* New York: Macmillan, 1927.

* Burke, Kenneth. *The Philosophy of Literary Form.* Baton Rouge: Louisiana State University Press, 1941.

* ————. *A Grammar of Motives.* Englewood Cliffs, N.J.: Prentice-Hall, 1945.

Burrow, Trigant. *The Social Basis of Consciousness.* New York: Harcourt, Brace & World, 1927.

Carnap, Rudolf. *Philosophy and Logical Syntax.* London: Psyche Miniatures, 1935.

* Cassirer, Ernst. *An Essay on Man.* New Haven, Conn.: Yale University Press, 1944.

Chase, Stuart. *Roads to Agreement.* New York: Harper, 1951.

————. *Power of Words.* New York: Harcourt, Brace & World, 1954.

————. *Guides to Straight Thinking.* New York: Harper, 1956.

Asterisk indicates titles obtainable in paperback editions.

* Cherry, Colin. *On Human Communication*. New York: Science Editions, 1957.

Chisholm, Francis P. *Introductory Lectures on General Semantics*. Lakeville, Conn.: Institute of General Semantics, 1945.

* Dantzig, Tobias. *Number: The Language of Science*. New York: Macmillan, 1933.

Deutsch, Karl W. *Nationalism and Social Communication*. New York: John Wiley, 1953.

Doob, Leonard W. *Public Opinion and Propaganda*. New York: Henry Holt, 1948.

* Empson, William. *Seven Types of Ambiguity*. London: Chatto and Windus, 1930.

ETC.: A Review of General Semantics (quarterly); edited by S. I. Hayakawa. Published since 1943 by the International Society for General Semantics, San Francisco State College, San Francisco, California.

* Frank, Jerome. *Law and the Modern Mind*. New York: Brentano, 1930.

Fromm, Erich. *Escape from Freedom*. New York: Rinehart, 1941.

Garey, Doris. *Putting Words in Their Places*. Chicago: Scott, Foresman, 1957.

Gordon, Thomas. *Group-Centered Leadership*. Boston: Houghton Mifflin, 1955.

* Gorman, Margaret. *General Semantics and Contemporary Thomism*. Lincoln, Nebr.: University of Nebraska Press, 1962.

Haney, William V. *Communication: Patterns and Incidents*. Homewood, Ill.: Richard D. Irwin, 1960.

Hayakawa, S. I. (ed.). *Language, Meaning and Maturity: Selections from ETC., 1943–1953*. New York: Harper, 1954.

———— (ed.). *Our Language and Our World: Selections from ETC., 1953–1958*. New York: Harper, 1959.

* ———— (ed.). *The Use and Misuse of Language*. New York: Fawcett, 1962. Selections from *Language, Meaning and Maturity* and *Our Language and Our World*.

Hockett, C. F. *A Course in Modern Linguistics*. New York: Macmillan, 1958.

Horney, Karen. *The Neurotic Personality of Our Time*. New York: W. W. Norton, 1937.

Huse, H. R. *The Illiteracy of the Literate*. New York: D. Appleton-Century, 1933.

Huxley, Aldous. *Words and Their Meanings*. Los Angeles: Jake Zeitlin, 1940.

Huxley, Julian. *Evolution: The Modern Synthesis*. New York: Harper, 1942.

* Isaacs, Harold R. *Images of Asia: American Views of China and India* (Scratches on Our Minds). New York: John Day, 1958.

Jacobs, Noah Jonathan. *Naming-Day in Eden*. New York: Macmillan, 1958.

* Johnson, Alexander Bryan. *A Treatise on Language* (1836); edited by David Rynin. Berkeley: University of California Press, 1947.

———. *The Meaning of Words* (1854); with introduction by Irving J. Lee. Milwaukee, Wisc.: John W. Chamberlin, 1948.

Johnson, Wendell. *People in Quandaries: The Semantics of Personal Adjustment*. New York: Harper, 1946.

———. *Your Most Enchanted Listener*. New York: Harper, 1956.

Kelley, Earl C. *Education for What Is Real*. New York: Harper, 1947.

Kepes, Gyorgy. *Language of Vision;* with introductory essays by Siegfried Giedion and S. I. Hayakawa. Chicago: Paul Theobald, 1944.

Keyes, Kenneth S., Jr. *How To Develop Your Thinking Ability*. New York: McGraw-Hill, 1950.

Korzybski, Alfred. *The Manhood of Humanity*. New York: E. P. Dutton, 1921.

———. *Science and Sanity: An Introduction to Non-Aristotelian Systems and General Semantics*. Lancaster, Pa.: Science Press Printing Company, 1933.

Kropotkin, Petr. *Mutual Aid, A Factor of Evolution;* with foreword by Ashley Montagu. Boston: Extending Horizons Books, 1955.

* La Barre, Weston. *The Human Animal*. Chicago: University of Chicago Press, 1954.

* Langer, Susanne K. *Philosophy in a New Key*. Cambridge, Mass.: Harvard University Press, 1942.

* Lasswell, Harold D. *Psychopathology and Politics*. Chicago: University of Chicago Press, 1930.

Leavis, Q. D. *Fiction and the Reading Public*. London: Chatto and Windus, 1932.

Lecky, Prescott. *Self-Consistency: A Theory of Personality*. New York: Island Press, 1945.

Lee, Irving J. *Language Habits in Human Affairs*. New York: Harper, 1941.

———. *The Language of Wisdom and Folly*. New York: Harper, 1949.

———. *How to Talk with People*. New York: Harper, 1952.

———. *Handling Barriers to Communication*. New York: Harper, 1957.

Lévy-Bruhl, Lucien. *How Natives Think*. New York: Knopf, 1926.

Lewin, Kurt. *Principles of Topological Psychology*. New York: McGraw-Hill, 1936.

Lieber, Lillian R. *The Einstein Theory of Relativity*. New York: Farrar & Rinehart, 1945.

———. *The Education of T. C. Mits*. New York: W. W. Norton, 1944.

* Maier, Norman R. F. *Frustration: The Study of Behavior Without a Goal*. New York: McGraw-Hill, 1949.

Malinowski, Bronislaw. *The Problem of Meaning in Primitive Lan-*

guages; Supplement I in Ogden and Richards, *The Meaning of Meaning.*

Maslow, A. H. *Motivation and Personality.* New York: Harper, 1954.

Masserman, Jules. *Behavior and Neurosis.* Chicago: University of Chicago Press, 1943.

* Mayer, Martin. *Madison Avenue, U.S.A.* New York: Harper, 1958.

* Mead, Margaret (ed.). *Cooperation and Competition Among Primitive People.* New York: McGraw-Hill, 1936.

* Menninger, Karl. *Love Against Hate.* New York: Harcourt, Brace & World, 1942.

* Miller, George A. *Language and Communication.* New York: McGraw-Hill, 1951.

Minteer, Catherine. *Words and What They Do to You.* Evanston, Ill.: Row, Peterson, 1952.

Morris, Charles. *Signs, Language and Behavior.* Englewood Cliffs, N.J.: Prentice-Hall, 1946.

Murphy, Gardner. *Personality: A Biosocial Approach to Origins and Structure.* New York: Harper, 1947.

Newton, Norman. *An Approach to Design.* Cambridge, Mass.: Addison-Wesley, 1951.

* Ogden, C. K., and I. A. Richards. *The Meaning of Meaning,* 3rd ed., rev. New York: Harcourt, Brace & World, 1930.

Osgood, Charles E., G. J. Suci, and P. H. Tannenbaum. *The Measurement of Meaning.* Urbana, Ill.: University of Illinois Press, 1957.

* Packard, Vance. *The Hidden Persuaders.* New York: David McKay, 1957.

* Piaget, Jean. *The Language and Thought of the Child.* New York: Harcourt, Brace & World, 1926.

* ———. *The Child's Conception of the World.* New York: Harcourt, Brace & World, 1929.

Pollock, Thomas Clark. *The Nature of Literature.* Princeton, N.J.: Princeton University Press, 1942.

* Popper, Karl R. *The Open Society and Its Enemies.* London: Hutchinson, 1950.

Rapoport, Anatol. *Science and the Goals of Man.* New York: Harper, 1950.

———. *Operational Philosophy.* New York: Harper, 1953.

———. *Fights, Games, and Debates.* New York: Harper, 1960.

Richards, I. A. *Science and Poetry.* New York: W. W. Norton, 1926.

* ———. *Practical Criticism, A Study of Literary Judgment.* New York: Harcourt, Brace & World, 1929.

———. *The Philosophy of Rhetoric.* New York: Oxford University Press, 1936.

———. *Interpretation in Teaching.* New York: Harcourt, Brace & World, 1938.

Rogers, Carl R. *Counseling and Psychotherapy.* Boston: Houghton Mifflin, 1942.

————. *Client-Centered Therapy.* Boston: Houghton Mifflin, 1951.

————. *On Becoming a Person.* Boston: Houghton Mifflin, 1961.

Rokeach, Milton. *The Open and Closed Mind.* New York: Basic Books, 1960.

Ruesch, Jurgen. *Disturbed Communication.* New York: W. W. Norton, 1957.

————. *Therapeutic Communication.* New York: W. W. Norton, 1961.

————, and Gregory Bateson. *Communication: The Social Matrix of Psychiatry.* New York: W. W. Norton, 1951.

————, and Weldon Kees. *Nonverbal Communication.* Berkeley: University of California Press, 1956.

Sapir, Edward. *Language: An Introduction to the Study of Speech.* New York: Harcourt, Brace & World, 1921.

Schaff, Adam. *Introduction to Semantics.* New York: Pergamon Press, 1962.

Skinner, B. F. *Verbal Behavior.* New York: Appleton-Century-Crofts, 1957.

Smith, Bruce L., Harold D. Lasswell, and Ralph D. Casey. *Propaganda, Communication, and Public Opinion: A Comprehensive Reference Guide.* Princeton, N.J.: Princeton University Press, 1946.

Snygg, Donald, and Arthur Combs. *Individual Behavior.* New York: Harper, 1949.

Stefansson, Vilhjalmur. *The Standardization of Error.* New York: W. W. Norton, 1927.

Szasz, Hans. *The Myth of Mental Illness.* New York: Harper, 1961.

Taylor, Edmond. *The Strategy of Terror.* Boston, Mass.: Houghton Mifflin, 1940.

Thurman, Kelly. *Semantics.* Boston: Houghton Mifflin, 1960.

Upward, Allen. *The New Word: An Open Letter Addressed to the Swedish Academy in Stockholm on the Meaning of the Word IDEALIST.* New York: Mitchell Kennerley, 1910.

Vaihinger, Hans. *The Philosophy of "As If."* New York: Harcourt, Brace & World, 1924.

Veblen, Thorstein. *The Theory of the Leisure Class.* New York: Modern Library, 1934.

Vygotsky, L. S. *Thought and Language.* New York: John Wiley, 1962.

Walpole, Hugh R. *Semantics.* New York: W. W. Norton, 1941.

Weinberg, Harry L. *Levels of Knowing and Existence.* New York: Harper, 1959.

Welby, V. *What Is Meaning?* New York: Macmillan, 1903.

Whorf, Benjamin Lee. *Language, Thought and Reality: Selected Writings of B. L. Whorf;* edited by John B. Carroll. New York: John Wiley, 1956.

* **Wiener, Norbert.** *Human Use of Human Beings: Cybernetics and Society.* Boston: Houghton Mifflin, 1950.

Yerkes, Robert M. *Chimpanzees: A Laboratory Colony.* New Haven, Conn.: Yale University Press, 1943.

* **Young, J. Z.** *Doubt and Certainty in Science: A Biologist's Reflections on the Brain.* New York: Oxford University Press, 1951.

Index

Doob, Leonard, *Public Opinion and Propaganda,* 117
Dostoyevsky, Fyodor, 150
Douglas, Kirk, 133
Doyle, Sir Arthur Conan, cited, 52–53
Drama, and symbolic process, 27–28
Drifters, 318
Duerrenmatt, Friedrich, *The Pledge,* cited, 166

Ecological balance, 9–10
Economic order, 301
Education, higher, 286–88
Einstein, Albert, 234, 238, 240
Eisenhower, Dwight, 257
Eisenhower, Dwight, and Harold Macmillan, "Issues Confronting the West," Television discussion, cited, 196
Eldridge, Florence, 28
Eliot, T. S., 267; cited, 115, 118
Elliot, Don, "Roadhouse Girl," cited, 139–40
Ellison, Ralph, *The Invisible Man,* 205
Emergency, and institutional change, 303
Emerson, Ralph Waldo, 130
Emotion, and two-valued orientation, 251–52
Empson, William, *Seven Types of Ambiguity,* 262–63
Enthymeme, 248
Environment, semantic, 18, 29
Ethics, 187
Euphemism, 86
Evaluation, 314–16
   discredited patterns of, 92
   self-, 320–21
Evans, Bergen, *The Natural History of Nonsense,* 37
Evolution, linguistic, 69
Ewing, Oscar, 280 *n.*
Excretion, and verbal inhibition, 86
Experience
   data of, 153
   extensional, 184

Experience (cont.)
   symbolic, 132–35
   symbolizing, 155
   as teacher, 327
Extensional and intensional meaning. *See* Meaning
Extensional and verbal worlds, 30
Extensional approach, 303–05

Fact
   affectiveness of, 127–28
   and judgment, 47
   and opinion, 43
   and word, 279
Fallacy, "One Word, One Meaning," 60–62
Farago, Ladislas, *German Psychological Warfare,* 117
Faulkner, William, 327
Fear, of change, 300–02
   and institutional rigidity, 302
Federal Deposit Insurance Corporation, 301
Figures of speech. *See* Metaphor; Simile
Fixation and adaptation, 306
Flynn, John T., *Country Squire in the White House,* cited, 244
Food, as a symbol, 25
Formulas, verbal, dependence on, 319
Frank, Jerome, cited, 101, 230
   Law and the Modern Mind, 117
Freedom Riders, 147 *n.*
Fromm, Erich, *May Man Prevail?* 117
Frost, Robert, 269
Frustration, 145, 295–97
Future, control of by words, 102
   and directive language, 104

Galbraith, John Kenneth, "The Age of the Wordfact," cited, 210–11
Generalizations, 154
Genesis 11:11–18, cited, 194
Germany, 232–34
   anti-Semitism in, 233, 235
   two-valued orientation in, 232, 234

Maladjustment (cont.)
social, 305–06
Malinowski, Bronislaw, cited, 69
Mann, Thomas, "Dostoyevsky—*in Moderation*," cited, 155–56
Joseph and His Brethren, cited, 88–89
Mannes, Marya, "The Case of the Orange Orange," cited, 143
"Maps" and "territories," 30–32, 40, 93, 102, 104, 109, 111, 130, 135, 150, 208, 301, 307, 314, 319, 320, 321, 325, 328
March, Fredric, 28
Markel, Lester, "The Real Sins of the Press," 305 *n.*
Marshall, General George C., 257
Marx, Karl, 236
Masserman, Jules, *Behavior and Neurosis,* 145 *n.*
Principles of Dynamic Psychiatry, cited, 192
Mathematics, 186
and two-valued logic, 240–41
Matthew 12:36–37, cited, 314
13:3–9, cited, 197
Maturity, intellectual, 317, 319–20
Maurel, Micheline, *An Ordinary Camp,* 21
Mayer, Martin, *Madison Avenue, U.S.A.,* 117
Meaning
affective, 271
allocation of, 45
areas of, 64
and context, 56–57, 60–62
extensional, 58–60, 184, 216, 316
fallacy of single, 60–62
intensional, 58–60, 316
and interpretation, 61–62
symbolic, 271
of words, 314
Mearns, Hughes, cited, 199
Meerloo, Joost, *The Rape of The Mind,* 117
Melman, Seymour, *The Peace Race,* 117

Memory, and directive language, 109
Mencken, H. L., *The American Language, Supplement II,* 20
Menninger, Dr. Karl, *Love Against Hate,* cited, 78 *n.*
Metaphor, 121–23
dead, 124–25
"Mexican," connotative meaning of, 89
Milton, John, 127
Paradise Lost, cited, 244, 264
"When I Consider How My Light Is Spent," cited, 162–63
Mind
blocked, 218–19
closed, definition of, 257
open and closed, 255–58
open, definition of, 256
Misevaluation, 278, 315, 325
"Mits" and "Wits," 15–18
Money, and verbal inhibition, 86
Moore, Thomas, "At the Mid Hour of Night," cited, 136
Mother Goose, cited, 69
Motion pictures
bibliography of, 142
symbolization in, 27–28
Muni, Paul, 28
Murphy, Gardner, *Personality: A Biosocial Approach to Origins and Structure,* 321 *n.*

Names
inventing, 214–17
and symbol confusion, 88–89
National Socialist Party (Germany), 232–34
"Nationality," 216–17
Nazis. *See* National Socialist Party
Negro, 90–92, 147, 218–19
as classification term, 217
persecution of, 297
and symbolic attitudes, 25–26
Nehru, Jawaharlal, cited, 311
Neill, A. S., *Summerhill: A Radical Approach to Child Rearing,* cited, 140–41

Symbol (cont.)
symbols of, 152–53
and thing symbolized, 26, 185
and word confusion, bibliography of, 37
Symbolic process, 23–26
Symbolism, and language, 26–27
Symbolization, and human tension, 145–46

Taboo, in language, 86–88
social value of, 87
Talking. *See* Conversation
Tannenbaum, Frank, "An American Dilemma," cited, 312
Taylor, Edmond, *The Strategy of Terror*, 117
Taylor, Elizabeth, 133
Taylor, Henry J., cited, 292
Tedlock, E. W., Jr., *The Frieda Lawrence Collection of D. H. Lawrence Manuscripts: A Descriptive Bibliography*, 96
Tennyson, Alfred, Lord, 269
"Ode on the Death of the Duke of Wellington," cited, 265–66
Tension, 144–53
See also Art; Literature
"Territories" and "maps." *See* "Maps"
Thelen, Herbert A., *The Dynamics of Groups at Work*, 212
Thinking, associative, 280
Thompson, Francis, cited, 123
Thoreau, Henry David, *Walden*, cited, 139
Thought and language, bibliography of, 22
Thouless, Robert H., *How To Think Straight*, 248
Time, cited, 51, 98–99, 100, 103
Tolstoy, Count Leo, *War and Peace*, cited, 49–50
Translation, reasons for difficulty in, 121–22
True Confessions, cited, 129
"True," concepts of, 315
Truth, ascertaining, 220–23

Tuchman, Barbara W., *The Guns of August*, cited, 35

Ulanov, Barry, *A History of Jazz in America*, cited, 197
Understanding, and order, 154
United States, two-party system in, 231–32
Unknown Soldier of World War II, 266
Utterance, two-valued, 243, 305

Validity, descriptive, 190
Vaughan, Henry, cited, 124
Veblen, Thorstein, *Theory of The Leisure Class*, 24
Vendryes, Joseph, *Language: A Linguistic Introduction to History*, 22
Verbal assault, 231
Verbal circles, 184–86
Verbal climate, effect on individual, 16–17
Verbal taboo, 86–88
Verbalization, 17
Verifiability, of reports, 39–40
Virgil, *The Aeneid*, 265
Vocabulary
archaic and obsolete, 107
and "law of identity," 240
learned, functions of, 286–87
Vows, 107–08
Vulgarism, 123

Wagner, Geoffrey, 80
Walpole, Hugh R., 118
War, and institutional change, 303
Warren, Robert Penn, *Wilderness*, cited, 49
Waskow, Arthur, *The Limits of Defense*, 117
"We" device, 120–21
Wealth, and cultural lag, 302
Weapons, atomic and thermonuclear, 298 *n.*
Weinberg, Alvin M., cited, 295
Welch, Robert, 257–58
The Blue Book of the John Birch Society, 257–58
The Politician, 257 *n.*

Wellek, René, and Austin Warren, *Theory of Literature*, 21; cited, 157

White, E. B., cited, 50
"One Man's Meat," cited, 140

White, William Allen, *Forty Years on Main Street*, cited, 245

White, William S., cited, 191

Whitehead, Alfred North, *Science and the Modern World*, 307 *n*.

Whorf, Benjamin Lee, 260; cited, 5, 8

Wilde, Oscar, 264

Wish-fulfillment, bibliography of, 142

Wolfenstein, Martha, and Nathan Leites, *Movies: A Psychological Study*, 37, 142

Word-magic, 202

Words
abstract sense of, 179
and abstraction confusion, 201, 203
are not things, 28–30, 314
confusion of notion and reality, 178, 203–05, 208
dictionary definition of, 55
and future events, 101–04
interaction of, 64

Words (cont.)
invention and need of, 124, 179
as parent-symbol, 319
prejudice-laden, 207
and previous experience, 177
reaction to, 201, 203
relation between, 177
unique meaning of, 315
and verbal abstraction, 178

Wordsworth, William, 125, 144, 327; cited, 263, 268
"Composed Upon Westminster Bridge," cited, 162

Works Progress Administration, 281

World
delusional, 207–08
extensional, 30–31
verbal, 30–31

World War II, 234

Worry, 316

Wright, Richard, *Native Son*, 132

Writing
communication by, 11–14
levels of, 128–30
teaching of, 297

Yerkes, Robert M., *Chimpanzees: A Laboratory Colony*, 23 *n*.

"You" device, 120

M 1
N 2
O 3
P 4
Q 5
R 6
S 7
T 8